Unprotected
TEXTS

Unprotected
TEXTS

The Bible's Surprising Contradictions

About Sex and Desire

Jennifer Wright Knust

HarperOne
An Imprint of HarperCollinsPublishers

HarperOne

HarperCollins books may be purchased for educational, business, or sales promotional use. For information please write: Special Markets Department, HarperCollins Publishers, 10 East 53rd Street, New York, NY 10022.

HarperCollins website: http://www.harpercollins.com

HarperCollins®, 📖®, and HarperOne™ are trademarks of HarperCollins Publishers

FIRST EDITION

Library of Congress Cataloging-in-Publication Data

Knust, Jennifer Wright.
   Unprotected texts : the Bible's surprising contradictions about sex and desire / Jennifer Wright Knust—1st ed.
      p.   cm.
   ISBN 978–0–06–172558–6
   1. Sex—Biblical teaching. I. Title.
   BS680.S5K58   2011
   220.8'3067—dc22   2010027064

11   12   13   14   15   RRD(H)   10   9   8   7   6   5   4   3   2   1

For Stefan, of course

Contents

Introduction

Why the Bible Is Not a Sexual Guidebook

Just before I turned twelve, my dad got a promotion at work. Moving up in the company meant moving in general, so off we went, from Warren, New Jersey, to Evanston, Illinois. At the time, Warren was a rural town. I had spent my days playing in the forest behind our house and building forts with my friend Nancy. My mom made my dresses, I took horseback-riding lessons, and my brother and I rode a yellow school bus to school. Evanston is the first suburb north of Chicago, a small city really, and the kids there took the "L" (Chicago's subway system), wore jeans to school (only particular brands, of course), and hung out at fast-food joints. I was doomed, a total misfit with no hope of making friends, at least not initially. I did okay for the first month or so, but then some of the popular girls noticed my existence. Soon the taunting started. "Slut!" was whispered in the hall. Or, "Jenny, Jenny, she's a slut. Look at how she can switch that butt." And this toward a girl whose mother made her dresses and who hadn't attended a boy-girl party since she was five years old.

As studies of the slut phenomenon in American high schools have shown, when it comes to being called a slut, the story is pretty much the same: A girl who is a misfit for one reason or another is selected (she's the new girl, she develops breasts earlier than the other girls, her hair is different—whatever). Then the stories start, irrespective of what this girl has or has not done. "She gives blowjobs in the boys' bathroom for cigarettes," is one common myth. "She'll do the whole football team if given the chance," is another. In any case, the rumors imply, she wants it all the time.[1] As a twelve-year-old "slut" with loving parents, I was lucky. My mom told me to hold my head high, keep walking straight on to class, and remember that I am not a slut. I am her daughter. My dad bought me some new jeans, let me get the cool but expensive shoes all the kids were wearing, and signed me up for more ballet classes; by eighth grade, all was forgotten. I had settled in to become the hardworking nerd I remain to this day. The popular girls had moved on to someone else.

Still, every time I hear people accuse one another of sexual misdeeds, I have to wonder: what is really going on here? My experience at twelve taught me that, when it comes to sex, people never simply report what others are doing or even what they themselves are doing. Those girls called me "slut" not because I was one—whatever that might mean—but because they were afraid of being labeled the slut themselves or, worse, of being asked to become one too.[2] Sex, I have since discovered, can be used as a public weapon. The tragedy of Phoebe Prince, a fifteen-year-old girl from South Hadley, Massachusetts, who committed suicide in January 2010 after repeated taunting for her allegedly "slutty" behavior is only the most recent example of the high price some girls pay for America's misogynistic double standards.[3]

At twelve, however, my Christian upbringing did little to help me handle the shame of being the designated slut. If anything, I had learned to hate sluts as much as the popular seventh-grade girls hated me. I was doing all I could to please God and my parents. I went to church on Sunday and sang in the choir. On Sunday nights I went to youth group and read the Bible, praying that Jesus might help me and the other girls in my class. But no one stood up for the slut in these contexts, not even when we read about how Jesus hung out with tax collectors and prostitutes. We all understood exactly what this biblical passage meant: we were supposed to be nice to tax collectors and prostitutes if we had the misfortune to run into one, but, for God's sake, we were never to become one ourselves. We might feel sorry for prostitutes—that was our Christian duty—but we should avoid them at all costs.

The real sluts in the Bible, we learned, were women like Jezebel, the evil wife of King Ahab of Israel and rival of the prophet Elijah. I knew this story well. King Ahab made the mistake of taking Jezebel, daughter of King Ethbaal of the Sidonians, as his wife. Following her lead, he went and served Baal, her idolatrous god (see 1 Kgs. 16:31). Seduced by the foreign queen, Ahab abandoned the one true God, Yhwh, for Baal, the perverse god of the Canaanites, and pretty soon both Israel and Ahab's morals were on their way down a slippery slope from which it would not be easy to recover. Ruthlessly persecuting Elijah and other legitimate prophets of Yhwh, Jezebel invited 450 prophets of Baal and 400 prophets of the goddess Asherah to join the royal court. But, the Bible assured us, she would not succeed forever. As Yhwh promised, she would eventually be overthrown—tossed over the palace walls, her flesh to be eaten by dogs. Even so, when the day of her demise finally arrived, she flaunted her slutty ways one more time. Hearing that the royal family had been massacred by Yhwh's choice prince Jehu, she "painted her eyes, and adorned her head, and looked out of the window" (2 Kgs. 9:30), taunting the new claimant to the throne. Unluckily for her, however, the palace eunuchs had changed sides, and they pushed her out this very window. She was trampled to death by horses and then left for the dogs. By the time the dogs were done with her, only her skull, her feet, and the palms of her hands remained. Sluts, the Bible taught us, deserved what they got.

Good Christian Girls

As I recently discovered, the teachings presented to American Protestant teenagers as both biblical and Christian haven't changed much since I was a kid. In 2007, while teaching my class on the history of the Christian Bible, my student Kathryn asked if I had heard about *Revolve,* a "Biblezine" (Bible magazine) published by Thomas Nelson. (Since it is a "zine," there is a new edition published each year.) As the mother of boys, I had missed this hot new product, which is marketed to conservative Christian girls and their families. Kathryn had sources back home and

brought one in to show me. "Can you believe it?" she said. "Beauty advice
and Jesus in the same book!" A New Testament filled with glossy images
and tips on "what guys *really* think" (emphasis in the original), *Revolve*
is a Bible-focused version of *Seventeen,* a complete New Century Version
New Testament accompanied by "stories about girls and guys who make
it their biggest priority to know God" in the margins of every page.[4]

Looking through *Revolve* together, Kathryn and I reminisced about
what it had been like to grow up female and Baptist. The advice given to
girls in the margins of *Revolve* was pretty close to what the both of us had
learned. "Sexually active girls are nearly three times more likely to attempt suicide than girls who are not sexually active," *Revolve* warns in the
margins of Luke 12:46–13:24.[5] Better not be a slut, girls! You may end up
dead. Sex is dangerous, *Revolve* advises, but being pretty is a top priority.
Why not put on "a pair of funky earrings or a super cool bangle brace-
let," and then, "as you add some color and splash to your appearance,
thank God for his transforming power in your inner life!"[6] You'll be so
beautiful inside and out that the guys and God will be sure to notice. Yet
a pretty girl should take care. While it's okay to be beautiful, sexiness is
wrong. "Guys are turned on by what they see," *Revolve* cautions. "If we're
doing everything out of love for God and others, then we'll be interested
in helping them *not* sin."[7] Nevertheless, on a special occasion, there is
nothing wrong with a glamorous "updo" and some sassy heels. Then,
shining with beauty, a girl can "walk the extra mile." "Give the shirt off
your back," *Revolve* exhorts. "Turn the other cheek. Don't hold back—
show the difference Jesus makes in your heart!"[8] From the perspective of
the editors of *Revolve,* then, a good girl serves God by being beautiful, but
not sexy. She is pleasing to boys, but she never tempts them to sin. Filled
with Christian love, she is ready to give away everything to others *but*
her body. A girl like this succeeds at being the good Christian that God
wants her to be, *Revolve* insists. If she fails, however, perhaps she, too, will
find herself tossed over a wall and eaten by dogs.

The Bible and the "Good Girl"

Grounding an impossible double standard in the New Testament, *Revolve* pretends that the Bible speaks with one voice about what God wants from teenage girls. But as an adult and a Bible scholar, I say that clearly *Revolve* is wrong. The Bible fails to offer girls—or anyone—a consistent message regarding sexual morals and God's priorities. Instead of learning about Jezebel, for example, girls could be taught about the woman in the Song of Songs, a love poem attributed to King Solomon. The lovers in this poem are not married, yet they eagerly seek one another out, uniting in gardens and reveling in the splendor of one another's bodies. "Open to me, my sister, my love" (5:2), the man pleads. "My beloved thrust his hand into the opening, and my inmost being yearned for him" (v. 4), she replies. This girl, at least, does not hesitate to announce her desires for her man, and she does not wait until marriage to fulfill them. Still, the Song never condemns her. Instead of calling her a slut, the "daughters of Jerusalem," who play the role of a backup chorus, encourage her decisions, urging her on by asking for a full description of her beloved's beauty. The woman is happy to comply: "My beloved is all radiant and ruddy, distinguished among ten thousand" (v. 10), she gushes. Can the Bible be used to support premarital sex, even for girls? The answer, I have now discovered, is yes.

Moreover, whatever I may have been taught about "sluts," the Bible does not object to prostitution, at least not consistently. The biblical patriarch Judah, for example, was quite content to solicit a prostitute while out on a business trip, offering her a kid from his flocks in payment for an opportunity to "go into" her. It was only later, when he learned that this "prostitute" was actually his daughter-in-law Tamar that he became angry. Sentenced to death for playing the whore, Tamar stood up to her father-in-law, proving to him that he had been her one customer. She was forced into the ruse by Judah, she explained, since he failed to give her the support she was due after the death of her husband, Judah's son. Repenting of his mistake, Judah let her live, admitting, "She is more in the right than I, since I did not give her to my [living] son Shelah" (Gen. 38:26).

With her life spared and pregnant with Judah's sons, Tamar went on to bear twins, Perez and Zerah, one of whom became an ancestor of both King David and Jesus. Does the Bible have a problem with prostitutes or prostitution? Not necessarily, I have come to learn.

Still, according to some biblical books, marriage is the only valid context for sexual intercourse, especially for women. Exodus and Deuteronomy assume that polygamy is the norm and thus that men will have multiple sexual partners. If a man takes another wife, Exodus 21:10 instructs, "he shall not diminish the food, clothing or marital rights of the first wife." If a man has two wives, Deuteronomy advises, he must treat sons born to each wife equitably. These laws find their fulfillment in the biblical patriarchs. Abraham, for example, fathers children with Hagar, Keturah, and Sarah. Jacob marries sisters Rachel and Leah and then takes two slave concubines, Bilhah and Zilpah. The kings of Israel also took multiple wives and concubines. David, for example, was married to Abigail, Ahinoam, Maacah, Haggith, Albitah, Elgah, and Bathsheba, among others. According to 1 Kings, Solomon's harem included seven hundred princesses and three hundred concubines. Women, however, are permitted only one husband at a time. Deuteronomy commands Israelite men to stone to death any young woman who fails to remain a virgin prior to marriage. If the woman does not bleed on her wedding night, she is to be executed on the doorstep of her paternal home "because she committed a disgraceful act in Israel by prostituting herself in her father's house" (Deut. 22:21).

The New Testament letter 1 Timothy also promotes marriage as the only appropriate context for sex, but it goes further, linking the state of a woman's soul before God to her status as a wife and mother. Writing in the name of the apostle Paul, the author states:

> *Women should dress themselves modestly and decently in suitable clothing, not with their hair braided, or with gold, pearls, or expensive clothes. . . . Let a woman learn in silence with full submission. . . . For Adam was formed first, then Eve; and Adam was not deceived, but the woman was deceived and became a transgressor. Yet she will be saved*

through childbearing, provided they continue in faith and love and holiness, with modesty. (1 Tim. 2:9–15)

Since Eve sinned, women will be saved by God only if they bear children, this author argues, presumably because Eve's punishment involved pain in childbirth (see Gen. 3:16). Giving birth, women experience the divinely mandated punishment of labor, meted out to all women from Eve onward.

To confuse matters further, however, Paul himself wasn't interested in promoting either marriage or childbearing. Instead, he teaches the followers of Jesus that they should avoid marriage—it is a distraction that keeps wives and husbands anxious about how to please their partners. By contrast, celibacy demonstrates both superior self-control and a more advanced commitment to Christ. According to the Gospels, Jesus agreed with Paul's assessment. Christians, Matthew, Mark, and Luke insist, are to privilege their commitment to Jesus Christ above their families. And the Gospel of Luke goes the furthest, stating, "Whoever comes to me and does not hate father and mother, wife and children, brothers and sisters, yes, and even life itself, cannot be my disciple" (14:26). Marriage is presented as a waste of time, though once married, divorce is not permitted. Spreading the good news about Jesus is more important than getting married. After all, when the resurrection comes, people "neither marry nor are given in marriage," but will be "like the angels in heaven" (Matt. 22:30), who avoid sexual intercourse altogether.

Whatever *Revolve* might suggest, then, the Bible does not speak with one voice when it comes to marriage, women's roles, sexy clothes, and the importance of remaining a pure virgin for one's (future) spouse. According to Genesis, a woman who sleeps with her father-in-law can be a heroine. Visits to prostitutes are also not a problem, so long as the prostitute in question is not a proper Israelite woman. According to the Song of Songs, a beautiful girl who enjoys making love can fulfill her desires outside of marriage and still be honored both by God and by her larger community. Sex is a good thing, and sexual desire is a blessing, not an embarrassment. Yet according to Exodus and Deuteronomy, sex is a matter of male property rights. Men can have sex with as many women as they like, so long as these women are their wives, slaves, or prostitutes, but a woman must guard her virginity for the sake of her father and then remain sexually faithful to one man after marriage. First Timothy offers yet another perspective: a woman must marry not so that she can express her desires appropriately but so that she can become pregnant and suffer the pangs of childbirth. God requires women to suffer in this way, and has demanded labor pains from them since Eve first sinned in Eden. Nevertheless, other New Testament books argue that the faithful followers of Jesus should avoid marriage if possible, in anticipation of a time when sexual intercourse will be eliminated altogether. Could one imagine a more contradictory set of teachings collected within one set of sacred texts?

Misrepresenting the Bible

Still, the fiction that there is a single biblical sexual standard is repeatedly invoked, and not only in the pages of *Revolve*. In January 2010, for example, the Ethics and Religious Liberty Commission (ERLC) of the Southern Baptist Convention filed a "friend of the court" brief before the Northern California United States District Court in favor of Proposition 8, the California ballot initiative specifying that marriage must be between one man and one woman. According to this brief, the Southern Baptists have no choice but to oppose same-sex marriage—they are duty bound to defend an understanding of marriage that is rooted in "biblical standards." Though the ceremonial and civil laws given to Moses in the Old Testament are no longer in force, the brief argues, divinely given moral laws, which are characterized by the ERLC as eternal and unchanging, must be obeyed. Citing but not quoting several biblical books, the ERLC claims that sexual conduct outside of the bonds of a marriage between one man and one woman fails to meet the Bible's mandates, demeans the dignity of the individual, and is an expression of sin.[9] If the court overturns Proposition 8, the free participation of Christians in public life will be threatened, since such a decision by the court necessarily mischaracterizes Christians as bigoted and antihomosexual.[10]

Yet it is this brief that engages in mischaracterization, and not only of "mainstream" Christianity but also of the Bible. Not all Christians agree with the ERLC on the points outlined in this brief, not even all Baptist Christians.[11] More important, however, the notion that the long list of biblical books named in this brief actually treat sexual morals, family norms, and marriage in precisely the same way is seriously misleading.

As we will see throughout this book, there is so much more to the passages listed in the ERLC brief than a set of simplistic statements about sex and marriage. In fact, among the texts cited, not one addresses "biblical marriage" directly, at least not as this brief defines it. These passages present: the creation of humankind by God (see Gen. 1:26–28; 2:18–25); the proper treatment of parents (see Exod. 20:12); the punishments specified by God for various sexual infractions (see Lev. 18 [sex with a menstruating woman, "lying with a man as with a woman," adultery, bestiality]); the importance of keeping the laws given to Israel in the covenant of Moses (see Exod. 20:14; Deut. 6:4–9); the necessity of bringing up children carefully (see Prov. 22:6); the value of marrying women from one's own community (see Mal. 2:10–16); Jesus's instructions regarding divorce (see Matt. 19:3–9); the illicit sexual behaviors that allegedly arise from idolatry (see Rom. 1:24–27); the importance of avoiding prostitutes (see 1 Cor. 6:18); the obedient behavior demanded from Christian wives, slaves, and children (see Eph. 5:21–33; 6:1–9; Col. 3:18–21); and the importance of honoring both married and celibate followers of Christ (see Heb. 13:1–6). These passages do not promote a single definition of marriage, let alone one sexual standard, and none addresses the set of cultural and historical circumstances currently informing the United States District Court of the Northern District of California in 2010. To argue that they do is not only disingenuous but demeaning to the complexity and richness of the biblical books. When the ERLC brief cites the Bible in this way, the point is not to represent the contents of the Bible adequately, but to grant a veneer of certainty and righteousness to the positions it puts forward, just as *Revolve* seeks to convince "good Christian girls" that sluts get what they deserve.

Taking the Bible Seriously

In our house, growing up, we had a big gold couch with olive-green flower embroidery. From the ages of seven to about ten, my mom and I would sit on this couch and read the Bible together before school. We had an oversize two-volume *Treasury of Bible Stories* with lengthy excerpts from the whole Bible illustrated with larger-than-life paintings on nearly every page.[12] Sitting on that couch, never once did my mom ask me to silence my questions about the Bible and its stories, nor did she tell me that I was silly or bad to wonder what these stories might be teaching me. My mom took me and my questions seriously. The Bible was ours to read, question, wonder about, and deliberate, and sometimes it was the questions that mattered more than the answers. On those weekday mornings before school, the Bible was not a collection of policy statements that had to be obeyed or a weapon designed to enforce particular views about morality, but an invitation to think about who God might be and what it means to be human.

Inspired, in part, by my mom and those mornings on the big gold couch, I am now a Bible scholar, an ordained American Baptist pastor, and a professor of religion. I have the good fortune of contemplating these and other questions full-time. With this in mind, I'm tired of watching those who are supposed to care about the Bible reduce its stories and its teachings to slogans. The only way that the Bible can be regarded as straightforward and simple is if no one bothers to read it. As I had already gathered as a child, the Bible is not only contradictory but complex. Biblical books take sides, they disagree with one another, they intentionally change earlier teachings, and they make irreconcilable claims about human life and the nature of God. In some cases, they promote points of view that, from a modern perspective anyway, are patently immoral.

This is no less true when it comes to sex than for any other topic. One cannot and should not expect easy answers from the Bible, a lesson that Americans, at least, should have learned a century ago.

Slaves Obey Your Masters

In 1779, reflecting on slavery in the state of Virginia, Thomas Jefferson declared:

> *I tremble for my country when I reflect that God is just: that his justice cannot sleep forever: that considering numbers, nature and natural means only, a revolution of the wheel of fortune, an exchange of situation, is among possible events: that it may become probable by supernatural interference! The Almighty has no attribute which can take side with us in such a contest.*[13]

Jefferson and his family would own slaves for generations, but now, 230 years later, a majority of American Christians would agree: if given the opportunity, God would most certainly take the side of the slaves, not that of the slave-owning "us" identified in Jefferson's comments. Yet it was not always so. Throughout the seventeenth, eighteenth, and nineteenth centuries, numerous biblical scholars, theologians, and pastors argued that God was on the side of slavery, and the Bible was repeatedly invoked to support their arguments. For example, quoting the New Testament letter to the Ephesians in 1836, writer and editor J. K. Paulding insisted that Paul, the "most eloquent, efficient and indefatigable defender of Christianity that ever adorned the world," most certainly did support slavery, as did every other book of the Bible.[14] Here Paulding depended upon the very same passage from Ephesians invoked by the ERLC in support of "biblical marriage." As Paulding knew but the ERLC seems to have forgotten, this passage is not only about marriage, but it is also about slaves.

The emphatic endorsement of marriage in Ephesians cannot be separated from an equally emphatic endorsement of slavery a few verses later.

Distinguishing between slaves, wives, and husbands in an extended passage about appropriate submission, Ephesians acknowledges that slaves could not marry. They belong to a separate category altogether. The overall principle of the passage is stated early on: "Be subject to one another out of reverence for Christ" (5:21). The mutual subjections the author has in mind are then outlined, one after another: Wives are to be subject to their husbands, "for the husband is the head of the wife just as Christ is the head of the church" (5:22–24). Children are to be subject to their parents in obedience to the commandment "honor your father and mother" (6:1–3; see also Deut. 6:7). Finally, slaves are to obey their earthly masters "with fear and trembling in singleness of heart," just as they obey Christ. Slave submission is to be so complete that those who are enslaved will comply with their master's orders even when he is away (see 6:5–9). Wives, children, and slaves, then, are separate categories, though each must submit to the male head of the household. Since slaves were the full sexual property of their masters, any sexual relationships between them would require the permission of their owners. Therefore, this letter does not support marriage between one man and one woman but between one free man and one free woman, who then live together in a hierarchical household populated by a husband, a wife, their children, and their slaves. Since they are property, the sexual lives of slaves belong to the master, who has full sexual access to them, if he so desires.

Though ancient slavery was not identical to slavery as practiced and enforced in an American context, it, too, was an abusive and inherently violent system designed to exploit some human lives and bodies for the benefit of others.[15] Slave women were bred, slave families were torn apart by means of sale and capture, slave torture was considered entirely acceptable, and escaped slaves were first returned to their masters and then tattooed or forced to wear lead collars.[16] Extant slave collars from late antiquity suggest that many ancient Christians took biblical endorsements of slavery quite literally: many fourth- and fifth-century collars are adorned with crosses or other Christian insignia, and at least one collar belonged to a slave owned by a Christian church.[17] The reuse of this very same New Testament passage to promote and defend North American slavery some seventeen centuries later only heightens the distressing implications of Ephesians and other, similar biblical passages.[18]

Aware of the death-dealing potential of commandments like "slaves, obey your masters," abolitionists like Daniel Goodwin argued that Christianity must be founded not in particular passages but in general principles drawn from the whole of the New Testament witness. As he put it in 1864, "all these negative arguments from the New Testament in favour of the law and practice of slavery, vanish away as smoke before the general spirit and tendency of its teaching," which could be boiled down to Jesus's commandment to "love thy neighbor as thyself."[19] The Bible was far too dangerous a document to be read simply, or simply read, abolitionists concluded. Instead, proper interpretation required a set of principles that could determine what the Bible must, in the end, say. For them, that principle was the Golden Rule. Since one could not love a neighbor and own him at the same time, Jesus can only have intended slavery to end. With this principle in mind, Frederick Douglass could then declare that abolitionists should "press [the Bible] to [their] bosoms all the more closely." They should "read it all the more diligently and prove from its pages that it is on the side of liberty—and not on the side of slavery."[20] If the Bible is to remain, as my denomination puts it, "the authoritative guide to knowing and serving the triune God: Father, Son and Holy Spirit," the "divinely-inspired word of God," and the "revelation of the Christian faith,"[21] it seems to me that it is time to apply lessons learned during abolition to other passages as well. It is time to stop pretending that, read uncritically and out of context, the Bible will set anyone free. Some kind of larger principle like "love thy neighbor" is required if an ethical compass is to be extracted from the biblical witness.

Siding with Queen Esther

According to the biblical book of Esther, there was once a beautiful young Judean named Esther who, with the help of her adoptive father, Mordecai, rescued fellow Jews from the evil schemes of Haman the Agagite, an assistant to the Persian king Ahasuerus (Xerxes I, reigned 486–464 BCE). As the story goes, after dismissing his Persian wife, Vashti, for refusing to appear before the court in all her beauty, Ahasuerus decides to choose a new wife for himself from among the most beautiful virgins in his kingdom. Esther is selected and given into the king's harem, where she undergoes various cosmetic treatments in preparation of her audience with the king. Living in the harem, she nevertheless refuses to abandon her fidelity to her ancestral god, Yhwh, keeping her ethnic identity and her religious commitments secret at the instructions of her father, Mordecai. When it is her turn to be brought before King Ahasuerus, he finds her to be the most pleasing of all the virgins and chooses her to be his queen. Well placed in the king's court, she is then ready to intervene when the Jews living in the Persian kingdom are threatened by Mordecai's refusal to bow down and worship the king's assistant, Haman. Infuriated by Mordecai's insubordination, Haman appeals to Ahasuerus to allow him to destroy all the Jews in his lands, a request the king grants (see Esther 3:6–15). When Mordecai gets word of Haman's plots to Esther, she begins her own campaign on behalf of her people, wining and dining the king and his court for three separate nights until finally revealing her request: "If I have won your favor, O king, and if it pleases the king, let my life be given me—that is my petition—and the lives of my people—that is my request" (7:3). After Esther discloses her Jewish identity and exposes Haman's schemes, the king chooses to side with her, hanging Haman on a gallows and allowing the Jews to execute all those who seek to destroy them. The book ends with Esther and Mordecai founding the Jewish festival of Purim in celebration of these great events, which are to be commemorated each year. Indeed, Purim is celebrated to this day.

If Jezebel is portrayed in 1 and 2 Kings as the nightmare that every Israelite should avoid, Esther is portrayed as her opposite. On the one hand is Esther, a heroine who protects her people by preserving their right to worship Yhwh alone, even though they dwell in a foreign land. She advances the cause of Jews who live outside of Israel and assists her adoptive father Mordecai in attaining the rank of chief assistant to the

Persian king, a position from which he seeks the good of his people. Becoming justly famous, she and her father are widely revered, especially among Jews living abroad. Like Esther and Mordecai, these Jews have no choice but to negotiate the complex problems faced by a minority people inhabiting a much larger and more powerful empire.[22] On the other hand is Jezebel, a daughter of the king of Sidon who arrogantly seeks to promote the worship of a foreign god within the holy land of Israel. Justly infamous, her name becomes a curse, both in the way it is translated in Hebrew and as it was applied by later Jewish and Christian authors to other detested women (e.g., Rev. 2:20). Rendered in her own tongue, Jezebel's name means "Where is the Prince?" an echo of the call that resounded throughout her homeland during the celebration of the release of the god Baal from Mot, the god of death. Rendered in biblical Hebrew, however, "Jezebel" means "dung," an obscenity meant to degrade her royal status.[23] The contrast between Esther and Jezebel could not have been made more obvious by biblical writers.

Yet how different were these two women really? Though one was Jewish and the other Phoenician, one royal and the other the orphan daughter of resident aliens, they share a great deal in common. As the daughter of a Phoenician king, Jezebel would have been appointed as a high priestess of her ancestral god, Baal Melquart, and asked to serve as a representative of her religious faith from a young age.[24] Like Esther, she obeyed her father by remaining faithful to her ancestral god once she was placed in the court of a foreign king. Given to Ahab, the king of Israel, by her father, the king of Sidon, she, like Esther, was not asked to agree to the match. Installed as queen of Israel, she brought her culture, her gods, and her companions with her, refusing to abandon her devotion to Baal, just as Esther had refused to abandon Yhwh or her adoptive father, Mordecai. Given the opportunity, Jezebel worked to promote Baal worship in Israel, her new home, over the objections of the prophet Elijah. Similarly, Esther worked to promote the good fortune of her people, resident aliens in Persia, over the objections of Haman the Agagite. Both Jezebel and Esther arranged for the deaths of their enemies, and both employed their feminine wiles to advance their goals.[25] Unlike Esther, however, Jezebel was reviled as the worst sort of foreign queen. Like the seventh-grade girls of Evanston, Illinois, biblical writers took sides, designating one woman as the shameful slut Jezebel and the other as the heroic queen Esther.

Opening the Bible

As interpreters, readers of the Bible today are asked to take sides too: for or against Jezebel, for or against slavery, and for or against particular kinds of marriages, to offer just a few examples. A hundred and fifty years ago, the most important biblical battles were fought over the question of slavery, with abolitionists arguing against the enslavement of other human beings and slave apologists lobbying strenuously for the perpetuation of America's most "peculiar institution." At the moment, sexuality is the central biblical battleground, as interpreters everywhere are asked to take sides on a whole host of sexual-political questions: Should we be for or against gay marriage, for or against the availability of abortion, for or against the submission of women to their husbands, and for or against women's political leadership? Should we openly declare our commitment to premarital virginity and abstinence, or will sex education and informed consent lead young people to make healthy sexual choices? Should we prevent gays and lesbians from serving as ordained ministers and bishops, or can God's call include everyone, irrespective of sexual orientation or gender identity? Whose side is the Bible on anyway?

Rather than getting caught up in these debates by attempting to pull the Bible over to a particular side, this book invites readers to encounter the full complexity of the biblical witness, taking both the diversity and the peculiarity of the Bible into account. Instead of repeating slogans and sound bites about sex and the Bible, this book presents a detailed analysis of biblical attitudes and assumptions while also exploring the reception of biblical narratives by later Christian and Jewish interpreters, each of whom had his or her own, unique approach to what were already a diverse set of biblical traditions. As we will see, biblical teachings regarding desire, marriage, and the human body are entirely inconsistent and yet thoroughly fascinating. If one book recommends polygamy, the next recommends celibacy. If one revels in erotic desire, the next warns that desire is evil, a source of nothing but trouble. If one assumes that women should be prophets, the next tells women to sit down and remain silent. If one assumes that children and property are the aim of human life, the next longs for the sex-free life of angels. And so on. The Bible does not offer a systematic set of teachings or a single sexual code, but it does reveal sometimes conflicting attempts on the part of people and groups to define sexual morality, and to do so in the name of God.

If I could meet my twelve-year-old self now, I would like to invite her to sit with me on a big gold couch with olive-green flowers. After snuggling in and getting comfortable, we would read the Bible together, asking whatever questions might occur to us. Along the way, we would discover that biblical writers told stories and presented teachings that are much more complex and fantastic than anything we could have imagined. Bound by their own histories, languages, and concerns, ancient writers, we would notice, were as worried as we are about the nature of human bodies, the meanings of sex and desire, and what might constitute an ethical sexual life. We would not hesitate, however, to call some of their answers into question, particularly when those answers seem to demand suffering, destruction, or death. We would not rejoice when Jezebel was finally thrown over the palace walls and eaten by dogs. We would not agree that God imposed labor pains as a punishment for Eve's sin. We would not decide that fidelity to the Bible requires that we take Esther's side, but not Jezebel's, any more than we would support the view that chattel slavery is divinely ordained simply because Ephesians suggests that it is. Finally, sitting together on that couch, before we even opened our Bible and began to read, I would insist that, as far as I'm concerned and whatever the Bible might say, sluts should live.

A Few Fantastic Things, or, a Preview of Coming Attractions

As we will see in chapter 1 of this book, the Bible has a much more expansive understanding of sex and sexual desire than is often thought. The Song of Songs, an ancient erotic poem that was once considered the holiest of all the holy books, will serve as our first example. This amazing poem is filled with luscious imagery designed to awaken the desires of lovers for each other, whether those lovers are imagined as a human couple or as a metaphorical pairing expressive of the erotic charge between humanity and God. Turning to the book of Ruth and stories about King David, we will meet protagonists who eagerly engage in sexual intercourse outside the bonds of marriage and are blessed as a result. As chapter 2 will show, marriage was held up as an ideal by many biblical writers, but their ideas about "good marriage" consistently fail to correspond to our own. Exodus and Deuteronomy assumed polygamy to be the normal Israelite practice, with instructions given regarding how to treat slave concubines and second wives. Jesus and his followers then "corrected" these teachings, but not by recommending marriage between one man and one woman. Instead, New Testament writers instructed Jesus's followers to avoid marriage if at all possible. Why? Because, as chapter 3 demonstrates, by the time the New Testament was written, many Jews and Christians thought that sexual desire was a problem to be solved, not a blessing given by God. The truly faithful should therefore attempt to overcome desire altogether.

The girls of Evanston once made fun of me for being a "slut." As we will see in chapter 4, biblical writers made fun of their own enemies as well, accusing them of all sorts of sexual misconduct. Biblical books like Leviticus, Joshua, and Revelation represented the enemies of Israel or the opponents of the Christians as sexual deviants, suggesting that worship of any God other than Yhwh inevitably leads to sexual excess. But these tales of sexual overindulgence are not innocent fun. They were employed to mischaracterize outsiders or, worse, to excuse the slaughter of persons who were depicted as abhorrent to the one true God. Yet, as chapter 5 will show, from the perspective of the Bible, the worst form of sexual deviance was not sex outside of marriage or even incest and bestiality but sex with angels. Sexual mixing between Israelites and foreign women or, even more troubling, between God's people and angels was widely denounced, with the attempted rape of angels by the men of Sodom recalled as a particularly egregious example of improper human lust.

In chapter 6, biblical teachings regarding menstruation, semen, and circumcision will be scrutinized. Why were Israelites circumcised? Why was menstrual blood considered polluting? And why was semen polluting as well, though it was also regarded as a precious resource? As we will see, answers to these questions shifted over time, as Jews and Christians applied changing "scientific" and cultural knowledge about the human body to their sacred texts. Circumcision, a practice that was once common to all men living in the land of Canaan, came to stand for Jewish identity so thoroughly that the apostle Paul could call Jews "the circumcised" and non-Jews "the foreskinned" (a more literal translation of the Greek word *akrobystiai,* usually translated "the uncircumcised"), as if these titles were perfectly normal. An earlier concern to protect the temple in Jerusalem from the contagious pollution of menstrual blood became a metaphor for pollution in general by New Testament times. Once the temple was destroyed altogether, both Jews and Christians found new ways to regulate their genital discharges, with some ruling that menstruants and ejaculants could attend worship at the synagogue or church and others ruling that they could not.

Letting in Some Good News

In January of 2005, my home church in Boston burned, nearly to the ground. As the *Boston Globe* reported, "A fire tore through First Baptist Church in Jamaica Plain last night, severely damaging the pre–Civil War landmark, and possibly destroying a treasured pipe organ that was spared in an earlier blaze almost 30 years ago."[26] Luckily no one was hurt, but by 5:30 the next morning, it was clear that almost nothing could be saved. The organ was gone, the thrift store was a total loss, and the sanctuary was ruined. All that was left standing was the steeple and an empty shell of masonry walls, covered in ashes and ice. After the loss of our beloved church, we met in a trailer on our lot, with the shell of our building behind us and the hope that someday we might rebuild. We held Sunday services and our regular weekly programs, sharing the "sacred double-wide" with Eglise Baptiste Pierre Anguilaire, the wonderful Haitian congregation that has been worshipping with us for years. Five years later, on Sunday, January 17, 2010, the building was finally ready, or at least ready enough for us to move in. This time the *Globe* could report, "Five years after fire, Jamaica Plain church set to rise from ashes."[27]

Preaching that Sunday, the Reverend Ashlee Wiest-Laird, our pastor, observed that God's generosity will not be limited. "The best things, like good wine at the end of the party," she remarked, "are still to come."[28] But then she added:

> *Of course, you know as well as I do, that living life as a celebration has nothing to do with the kind of fake happiness that paints on a plastic grin in the denial of the struggle, pain, and hardship each of us must face. Those are, unfortunately, realities in life and especially in a life of faith. Whoever says otherwise is, as they say, selling something.*

She then quoted Martin Luther King Jr.: "a positive religious faith does not offer an illusion that we shall be exempt from pain and suffering . . . rather it instills us with the inner equilibrium needed to face strains, burdens, and fears that inevitably come."[29] As Pastor Ashlee reminded us, the intoxication we felt upon entering our building again for the first time in five years was to be celebrated, and celebrated extravagantly. But still, not all was well that Sunday. Our Haitian brothers and sisters had suffered immensely a few days earlier, victims of the most terrible earthquake to hit their homeland in generations. Many members of Eglise Baptiste had lost loved ones, and many more had lost everything they ever owned. At First Baptist, we still had many bills to pay, sick members, losses and struggles to face, and a main sanctuary that is still incomplete. Yet so many people were there in our new multipurpose room, warm and dry under our new roof and refurbished steeple, glad to be alive. For the moment, we could rejoice. For the moment, we could enjoy the party.

Reading about sex in the Bible is akin to taking on a life of faith as Pastor Ashlee and Martin Luther King Jr. describe it. Pasting a plastic smile on what are sometimes death-dealing commandments and disturbing stories will not lessen their potential for harm. Ignoring the passages we don't like and holding on to the passages we love will not make what we hate go away. Similarly, selectively citing what is uplifting and wonderful, however well meaning our intentions, will not teach us what the Bible truly means or what the Bible must truly say. The Bible is complicated enough, ancient enough, and flexible enough to support an almost endless set of interpretive agendas. That's why abolitionists could find inspiration in the Bible's pages despite centuries of biblically sanctioned argumentation in favor of the enslavement of fellow human beings. Even today, progressives can cite scripture to celebrate the consecration of gay marriage just as effortlessly as conservatives can argue that God refuses to accept anything other than marriage between one man and one woman. It wasn't the Bible that brought emancipation, and it won't be the Bible that determines our sexual ethics. Rather, we ourselves must decide what kind of people we will become, what kinds of weddings should be celebrated, and how best to love one another.

By writing this book, I hope to move the current conversation about sex and the Bible past the polemical and shortsighted claims of the ERLC, the simplistic and harmful messages of Biblezines, and the confident pronouncements of slave apologists toward a larger understanding of what the Bible does have to say about bodies, sex, and gender. Though biblical teachings are rarely easy or consistent, they can continue to resonate with our own concerns and experiences. Ancient people had bodies, too, and their bodies were as vulnerable to wounds and as in need of caresses as ours are today. If sexuality is a way of being for one another and in relationship with one another, it is also a way of being for ourselves and in ourselves. The Bible doesn't have to be an invader, conquering bodies and wills with its pronouncements and demands. It can also be a partner in the complicated dance of figuring out what it means to live in bodies that are filled with longing, both to touch and to be touched.

CHAPTER 1

The Bible and the Joy of Sex

Desire In and Out of Control

E very time you have sex," Christian educator Bonnie Park warns teenagers in a recent video, you are playing Russian roulette. "What if I want to have sex before I get married?" one boy asks. "Well," Ms. Park replies, "I guess you'll just have to be prepared to die, and you'll probably take you and your spouse and one or more of your children with you."[1] The scare tactics employed in abstinence-only education programs developed by Ms. Park and others are not always this threatening, but the overall message is clear: teenagers who engage in premarital sex are risking both their lives and their bodies.[2] Boys, abstinence-only educators argue, cannot possibly control their animalistic impulses without the assistance of God, strong parenting, and a godly girl. Since girls are responsible for monitoring both their own desires and those of the boys who long to touch them, parents must supervise their girls closely, ensuring that girls' bodies and minds remain pure for their future husbands. If either parents or children fail in this crucial endeavor, educators warn, disaster is sure to follow. But by claiming that the Bible supports their point of view, these educators are selling both kids and their parents a bill of goods. As this chapter shows, passages celebrating sexual pleasure outside the bonds of marriage *can* be found within the Bible and, remarkably, no one dies. In fact, two of Jesus's ancestors risked the conception of children out of wedlock—Ruth and Bathsheba—and yet neither these women nor their partners were killed. In these texts, extramarital sexual expression leads to God's blessing, not God's curse, and sexual longing is both productive and positive. There is so much more to the Bible's teachings on sex and desire than current fearmongering suggests.

The Song of Songs, an ancient biblical love poem that speaks frankly of towering breasts, flowing black locks, kissable lips, and the joy of sexual fulfillment, offers a particularly striking example of this phenomenon, but other biblical passages are nearly as forthright. Ruth, King David's grandmother, conspires with her mother-in-law, Naomi, to seduce Boaz, one of Naomi's wealthy relatives. "Uncovering his feet," a Hebrew euphemism for uncovering a man's genitals, Ruth succeeds at gaining a home for herself and for Naomi, a woman she has promised to love until they are parted by death. By loving both her mother-in-law and her partner, Boaz, Ruth's bold desire secures a future for herself and her family. The love between Naomi and Ruth is paralleled by the devotion of Jonathan to David, a friendship so strong that Jonathan comes to love David more than he loves women. After Jonathan's death, when David spies the beautiful Bathsheba bathing, he invites her for a sexual rendezvous in the palace, though he already had many other wives to enjoy. The child of their adultery dies, but Bathsheba later becomes pregnant with Solomon, the famously wise king and the purported author of the Song. In these biblical passages, sexual longing refuses to be limited to the love between a husband and wife, or even between a man and a woman. In the case of the Song of Songs, desire's heat can be applied not only to the love between a woman and a man, but also between humanity and God.

Many Waters Cannot Quench Love:
Desire and the Song of Songs

"Let him kiss me with the kisses of his mouth!" So begins the Song of Songs, an erotic poem that revels in desire postponed, fulfilled, and postponed again. "I come to my garden," the woman's lover proclaims, "I eat my honeycomb with my honey" (5:1). "Open to me, my sister, my love, my dove, my perfect one" (v. 2), he pleads, using a double entendre few could miss.³ "My beloved thrust his hand into the opening," the woman responds, "and my inmost being yearned for him" (v. 4). But then he withdraws, and so she laments, "I opened to my beloved, but my beloved had turned and was gone" (v. 6). Hoping to find him again, she searches throughout the city, faint with love, only to be beaten and wounded for her pains. Reunited, the man caresses her with his gaze from her sandaled feet to her purple tresses, describing her thighs, navel, breasts, and neck. Pledging her love in return, the woman promises spiced wine and strong scents, warm embraces in a budding vineyard, and the juice of her own pomegranates. At the close of the poem, she calls to him again, her desire as of yet unquenched. The frank eroticism of this poem, rare among the biblical books, suggests that the Bible's sexual mores can include sex outside of marriage. The Song of Songs, perhaps more than any other biblical book, refuses to be limited by common notions of "family values." Instead, this book celebrates pleasure for pleasure's sake.

Modern readers are sometimes surprised that this book is canonical at all. Can a book this sexy be biblical? Surely someone tried to keep it out of the Bible! But, in fact, the Song of Songs has been among the most widely read and closely studied of all the canonical books. Copies of the Song were found among the Dead Sea Scrolls, the collection of books hidden in caves in the desert outside of Jerusalem sometime before 73 CE, and it was included among the list of sacred books mentioned by an important first-century Jewish historian named Josephus.⁴ A Greek translation of the Song also appears in the very early fourth- and fifth-century copies of the Christian Bible, and it was included among the sacred books of the Christians listed by a fourth-century Egyptian bishop called Athanasius of Alexandria.⁵ In other words, however risqué the Song of Songs may be, its canonical status has never seriously been questioned.

The Writing of the Song

Though attributed to King Solomon, the Song was probably written much later, after the Babylonian exile and while Israel was a vassal state of either Persia (539–323 BCE) or of the heirs of Alexander the Great (323–63 BCE).[6] As such, the Song may express Israel's longing for a time when Jerusalem was independent of foreign domination and Solomon's original temple still stood tall, at the height of its glory. References to "the curtains of Solomon," the "wood of Lebanon," and the "orchard of pomegranates" can be understood as allusions not to the woman or the man per se but to the curtain separating the Holy of Holies from view, the cedar from Lebanon that adorned the temple walls, and the lattice-work, ripe with bronze pomegranates, that once surrounded the temple courts.[7] If this interpretation is correct, the Song employs human desire to offer a poetic description of Israel's love for her land while also expressing a sentimental longing for the glory the nation once enjoyed. Imagining the restoration of God's garden (Israel) and the centerpiece to that garden (the temple), the Song of Songs recalls the golden age of the time of Solomon and envisions a return to the productive "marriage" of God and his people in a peaceful homeland.

But the Song also recalls the great love poetry of ancient Egypt and Mesopotamia, in which lovers are "honey-sweet" and sexual consummation is urgently sought and then vividly described.[8] These ancient Near Eastern poems are significantly older than the Song, but their language and poetic forms have left a mark nonetheless. Like these earlier poems, the Song does not shrink from describing genitalia, sexual intimacy, and climax. Read this way, "With great delight I sat in his shadow, and his fruit was sweet to my taste" can be understood as a reference to oral sex offered by the woman to the man's "tree";[9] "His left hand is under my head and his right hand caresses me" may describe the man caressing the woman's vulva;[10] and "Let my beloved come into his garden, and eat its choicest fruits" (4:16) should be read as a frank invitation to sexual intercourse.[11] The phrase "I compare you, my love, to a mare among the Pharaoh's chariots" (1:9) is also explicit, invoking the ancient military practice of sending a mare in heat amid the stallions as a distraction.[12] Apparently, the woman's scent drives men equally wild.

But What Does the Song Mean?

Still, the metaphorical language of the Song does not require readers to envision particular sex acts and positions.[13] Sexually explicit interpretations are possible, not obvious, and ready to be discovered by an enterprising reader eager to find them.[14] Certainly the ancient Christian theologian Origen of Alexandria was worried that an immature reader might get the wrong impression:

> For this reason I give warning and advice to everyone who is not yet free of the vexations of the flesh and blood and who has not withdrawn from desire for corporeal nature that he completely abstain from reading this book.[15]

The Song of Songs is a poem, and, as such, interpretation is left open. Its metaphors remain ambiguous, even as they heighten desire through text, pattern, and language, mimicking the rhythm of sexual intercourse and titillating with sensual, luxuriant imagery. Climax is hinted at rather than described, leaving it to readers to supply what the poem refuses explicitly to reveal.[16] Nevertheless, both the poem's beauty and its force depend upon sensual arousal and the awakening of erotic sentiments. And, interestingly enough, once awakened, *desire*—not marriage or childbearing—remains the focus. Voluntary intimacy and pleasure are the goal of these lovers, and social norms appear to be irrelevant to the delight they intend to pursue.

In addition to the lovers, other characters appear throughout the poem, who either encourage or interrupt the fulfillment of the couple's sexual longing. Their involvement, even more than the speeches of the lovers, hints at the fundamentally open perspective to sexual satisfaction adopted by the Song. Attributed to Solomon, the poem mentions his curtains, palanquin, crown, and vineyard, yet the poem also resists close affiliation with the famous Israelite king. The lover is not a king; he is a shepherd, or a gardener. At the end of the poem, the lover derides King Solomon's multiple vineyards/lovers, claiming to prefer his very own vineyard/ beloved, which he keeps for himself. The woman's mother is also mentioned, though she never appears. Her daughter imagines that she will offer her home for their encounters. A group called the "daughters of Jerusalem" is also supportive, asking the woman to describe her beloved to them. They serve as witnesses to her devotion and as dialogue partners regarding the nature of love. Daughters and mothers cheer the lovers on. By contrast, a series of meddling, violent men interrupt the woman's pursuit of desire, attempting to exercise control over her, though, in the end, their efforts are futile. The ancient purveyors of "abstinence-only education" do not succeed in controlling this woman by either fear or violence.

Early on, the woman complains that her "mother's sons" have kept her from caring for her vineyard, forcing her to care for their vineyards instead. Defiant in the face of their flagrant abuse of her body, the woman declares, "I am black and beautiful, O daughters of Jerusalem" (1:5). Later, the brothers insist on their right to police her behavior, promising to enclose their "little sister" with "boards of cedar" (8:8–9), presumably to protect her from illegitimate suitors. In ancient Israel, the writers of the Song knew, brothers could control young women still living in their family's house. Since the lovers live apart, they must therefore contend with her brothers' objections. As the poet has already intimated, however, this woman is beyond their protection, which she rejects. She has already invited her beloved to "go forth into the fields, and lodge in the villages" (7:11), offering him her "choice fruits" without their permission. True to form, she defies them again, rejecting their assessment of her status by announcing, "I was a wall, and my breasts were like towers; then I was in his eyes as one who brings peace" (8:10).

Male representatives of the city also try to control her. Venturing out at night to find her beloved, she is discovered by the city's guards, who then beat her, wound her, and strip her of her garment.[17] Undaunted, she appeals to the daughters of Jerusalem for support and, a few verses later, is reunited with her lover in a garden. Neither her brothers nor the watchmen could keep her from her goal. Ending where it began, the Song of Songs closes with an exhortation to the male lover to attend to the woman: "Make haste, my beloved, and be like a gazelle or a young stag upon the mountains of spices!" (8:14). The poem therefore rejects the view that men can or should control women. It also displays no interest whatsoever in defending marriage as the only appropriate setting for love.[18] These lovers pursue their love urgently, without consulting the wishes of others. Marriage is beside the point.

Who Is the Man? Who Is the Woman?

In addition to undermining the importance of marriage, the Song of Songs fails to meet expectations about male and female roles, exhibiting a remarkably open attitude toward gender. The dialogue form of the poem introduces the phenomenon. Though it is usually possible to detect whether the poet is speaking in the voice of a man or a woman in the original Hebrew (like many other languages, Hebrew nouns, pronouns, adjectives, and verbal forms have gender), some verses remain opaque, and so it can be difficult to discern who, exactly, is speaking.[19] The male lover elides into the female and vice versa, in a pattern that is not always clear.[20] By employing imagery drawn from architecture, war, and nature, the poet's vision of beauty can also seem strangely gendered, even grotesque.[21] The man is "radiant and ruddy," with "eyes like doves" and "cheeks . . . like beds of spices." The woman has hair "like a flock of goats," teeth "like a flock of shorn ewes," a neck "like the tower of David," and breasts "like two fawns." Her appearance is "terrible as an army with banners," her eyes are like pools of water by "the gate of Bath-rabbim," and her nose is like a tower of Lebanon, from which Damascus can be surveyed. Many of these images are rooted in ancient tastes and ideals, some of which no longer resonate. They are also metaphorical, intended to provoke admiration and awe, not to describe a "real" woman or man. Still, the woman's body in particular has troubled interpreters, who have wanted to explain how, exactly, breasts can be compared to fawns or teeth to a flock of shorn sheep.

These beautiful and yet strange metaphors have encouraged remarkably creative interpretations. According to the fifth-century Christian bishop Augustine of Hippo, the woman's teeth represent (male) church leaders, who bite and tear sinners away from their errors, shearing them of their worldly burdens.[22] According to the important eleventh-century Jewish interpreter Rashi, the pools of the woman's eyes signify the wisdom that flowed from Israel's (male) sages as they sat at the gates of the city.[23] Nicholas of Lyra, a twelfth-century Christian scholar who borrowed from Rashi, understood her neck as a reference to the (male) teachers of the Law, fortified by their studies as shields fortify a tower.[24] The fourteenth-century *Glossa Ordinaria*—interpretive statements that literally surround late-medieval biblical texts with definitions and commentary—suggested that the woman's pomegranate cheeks describe not cheeks per se but the red blood of Christ's passion and the blushing of the personified Church whenever "she" recalls the saving grace he offers.[25] Ancient and medieval interpreters replaced the woman's features with a man, men, or male-dominated institutions, imagining an entire church or people as the "woman." In this way, the hot desire of the woman for the man and the man for the woman was interpreted allegorically, an ancient and popular way of reading that claims there is a deeper, hidden meaning that is more important than the obvious or literal meaning. So interpreted, the seductive prose of the Song was marshaled to other ends, and, in the process, it became one of the most important books of the Bible.

The Love Between God and His Wife

Interpreting the Song not as an erotic dialogue between a man and a woman but as a description of the love affair between God and Israel, the second-century Rabbi Akiva declared that the Song of Songs is not only an important book, but the "holiest of the holies." Here Rabbi Akiva drew an explicit comparison between the poem and the temple's Holy of Holies, a location so sacred that, when the Jerusalem temple was still standing, the high priest entered it only once per year.[26] Other rabbis shared Rabbi Akiva's high estimation, arguing that the Song provides the interpretive key to the Torah, the five sacred books of Moses given at Sinai (Genesis–Deuteronomy) and preserved by faithful Israel. Celebrating the marriage between God the Bridegroom and Israel the Bride on their shared wedding day—the day when God gave the covenant at Sinai and appeared to Israel in all his glory—in their opinion the Song communicated the joy of the Exodus experience and the loving response of faithful Israel to "her" God.[27]

Revered as a wedding song by early Christians as well, the Song was applied not to the marriage of God and Israel or of God and the Synagogue, but of Christ and the Church or Christ and the believer's soul. As the third-century theologian Origen of Alexandria put it, the Song reveals the great mystery of God's love for humanity and of the faithful soul for God. Led by "heavenly love," the soul is transfixed by the magnificence of God's brilliance.[28] This "love" also anticipates the reunification of the Jews and Gentiles, symbolized by Christ's courtship first of the Jews through the Law and the Prophets and then of the Gentiles through his glorious incarnation.[29] A century later, Gregory of Nyssa followed Origen's lead, reading the Song as a description of the romance between God and the soul. To him, the Christian's spiritual life reaches its zenith when reading this Song, which sums up the soul's deep desire for union with the divine.[30] Ancient rabbis and Christian teachers may have warned that only mature believers are fully capable of understanding the Song's true meaning, but they did not hesitate to extol its sublime beauty. They even argued that it was the most sacred book of all.

But if God is essentially male, as is often assumed, and if the Song celebrates the nuptials of God and (his) "spouse" Israel, the Church, or the soul, then the anticipated wedding appears to be a marriage between "men." Allegorical interpretation takes the slippery gender roles of the Song even further, troubling the notion of who desires whom. In rabbinic readings, the leaders of Israel—Moses, Abraham, Isaac, Jacob, and so on—could be understood as God's "wives," the "pride and beauty of Israel."[31] Male Christians also cast themselves in the role of the "woman" to God's or Christ's man, imagining their souls panting after their beloved in the streets. "O that the Bridegroom's more perfect embrace may enfold my Bride!" Origen implored. "And if He will condescend to make my soul His Bride too and come to her!"[32] Medieval interpreters took this tradition even further: William of St. Thierry envisioned his soul ascending to the house of God, where the union of his soul with Christ could commence without restraint.[33] His companion Bernard of Clairvaux was equally effusive, "If anyone has received this mystical kiss from the mouth of Christ even one time, he seeks again that intimate experience, and repeats it willingly."[34] Men kissing men in advance of their passionate marriage to the (male) divine became a principal way of describing the mystical union of the human soul and God as depicted by the Song. Christ could switch genders and poetic roles as well. Envisioning Christ as a "woman," medieval mystics imagined Christ's wounds as fissures from which honey could be sucked and within which the soul could find refuge.[35] They also imagined themselves receiving milk from Christ's fecund breasts, an image they inherited from ancient Christian reflections on the Eucharist.[36] Female nuns and mystics could place themselves in the poem as well, taking on the role of the female beloved to the divine man. As virgin lovers of the Bridegroom, they awaited consummation in the closed garden of the convent. As beloved daughters of Christ the Mother, they received heavenly milk from his breasts.[37] In this way, medieval readers of the Song took on male and female roles at will, pursuing erotic fulfillment in the arms/breasts/wounds of a loving God.

Allegorical readings of the Bible are not as popular as they once were, and thus the playful role-switching of ancient and medieval interpreters can seem odd to readers today.[38] Nevertheless, the remarkable openness of the Song of Songs to diverse interpretations—historical, literary, or allegorical—mirrors the remarkable openness to erotic desire that pervades this poem. Whatever this sacred poem means, whenever it was written, and whoever composed it, the Song refuses to limit human desire to marriage or even to the love between a man and a woman. Sexually forthcoming and erotically charged, the poem experiments with both language and bodies in ways that have remained provocative and fertile to generations of readers, whether they prefer to read the poem literally, as a frank description of sexual longing, or spiritually, as an extended metaphor expressive of the love between humanity and God. As we will see, the Song is not the only biblical text capable of entertaining the joys and possibilities of love, longing, and touch. The Song may offer the most obvious example, but other texts are nearly as stimulating. The Bible exceeds whatever limits contemporary "family values" campaigns attempt to place upon it.

But Ruth Clung to Her: The Love Affair of Ruth and Naomi

For too long, scholar Sara Ahmed has suggested, family has been envisioned as an achievement toward which all should aim but which, thanks to culturally informed norms and ideals, only a few can enjoy. Those who fail to embody their proper roles within a narrow image of family as husband, wife, and children living in ordered harmony do not have "families," not really, and so are to be pitied or regarded with scorn. "Family," however, can be imagined another way. For example, one might understand family to be a "doing word and a word for doing"[39] that can include diverse configurations of shared bonds and responsibilities, all which qualify as "family."[40] So long as people love one another and care for one another, they are a family, irrespective of their biological ties or their legal recognition by the state in which they live. Though written in a very different context and more than two millennia before our own time, the book of Ruth seems to share Ahmed's basic insight: families can be formed by love and desire, whether or not they are recognized by institutional bodies. To the writer of Ruth, family can consist of an older woman and her beloved immigrant daughter-in-law, women can easily raise children on their own, and men can be seduced if it serves the interests of women.

Placed directly before the Song in Jewish copies of the Bible, the book of Ruth is the only book in the Hebrew Bible devoted to telling the story of a non-Israelite woman. Ruth is a descendant not of Abraham, the ancestor of the Israelites, but of Lot, Abraham's brother. Therefore she is a Moabite, a people the Israelites were explicitly commanded elsewhere in the Bible to avoid. Described as descendants of the incestuous union of Lot and one of his daughters (see Gen. 19:30–38), the Moabites are relatives of the people of Israel, but also hated rivals and enemies. The Moabites cannot be admitted into the assembly of Yhwh, Deuteronomy instructs (23:3–5), advice that was repeated by both Ezra and Nehemiah (Ezra 9:1; Neh. 13:1). According to Numbers, the Moabites seduced the Israelites into idolatry with their god Baal of Peor, resulting in the execution of all the chiefs of the people by the direct order of Yhwh (25:1–5). Moab will be laid to waste, the prophet Zephaniah predicted, because they scoff at both the Lord and his people (2:9–11). From the perspective of much of the Hebrew Bible, then, Moabites are to be avoided and shunned. The book of Ruth, however, takes quite a different approach, and not only to Moabites.

Ruth begins by reporting that, during the time of the judges, there was a famine so severe that the Judean Elimelech and his wife, Naomi, went to Moab to seek relief. Settling there, their sons, Mahlon and Chilion, married local women. Then, tragically, all three men died, leaving Naomi and her two daughters-in-law to fend for themselves. When Naomi hears that the famine has ended, she decides to return to Judah, encouraging her daughters-in-law to remain behind with their Moabite families. They resist, and so she points out that she has no sons left for them to marry. Here Naomi refers to an ancient biblical tradition called "Levirate marriage," in which a widow was to be married to a surviving brother of her husband, thereby keeping the first husband's wealth and property in the family. By following Levirate marriage customs, the widows of Mahlon and Chilion might also produce heirs, continuing the family line. But, Naomi points out, she has no sons, and so both she and her daughters-in-law can have no future together. Ruth's fellow sister-in-law, Orpah, takes Naomi's advice, but Ruth refuses, pleading, "Do not press me to leave you or to turn back from following you!" (1:16). Ruth vows to adopt Naomi's people as her people and Naomi's God as her God, promising, "Where you die, I will die—there will I be buried," and ending her pledge with an oath, "May the LORD do thus and so to me, and more as well, if even death parts me from you!" (v. 17).[41] This covenant between Ruth and Naomi, so often read in marriage ceremonies today, is therefore actually a covenant between two women whose steadfast love for each other brings blessings not only to the two of them but to Israel as a whole. By the end of the book, Ruth and Naomi have returned to Israel, secured an inheritance for themselves, and, with the assistance of Boaz, one of Elimelech's relatives, given birth to a son, Obed, the grandfather of David.

Continuing the Family Line

As with the Song of Songs, it is difficult to determine precisely how to interpret this carefully constructed story. Is the emphasis on Ruth and Naomi, their devotion to each other and the fertility of their unwavering love?[42] Or perhaps the story is concerned with the intricacies of Levirate marriage laws and Judean inheritance customs, both of which are appropriately observed by Naomi, Ruth, and Boaz.[43] The story might also offer a way to bring faithful Moabites into David's kinship line legitimately, despite their objectionable former behavior, a strategy that could justify David's conquest of their territory during his reign.[44] Nevertheless, one narrative feature seems crystal clear: the main characters of this story are women, deeply devoted to each other and the agents of their own destiny. These two women—one Israelite and one Moabite—arrange for the continuation of the family line first by their fierce love for each other and then by means of a daring sexual overture.

When Ruth and Naomi enter Judah, they are impoverished and without male support, and so Ruth resorts to gleaning barley in the fields of Boaz, Naomi's kinsman. According to Israelite law, the poor were permitted to glean fields for remaining grain after the harvest (see Lev. 19:9–10;

Deut. 24:19–22), and this is precisely what Ruth does, feeding both her-self and her mother-in-law. But when Ruth sees an opportunity to im-prove her circumstances, she takes it. Catching Boaz's eye, she receives his promise to serve as her protector, and he invites her to glean in his fields unaccosted. Then, after sharing a meal together, he offers her even greater honor, allowing her to glean among the standing sheaves, a prac-tice she continues throughout the barley and wheat harvests. Pleased with her daughter-in-law's good fortune, Naomi notes that Boaz is a relative, implying that he has the right to redeem Ruth for himself (see Ruth 2:20). In other words, according to Levirate marriage laws, Boaz is next in line to marry Ruth. He can continue Ruth's first husband Mahlon's line and inherit Mahlon's property. At the end of the harvest season, therefore, Naomi presents Ruth with some surprising instructions: "Wash and anoint yourself," she suggests, "and put on your best clothes and go down to the threshing floor." Waiting until after Boaz is asleep, Ruth is to "un-cover his feet and lie down" (3:3–4). By directing her to "uncover his feet," which actually means "uncover his genitals," Naomi seems to be recom-mending to Ruth that she openly proposition their relative Boaz.[45] At-tractively adorned, Ruth is to uncover Boaz's feet/genitals while he is lying alone, relaxed and comfortable after a full harvest meal.

Ruth takes Naomi's advice. When her intended lover awakens, he is startled to find a young woman lying at his "feet." "Who are you?" he asks. Identifying herself, Ruth requests that he spread his cloak over her, a forthright request that he take her in marriage. He responds by prais-ing her for the steadfast love she has displayed. Calling her a "valorous woman," a term employed elsewhere in the Bible to praise a good woman for her generosity, dignity, and kindness (see Prov. 31:25–31),[46] he agrees to fulfill her request, so long as another relative with a previous right to redeem does not choose to marry her instead. Boaz, like Naomi, carefully observes Levirate marriage laws , making sure that an even closer rela-tive has the opportunity to claim Mahlon's widow first. Still, Ruth then "lay at his feet" until the morning, getting up to return home "before one person could recognize another" so as to avoid a scandal (3:14). Did Ruth and Boaz enjoy a sexual encounter? The language suggests that they did, even though a chance remained that Boaz would not be able to marry Ruth in the end.

Arrangements between Boaz, Ruth, and Naomi then proceed as planned: Boaz and Naomi's closer male kin negotiate over Ruth's first husband, Mahlon's, inheritance (Ruth and a piece of property belonging to his father, Elimelech); when this unnamed close relative learns that Ruth will be part of the deal, he surrenders both Ruth and the land to Boaz, with the elders and all the people serving as witnesses to the transaction; Boaz then takes Ruth as his wife and she conceives a child; when the child is born, the women of Judah congratulate Naomi on her success, exclaiming that Ruth is "more to you than seven sons" (4:15); Naomi then becomes the child's wet nurse, and the women name the baby Obed. The book closes with a reminder from the narrator that this same Obed will be the father of Jesse and the grandfather of King David.

Nursing Obed

The devotion of Ruth to Naomi may well be the central lesson of this story: through their love, boundaries of nation, age, and religion are crossed and a child is created who is raised not by a married couple, but by the women, including Naomi, who nurses Obed at her breast.[47] To the book of Ruth, the family of Israel can include a family made up of two women and a baby, conceived at their initiative. Ruth and Naomi are in this way the conduits of wholeness and well-being, and not only for themselves, but also for the whole community, particularly the women, who rejoice at their good fortune.[48] Aware of the constraints of their male-dominated society—without a man to support them, they will remain impoverished—the enterprising pair refuse to be left destitute. Instead, they work within existing structures in surprising, bold ways, taking the initiative and working out their own destiny. They go so far as to seduce Naomi's kinsman Boaz at night, when he is drunk. Perhaps they even intend to force Boaz into marrying Ruth since, as a respectable man, he will want to avoid a scandal, especially if Ruth becomes pregnant.[49] Against the odds, the love and determination of these two women secure their own futures and also the future of the line of Perez/Elimelech/Mahlon, which turns out to be the line of King David.

Lurking behind the book of Ruth, however, is a story not only of successful female love and empowerment, but also of male-dominated property rights and inheritance. Together the women place themselves within an established, male-led household, manipulating existing property laws in their favor, but without challenging the basic validity of these same laws. The book never questions the view that women are property, subject to exchange between men; the legal transaction between Boaz and Naomi's other male relative includes Ruth and a plot of land as a combined purchase, treating them as equivalent "goods."[50] Moreover, the final sign of blessing in this book is a male child, through whom property—and women—can pass to the next generation of propertied men.

The book also never really undermines the secondary status of Moabites. Naomi does not contradict Ruth's own stated perspective—that she is Naomi's maidservant, subject to the will of her mother-in-law and obedient to her in all matters—and Naomi is willing to put her daughter-in-law at significant risk by encouraging her to play the role of a loose woman who travels alone at night adorned for an assignation. As already noted when discussing the Song of Songs, such behavior could lead to abuse and violence against women, as the woman of the Song discovered when searching for her beloved in the city. Perhaps Ruth's identity as a Moabite makes these extraordinary measures necessary. After all, Naomi's closer kinsman renounces his claim to Mahlon's land once he realizes he will need to redeem (that is, marry) Ruth to gain access to the estate.[51] The rabbis intensified this exact point, blaming the deaths of Naomi's sons on their decision to marry Moabite women to begin with.[52] The ancient Christian bishop John Chrysostom also understood Ruth's identity to be disgraceful; he argued that Boaz's response to her was exceptionally kind, since Boaz, "neither despised her poverty nor abhorred her mean birth."[53] Finally, Obed is brought up not by Ruth, a Moabite maidservant, but by Naomi herself, whose identity as a Judean is never in question.[54] Ruth gains her status as a (surrogate) member of Israelite society by denying her own people, caring for her mother-in-law at significant risk to herself, and, as the local women confirm, bearing a child not for herself but for Naomi ("A son has been born to Naomi." 4:17).[55]

Still, despite these undercurrents, like the Song of Songs, the book of Ruth presents an unexpected understanding of the place of desire in human life while also redefining what a proper family might look like. Neither book limits sexual intercourse to marriage, and this book in particular seems to assume that extraordinary circumstances—a famine, a childless family, and the absence of an available redeemer—justifies extraordinary measures, including sexual assertiveness on the part of women. Ruth's seduction of Boaz at the instigation of her mother-in-law, at night, and before a betrothal has been successfully arranged, is key to the narrative and central to the genealogy of the Davidic royal family. Apart from Naomi and Ruth, there would have been no David, and their example is extolled throughout the book. It is therefore the devotion of two women—one Israelite, one Moabite—for each other that makes Israelite royalty possible, and in direct violation of Israelite law.[56] Not only does David's line include a Moabite, though Israelites are specifically ordered not to associate with Moabites, but his birth also depends upon Ruth's willingness to "uncover the feet" of a man who is not her husband. Two generations later, David will also violate social norms, first by entering into a loving covenant with the son of King Saul and then by engaging in a seduction of his own. Like Ruth, the story of David refuses to define family as an ordered grouping of one husband, one wife, and their obedient children and, like both the book of Ruth and the Song of Songs, sex outside of marriage is not only practiced, it is encouraged.

Your Love to Me Was Wonderful:
Desire and the Love of King David

Sexual intrigue is central to the story of King David, a story told through a series of contradictory accounts now collected within 1 and 2 Samuel.[57] Written and edited long after his reign, these books do not conform to

modern notions of history, nor do they progress according to modern
logics of narrative and plot. Nevertheless, there is an obvious and over-
whelming focus on King David, his rise, his exploits, and his military
successes. Throughout both books, David's sexual partnerships and erotic
alliances serve to cement political ties or undermine them, demonstrating God's favor or carrying out God's punishments, and displaying the
overarching perspective of the editor: monarchy comes at a cost. David
ascends to the throne by means of an erotic attachment to Jonathan, the
son of the current king. Once on the throne, he displays his status as king
by marrying the former wives of his rivals, and, when these women are
not enough, by initiating an adulterous affair with Bathsheba, the wife of
one of his military commanders, Uriah the Hittite. When she becomes
pregnant, he arranges for the death of her husband and then marries her
himself. The book of Deuteronomy may prescribe death for adulterers
(22:22), but the liaison of David and Bathsheba ultimately produces the
heir to the throne.

Early in 1 Samuel, the people of Israel appeal to their judge/prophet
Samuel to appoint a king for them, despite Yhwh's warnings. A king
will "take your sons and appoint them to his chariots and to be his
horsemen. . . . He will take your daughters to be perfumers and cooks
and bakers. . . . He will take one-tenth of your grain and of your vineyards. . . . He will take your male and female slaves, and the best of your
cattle and donkeys. . . . He will take one-tenth of your flocks" (8:11–17).
In the end, Yhwh cautions, you will be his slaves. The people, however,
ignore these dangers, seeking instead a king who will protect them from
other nations, particularly the Philistines. Acquiescing to their pleas,
Samuel appoints Saul, a man "head and shoulders above everyone else"
(9:2), a decision that is affirmed by the casting of lots and by his exceptional military prowess. Saul's success, however, begins to falter, and
after Saul engages in a series of improper religious rituals, Yhwh's favor
is transferred from Saul to David, who, unbeknownst to Saul, has been
anointed king by Nathan, Samuel's successor. The handsome David is
brought to Saul's court, where he pleases everyone, defeats the Philistine
giant, Goliath, and forms a bond of friendship with Jonathan, Saul's son

and heir. The bond between David and Jonathan is exceptionally strong, so strong that Jonathan takes off his robe, armor, sword, and bow and gives them to his friend. In fact, his extravagant gesture suggests more than friendship; here Jonathan expresses a willingness to transfer his right of succession to David, whom "he loved . . . as his own soul" (18:3).[58]

The Love Affair of Jonathan and David

The deep attachment between Jonathan and David serves as a backdrop to the struggles between David and King Saul. Jonathan remains loyal to David throughout Saul's rule, despite the king's growing jealousy and hostility toward his younger and more accomplished rival. Jonathan takes "great delight in David," foiling Saul's various attempts to arrange for David's death and repeatedly choosing his friend over his own father (19:1–7; 20:1–42). Sensing that his father's reign will fail, he makes a formal covenant with David, asking his friend to remain faithful to him and to his descendants, whatever happens over the course of the struggles with Saul. Sealing the covenant with an oath, David swears by his love for Jonathan, "for he loved him as he loved his own life" (20:17). Then, when Jonathan is killed by the Philistines and his father, Saul, falls on his sword, David sings a formal lament for them both, calling them "beloved and lovely . . . swifter than eagles" and "stronger than lions." The song ends with special praise for Jonathan: "I am distressed for you, my brother Jonathan; greatly beloved were you to me; your love to me was wonderful, passing the love of women" (2 Sam. 1:23–26).

The story of David and Jonathan is illustrative of the pro-David stance of much of 1 and 2 Samuel, implying as it does that King Saul's son willingly gave up his claim to the throne, and thus that David, a shepherd with no formal ties to Saul, was the rightful heir to the throne and not a usurper, as some might (naturally) conclude. Their deep love and devotion is also hierarchical; it is Jonathan whose love for David surpassed his love of women and Jonathan who is accused by his father of an improper relationship with the charismatic David. Catching him taking David's side against his father, King Saul upbraids Jonathan: "You son of a perverse, rebellious woman! Do I not know that you have chosen the son of Jesse to your own shame, and to the shame of your mother's nakedness?" (1 Sam. 20:30). This charged vocabulary of shame and nakedness implies that Jonathan's disgrace is sexual as well as political, at least from the king's perspective.[59] In this way, the writers of 1 and 2 Samuel imply that the intimacy of the two men extended beyond close friendship to include an erotic dimension that, from Saul's point of view, shamed his son.[60] Jonathan's love for David, a love that surpassed his love of women, appears to have included an erotic attachment.

Some historians have resisted this interpretation. Noting that the language of love is actually quite typical of the vocabulary employed in ancient covenant contexts, these scholars have argued that the "love" of Jonathan for David is no more erotic than the love of a king for his subjects or of one political ally for another.[61] Jonathan loves David, but so does Saul, at least initially. The people also love David, and later when, as king, David makes a treaty with the king of Tyre, this king also becomes a "lover of David."[62] In other words, love language does not necessarily refer to erotic intimacy and desire. Or does it? As other historians have also pointed out, Saul's daughter Michal, David's first wife, is said to love David too, so much so that she, like her brother, conspires to protect him from her father. Michal's love clearly includes marital and sexual love, though their union fails to produce an heir. Moreover, David's assertion that Jonathan's love for him was better than his love for women cannot be explained in terms of ancient covenant terminology.[63] As biblical scholar Susan Ackerman observes, Jonathan is presented as womanlike or wifelike in his relationship to David, making his death—and the loss of his wonderful love—worthy of David's tender eulogy.[64] Jonathan's love for David justifies David's superiority over him and his willingness to take the throne of Israel from his friend. Their love also implies that before becoming king, David, the beautiful musician and shepherd, enjoyed an intimate friendship with a man. According to this story, David enjoyed sexual satisfaction and intimate love with both his dear friend Jonathan and with his wives.

The Love Affair of David and Bathsheba

Following the deaths of Saul and Jonathan, David keeps his covenant with Jonathan, punishing those who seek to harm Jonathan's descendants. Initially, men loyal to King Saul attempt to prevent David's rise, but after Saul's son Ishbaal insults one of his commanders and the commander then switches sides, the tide turns and David emerges triumphant. All the leaders of Israel declare their loyalty to the new king, and he is installed in Jerusalem. Newly minted as king of Israel and residing in the capital city, David cements his political alliances by taking additional wives and concubines, displaying the wealth and stature befitting his new status.[65] He also undertakes several military and sexual conquests, including the conquest of Bathsheba, the wife of his Hittite commander.

One day while his troops are out battling the Ammonites, David views a beautiful woman bathing on her roof. A messenger informs him that she is already married, the wife of Uriah the Hittite, but David sends for her anyway. Lying together, she becomes pregnant, and so he calls for Uriah to return home. "Go down to your house, and wash your feet" (2 Sam. 11:8), David orders, implicitly encouraging the commander to have sexual intercourse with his wife. As we have seen, references to feet regularly point to sexual encounters. Uriah, however, refuses to visit his home and instead insists on maintaining his soldier's vow of celibacy. So long as his troops remain assembled for war, he will not "lie with" his wife (v. 11). With this first plan foiled, David then instructs his general, Joab, to place Uriah on the front lines, arranging for his rival's death so he can take Bathsheba as his own.

This sordid tale of adultery and arranged murder complicates the portrait of King David we have encountered thus far. Though much of 1 and 2 Samuel defends David against detractors, the adulterous liaison with Bathsheba leads inexorably to the demise of both David and his household. The child he fathers in the context of his adultery dies, and, as a result of his sin, Yhwh promises to "raise up trouble against you from within your house," taking David's wives and giving them to another, who will lie with them "in the sight of this very sun" (2 Sam. 12:11).

God also sends Nathan to tell David a parable involving a shepherd and a little ewe-lamb: A rich man with many flocks and cattle did not want to slaughter one of his own animals to feed a visiting guest, so he stole a ewe-lamb from a poor man, a lamb so beloved that "it used to eat of his meager fare, and drink from his cup, and lie in his bosom, and it was like a daughter to him" (2 Sam. 12:3). The love of the poor man did not prevent the rich man from exploiting his neighbor and stealing the beloved lamb, however, an action that infuriates David. "As Yhwh lives, the man who has done this deserves to die" (v. 5), David cries out, only to be informed by Nathan that he himself is the rich man, guilty of stealing the wife of Uriah the Hittite and arranging for Uriah's murder. The affair of David and Bathsheba, unlike the love between David and Jonathan, mars David's reign and causes him significant trouble. Yet, in contravention of other biblical laws, neither he nor Bathsheba is killed. Others pay for their adultery: first Uriah the Hittite is murdered, then the son they produce dies, and, finally, David's concubines are raped by one of his other sons.

Bathsheba the Ewe-Lamb

The comparison of Bathsheba to a ewe-lamb and David's infraction to theft may seem misplaced, but according to the logic of 1 and 2 Samuel, Bathsheba is the property of Uriah and her affair with David was a material as well as a sexual crime.[66] David did not simply enjoy sex with Bathsheba and then murder her husband; he stole another man's property. Yet, unlike Nathan's reading of these events, some biblical scholars place the blame not on David but on Bathsheba: She must have known that she could be seen by the king during his afternoon walk and so likely arranged for her own seduction. She displays no resistance to David's advances and no dismay when she learns of her pregnancy, though she must have known that she would likely be fertile during their encounter. Finally, as a wealthy woman from a family of high status, she knew that her association with the king would raise her status even further, opening up the possibility that her own offspring would become king. In other words, according to these interpreters, Bathsheba was a willing and equal partner in the adultery, if not a seductive temptress who forced David to misbehave against his own interests. After all, she was a foreign woman, and foreign women cannot be trusted.[67] The writers of 2 Samuel, however, adopt a different perspective, punishing David not directly, but through his harem. A few chapters later his son Absalom leads a revolt against him, displaying total disdain for his father's authority by "going into" (raping) his father's concubines on the roof of the palace "in the sight of all Israel" (2 Sam. 16:22).

In 1 and 2 Samuel, the rise of King David is therefore explained, in part, in terms of intimate friendships between men, political marriages, and sexual conquests. His close relationship with Jonathan legitimizes his usurpation of Jonathan's own role as heir to the throne. His marriage to Michal, daughter of Saul, and to the former wives of his rivals dramatizes his dominance over the men who stand in his way. His improper liaison with Bathsheba, however, demonstrates that he, too, is capable of betraying Yhwh, a betrayal that leads to his own unmanning in the form of the rape of his concubines by his son Absalom. As God predicted through the prophet Samuel at the beginning of 1 Samuel, King David turned his subjects into his personal property, demanding access to the wives and "sheep" of others. As God predicted through the prophet Nathan, David was punished for his murderous arrogance not by his own death or the death of his partner Bathsheba but by the death of their son and then by the exposure of David's harem to the violence of Absalom. Nevertheless, the royal line continued through Bathsheba and David, producing Solomon, the next king. The writers of 1 and 2 Samuel do not limit erotic entanglements to marriage or to the love between a man and a woman. They also portray David, the hero of most of the story, violating biblical laws against adultery. In these books, sex, betrayal, desire, and love are broad categories, despite the underlying assumption that women belong to their husbands or fathers. In the case of David, the love between two men—covenantal or erotic—turns out to be the most productive love of all.

Desire In and Out of Control

The Song of Songs, the book of Ruth, and the cycle of stories associated with King David demonstrate that biblical perspectives on sexual desire and family ties remain much more complicated than is often thought. The appropriate expression of desire is not limited to marriage between a man and a woman, but can include the love of a son of a king for his charismatic ally, the love of rabbis and theologians for God, their "husband," and the love of a faithful Moabite for her Israelite mother-in-law. The nuclear family is also not idealized: Naomi, Ruth, and Obed are a family, bound together by their common love for one another, and, in the Song of Songs, the woman's mother supports her daughter's premarital encounters over the objections of her sons, who seek to control their sister's sexuality and are overruled. King David never even bothers to pursue marriage as commonly envisioned today. His first erotic attachment is to the son of the king, he marries several women, and he engages in an extramarital affair with the wife of his general. Biblical desire refuses to be limited to marriage: the lovers of the Song consummate their longing before any marriage ceremony takes place, Ruth "uncovers Boaz's feet" before Boaz has established his "right to redeem," and David fathers a child with Bathsheba while she is still married to Uriah. In other words, when all the biblical books are taken into account, no simple message regarding the meaning and limits of desire can be found. In fact, the passages considered in this chapter suggest that nonmarital desire can be both limitless and productive. If Ruth, Naomi, Boaz, Jonathan, David, or Bathsheba had listened to Christian educator Bonnie Park, Obed and Solomon would never have been born. As we will see in the next chapter, however, in other biblical books, desire is a matter of property rights, especially the rights of men to the women and slaves in their care.

CHAPTER 2

Biblical Marriage

There Is No Single View on Marriage Presented in the Bible

Lately it seems that no serious political discussion can begin without the question, "Are you for or against gay marriage?" as if the answer given to this single question sums up one's politics, religion, and very identity. But surely marriage is more complicated than this. Certain groups have always been designated as ineligible for marriage, denied its privileges and its benefits. Indeed, it isn't only gay couples who cannot obtain the social, cultural, and economic advantages that accrue to heterosexual couples with access to recognized, state-issued marriage certificates. Common-law marriages and marriages between citizens and noncitizens are also recognized differently in different states, and, not too long ago, marriages between men and women of different races were patently illegal. Prior to 1967, when the Supreme Court ruled that antimiscegenation laws are unconstitutional, twelve states outlawed marriages between whites and Native Americans, fourteen states banned white-Asian marriage, and many more banned white–African American marriage.[1] The state of Texas, for example, which enacted its first antimiscegenation law in 1837, ruled that no person of "European blood or their descendants" could marry with "Africans or their descendants," a law that stood for more than a century.[2] In California, marriage between "white persons" and "Negroes, Mongolians, members of the Malay race or mulattos" was prohibited from 1850 until 1948, when a Mexican American resident attempted to marry an African American resident, only to be told that such a marriage would be prohibited since she was white.[3] Forty years ago, the pressing political question was, "Are you for or against miscegenation?" not "Are you for or against gay marriage?"

Whatever politicians and pastors might argue, then, state-sponsored marriage is not a matter of morality and piety but of privileges meted out to some and denied to others. Marriage certificates distribute goods and bodies in such a way that certain resources are kept "in the family," or "among the citizens"; they do not define which human ties are recognized by God. The promotion of heterosexual marriage over and against gay marriage is just the latest in a series of exclusionary marriage regulations that attempt to define what a "real" marriage is supposed to look like over and against the inadmissible couplings of other intimate partners. Again and again, the Bible is inserted into these discussions, just as it was in miscegenation controversies several decades ago, as if biblical teachings can solve the problem of which marriages the state should or should not recognize. This strategy needs to stop, not only because the separation of church and state is a central democratic value, but also because the Bible offers no viable solution to our marriage dilemmas. There is no such thing as a single, biblically based view of legitimate marriage.

As we observed in the previous chapter, the assumption that women are the property of the men in their families, to be disposed of as their fathers, brothers, and husbands see fit, informs much of biblical literature. The Song of Songs reacts against this assumption by refusing to limit sexual desire to marriage, even for the woman. By contrast, both the book of Ruth and the story of David presuppose that, in the end, the point of marriage and family is to continue the male line. In Ruth, this goal must be managed with the assistance of women, but only after the men who "own" them agree to the arrangement. Thus, Boaz must check with another male relative of Naomi's before he can take Ruth as his wife. Similarly, in 2 Samuel, the prophet Nathan accuses David of violating Uriah's property rights, not Bathsheba, when the king seduces her. In these stories, women function as units of exchange in negotiations between men, though these same texts are willing to entertain the productivity of extramarital sex and homoerotic love. Biblical marriage law is even more emphatic: women belong to men; male honor is tied, in part, to how well men supervise the women in their care; and men demonstrate their wealth and success by the number of legitimate wives and children they are able to acquire. Though the practice of polygamy disappears from later biblical writings, the view that men are supposed to control their wives, whom they own, does not. New Testament writings often adopt this same perspective, but with a proviso: though marriage is acceptable, celibacy is even better. Adjusting previous teachings regarding marriage and family, Jesus and his followers emphasize not marriage, property, and genealogical relationships but the sexual self-control that comes with faith in Christ. When it comes to marriage, biblical laws are almost entirely contradictory.

One Flesh: The Book of Genesis and "Biblical Marriage"

In the second and third chapters of Genesis, a rationale for sexual intercourse is offered that is still quoted today: "Therefore a man leaves his father and his mother and clings to his woman, and they become one flesh" (2:24, my translation). According to this view, sexual union overcomes a division that was created when God made two beings, male and female, from one human person, Adam. Their primordial companionship, cemented when Yhwh resolved to make a helper for Adam out of Adam's own rib, was disastrously interrupted by their decision to eat from the forbidden tree of the knowledge of good and evil. Among other punishments for their disobedience, Yhwh declares to the woman, "your desire shall be for your man, and he shall rule over you" (3:16, my translation). Embedded within the creation story, then, are two seemingly immutable principles: in sexual intercourse, men and women seek to reunite the flesh they once shared, and, in marriage, women necessarily accept subordination, which is rooted in their desire for their husbands.

Yet these principles, supposedly designed into the very fabric of male and female natures, are not quite so clear-cut. The story of the garden of Eden is the second of two creation stories, the first of which offers quite a different picture of male-female creation, one in which God, called here Elohim rather than Yhwh, creates humankind all at once: "So God created humankind (*adam*) in his image, in the image of God (*Elohim*) he created them; male and female he created them" (1:27).[4] If God/Elohim created humankind at once, male and female, and both were made in God's image, then why did Yhwh need to create the female a second time, fashioning the woman from the rib of the *adam*? The first creation story implies that *adam*, translated here as "humankind" rather than as the proper name Adam, could be both male and female, not that there was first a male *adam* and then a female created as his helper. In other words, the first human was not a man at all: he (or it) was simply an earth creature, an *adam*, without a discernible gender, until we learn that "male (*ish*) and female (*ishah*), God created them."[5] Male and female may be "one flesh," but the way in which they are one flesh differs. In the first account of human creation, they are one flesh because they are both made of the same material (*adamah*—fertile soil)[6] and in the image of God. In the second, they are one flesh because God forms the female from the *adam* he had already created. The explanation given for sexual intercourse in Genesis 2 is therefore contradicted by the creation account given in Genesis 1.

Nevertheless, these same stories continue to be cited today as definitive sources for God's understanding of human sexuality. As one Christian theologian recently argued, Genesis "remains authoritative for conveying that the obvious complementarity (and concordant sexual attraction) of male and female witness to God's intent for human sexuality."[7] Or, as another puts it, "the one ineluctable fact of human nature, of being human . . . is that we are all created male and female," and thus that, "maleness and femaleness is what sexual longing is fundamentally about."[8] Read in this way, the creation stories purportedly describe marriage as God intended it: "Adam and Eve made commitments to each other and made love in celebration of those commitments. Marriage, like our creation as male and female, is a gift of God's love."[9] But not only do these interpretations gloss over the differences between Genesis 1 and

Genesis 2, but they also fail to notice the implications of Genesis 3: the desire of the woman for her husband is not rooted in complementarity, nor does it originate in a recognition of the flesh she once shared with the man, nor does it celebrate her commitment of love. Instead, desire accompanies her subordination to her husband, for whom she now must bear children in pain. As Yhwh puts it, "I will greatly increase your pangs in childbearing, in pain you shall bring forth children, yet your desire shall be for your husband, and he shall rule over you" (3:16). Female desire is therefore a punishment, not a blessing, and it is male desire that initiates sexual coupling. It is the man who "leaves his father and his mother and clings to his woman" and the *adam* who remarks "this at last is bone of my bones and flesh of my flesh" (2:23). Recognizing, perhaps, that childbirth is a dangerous proposition for women, especially in premodern times, those who composed the story of Adam and Eve interpreted female desire as a source of risk, not as a blessing.[10]

Primal Androgyny and the First Human Person

The view that Genesis 1:27 is about gender complementarity, so prevalent today, is only one possible interpretation among many, and a relatively new one as well. From the perspective of late-antique Jewish rabbis, the phrase "in the image of God he created them, male and female he created them" refers not to the creation of two complementary sexes, but one. As Rabbi Samuel bar Nahman explained in Genesis Rabbah, a verse-by-verse commentary on Genesis compiled in the mid-fifth century CE, "When the Holy One, blessed be he, created the first man, he created him with two faces. Then he split him and made two bodies, one on each side, and turned them about."[11] In other words, the first human being was androgynous, possessing the genitals of both sexes, but then in Genesis 2, when God took the *adam*'s rib—interpreted here as one of *adam*'s sides—God cut the androgynous being in two.[12] This reading deals with the problem of the two creation stories by positing two steps in God's fashioning of humanity: first, the human person was androgynous, then the human person was divided into two, making two incomplete beings from one, primal, unified, and dually sexed creature.

Many ancient Christians shared this same point of view, imagining an initial androgynous being followed by secondary division, a separation that some hoped to overcome. As the apostle Paul put it when writing to the church in Galatia, in Christ "there is no male and female" (3:28, my translation). Like some of his Jewish contemporaries, Paul expected a return to primal androgyny once God's elect received their heavenly bodies.[13] Among later Christians, the separation of the two genders was sometimes interpreted as the moment in which death and sorrow entered the world: "If the female had not separated from the male," declares the third-century Gospel of Philip, "she and the male would not die. That being's separation became the source of death." From the perspective of the Gospel of Philip, Christ came to reunite the two, making life available for those who understand this truth (Gospel of Philip 70).[14] The third-century "Gnostic" Gospel of Philip presents an understanding of creation that was ultimately rejected by orthodox Christians, but the longing for a presexual, androgynous, and virginal unity of "no male and female" was retained by later theologians.[15]

The claim that together the creation stories necessarily serve as a warrant for heterosexual love and marriage is therefore a modern invention, unfamiliar to the founders of both Christianity and Judaism. Ancient rabbis did interpret the separation of the male from the female in Genesis 2 as an explanation for male-female sexual intercourse—the purpose of marriage was to return the pair to a state of unity—but this did not prevent them from imagining the original human form as dually sexed.[16] Moreover, from the ancient Christian perspective, the lesson of the separation from primal androgyny to secondary sexual difference was not that marriage is both natural and good, but that sexual abstinence is preferable to sexual activity. By avoiding sex acts, human beings not only anticipate the heavenly state, in which "they neither marry nor are given in marriage," but they also imitate the lives of Adam and Eve before their expulsion from the garden. Offering an interpretation that is nearly opposite to some interpretations today, these

Christians concluded that, prior to their punishment, Adam and Eve never engaged in sexual activity at all.[17]

Genesis 1–3 Is Not Necessarily About Marriage: It's a Story About Farming

Extracting a normative vision of biblical marriage from the Genesis creation accounts is therefore not as straightforward as many today assume. In fact, the fascination with biblical creation accounts as a source for marriage law begins only in the first century BCE, long after these stories were first told and written down. Greek-speaking Jews, early Christians, and rabbis may have turned to Genesis again and again as they worked out what sexuality might mean, but no pre-Christian biblical book employs Genesis in this way.[18] Instead, in dialogue with other ancient Near Eastern creation myths, Genesis creation stories respond to questions like: What are the differences between human beings and animals? Why aren't human beings immortal? Why is it so difficult to farm the land? And why do women labor in childbirth?[19] To answer these questions, the writers of the Genesis accounts compared their God to other Mesopotamian gods and earlier creation stories, and the similarities between them are striking.

In one ancient Babylonian creation myth, the story of *Atrahasis,* humanity is created to till the land for the gods. According to the myth, the goddess created primeval man "so that he may bear the yoke," that is, that he may till the soil, and that he may do so in place of the gods. "Let man bear the yoke of the gods!" Atrahasis exclaims.[20] This explanation is quite similar to the reason given for Adam's creation in the second Genesis story: "Yhwh took the *adam* and put him in the garden of Eden to till it and keep it." In the Babylonian *Epic of Gilgamesh,* man becomes civilized only after intercourse with a woman: the character Enkidu feeds on the milk of wild animals and wanders through the world naked until he encounters a woman, who teaches him to copulate, to eat bread, and to drink wine.[21] Similarly, in Genesis 2, the *adam* becomes fully civilized and fully human only after engaging in sexual intercourse with a female, the woman created from his side. Expelled from the garden, Adam and Eve wear clothing, beget children, and raise flocks. Finally, as in Genesis 3, in the *Epic of Gilgamesh* humanity misses a chance at immortality after losing access to a particular plant. A clever snake steals the plant from the hero, Gilgamesh: "A serpent perceived the fragrance of the plant [of immortality]; it came up and snatched the plant, sloughing [its] skin on its return."[22] Apparently, the snake's ability to shed its skin was interpreted as a sign of its immortality, a point of view that may have influenced Genesis 3. While it may be possible to interpret Genesis as "about sex," then, it is also about the loss of immortality, the importance of farming, the difficulties of fertility, and, from an ancient Israelite perspective, the character of their God, Elohim/Yhwh, in comparison with local Babylonian, Sumerian, and Assyrian gods about whom other, similar stories were told.

Placed in an ancient context, the Genesis stories can also be read not as explanations for human sexuality but as responses to the perils of the ancient agricultural economy. Farming and fertility are a major concern of both stories, particularly the story of Adam and Eve. In the first creation story, humankind is placed in charge of every creature and every plant and then urged to "be fruitful and multiply"; in other words, humanity is created, in part, to populate the land and care for it. In the second, the writer indicates that the purpose of humankind is to till the soil. Then, following human disobedience, the god Yhwh curses the same soil from which he formed the *adam,* promising fertility problems for both the man and the woman: the woman will bring forth children in pain, and the man will have to extract grain "by the sweat of his brow" as opposed to simply enjoying the abundant fruit of the primeval garden.[23] Ordered to populate and cultivate the earth and then warned that the effort will be harrowing, humankind leaves the garden with a daunting task ahead.

Yhwh's curse, however harsh, resonates with the actual experiences of early Israel: unlike other Mesopotamian peoples, the Israelites farmed on mountainous steppes, which required terracing and the careful conservation of water.[24] The successful cultivation of grain was therefore hard work, as Genesis 3:17–18 acknowledges. Childbearing was also a fundamentally important but exceedingly dangerous activity for ancient Israelites. Multiple children successfully birthed and brought past infancy ensured community survival, since children could offer assistance for the intensive, subsistence-level farming of the period and provide the numbers required to occupy and then secure the land.[25] Yet a high infant mortality rate and a high rate of death in childbirth made the injunction to "be fruitful and multiply" a difficult commandment to fulfill. If there is a rationale for sexual intercourse, then, it appears to be compelled not by a worry about a particular sexual order but by an interest in encouraging procreation, despite the risks involved. For the land and the community to prosper, men must sow their seeds, both in the arable land and in a fertile female. To fulfill their appointed lot, Genesis suggests, women have no choice but to dedicate their bodies to this purpose.[26]

The stories told of the biblical patriarchs and their marriage arrangements throughout the rest of the book confirm this point of view. The patriarchs marry more than one wife, take concubines as well as wives, and attempt to father as many children as possible. Thus, Abraham marries Sarah and fathers Isaac, but before that, when Sarah fails to conceive, he also fathers a son with Sarah's slave Hagar. Near the end of his life, Abraham takes a second wife, named Keturah, with whom he fathers four more sons. Genesis concludes: "Abraham gave all he had to Isaac. But to the sons of his concubines Abraham gave gifts, while he was still living, and he sent them away from his son Isaac, eastward to the east country" (Gen. 25:6). In other words, though God's blessings and Abraham's inheritance belong exclusively to Isaac, Abraham's wealth and accomplishment were expressed through his multiple progeny, born to multiple women. Isaac's twin sons, Esau and Jacob, also take multiple wives and concubines. Jacob marries the sisters Leah and Rachel as well as their two maids, Bilhah and Zilpah. Jacob fathers a total of twelve sons with his wives and concubines, as well as a number of daughters, though only one is named. Esau marries three women, Adah, Oholibamah, and Basemath, and fathers five sons as well as several daughters, who are neither numbered nor named. The importance given to progeny, especially sons, is further emphasized by the organization of the book: upon the death of each patriarch, Genesis offers a list of his wives and descendants, with notice given regarding where they settled and the amount of wealth they accumulated.

Situating the Genesis creation accounts within a context of ancient myth and within the demands of ancient agriculture reminds us that these are ancient stories designed to address the needs and circumstances of Israel, not twenty-first-century Christians and Jews. Nevertheless, these stories are no more "about" farming than they are about sex. Subject to several centuries of interpretation, the meanings associated with the statements "Therefore a man leaves his father and his mother and clings to his wife," and "in the image of God he created them, male and female he created them" can and do change. Neither statement has settled the question of God's plan for human sexuality, nor have they provided a fixed definition of human marriage. Instead they have offered interpreters fertile ground for thinking through questions about fertility, sexuality, and human life, whether one finds in God's first human person a dual-sexed earth creature, an androgynous virgin who avoids sexual intercourse altogether, or a mandate for heterosexual marriage. Genesis does not so much settle the question of human sexuality as raise it in striking, interesting ways. To find direct commandments of the biblical God concerning marriage, we need to turn not to Genesis but to the covenant instructions (purportedly) given to the Hebrew people by Moses and collected in the books of Exodus and Deuteronomy.

Moses and Biblical Marriage Laws

The creation stories may not offer a straightforward set of rules and regulations for marriage, but the Hebrew Bible does have quite a bit to say to free Israelite men about the disposition of their women, slaves, and other property. Commanded not to commit adultery and not to covet a neighbor's wife, slave, ox, or donkey, Israelite men were also instructed to honor the marriage arrangements of male Hebrew slaves, treat slave wives equitably, and pay a full bride-price penalty to the father of any young unmarried woman they dare to seduce. Adulterous men and women were to be executed, and a man who slept with a wife of his father was to be cursed, since he had "uncovered his father's skirt" (Deut. 22:30, my translation). Legally, virgins were the highly prized responsibility of their fathers: a father was injured when his daughter's virginity was violated before her marriage, and a man who falsely accused his wife of premarital sex paid a heavy fine if her parents could produce evidence of her virginity in the form of bloodied sheets preserved from their wedding night. If, however, the charge was true and the woman was not a virgin at first marriage, she was to be stoned to death by the men of the village and at the entrance to her father's house. In this way, the father was punished as well, for he had failed to supervise his daughter and his negligence injured the entire (male) Israelite community.[27]

Two Covenant Codes on Marriage and Slaves

Preserved in two different books, the Sinai marriage laws are not always consistent: Exodus and Deuteronomy differ in the reasons they give for particular commandments, in the punishments they recommend, and in the types of incidents that are legislated. Though both books are associated with Moses and both sets of laws are described as having been given to the Hebrew people while they were wandering in the wilderness, the two law codes address different circumstances and concerns, perhaps because they were written at very different moments in Israelite history. The laws preserved in Exodus were likely collected earlier, even before the founding of the Israelite monarchy (before 1025 BCE), when local tribal judges ruled on cases and the law was viewed as a treaty between a divine ruler (Yhwh) and his vassal (Israel). Deuteronomy was probably composed in a later period, when kings ruled Judea and older legal practices needed reinterpretation.[28] Deuteronomy may even be the very book found (or composed) by a priest during the reign of the Judean king Josiah (641/640–609 BCE). Shaken by the fall of the Northern Kingdom of Israel to the Assyrians in 722 BCE,

King Josiah used this book of the law to institute a series of reforms, including a sweeping abolition of the worship of any god but Yhwh within Judah's borders.[29] Whichever book came first, however, they are clearly related, with one book's employing the other as a source, reinterpreting Moses's laws in light of new concerns.[30]

In Exodus, detailed instructions regarding marriage begin not with laws on adultery, as might be expected given the general prohibition of the practice in the context of the Ten Commandments, but with commandments involving the treatment of male Hebrew slaves and their wives. "When you buy a male Hebrew slave," Exodus instructs free Israelites, "in the seventh [year] he shall go out a free person, without debt" (21:2).[31] If the slave was married when purchased, Exodus then commands, his wife is to be released with him. In other words, though only the man is addressed initially, it turns out that he and his wife, if he has one, would be sold into slavery at the same time. By contrast, if the master gives the man a wife while he is enslaved, the wife and her children remain the property of the master, and he alone is released. Exodus then offers an exception: "If the slave declares, 'I love my master, my wife, and my children; I will not go out a free person'" (v. 5), then the man may opt to stay enslaved in perpetuity, a decision that is formalized by piercing his earlobe with an awl.

As is evident from this law, and others as well, Israelites became slaves of other Israelites not through capture as war booty or by breeding, but through debt: a man who had become overwhelmed with debt and poverty could sell himself or a member of his family to another Israelite man, serving as a slave for six years before being released, his debts clear. This practice is similar to what can be found in other ancient Mesopotamian cultures. For example, according to the Laws of King Hammurabi of Babylon (ruled 1792–1740 BCE), if a Babylonian man sells a wife, son, or daughter to another to pay off his debts, his (human) property is to be returned to him after three years of service and the debt forgiven.[32] Noticeably absent from the Exodus law, however, is any mention of an Israelite woman's selling herself. Presumably, she did not own her own body, and so debt slavery was not an option she could choose. Yet she could be enslaved. If married, she would be sold with her husband.[33] If unmarried, the decision to sell her belonged to her father, a conclusion that is confirmed in the next section of the covenant.

"When a man sells his daughter as a slave," Exodus continues a few verses later, "she shall not go out as the male slaves do" (21:7). Apparently, the rule that Israelite debt slaves are to be released on the seventh year of service does not apply to Israelite daughters. Instead, Exodus encourages her master to marry her, either to himself or to his son. If neither of these options is desirable, she may be "redeemed," that is, sold back to her father, or married or sold to another Israelite (sale to a non-Israelite is expressly forbidden).[34] In this way, the woman's father or master determine who will benefit from her labor and her sexuality. Still, her master is required to care for her appropriately. If he takes her as a wife, he is not permitted to mistreat her when he takes another, but must provide comparable food, clothing, and sexual intercourse to her as well. Moreover, if he gives her to his son as a wife, he must treat her as a daughter. Non-Israelite slaves, however, were not protected in this way. These slaves were the permanent property of their masters, and any children born to them were also enslaved. That is why a Hebrew slave married to a non-Hebrew slave woman by his master could remain with his family only if he, too, became a slave for life.[35]

Laws Are Not Necessarily Observed

Whether or not the Exodus regulations regarding slave marriage were ever followed cannot easily be determined. As is the case today as well, law prescribes what people *should* do, but it does not describe what they *actually* do, and practice regularly differs from the ideal espoused in law. Miscegenation may have been outlawed in the United States over the course of the nineteenth century, for example, but marriages between couples of every sort were tolerated anyway, whether or not they were legally recognized. Discrepancies between ancient laws and surviving ancient contracts are also not unusual. For example, as in Israelite law, only Assyrian fathers were given express permission to sell their daughters into debt slavery, but contracts between mothers and buyers have also been found. Similarly, though the Babylonian Laws of Hammurabi required debt slaves to be released after three years, extant Babylonian contracts suggest that this practice was not always honored.[36]

Apparently, Israelites were equally reluctant to release their slaves. Revisiting the Exodus covenant, the writers of Deuteronomy had to insist that the release requirement be observed, even though the Exodus version of the law had likely been in force for centuries. The affair of David and Bathsheba offers another helpful example. The Sinai covenant may expressly forbid adultery, but the heroic king David acquired Bathsheba as a wife only after first coveting his neighbor's wife and then impregnating her while she was married to another man. Neither David nor Bathsheba was accused by the prophet Nathan of violating covenant commandments, however, perhaps because, strictly speaking, they did not break either set of laws. Since Bathsheba's husband, Uriah, was a Hittite, the Sinai codes did not apply. Non-Israelite generals, like non-Israelite slaves, belonged to a separate legal category from free Israelites. Therefore, an Israelite man would not technically commit adultery if he slept with the wife of a foreigner. David and Bathsheba violated the spirit of the law, but they did not disobey its letter. And so, when offering his rebuke of the king, Nathan emphasized David's violation of Uriah's property rights not the gravity of his adulterous affair.

Marriage and Slave Law (Again)

Focusing on the obligation to let Hebrew slaves go free instead of on the treatment of slave families, Deuteronomy's version of the laws regarding slave release is quite different from what is found in Exodus. Mentioning nothing about slave wives and omitting instructions regarding Hebrew daughters sold into slavery, Deuteronomy reaffirms the principle that Hebrews who sell themselves into slavery must be released during the seventh year. But, unlike Exodus, Deuteronomy explicitly includes Hebrew women in the commandment: "If a member of your community, whether a Hebrew man or a Hebrew woman, is sold to you and works for you six years, in the seventh year you shall set that person free" (15:12). From Deuteronomy's perspective, then, female Hebrew debt slaves must be released as well, an apparent contradiction of the Exodus code. Masters are then warned "you shall not send him out empty-handed" (v. 13) but with produce from the land and animals from your flocks. Not only are masters expected to release their Hebrew slaves, they are expected to pay them for their service. A rationale for this required generosity is included, "Remember that you were a slave in the land of Egypt, and the Lord your God redeemed you" (v. 15). Slave redemption was therefore a moral obligation, binding on all free Israelite men and extended to include female Hebrew slaves as well. Still, as in Exodus, Hebrew slaves were offered the option of electing permanent slavery: if a slave "loves you and your household," he may choose to remain with his master's family. Then his ear will be pierced with an awl, marking him as a slave forever. The writers of Deuteronomy expect Hebrew debt slaves to stay not because they want to retain a relationship with their own families but because they love the master's family. Slave marriage is no longer part of the equation.[37]

Protecting Virgin Property

Deuteronomy may not offer specific advice regarding slave marriage, but the book does significantly expand regulations involving the sexual behavior of free Israelites. Addressing the fathers of Israelite virgins, an Exodus law had already sought to guard the honor of the girl's family of origin by protecting her from seduction. Legally, she should only be sexually available to an Israelite man chosen for her by her father. If a young woman, not yet betrothed to another man, lies with an Israelite without her father's permission, this man must marry her, giving the bride-price to her father. If, however, her father does not want to give his daughter in marriage to the man, the father can demand payment instead, and the seducer must pay him the full bride-price anyway.[38] This commandment reasserts the control of the father over his daughter by giving him the right to decide how to treat the girl's seducer. The daughter's value as a marriageable girl is therefore retained and the seducer is "punished" by forcing him to take her as his wife, if the father wills it.[39] Deuteronomy surrounds a version of this same law with several other laws, each of which seeks to protect the honor of the father and make the seduction or slander of an Israelite virgin an expensive proposition.

First, Deuteronomy addresses a scenario whereby a malicious Israelite husband offers a trumped-up charge of premarital sex against a wife who displeases him. In this case, Deuteronomy recommends that the father of the young woman present evidence of his daughter's virginity to the elders of the city, in the form of bloodied sheets saved from her wedding night. After examining the cloth, the elders are to fine the husband one hundred shekels, which are given to the father, and the husband is to be forbidden to divorce his wife then or in the future. If she is guilty, however, she is to be stoned to death. Second, Deuteronomy rules on the problem of the intentional deflowering of a virgin without the permission of her family of origin. Expanding Exodus, two types of virgins are addressed—those betrothed and those not yet promised by their fathers to another man— and three sets of circumstances are considered: (1) An engaged woman is seized by a man, and he lies with her in a town. In this case, both are to be stoned to death, the man because he violated his neighbor's wife (an engagement is treated as an equivalent to marriage), and the woman because she did not cry for help; (2) An engaged woman is seized by a man in the open country. Once they are discovered, only the man is to be executed, since the woman may well have cried out, but no one could hear her; (3) A virgin who is not yet engaged is seized by a man, and they are caught in the act. The man must pay fifty shekels to the woman's father and marry her, keeping her as his wife without the possibility of divorce. Of these, only scenario three is similar to what is considered in the context of Exodus, and, as in Exodus, the man who seduces her must marry her and pay a fine to her father. Exodus's resolution to the problem, however, has been amended. According to Deuteronomy, the father no longer has the option of denying his daughter's marriage to her seducer, and the seducer has no opportunity to divorce the woman in the future. In effect, by raping a virgin, the rapist makes her his permanent wife.

Keeping Women in Line

Though quite different, the marriage laws collected in Exodus and Deuteronomy do share a common point of view: Both versions of the Sinai covenant presuppose the importance of preserving the control of free Israelite fathers, husbands, and masters over the women, slaves, and children under their direct supervision. Their control comes with responsibilities and obligations, which were to be enforced by other free male Israelites, but it is male Israelites who act on God's behalf by executing adulterers, collecting fines, or examining bloody sheets.[40] Women and slaves were protected, but only so long as Israelite men policed themselves and one another. When it comes to their sexuality, the consent of women, slaves, and foreigners was not sought. As such, the Sinai covenant codes accord well with other ancient legal systems. Focused on the privileges and responsibilities of free men and working to preserve ties between the men of a particular kinship group, Babylonian, Sumerian, and Assyrian laws also make adultery punishable by death, protect the honor of men whose wives or daughters are accused of a sexual indiscretion, and punish free men who violate the wives and slaves of others.[41] As valuable property, wives, daughters, and slaves must be protected, even from other men in the group.[42]

Provisions for the care of widows and orphans in the Sinai covenant laws make this same point, but from another angle. Since widows and orphans have no father, husband, or master to protect them, and since, in theory anyway, they cannot care for themselves, they are the direct responsibility of no one. Thus, in terms of covenant law, they are treated as outsiders, of the same category as non-Israelites. Protecting them is up to God. Exodus explains: "You [Israelites] shall not wrong or oppress a resident alien. . . . You shall not abuse any widow or orphan. If you do abuse them, when they cry out to me, I [God] will surely heed their cry" (Exod. 22:21–23). As the principal and divine (male) Israelite, God takes responsibility for those without an actual Israelite male to protect them, a point also made in Deuteronomy. The God of Israel is so generous that he "executes justice for the orphan and the widow," and "loves the strangers, providing them food and clothing" (Deut. 10:18). Since outsiders belong to Israel's God, but not to a particular Israelite man, from the perspective of Exodus and Deuteronomy they also belong to the entire (male) Israelite community. With this principle in mind, Deuteronomy instructs Israelite farmers to allow resident aliens, orphans, and widows to take their fill from a portion of the harvest set aside especially for them. God's protection and care is to be extended like a father's care for his children or a husband's care for his wives.

In this way, free Israelite men determine the legal status of all the residents of the land, and they are responsible for receiving and enforcing the Sinai covenant. A woman's status and obligations are defined by her relationship to the free man who supervises and cares for her in her role of unmarried daughter, wife, mother, or slave. If she is a widow, her only recourse is God and the goodwill of the Israelite men. By contrast, a man's legal status is determined by his role as father in charge of a household, husband in charge of a wife or wives, free man responsible to himself, or debt slave responsible to his master for a set period of time. Marriage, as the Sinai covenant codes imagine it, is therefore a legal arrangement guaranteeing the rights of fathers, husbands, and masters over Israelite women, children, and slaves. Marriage does not unite one man and one woman in one flesh for the purposes of procreation and sexual enjoyment. Instead, marriage unites free Israelite men with as many women and slaves as they can reasonably support. Hebrew slaves may be released every seven years, at least in theory, but women and foreign slaves are objects of exchange rather than people who choose to live and love as they will.

Jesus of Nazareth and Biblical Marriage Reconsidered

In the canonical Gospels, Jesus has very little to say about marriage, and what he does say tends to discount the importance of marriage and family relationships. Gone is the encouragement to "be fruitful and multiply." Gone are references to the obligations of men to care for wives, daughters, and slaves. Instead, Jesus promotes the ties of his followers to one another, undermining their ties to their families and their obligation to marry and

produce children. Jesus's statements about household relationships are especially stark. In the Gospels of Matthew and Luke, Jesus warns that he sets
fathers against sons, sons against fathers, mothers against daughters, and
daughters against mothers. In Matthew, Jesus cautions that those who love
their fathers, mothers, sons, or daughters more than they love him are not
worthy to receive him. Luke's version of the same saying is even more striking: "Whoever comes to me and does not hate father and mother, wife and
children, brothers and sisters, yes, and even life itself, cannot be my disciple"
(14:26). The Gospels of Matthew, Mark, and Luke include a story to il-
lustrate this principle: One day while teaching, Jesus is told that his mother
and brothers are standing outside, looking for him. Rather than going out
to see them, he states, "Who is my mother and who are my brothers? . . .
Here are my mother and my brothers! For whoever does the will of my
Father in heaven is my brother and sister and mother" (Matt. 12:48–50).
From Jesus's perspective, then, the family is made up of fellow believers,
not kin with formal ties outsiders might recognize. The Gospels push this
point in other ways as well, linking Jesus the Messiah to King David, from
whom the Messiah must be descended, not through Mary but through his
adoptive father, Joseph, and presenting the followers of Jesus as brothers
and sisters of one another, irrespective of their families of origin.[43]

In the Gospels, then, one becomes a true parent, a child, a sister, or a
brother not through marriage and childbirth but through joining forces
with those who follow and obey Jesus's teachings. As Jesus warned the
Pharisees and Sadducees, family ties will not guarantee salvation to anyone:
"God is able from these stones to raise up children to Abraham" (Matt. 3:9),
and therefore all people must "bear fruit worthy of repentance" (v. 8). He
makes a similar point later on in his ministry: When a disciple promises
to follow Jesus after first burying his father, Jesus responds, "Follow me,
and let the dead bury their own dead" (Matt. 8:22). Jesus devalues literal
family ties to the extent that he would rather his followers ignore the death
of a parent than miss the chance to follow him. His opinion on marriage
is equally unexpected: He counsels his followers to avoid it if they possibly
can, even while he insists that those who are married should either stay
married or, if separated, refrain from the "adultery" of marrying again.

Jesus's instructions regarding marriage are most clearly presented in the Gospels of Matthew, Mark, and Luke. These three Gospels appear to be related to one another, probably because the authors of Matthew and Luke used Mark as a source, while also sharing a separate collection of Jesus's sayings, which has now been lost. They are so similar that they are usually referred to as the Synoptic Gospels, an English label that employs a Greek term meaning "to see together" or "to see from one point of view" (*syn*—"together or with"; *optic*—from *horaô*, the verb "to see"). A theory of shared sources behind Matthew and Luke can explain why the basic narrative structure of these three gospels is so similar and also why Matthew and Luke share versions of Jesus's sayings that are missing from Mark. The author of the Gospel of Luke actually acknowledges his use of oral and written sources, stating in the very first lines of his book, "many have undertaken to set down an orderly account of the events that have been fulfilled among us" and "I too decided, after investigating everything carefully from the first, to write an orderly account." Reading these three Gospels together shows that ancient Christians were collecting the sayings of Jesus and sharing diverse accounts of his life with one another, sometimes in the context of written books. The Gospel of John, the last of the four canonical Gospels, however, is quite different from Matthew, Mark, and Luke and includes no straightforward statements by Jesus on the topic of marriage. Still, even the Synoptic Gospels present Jesus's specific teachings regarding marriage quite differently.

The End of Marriage

To Jesus, marriage is something that will ultimately be overcome. As the Gospels suggest, he looked forward to the day when, enjoying the benefits of androgynous heavenly bodies, marriages will no longer take place: "When they rise from the dead, they neither marry nor are given in marriage, but are like angels in heaven" (Mark 12:25). He did acknowledge that those in the present age do marry, but only because, as he saw it, they are unaware that God's end-time judgment will soon take place. Recalling the time of Noah just before the flood, Jesus offered marriage as an example of the ignorance of those who refused to see the threat of God's judgment: "they were eating and drinking, marrying and giving in marriage, until the day Noah entered the ark, and they knew nothing until the flood came and swept them all away" (Matt. 24:38–39). Warning that a second judgment is imminent, he implies that marriage is equally unimportant in his own time: "Keep awake therefore, for you do not know on what day your Lord is coming" (v. 42). Those who know that the Son of Man is about to return in judgment do not waste their time marrying, or so Jesus suggested.[44]

A saying of Jesus found only in the Gospel of Mathew makes a similar point, and even more dramatically. Following a general teaching regarding divorce (discussed at greater length below), Jesus offers an esoteric teaching to his disciples alone:

> Not everyone can accept this teaching, but only those to whom it is given. For there are eunuchs who have been so from birth, and there are eunuchs who have been made eunuchs by others, and there are eunuchs who have made themselves eunuchs for the sake of the kingdom of heaven. Let anyone accept this who can. (Matt. 19:11–12)

According to Matthew's Jesus, then, voluntary castration would be a good option for those dedicated to attaining the kingdom of heaven. Some Christians took this recommendation quite seriously: The second-century Christian Justin Martyr tells a story involving a Christian man who sought permission to castrate himself so that his celibacy would be guaranteed. Though permission was denied (according to Roman law, castration was illegal for Roman citizens), Justin reports, "the youth remained single . . . satisfied with the testimony of his own conscience and that of his fellow believers."[45] In other words, though he was forced to keep his testicles, help from his fellow believers gave him confidence that his goal of sexual continence could be kept.

The illegality of castration did not prevent some Christians from taking the passage from Matthew literally. The third-century Christian theologian Origen was accused of excising his testicles in his youth, though in his later years he recommended reading Jesus's saying as an exhortation to sexual self-control.[46] Whether or not Origin did, in fact, castrate himself, it is clear that some did. Thus, the fourth-century bishops assembled at the Council of Nicaea (325 CE) specifically forbid free members of the Christian clergy to become eunuchs.[47] Apparently, the practice needed to be stamped out, at least in some quarters. Interpreting Jesus's saying as a recommendation for celibacy, however, most early Christians argued that becoming a voluntary eunuch involved not castration but the adoption of a sexually ascetic lifestyle. They sought to obey the saying either by avoiding sex altogether or by refraining from second marriage after the death of a spouse.[48]

Eunuchs for the Kingdom of Heaven

Whatever Jesus intended, the saying in Matthew was clearly intended to shock the reader. The Gospel of Matthew challenges the audience to notice how odd the saying was, framing it with two cautions, "not everyone can accept this reading" and "let everyone accept this who can." As the Gospel author knew, the idea of becoming a eunuch by choice would have had significant shock value: eunuchs were much reviled and yet well-known figures in antiquity, represented as not-men who were either overly sexed or not sexed at all.[49] Since castration was illegal for citizen men, to become a eunuch would also involve a loss of status. Eunuchs were presumed to be either foreigners or slaves, castrated by their masters. Nevertheless, this saying also fits well with Jesus's expressed indifference to becoming married. Also, by mentioning eunuchs, the Gospel of Matthew reemphasizes the importance of joining the "family" of Jesus. Recalling a prophecy of Isaiah, Matthew envisions a time when all peoples will worship Yhwh, irrespective of their genitalia, their ability to reproduce, or their families of origin. Isaiah stated:

Do not let the eunuch say, "I am just a dry tree." For thus says the LORD: To the eunuchs who keep my sabbaths, who choose the things that please me and hold fast my covenant, I will give, in my house and within my walls, a monument and a name better than sons and daughters; I will give them an everlasting name that shall not be cut off. (Isa. 56:3b–5)

In other words, when the kingdom of heaven arrives, eunuchs who observe God's commandments will be shown to be fertile, not "dry trees." They will bear fruit for God whether or not they are capable of producing actual children. Sex, procreation, and marriage are therefore secondary concerns. Anticipating the gift of androgynous resurrection bodies, depicting marriage as a distraction characteristic of those ignorant of the coming judgment of God, and devaluing family ties, Jesus did not legislate against marriage, but he certainly did not recommend it to his followers.

Jesus and the Sanctity of Marriage

Still, when Jesus did offer instructions regarding marriage, his teachings were exceptionally strict, so strict that he regularly contradicted earlier biblical precedents. Equating illicit sexual desire with illicit sex, Jesus forbade not only adultery but also lust: "You have heard that it was said, 'You shall not commit adultery.' But I say to you that everyone who looks at a woman with lust has already committed adultery with her in his heart" (Matt. 5:27–28). He then goes on to recommend plucking out an eye or cutting off a hand that causes one to sin, for "it is better for you to lose one of your [bodily] members than for your whole body to go into hell" (v. 30). Illicit acts are considered sinful; so are the inward thoughts that lead to these acts. These thoughts are so dangerous that it would be better to cut off a body part than to succumb to them. Perhaps Jesus did want some of his followers to self-castrate.

Jesus's attitude toward divorce is equally stringent. Though the Sinai covenant allows men to divorce their wives, the Gospels suggest that divorce ought to be forbidden, labeling remarriage "adultery." Yet there are so many different versions of these teachings, both in the Gospels and in the ancient manuscripts that preserve them, that it is impossible to determine precisely what Jesus himself intended to demand from his followers. There are four passages in the Gospels with instructions regarding divorce: one in Mark, two in Matthew, and one in Luke. A similar teaching, preserved by Paul and ascribed directly to Jesus, shares much in common with these other passages and will be considered in the next chapter. Since Mark is usually thought to be the earliest Gospel, written sometime around 70 CE, we will begin there.

Divorce Is Not Permitted

According to Mark, Jesus's opinion regarding divorce was offered in the context of a controversy with the Pharisees, a sect of Jews active during the first century. The Pharisees ask him a question: "Is it lawful for a man to divorce his wife?" (Mark 10:2). Jesus replies by suggesting that God allows divorce only because of "hardness of heart" (v. 5). God's true intention is an indivisible marriage bond. Changing the topic to marriage, he invokes Genesis 1:27 and 2:24:

From the beginning of creation, "God made them male and female." "For this reason a man shall leave his father and mother and be joined to his wife, and the two shall become one flesh." So they are no longer two, but one flesh. Therefore what God has joined together, let no one separate. (vv. 6–9)

Here Jesus offers a rationale for marriage that is similar to what will be presented in later rabbinic literature, a rationale we've already considered: Since the first human being was androgynous, and, dividing Eve from Adam, God made two from one, sexual intercourse enacts a re-unification of the two fleshly creatures into their original state as one, dually sexed flesh. Marriage, then, anticipates the resurrection to come, as Jesus describes it a few paragraphs later. Whereas celibate flesh points to the virginal state of bodies that will soon be like the bodies of angels, which neither marry nor are given in marriage, married flesh overcomes divided flesh, embodying the one, androgynous flesh that believers will someday attain. Jesus's primary concern is therefore not divorce per se, but the state of human flesh prior to and after the resurrection.

Nevertheless, when it comes to divorce, Jesus's teachings depart from biblical precedent and from what is recommended by the Pharisees, who do permit divorce. Summarizing a process based in Deuteronomy and similar to what is found in later rabbinic legal theory, the Pharisees remind Jesus that, according to Moses, divorce is permissible and initiated by Jewish men: "Moses allowed a man to write a certificate of dismissal and to divorce her" (10:4). As this statement implies, Jewish tradition expected men to initiate divorce,[50] though actual practice was much more complex. Enslaved Jews were not eligible for legal marriage in any case, and Jewish women did sometimes seek divorce from their husbands.[51] Jesus, however, forbids remarriage for both husbands and wives. Clarifying his instructions to the disciples in private a few sentences later, he adds:

Whoever divorces his wife and marries another commits adultery against her; and if she divorces her husband and marries another, she commits adultery. (vv. 10–12)

Jesus makes remarriage following divorce tantamount to adultery. Perhaps, having transformed married flesh into a sign of the resurrection, the additional mixing of one flesh with another could not be tolerated.

Except If One's Wife Fornicates

Jesus forbids divorce in the Gospel of Matthew as well, but in a very different way. Matthew includes not one but two instructions on divorce, the first in the context of a collection of commandments known as the Sermon on the Mount and then in response to a controversy with the Pharisees similar to what is found in Mark. In the Sermon on the Mount, Jesus alludes to Deuteronomy, saying, "It was also said, 'Whoever divorces his wife, let him give her a certificate of divorce'" (5:31), and then he amends the saying:

But I say to you that anyone who divorces his wife, except on the ground
*of unchastity (*porneia*), causes her to commit adultery; and whoever*
marries a divorced woman commits adultery. (v. 32)

From Matthew's perspective, then, Jesus permits a husband to divorce his wife if she has engaged in any kind of sexual immorality (*porneia*), though he still equates remarriage with adultery. A similar saying appears later in the Gospel, during Jesus's argument with the Pharisees. They ask, "Is it lawful for a man to divorce his wife for any cause?" (19:3), and, as in Mark, Jesus changes the topic, quoting Genesis 1:27 and 2:24 and ruling, "what God has joined together, let no one separate" (19:6). He then accuses the Pharisees of hard-heartedness, offering a general teaching regarding divorce that is presented to both his disciples and the Pharisees:

*Whoever divorces his wife, except for unchastity (*porneia*), and marries*
another commits adultery. (v. 9)

In these teachings, Jesus and the Pharisees both assume that only men can initiate divorce; the provision regarding the behavior of women is omitted. Also, unlike in Mark, Jesus offers an exception to the command "let no one separate," adding special instructions directed at men with sexually immoral wives.[52] Finally, and also unlike in Mark, Jesus presents his teachings publicly, in front of the Pharisees and others, rather than privately to the disciples alone. (In Matthew, the private teaching that follows involves eunuchs who castrate themselves for the sake of the kingdom of heaven, not a strict saying involving adultery and divorce.) Though according to Mark, remarriage is impossible, in Matthew remarriage remains an option for some men, so long as the initial divorce was prompted by a wife's illicit behavior.[53]

Separation Is to Be Recommended

The Gospel of Luke offers only the briefest treatment of Jesus's teachings regarding divorce and marriage. Even so, his version of these sayings differs significantly from what is found in Mark and Matthew. Most important, Luke actually permits husbands and wives to separate. Jesus simply states:

Anyone who divorces his wife and marries another commits adultery, and whoever marries a woman divorced from her husband commits adultery (16:18).

To Luke, then, it is only remarriage that is the problem. Divorce is not forbidden, and Jesus does nothing to undermine earlier biblical teachings. As in Matthew, Jesus's teaching is directed exclusively at husbands, who are assumed to initiate both divorce and remarriage, and wives are overlooked. As in Mark and Matthew, remarriage is compared to adultery, though unlike in Matthew, no exception is given that would allow men with sexually immoral first wives to marry again. Moreover, Luke makes no explicit association between marriage and the reunification of male and female flesh, either by means of sexual intercourse or by God at the end of time. Finally, Luke presents Jesus's decree among a series of other teachings involving possessions, following up the saying not with a general statement about marriage but with a story involving a selfish rich man who refuses to share his wealth with the poor. As Dale Martin has pointed out, according to Luke, family members "are possessions disciples are called to forsake."[54] Separation, then, is acceptable, even encouraged, but remarriage is not.

The contradictions among these sayings—Is separation allowed or not? Is remarriage permitted or not? Are Jesus's teachings different from those of Moses or not? In what ways?—have left a confusing record, made even more complicated by surviving manuscripts, which preserve multiple versions of these same verses. (See table 1.) Jesus's teachings on divorce are among the most variable passages in the entire New Testament, with scribes altering and editing the traditions they had received, sometimes in an effort to harmonize what was found in one gospel with what was found in another.[55] (See table 2.) Contemporary readers are therefore not the first audience to notice that Jesus's teachings in the Gospels do not agree. The difficulty of these sayings and the differences among them point to the continuing development of Jesus's teachings over time.

TABLE 1. A COMPARISON OF TEACHINGS ON MARRIAGE AND DIVORCE IN MARK, MATTHEW, AND LUKE

	Mark	Matthew	Luke
Who belongs to one's family?	Those who follow Jesus	Those who follow Jesus	Those who follow Jesus
Is marriage important?	Not at the end-time, when no one will marry	Not to those who are aware that the end-time is near	Not to those who are aware that the end-time is near
Should one marry?	No recommendation offered.	Not if one is capable of becoming a "eunuch for the kingdom of heaven"	No recommendation offered.
Is divorce permissible?	No	Yes, if the wife is guilty of sexual immorality	No, but separation is acceptable.
Is remarriage permissible?	No. Remarriage is adultery.	No. Remarriage is adultery.	No. Remarriage is adultery.

TABLE 2. TEXTUAL VARIATIONS IN JESUS'S SAYINGS ON DIVORCE[56]

Mark 10:10-12, oldest textual witnesses	Whoever divorces his wife and marries another commits adultery against her; and if she, divorcing her husband marries another, she commits adultery.
Mark 10:10-12, a fifth-century manuscript and some Latin manuscripts	Whoever divorces his wife and marries another commits adultery against her; and if a woman goes out from her husband and marries another, she commits adultery.
Mark 10:10-12, a fifth-century manuscript and several medieval Greek manuscripts	Whoever divorces his wife and marries another commits adultery against her; and if a woman divorces her husband to be married to another, she commits adultery.
Mark 10:10-12, the Freer Gospels	If a woman divorces her husband and marries another, she commits adultery; and if a man divorces his wife, he commits adultery.
Mark 10:10-12, three Old Latin manuscripts	If a man divorces his wife and marries another, he commits adultery against her, and if a woman separates from her husband and marries another, she commits adultery against him; likewise also he who marries a woman divorced from her husband commits adultery.
Matthew 19:9, the oldest textual witnesses	Whoever divorces his wife, except for sexual immorality, and marries another commits adultery.
Matthew 19:9, a fifth-century manuscript and Old Latin manuscripts	Whoever divorces his wife, except for sexual immorality, and marries another commits adultery.

Matthew 19:9, a medieval Greek manuscript plus a few others	Whoever divorces his wife, except for sexual immorality, makes her an adulteress; and the person marrying a divorced woman commits adultery.
Luke 16:18, most textual witnesses	Whoever divorces his wife and marries another commits adultery, and whoever marries a woman divorced from her husband commits adultery. [note: the problem is remarriage]
Luke 16:18, a fifth-century manuscript and a few others	Whoever divorces his wife and marries another commits adultery, and whoever marries a divorced woman commits adultery.
Luke 16:18, a fourth-century Latin manuscript and a few others in Greek and Latin	Whoever divorces his wife and marries another commits adultery.

Collected together, diverse sayings on divorce, remarriage, adultery, husbands, and wives in Mark, Matthew, and Luke offer not one teaching but several. Eunuchs for the kingdom of heaven, haters of fathers, mothers, wives, daughters, and sons, or "one flesh" with a spouse whom one can never leave, the followers of Jesus were offered a puzzling collection of sayings encouraging them to replace current family arrangements with a new family, made up of believers instead of blood relatives. Rather than standing with earlier biblical traditions, Jesus and his followers appear to have stood apart from them. Even so, they could not agree on precisely what these new arrangements ought to look like.

Conclusion: There Is No Single View on Marriage Presented in the Bible

In the end, Genesis, Exodus, Deuteronomy, and the Synoptic Gospels simply do not promote the same meanings and purposes for marriage.

They certainly do not argue that marriage should be contracted between one man and one woman for the purpose of procreation. Exodus and Deuteronomy assume that, given a chance, men will take multiple wives and have intercourse with as many of their slaves as they like. The Gospels do not promote procreation at all, but instead look forward to resurrection bodies that do not produce children. Moreover, though the laws recorded in Exodus and Deuteronomy differ, both books suggest that marriage is a property arrangement, designed to protect the interests of free Israelite men who are responsible for the women and slaves in their care. In the Genesis creation accounts, however, the emphasis is not on property but the importance of the fertility of both the land and the people created to till it. Female desire is therefore presented as a punishment guaranteeing both childbirth and the painful labor it entails. For Jesus and the Gospel writers, the primal androgyny of Genesis 1 could be achieved either through marriage or through the practice of celibacy. And yet Jesus's teachings regarding marriage, celibacy, divorce, and remarriage are presented quite differently in the Gospels. The evangelists agree that a choice for Jesus should override all other family obligations, but they do not agree regarding the permissibility of divorce and remarriage. Such a diverse body of teaching simply cannot be reconciled into a single statement summing up "God's view of marriage," let alone "God's view of human sexuality." The Bible provides no clear answer to questions like "Are you for or against gay marriage?"

As the next chapter shows, contradictory debates regarding the meaning and significance of sexuality extend beyond discussions of marriage to include a reconsideration of the meaning and significance of desire itself. The Song of Songs, the story of Ruth, and the love between David and his companions may suggest that desire is delightful, reaching beyond the bonds of marriage to include the love of women for men, men for men, and women for women, but later Jewish and Christian texts often viewed desire as a problem, an evil impulse best overcome. For these writers, sex was justified as a technique for overcoming unwanted passion.

CHAPTER 3

The Evil Impulse

Disordered and Ordered Desire

In November of 2008, the Reverend Ed Young, pastor of the Fellowship Church of Grapevine, Texas, developed a novel approach to the crisis in the U.S. financial system. He encouraged married members of his flock to "move from whining about the economy to whoopee!"[1] More married sex, he argued, offers the best solution to difficulties at work or at home.[2] "We should try to double up the amount of intimacy we have in marriage," he advised. "And when I say intimacy, I don't mean holding hands in the park or a back rub." In the process, rampant divorce, complaints about the financial crisis, and debates about same-sex marriage will finally be brought to an end. From Reverend Young's perspective, heterosexual, married sex is the salve that God has provided to cure the ills of contemporary America. As for single people without access to a sexual partner, they might try eating chocolate cake.[3] Supporting this call for a "sexperiment," involving sex seven days a week, with quotes from the Song of Songs, Genesis 2, and 1 Corinthians, Reverend Young observed that, "God thought it up, it was his idea," and so the more couples do it, the better.[4]

Working within an evangelical North American Christian tradition that links heterosexual, married sex to a gendered order supposedly given by God, Reverend Young's instructions make perfect sense: the more often wives submit to their husbands in bed, the more often the couple performs and consecrates a divinely ordered hierarchy of Creator-creation. The pairing of man (who corresponds to God the Creator or Christ his Son) with woman (who corresponds to creation) in the act of sexual intercourse reenacts and reaffirms God's own relationship to humanity and therefore attracts God's blessing. Or so some contemporary Protestant Christians like Reverend Young assume.[5] Ancient Christians, however, would have balked at the reverend's suggestion. From their perspective, sexual intercourse, though given by God, was nevertheless an expression of an "evil impulse," best overcome. As early Christians saw it, the purpose of sexual intercourse was neither to encourage intimacy between heterosexual couples nor to call God's blessings upon an idealized notion of family and home, but to keep desire in check. Sex for its own sake was to be carefully avoided.

The sayings of Jesus regarding marriage and divorce discussed in the previous chapter have already indicated that sexual desire could be perceived by ancient Jews and Christians as a problem requiring careful control and management. Long before the Gospel of Matthew praised those who made themselves eunuchs for the kingdom of heaven, Jews living under Greek rule (323–164 BCE) composed warnings about the dangers of "the evil impulse" (*yetzer harah*). Desire, these Jewish authors argued, can cloud a man's judgment and make him susceptible to sin. Thus, the second-century BCE author Ben Sira prayed, "O Lord . . . do not give me haughty eyes, and remove evil desire from me. Let neither gluttony or lust overcome me, and do not give me over to shameless passion" (Sir. 23:4–6). To Ben Sira, passion all too easily leads to sin, and so Israelite men must carefully control their appetites by avoiding luxury, feasting, wine, women, and prostitutes (Sir. 18:30–19:3). Tobit, another second-century BCE Jewish book, blames foreign women for exposing men to such problems. In response, the author urges Judean men to marry Judean women, "not because of lust, but with sincerity" (Tob. 8:7).[6] Once married, the Judean hero Tobias is free to express his desire appropriately with his Judean wife, Sarah, with whom he fathers seven sons.[7] Though neither of these late biblical books made it into the Jewish canon of scriptures, ancient Christians did read them as sacred texts, and similar warnings about unrestrained lust were put forward by other early Christian and Jewish writings. The Sinai covenant codes may have presupposed that sexual intercourse is necessary for the acquisition of children and wealth, but these later writings presented sexual intercourse as a potential threat. If a man cannot master his sexual desire, these writings suggest, he has failed both as a follower of the God of Israel and as a man.

It Is Well for a Man Not to Touch a Woman: Paul and the Problem of Desire

Among the New Testament authors, the apostle Paul is most famous for his anxious response to sexual desire. Paul was a first-century Greek-speaking Jew who became convinced that Jesus of Nazareth was God's Messiah, promised by the prophets and sent to lead the Gentiles (that is, all non-Jews) to the worship of Israel's God. His deep conviction that he was uniquely appointed to bring the message about Jesus to Gentiles led him to found small communities of believers across Roman Asia Minor, in such cities as Corinth, Thessalonike, and Philippi and in the villages of Galatia. Some of these letters are now collected within the New Testament and are the earliest surviving writings by a follower of Jesus. Paul's letters are even earlier than the Gospels, which were written ten to thirty years after Paul had died and more than thirty years after the death of Jesus. But Paul and the authors of the Gospels held some ideas in common: like them, he, too, emphasized the ties of the Christian "family" over traditional kinship relations, calling Jesus's followers "brothers" and "sisters," and he, too, looked forward to a time when all of God's elect would be resurrected to eternal life, living in bodies that engaged in no sexual relations whatsoever. In the meantime, however, he instructed Jesus's Gentile followers to adopt the strictest possible standards of sexual morality, a morality he measured in terms of how well desire was brought under control.

Paul offered a set of explicit instructions regarding the importance of sexual self-mastery in response to questions and concerns raised by the followers of Jesus in Corinth, a port city outside of Athens that was re-founded by the Romans in the first century BCE. As a Roman-style city in the Greek-speaking eastern part of the Roman Empire, with a reputation for cosmopolitan attitudes and luxurious brothels, Corinth was a regular brunt of jokes by Greek citizens of more refined tastes. To this day, interpreters sometimes claim that the Corinthian Christians, like their non-Christian neighbors, must have been especially profligate, eager to visit prostitutes and to pursue their lusts with abandon.[8] Yet Paul's letters to them suggest the opposite problem: some Corinthian Christians were eager to avoid sex altogether, even with their wives.

Celibacy Is to Be Preferred

Responding to a letter written to him by the community, Paul offers the following statement:

> *Now concerning the matters about which you wrote: "It is well for a man not to touch a woman." But because of cases of sexual immorality (porneia), each man should have his own wife and each woman her own husband. (1 Cor. 7:1–2)*

Ancient manuscript copies of letters do not include punctuation like quotation marks around the statement "It is well for a man not to touch a woman," though they are added in many English translations today. Without quotation marks, however, it is not clear if Paul is quoting a Co-rinthian point of view or expressing his own opinion. In either case, how-ever, his answer implies that some men in the community were adopting a celibate lifestyle and requesting further advice about their decision. Responding to their concerns, the apostle agrees that avoiding sex with women is a good practice, but only for those capable of mastering their desires. (As he puts it later, "I wish that all were as I myself am" [v. 7], that is, celibate.) But, he argues, those who are married should engage in regular sexual intercourse, not for the sake of bearing children, but so that they might protect themselves from illicit desire:

> *Do not deprive one another except perhaps by agreement for a set time, to devote yourselves to prayer, and then come together again, so that Satan may not tempt you because of your lack of self-control." (7:5)*

In other words, while it might be appropriate to avoid sexual intercourse for a brief period, perhaps for prayer or another pious purpose, the temptation to engage in sex with someone else is simply too dangerous for married couples to avoid sex altogether. Encouraging those unmarried or widowed to remain single and abstinent, he nevertheless then conceded, "It is better to marry than to burn" (v. 9). In other words, it is better to be married and express desire appropriately than to be aflame with illicit passions. Once married, spouses should avoid the sin of desiring another by engaging in regular sex. Perhaps Paul, like Matthew, believed that even looking at a woman with lust was tantamount to adultery (compare Matt. 5:28). Whatever Reverend Young might suggest, however, Paul does not recommend seven-day sex as a salve to community problems. He prefers celibacy to marriage.

Like Ben Sira, then, Paul worried that sexual longing could lead to sexual immorality, defined here as sex outside of marriage, and so he instructed followers of Jesus to engage in sex if married or to go ahead and get married if single and yet incapable of firm self-control. In this way, believers would steer clear of the burning of forbidden passion and the burning of eternal punishment in hell. Marriage and sexual intercourse within marriage are not sins, Paul insists, but they are distractions that can lead husbands and wives to care more about the affairs of the world than the affairs of the Lord (see 1 Cor. 7:32–34). Since sexual desire is such a serious problem, however, "the man should give what he owes to his wife, and in the same way, the woman should give this to the man" (7:3, my translation). Paul certainly does not offer a strong endorsement of sex, but he was interested in controlling desire, and he viewed marriage as the second-best option to achieving this goal.

But Regular Sex Is Also Necessary

By speaking of sexual intercourse as an obligation owed by husbands to wives, Paul draws upon a common Jewish tradition, also preserved in a collection of second-century CE Jewish writings known as the Mishnah, advising husbands and wives to provide regular sex to each other. Husbands in particular were required to give their wives sexual satisfaction, and on a regular basis, a command second-century rabbis derived on the basis of Exodus 21:10 ("If [an Israelite man] takes another wife to himself, he shall not diminish the food, clothing, or marital rights of the first wife").[9] Later rabbis offered more specific advice, concluding from Genesis 3:16 ("your desire shall be for your husband") that women's excessive desire required special care and attention from their husbands. Thus, men forced by occupation to leave their homes for extended periods of time must nevertheless perform their sexual duties whenever possible, and men devoted to studying God's law must always return to satisfying their wives after a brief period of abstention. Rabbi Joshua ben Levi, an early-third-century rabbi, applied this principle to advice offered to men leaving on a journey:

> *It is a man's duty to pay a visit to his wife when he starts on a journey; for it is said; "And you shall know that your tent is in peace." Is this deduced from here? Surely it is deduced from the following: "And your desire shall be for your husband" teaches that a woman yearns for her husband when he sets out on a journey. (Yevamot 62b)*[10]

Paul introduced a similar point of view, but for a very different reason: Yes, husbands must satisfy their wives, and wives their husbands, but not because they have a sacred duty to provide sexual intercourse to each other. Rather, the danger of potential immorality brought on by sexual frustration was so strong that the important goal of avoiding sex altogether could be set aside in marriage. In the end, however, it was still better for a man not to touch a woman.[11]

Disordered Desire and the Death Penalty
in the Letters of Paul

Paul's determination to instill sexual self-mastery among the followers of
Jesus not only led him to recommend celibacy for the strong and marriage for the weak but also to threaten those who fail to control desire
with eternal death. As he warns the Corinthians:

> *Do you not know that wrongdoers will not inherit the kingdom of God?*
> *Do not be deceived! Neither fornicators/prostitutes* (pornoi), *nor idola-*
> *ters, nor adulterers, nor the effeminate* (malakoi), *nor man-beds[?]*
> (arsenokoitai), *nor thieves, nor the greedy, nor drunkards, revilers or*
> *robbers, none of these will inherit the kingdom of God. (1 Cor. 6:9–10,*
> *my translation)*

Adultery, prostitution, greed, robbery, and sexual exploitation of some
sort (whatever *arsenokoitês* might mean—the term is notoriously difficult
to translate)[12] are treated with a broad brush by Paul, as equally egregious
examples of the sins that flow from illicit desire. All who engage in them
are then warned that they will not inherit God's kingdom.

Paul's intolerance of most sexual pairings is further emphasized by
the attitude he takes toward a man sleeping with his father's "woman"
(*gynê*) a few verses earlier (1 Cor. 5:1, 5). This man must be driven out
of the community, even killed, the apostle insists, for members of the
community must not associate with any "brother" guilty of sexual immorality (*porneia*):

> *Everywhere it is heard that there is sexual immorality among you, and*
> *a kind of sexual immorality which is not even heard among the Gen-*
> *tiles, that a certain man has his father's woman. And you are arrogant!*
> *(1 Cor. 5:1–2a, my translation)*

But what, exactly, was this man guilty of? Since in Greek the word
for "wife" is identical to the word for "woman" (*gynê*), it is not clear how

the woman was related to the man's father. Was she the father's slave, concubine, widow, or wife? Perhaps the man was sleeping with his step-mother, a common interpretation of the passage. Perhaps she was his fa-ther's widow. It was not uncommon at the time for a much older man to marry a much younger woman, and therefore she may have been closer in age to the son than the father.[13] Or perhaps she was a slave given to the son by the father. As we observed when considering Exodus, this scenario was considered entirely appropriate in the Sinai covenant ("If [the father] designates [the female slave] for his son, he shall deal with her as with a daughter," Exod. 21:9). Roman slave law also approved of the arrange-ment: unauthorized sex with another man's slaves might be punished, but sexual access to one's own slaves was simply assumed.[14] If the father had given the slave to his son, then, no sexual misdeed would have taken place, at least not from a legal perspective. Unlike in the Sinai covenant, however, she would remain enslaved. Finally, perhaps the woman was a concubine who had first serviced his father. Such a situation was frowned upon but not unheard of in Roman settings. As the third-century CE Roman jurist Ulpian explained:

If a woman has been her patron's concubine and then becomes his son's or grandson's or vice versa, I do not think she is behaving properly, since a relationship of this kind is almost criminal. So this sort of bad behavior is prohibited.[15]

Any of these relationships between the man and his father's "woman" were possible and thus the character of the man's sexual immorality cannot easily be determined. Nevertheless, from Paul's perspective, the man needed to be expelled from the community, handed over "to Satan for the destruction of the flesh, so that his spirit may be saved in the day of the Lord" (1 Cor. 5:5, see also v. 13).[16] Displaying no concern at all for the woman, Paul recommends a (spiritual) death penalty for the man.[17]

Putting His Penis in the Wrong Place

Paul begins his letter to the brothers and sisters in Rome with a very similar argument, linking the inappropriate exercise of sexual desire to spiritual and physical death. Indicting all those who worship gods other than the God of Israel, he claims that these wicked fools "exchanged the glory of the immortal God for images resembling a mortal human being or birds or four-footed animals or reptiles," though they should have recognized God (1:23). Having given themselves over to gods that are not gods, the one true God punishes them by handing them over to dishonorable passions, which lead them to exchange "natural" for "unnatural" sex:

> *Their females exchanged their natural use for that which is against nature, and in the same way the men, having given up the natural use of females, were consumed with desire for one another, men in men achieving the shame and dishonor which, having receiving [it], bound their error to themselves. (1:26–27, my translation)*

The logic and the syntax of this passage are quite difficult.[18] Still, whatever the precise nuance of Paul's words, his description of "natural" sex presupposes that nature intends the use of (certain) female bodies by male bodies during the sexual act.

At issue in Romans 1 is what is "exchanged": the worship of the God of Israel is exchanged for the worship of idols; wisdom and self-mastery are exchanged for the uncontrollable exercise of desire; the natural use of women's bodies by men is exchanged for the use of men's bodies by men; and women's desire for their own "natural use" is exchanged for their desire for one another. As such, Paul depends upon a widespread ancient point of view—"maleness" involves penetration and "femaleness" involves being penetrated. He recycles this understanding of gender to make a particularly Christian argument: the God of Israel abandons those who do not worship him to "unnatural" lusts, and therefore they deserve to die.

Being a Man/Taking It Like a Woman: Male and Female Roles in the Letters of Paul

Women, Paul and other ancient authors often assumed, are "naturally" the passive recipients of a phallus during sexual intercourse; therefore, they should not seek to penetrate others. Citizen men, however, are "naturally" dominant, and they dramatize their status as free men whenever they take the active role in sex, whether they are partnering with women, slaves, or boys. From this perspective, women who imitate men by seeking sexual satisfaction through the penetration of other women—to quote Paul, "they exchange their natural use for that which is unnatural" (Rom. 1:26, my translation)—are unfortunate victims of disordered desire. They are imitation men, not women.[19] Similarly, since "natural" sex necessarily involves the penetration of women and other subordinates by free adult men, a free adult man who desires penetration loses honor and status, or, as Paul puts it in Romans, he receives his "error"—that is, a phallus—in himself.

Epictetus, a Stoic philosopher and contemporary of Paul, made a similar observation:

What is lost by the one who suffers the things of the kinaidos *[that is, the man who enjoys playing the passive role in a homoerotic sex act]? His manhood. And by the agent [*lit. *the one doing the placing]? Besides a good many other things, he also loses his manhood no less than the other.*[20]

From Epictetus's perspective, then, the man who desires penetration loses his manhood more decisively than the man doing the penetrating, though both have been dishonored. Paul and Epictetus agree: both male partners in a sexual encounter are shamed, though the passive partner suffers more decisively. Defining manhood as the ability to penetrate others, both writers assume that those who accept penetration are not men; they must be women, or slaves, or deficient in manliness.

Paul and Epictetus, however, promoted a minority perspective: to many Greek and Roman writers, men who engaged in sexual intercourse with one another retained their honor and continued to perform their manliness so long as the penetrator was of a higher status than the one who was penetrated. The sexual attraction of older men to those younger and more beautiful was presupposed. A common topic in Greek and Roman literature and art, the loveliness of young adolescent boys was praised in poetry, depicted in statues, on vases, in floor mosaics, and in wall paintings and was recalled in numerous retellings of the love of the god Zeus for his youthful male companion, Ganymede. A willing, virile, and respectable boy was a prized sexual object, worthy of praise. From this perspective, adult men would "naturally" desire both women and boys, as a humorous inscription to the Roman god Priapus confirms:

Grant me a flowering youth; grant that I may please good boys and girls with my naughty prick, and that with frequent fun and games I may chase away the worries that harm the soul, and that I may not fear old age too much.[21]

Both boys and girls are appropriate objects for adult male desire and appropriate receptacles of "naughty pricks," or so this author assumed.[22] By claiming that both the insertive and receptive partner are somehow shamed by homoerotic sex, Paul and Epictetus departed from other ancient understandings of male sexual morality. Still, their logic—shame and honor are tied to playing the appropriate role in a sexual act, with the dominant male "naturally" desiring to insert his phallus into his subordinates and the weaker, more "feminine" subordinate "naturally" seeking penetration—was consistent with their larger culture. Paul went on to apply this same logic to the sexual use of women.

Vessels of the Lord

A strange comment made by Paul to the Christians in Thessalonike applies the principle of active (male) and passive (female) roles to the sexual use of wives:

For this is the will of God, your sanctification, that you refrain from sexual immorality (porneia), *that each of you know your own wife* (skeuos, lit. *"vessel"*), *acquired in holiness and honor, not in the passion of lust like the Gentiles who do not know God. (1 Thess. 4:3–5, my translation)*

To Paul, the holiness of the followers of Jesus in Thessalonike was connected to their acquisition of a vessel/wife within whom the phallus could be placed. She alone was the appropriate container for this activity. Paul then contrasts this supposedly appropriate, holy behavior to the sexual intercourse pursued by Gentiles, who, he suggests, are fornicators.[23] Christian brothers will avoid fornication/sexual immorality/prostitution (*porneia* designates all three) by knowing their own "vessels." He makes a similar point in a letter to the Corinthians: the "brothers" in Christ must not place their "members," that is, their penises, within the body of a prostitute (a *pornê* or *pornos*). "Do you not know that your bodies are parts of Christ?" he asks. "Then, taking your bodily part, will you make part of Christ a part of a prostitute? Certainly not!" (1 Cor. 6:15, my translation). Here he envisions male Christian body parts within a metaphorical communal body, identifying each (male) believer—and each believer's "parts"—with the (spiritual) body of Christ. He can then compare placing one's penis within a prostitute to placing Christ within the body of a prostitute, a mixing he finds horrific. The prostitute's "parts," however, were less of a concern.

Directing his advice at Christian men, the "vessel"—be she a prostitute, a wife, or a virgin—was important to Paul largely for how she impacted male desire and male bodily parts. In Greco-Roman cities like Corinth, prostitution was legal and taxed. Enslaved to their pimps or to the local city brothel, prostitutes had no choice regarding the "members" penetrating them, yet Paul offers no advice concerning their plight. He simply assumes that they will be excluded from the community. Slaves, who could not legally marry, were also left out of Paul's moral scheme. Though some slaves did "marry," in the sense that they were permitted to carry on an extralegal marriage by their masters, legally speaking their bodies belonged not to their "spouses" but to their owners. It is striking, then, that Paul offers no explicit instructions to Christian masters regarding the sexual lives of their slaves. Presumably, his strict advice regarding marriage would prevent masters from engaging in sexual intercourse with slaves, but he never forbids it outright.

Paul, the Philosophers, and Sex with Slaves

Other philosophers in Paul's day did advise men to pursue sexual intercourse exclusively with wives, arguing that men better display their own self-control when they leave their slaves alone. The first-century teacher Musonius Rufus promoted this perspective:

> *There must be sheer wantonness in anyone yielding to the temptation of shameful pleasure and like swine rejoicing in his own vileness. In this category belongs the man who has relations with his own slave-maid, a thing which some people consider quite without blame, since every master is held to have it in his power to use his slave as he wishes.* ("On Sexual Indulgence," 12)[24]

Musonius's concern was the bodies of masters, not slaves, but he did try to discourage slave abuse. Musonius's and Paul's contemporary Plutarch, however, had no such qualms. Instead, Plutarch argued that wives ought to tolerate the sexual use of household slaves:

> *If a private citizen, intemperate and tasteless in his pleasures, commits an offense with a mistress or maidservant, his wife ought not to be angry or annoyed, but reflect that it is his respect for her that makes her husband share his intemperance or violent behavior with another woman.* ("Advice to the Bride and Groom," 16)[25]

Plutarch does suggest that only an intemperate man would want to sleep with his slaves, but he considers the abuse of slaves by morally weak men preferable to the sexual abuse of wives, and he encourages wives to feel the same way.

Paul never explicitly counters this line of reasoning, despite his claim that a wife "does not have authority over her own body, but the husband does," and, similarly, that the husband "does not have authority over his body, but the wife does" (1 Cor. 7:4). In fact, later in the letter he asks virgins to give up their decision to adopt celibacy, instructing them to marry their fiancés if the fiancé cannot control himself (see 7:28, 36–38).[26] As in Exodus and Deuteronomy, the "vessel" had little say about her sexual fate if the man who "owned" her needed her body, though in this case she was needed not for procreation but in order to protect men from their illicit desires.

To Paul, then, the proper ordering of desire is key to joining the "family" of Christ. Defining disordered desire in terms of the proper or improper placement of a phallus, Paul makes the desires of the flesh a central proof of the depravity of the world. This devaluing of fleshly desires, however, was justified by a different longing: firmly believing that Jesus Christ would soon return, Paul looked forward to a time when all the elect would receive renewed bodies and minds. These bodies would no longer be subject to the desires of the flesh, he claimed, but would enjoy spiritual, imperishable bodies that truly bear the image of God. As such, the marriage of the flesh was beside the point, necessary only as a temporary measure for the sake of keeping illicit sex under control. Soon both flesh and the phallus would be overcome.

Waiting on the Lord: Paul and the Nearness of the Resurrection

Arguing against marriage for the unmarried, Paul declared: "In whatever condition you were called, brothers and sisters, there remain with God" (1 Cor. 7:24). Remaining as one was called—free or enslaved, Jew or Gentile, male or female, married or unmarried—appears to be an overriding principle for Paul, an expression of his belief that "the appointed time has grown short" (1 Cor. 7:29). As he puts it at the end of a letter to the Corinthians, "*Maran atha,*" or, "Our Lord, come!" (1 Cor. 16:22), an Aramaic phrase that may go back to Jesus. (Aramaic was the language spoken in Judea at the time.) Paul makes a similar declaration in his letter to the followers of Jesus in Thessalonike, observing that, "the day of the Lord will come like a thief in the night" (1 Thess. 5:2). Referring directly to his own times, he then warns, "When they say, 'There is peace and security,' then suddenly destruction will come upon them, as labor pains come upon a pregnant woman, and there will be no escape!" (v. 3). As Paul and his audience well knew, "peace and security" was a Roman imperial slogan. In other words, at the very moment Paul was writing these words, "they" were saying, "there is peace and security."[27] Since time was short, the resurrection near, and judgment inevitable, mundane matters like setting up households and bearing children had become irrelevant. The "affairs of the Lord" were paramount.[28]

Paul also applied his sense that God's judgment was near, and so one should remain "in whatever condition you were called," to Jesus's teachings on divorce. Offering a rare direct citation of Jesus, he states: "To the married I give this command—not I but the Lord—that the wife should not separate from her husband (but if she does separate, let her remain unmarried or else be reconciled to her husband), and the husband should not divorce his wife" (1 Cor. 7:10–11). Like Mark, Paul assumes that the wife will initiate the divorce and, like Matthew and Luke, he suggests that divorce is forbidden. Offering his own rationale for this principle, he claims that the physical union of Gentile Christians with nonbelieving spouses can sanctify the bodies of both, and of their children as well: "For the unbelieving husband is made holy through the wife, and the unbelieving wife is made holy through her husband [*lit.* 'brother']" (v. 14). Separation is possible when the marriage is mixed ("if the unbelieving partner separates, let it be so"), but still, "let each of you lead the life that the Lord has assigned" (vv. 15, 17). Again, Paul ties his sexual logic to his understanding of bodily parts, but in this case he concludes that the mixing of holy, Christian bodily parts with unholy, Gentile bodily parts brings not pollution and judgment but salvation. Apparently, the union of holy flesh within the context of a legal marriage sanctifies: ("Wife, for all you know, you might save your husband. Husband, . . . you might save your wife," v. 16), but the union of this same flesh with a prostitute is dangerously contagious, bringing judgment not only on the believer but also on the entire community.

Desire and the Christian Household: Later Interpretations of Paul's Teachings

A decade or two after Paul's death—he was likely killed in Rome in the early sixties CE—a new generation of Christians influenced by his teachings sought to apply his message to the changing circumstances of the churches in Roman Asia Minor. Paul's expectation that God's judgment was imminent, along with an accompanying resurrection of the elect, had not been realized. Instead, a disastrous war in Judea (66–73 CE) had left the Jerusalem temple in ruins and the God of Israel without a clear homeland. In this context, the argument that one ought to "remain in the condition in which you were called," waiting for the Lord and the resurrection bodies he had promised, no longer had the same impact. The followers of Jesus developed new ways to manage the problem of desire, reinterpreting sexual morality in such a way that marriage, not celibacy, became the preferred option for believers. In a series of letters written in Paul's name, his later disciples identified ordered desire with an ordered household, arguing that free men ought to firmly control their wives, slaves, and children. Now preserved in the New Testament and received by church tradition as Paul's own compositions, these letters measure a man's fitness as a church leader and Christian by how well he masters his household.[29]

The letters discussed in the next section are identified by many biblical scholars today as "pseudepigraphical"; that is, they are attributed to one author (Paul) but are not thought to have been written by him. The pseudepigraphical letters include: Colossians, Ephesians, 2 Thessalonians, 1 Timothy, 2 Timothy, Titus, and Hebrews. Ancient Christians also recognized that not every letter attributed to Paul was written by him. Describing the treatise known as Hebrews, Origen stated:

> *The diction [of Hebrews] does not exhibit the characteristic roughness of speech or phraseology admitted by the Apostle [Paul] himself, the construction of the sentences is closer to Greek usage, as anyone capable of recognizing differences of style would agree. On the other hand the matter of the epistle is wonderful, and quite equal to the Apostle's acknowledged writings.*[30]

In other words, though Origen knew that Paul did not write Hebrews, he was prepared to read the work as if it was by Paul. After all, Hebrews is beautiful and close to Paul's own thinking, or at least Origen thought it was.[31]

Perhaps late-first- and second-century Christian readers adopted a similar attitude toward pseudo-Pauline letters ultimately included within the New Testament, though they do not mention it. Instead, from the late second century on, readers like Irenaeus of Lyons and Tertullian, a North African Christian, accepted Colossians, Ephesians, 2 Thessalonians, 1 Timothy, 2 Timothy, and Titus as genuinely authored by Paul, even as they viewed other pseudo-Pauline works like 3 Corinthians, the Letter to the Laodiceans, and the correspondence between Paul and the Roman philosopher Seneca to be extracanonical forgeries.[32] Unlike Irenaeus and Tertullian, however, modern biblical scholars are skeptical about the authorship of these letters. Calling attention to the multiple differences in vocabulary, theme, and tone between the authentic Pauline epistles (Romans, Galatians, 1 and 2 Corinthians, Philippians, 1 Thessalonians, and Philemon) and those that may be spurious, historians argue that some or all of these letters were forged. A comparison between the views on women, marriage, and sex encountered thus far in Paul's letters, and those expressed in Colossians, Ephesians, 1 Timothy, 2 Timothy, and Titus seems to confirm this impression.

Colossians and the Well-Managed Home

The earliest of these pseudo-Pauline letters, the epistle to the Colossians, remains close in style to Paul's own writings but departs from Paul's teachings in significant ways.[33] As we have seen, Paul argues that a general resurrection will soon arrive, along with the gift of a renewed, imperishable body no longer bound by sex or gender. By contrast, this author suggests that the resurrection has already taken place, at least in a spiritual sense. In Colossians, resurrection is a spiritual, not a bodily condition and it can be achieved during the present age: "When you were buried with [Christ] in baptism, *you were also raised* with him through faith in the power of God, who raised him from the dead" (Col. 2:12, emphasis added), this author declares, a direct contradiction of Paul's statement in Romans, "For if we have been united with [Christ] in a death like this, *we will certainly be united* with him in a resurrection like his" (Rom. 6:5, emphasis added). In Romans, Paul suggests that resurrection is a future reality, but in Colossians, resurrection is something that has already been experienced.

Enjoying a spiritual resurrection instead of waiting eagerly for a swiftly approaching bodily resurrection, believers are to pursue not celibacy, as Paul recommended in 1 Corinthians, but marriage within a well-ordered household, where wives are subjected to husbands, children are obedient to parents, and slaves submit to their masters willingly, "fearing the Lord" (Col. 3:18–25). According to this scheme, marriage and family life are designed neither to prevent illicit desire, as Paul suggested, nor to provide the appropriate context for "seven-day sex," as Reverend Young supposes, but to display commendable conduct to outsiders, who will observe what they see and approve (see Col. 4:5–6). In this way, a hierarchically arranged Christian "family"—a church made up of "brothers and sisters in Christ"—is consecrated by hierarchically arranged Christian households, with a man at the head.

According to Colossians, sexual expression was a matter of household management and control of desire was an important mark of manliness:

Wives, be subject to your husbands, as is fitting in the Lord. Husbands, love your wives and never treat them harshly. Children, obey your parents in everything. . . . Slaves, obey your earthly masters in everything, not only while being watched and in order to please them, but wholeheartedly, fearing the Lord. (Col. 3:18–22)

This point of view, recognizable throughout the Greco-Roman world, judged the mastery of men by how well they mastered not only themselves but also their subordinates. As the first-century philosopher Musonius Rufus put it:

The attribute of a kingly person is obviously the ability to rule peoples and cities well and to be worthy to govern men. Well, then, who would be a more capable head of a city or more worthy to govern men than the philosopher? For it behooves him (if he is truly a philosopher) to be intelligent, disciplined, noble-minded, a good judge of what is just and what is seemly, efficient in putting his plans into effect, patient under hardship. . . . Even if he does not have many subjects obedient to him he is not for that reason less kingly, for it is enough to rule one's friends or one's wife and children or, for that matter, only oneself. ("That Kings Also Should Study Philosophy," 8)[34]

A man's self-control therefore justifies his control over others, making him appear "kingly" to his peers. In Musonius's opinion, philosophy makes this ideal behavior possible. In Colossians, however, it is Christ who instills this same type of behavior, training believers to adopt a moral life (see Col. 3:5–17). Loving their wives, caring for their children, and treating their slaves justly, men please their Master in heaven (see Col. 4:1) and attract outsiders with similar values to Christ (see vv. 5–6).

The Lord's Dominion

A comparable set of instructions was offered by the author of Ephesians, a general letter to Pauline Christians that was later associated with the city of Ephesus. Also attributed to Paul, but likely written twenty years after his death, this letter seems to have employed Colossians as a source, expanding the teachings of Colossians to address new concerns. As in Colossians, Ephesians suggests that believers are already experiencing the resurrection—they have been "raised up with [Christ]" and are seated with him "in the heavenly places" (2:6). With the benefits of the resurrection already in place, marriage and procreation can resume. Thus, Ephesians also claims that the moral life is best achieved within strictly ordered families made up of husbands, wives, slaves, and children.[35] The author explains:

> *Wives, be subject to your husbands as you are to the Lord. For the husband is the head of the wife just as Christ is the head of the church, the body of which he is the Savior. Just as the church is subject to Christ, so wives ought to be, in everything, to their husbands. Husbands, love your wives, just as Christ loved the church and gave himself up for her. . . . In the same way, husbands should love their wives as they do their own bodies. (5:22–28)*

In Colossians and even more so in Ephesians, the dominion of husbands over wives and masters over slaves is described as analogous to Christ's dominion over the cosmos, with divine and human rule ideally characterized by love. Love is therefore something that those in a superior position bestow on their subjects. Subjects are to respond with willing obedience, accepting the dominion of their own immediate superiors while submitting themselves to those who "own" them. Owned by God, free men—described as "slaves" with a master in heaven in Colossians (4:1)—willingly submit to the Lord Christ, who is the "head" of the church body. Under the control of husbands, wives freely submit their bodies "as is fitting in the Lord." Slaves of both God and a human master, slaves must obey their owners "with fear and trembling, in singleness of heart . . . not only while being watched, and in order to please them, but as slaves of Christ" (Eph. 6:5–6). This idealized structure, knit together by the love of God and free men for their subjects, controls desire by managing it within a strictly ordered household. This divinely given hierarchical order, however, is displayed not in the context of sexual intercourse between a husband and wife, as Reverend Young suggests, but in the context of a Greco-Roman household, complete with slaves, who could not marry, and masters, who had full access to the bodies of slaves.

Domesticating One's Wife

The view that sexuality and desire are best handled within a hierarchical household with a wise father at the helm had a long tradition in Greek-speaking contexts. For example, in the fourth-century BCE treatise "On Household Management" (*Oeconomicos*) Xenophon suggested that a husband should "tame" and "domesticate" his wife so that together they could govern a prosperous home. Properly disciplined, a wife learns to arrange the items of the house in a way that pleases her husband, including their slaves, who will seek to emulate the self-controlled behavior of their masters. Describing the best disciplinary procedures a family can adopt, the husband explains:

> *[My wife] asked me if I had any advice to give her about how she might look really beautiful and not merely seem to be so. . . . I advised her . . . to supervise the baker, and to stand next to the housekeeper while she was measuring out provisions, and also to go around inspecting whether everything was where it ought to be. . . . I said that mixing flour and kneading dough were excellent exercise, as were shaking and folding clothes and linens. . . . For compared with a slave, the appearance of a wife who is unadorned and suitably dressed becomes a sexual stimulant, especially when she is willing to please as well, whereas a slave is compelled to submit.*[36]

Though Xenophon wrote five centuries before Colossians and Ephesians were composed, he nevertheless presented an image of the ideal household that was quite similar to these later Christian writings: husbands train wives, whom they love; wives eagerly take the advice of husbands, whom they obey, displaying womanly virtues by managing a household well and comporting themselves modestly. At the same time, slaves obey both the mistress and the master fully, without complaint. As Xenophon points out, unlike wives, slaves are "compelled to submit."

The parallels between Christian writings and the writings of Xenophon are not surprising. Read as an important philosophical treatise during the Roman period, the *Oeconomicos* was widely appreciated and quoted by authors like the famously strict Roman senator the Elder Cato and the first-century orator Cicero.[37] Even those never directly exposed to Xenophon's writings would have been familiar with similar arguments. Since the topic "on household management" was a subject of school exercises, young men would learn to read and write, in part, by composing works that described the arrangement and government of a well-ordered, hierarchical home.[38] The views expressed in Colossians and Ephesians were therefore quite common, even stereotypical. Urging husbands to care for wives, wives to obey husbands, children to honor their parents, and slaves to submit to masters, Colossians and Ephesians put forward a familiar Greco-Roman sexual morality. Yet they also contradict Paul's own stated opinions. With the bodily resurrection imminent, Paul preferred not marriage but celibacy, and he described sexual morality not in terms of an ordered home life but in terms of the placement of particular bodily parts. Whereas Paul recommended the mutual subjection of married bodies to each other for the purpose of avoiding illicit sexual temptation, Colossians and Ephesians recommend the dominion of free men over women, slaves, and children, with everyone in the household kept under strict control by the ultimate Master, Jesus Christ. Desire continues to be represented as a problem that needs to be solved, whether or not Paul wrote these letters, and Christ continues to be put forward as the only viable solution to the evil impulse. But the ideal solution offered by Paul on the one hand and Colossians and Ephesians on the other is quite different. None of these letters, however, suggest that God wants believers to "just do it," as Reverend Young claimed in 2008.

Masters Who Are Above Reproach:
Ordered Desire in the Pastoral Epistles

A few decades after Ephesians was composed, yet another author—whom we will call the "Pastor"[39]—took it upon himself to interpret Paul's teachings.[40] Focused on those who "pastor" the churches, 1 Timothy, 2 Timothy, and Titus—often referred to as the Pastoral Epistles—pay particular attention to the duties of bishops, deacons, and other church leaders, who, it is argued, must defend against misleading doctrines, as well as other threats. Writing a set of three related letters and presenting himself as Paul, the Pastor offers advice and instruction to Paul's youthful companions Timothy and Titus regarding how churches should be governed. This is a pressing need, he argues, given the false teachings troubling the community. A beleaguered church needs strong male leaders; without them communities crumble, women and young people go astray, and desire runs amok. Thus, virtuous men should be appointed, chosen on the basis of how firmly they control both themselves and their subordinates. Then, with an honorable man in charge, churches will be protected from quarrels, false teachers, and external threats, and also from women and slaves incapable of controlling themselves. Women in particular must be kept in line; left on their own, their desires will surely overtake them.

By focusing on the discipline of wayward women, the Pastor introduces a common theme, familiar within both the Hebrew Bible and in earlier Greek writings: that of the wild woman who threatens both herself and her community with her excessive desire.[41] Deeply concerned about the trouble immodest women can introduce into the community, the Pastor insists that women must adorn themselves properly, avoiding gold, pearls, and expensive clothes, while clothing themselves with "good works, as is proper for women who profess reverence for God." Otherwise women bring shame upon themselves, their families, and the churches.

Since they are prone to sin, wives should "learn in silence, with full submission," listening to their husbands. After all, the Pastor argues, Eve, not Adam, was deceived and "became a transgressor" (1 Tim. 2:10–14).

Offering Eve's sin as a rationale for womanly subjection, the Pastor argues that, as descendants of Eve, women are inherently dangerous and therefore require husbands to control them. Through marriage, however, salvation becomes possible: wives can be "saved through childbearing, provided they continue in faith and love and holiness, with modesty" (v. 15). In contrast to Paul, who exhorts both women and men to remain virgins if they are able, this author views marriage and procreation as the only acceptable option for free Christian women. Older, respectable widows who have already raised children may choose to remain unmarried, the Pastor concedes, so long as they devote themselves to service to the church. But, he also insists, younger widows should marry again; there can be no vow of celibacy for them. If they do not remarry, they may well "behave wantonly"[42] before Christ, violating their "first pledge"—that is, their pledge to remain abstinent—by seeking remarriage anyway.[43] In this way, the Pastor directly contradicts not only Paul but also the teachings of Jesus put forward in the Gospels of Matthew, Mark, and Luke. In these writings, Jesus explicitly forbids remarriage, which is equated with adultery. Apparently, from the Pastor's perspective, unmarried women are so dangerous that Jesus's teachings should be ignored.

Manly Men Control Themselves

To the Pastor, female desire was truly threatening, demanding a strong response from husbands and male church leaders. Since young men are troubled by intense passions as well, the Pastor also exhorts Titus to "urge the younger men to be self-controlled" (2:6) and Timothy to "shun youthful passions" (2 Tim. 2:22). Offering himself as a model, the Pastor presents himself as formerly plagued by uncontrolled desire. He, "Paul," overcame this disease only through a disciplined relationship with Christ and the Church, he claims: "For we ourselves were once foolish, disobedient, led astray, slaves to various passions and pleasures, passing our days in malice and envy, despicable, hating one another" (Titus 3:3). But, thanks to God's mercy, "we" were given "the water of rebirth and renewal by the Holy Spirit" (v. 5) and so are now capable of devoting "ourselves" to good works. To the Pastor, then, training in the Christian life enables young men to achieve the kind of manly mastery expected from free citizens: they are to display integrity, gravity, sound speech, self-control, obedience to their superiors, piety toward God, endurance in the face of suffering, and an education in "sound doctrine."[44] When they succeed, the community will prosper, God will be pleased, and outsiders will be impressed, or so the Pastor claims.

Leaders in particular are to be held to a high standard. Community overseers, or "bishops" (episkopoi—not to be confused with the office of "bishop" as it develops in later centuries) should be "above reproach, married only once, temperate, sensible, respectable, [and] hospitable." They should manage their own households well, keeping their children "submissive and respectful in every way." Servants of the church, or "deacons" (diakonoi) must be "serious, not double-tongued, not indulging in much wine, not greedy for money." Elders (presbyteroi) should be "blameless, married only once," with believing children and "not accused of debauchery and not rebellious." These leaders are to be mature men, with demonstrable competence at ruling wives, children, and slaves. As such, they can be shown to be prepared to serve as God's "household manager" (oikonomian theou, 1 Tim. 1:4).[45] In contrast to women, who must marry or remarry, these male leaders may be either married heads of households or celibate, depending upon whether or not their one allotted wife has died. Presumably, widowers were not expected to remarry but could imitate their celibate hero Paul by applying their skills at household management to the household of God.[46] Perhaps the Pastor could afford to tolerate celibacy in widowed men since, unlike women, men could be trusted to control themselves.

"Real Widows"

Widows, however, were another story, at least from the perspective of the Pastor. The first letter to Timothy suggests that there was a distinct class of women, identified as "widows," who were given special roles in the Pastor's churches. Supported by church funds and put on a list, these women were given teaching and other responsibilities. The Pastor approves of this practice, at least to some degree: "Let a widow be put on the list," he advises, "if she is not less than sixty years old and has been married only once" (5:9). If she has raised her children, offered aid to the sick, and devoted herself to good works, then the church should be willing to accept her authority and support her, but if she has relatives to help, "let the church not be burdened, so that it can assist those who are real widows" (v. 16). Here the Pastor seems to be contrasting "real widows"— impoverished women without men to supervise or support them—with church "widows," a leadership office designed especially for women. According to the Pastor, however, younger widows are not eligible to apply. They must marry again, or else they will "learn to be idle, gadding about from house to house," becoming "gossips and busybodies, saying what they should not say" (v. 13). In this way, the Pastor required women to remain married until their procreative years had come to an end, even if their husbands should die.

References to "younger widows," "real widows," and "widows who are not widows" in 1 Timothy point to the possibility that honored groups of widow-virgins had already been established in churches identified with the apostle, a phenomenon known from later Christianity.[47] The English word "widow," meaning "a woman whose husband has died," cannot capture the range of possible meanings of the Greek word *chêra,* usually translated "widow." A *chêra* could also be a woman who had left her husband or even simply a woman who lives without a man. Thus, in Greek anyway, it was entirely possible for a woman to be designated as a "widow" even if she had never been married.[48] Ignatius of Antioch, an early-second-century Christian martyr, confirms this interpretation: he mentions "virgins called widows" among a list of persons to whom he sent greetings when writing a letter to the church of Smyrna: "I greet the households of my brothers, along with their wives and children, and the virgins who are called widows."[49] In another letter to the overseer (*episkopos*, "bishop") of this same city, he declares: "Do not allow the widows to be neglected. After the Lord, it is you who must be mindful of them" (*Letter to Polycarp* 4).[50] The role of the "virgin" is also celebrated by the later-second-century *Acts of Paul and Thecla*, an enormously popular story about a wealthy young woman who commits her life to both Christ and sexual abstinence after hearing the preaching of Paul. Captivated by the apostle's message, "Blessed are those who have kept the flesh chaste, for they will become a temple of God. . . . Blessed are the bodies of virgins, for they shall be pleasing to God," Thecla breaks off her engagement to the eligible bachelor Thamyris, follows Paul to Antioch, and is nearly martyred for her pains. By the end of the story, however, she has become a perpetual virgin commissioned by Paul to preach the good news in and around her home city, Iconium, a town to the north of Antioch.[51]

It would appear, then, that some young women took Paul's instructions to the Corinthians seriously, remaining abstinent while waiting upon the day of the Lord. In some cases, these women were designated "virgin widows" and were supported by church funds. Without the distractions of husbands or children, these women devoted themselves to the propagation of the Christian message, an activity degraded by the Pastor as mere "gossip." Not every follower of Paul, however, revered the widow-virgins as much as Ignatius of Antioch or the writers of the *Acts of Paul*. In fact, by the end of the second century, some Christians were actively campaigning against the practice, arguing that young virgins had not attained the status of "widows" and so must remain strictly under control of their fathers or mothers.[52] Though "virgins" would eventually become a distinct office as well, at this early stage, the title "widow" and "virgin" could be used interchangeably. The Pastor may be regarded as the Christian author responsible for launching the campaign to distinguish between them, while also ensuring that younger virgins marry and procreate.

The Rule of Women

By linking women's salvation to marriage and procreation, the Pastor not only places women's sexual lives under the strict control of free men, he also imitates a set of instructions present in first-century Roman law. Securing support following his defeat of Mark Antony at the Battle of Actium (31 BCE), Emperor Octavian Augustus instituted a set of laws designed to promote marriage and childbearing among Roman citizens, in part by repressing adultery and extramarital sex among free women. His legal reforms—the *lex Iulia de maridandis ordinibus* (Julian law on marriage orders, 18 BCE), the *lex Iulia de adulteriis* (Julian law on adultery, 18 BCE), and the *lex Papia Poppaea* (Papian-Popaean law, 9 CE, a statute that amended and completed his earlier legislation)—penalized Roman citizens who did not marry, required widows and divorcées to remarry, and made women's adultery a criminal offense. Like the Pastor, who granted older widows who had raised their children permission to be placed "on the list," the Emperor also granted special privileges to mature Roman mothers. A woman who successfully bore three or more children was released from the requirement that she obtain a guardian (a "tutor") when widowed; she could therefore control her own estate, apart from the supervision of a man, and inherit property directly from her husband.[53]

The second-century Roman law professor Gaius explains the rationale for *tutela* or "guardianship" of women:

> For the ancients wanted women, even if they are of full age, to be in guardianship (tutela) on account of their lightmindedness.[54]

In other words, womanly weakness, or "lightmindedness," required that a woman be under the care of a guardian at all times, be he her father, husband, or a special "tutor" appointed for her following her husband's death. Following Augustus's reforms, however, mothers of three or more children were exempted from this requirement. Such women were also granted permission to remain unmarried, though they were usually expected to marry anyway.[55] Nevertheless, the supervision of Roman women remained an important goal of the Augustan legislation: women caught in the act of adultery by their fathers could be executed on the spot, husbands with adulterous wives could be tried for the crime of "pimping" if they did not seek a divorce, and guilty wives were to be exiled forever to an island after first relinquishing half their dowries to their husbands. Moreover, Roman women who had not yet achieved the status of mother of three remained under the control of a father, husband, or guardian. They also could not inherit property from their husbands, and they had no choice but to remarry. As "father of the fatherland," the emperor demonstrated his superior skills at "household management" by controlling not only his own household but also the marital affairs of all his subjects. In the Pastorals, then, "Paul" has taken on a similar task.

Keeping Both Passion and People Under Control

In the Pastorals, the perfect control of passion is achieved not through spiritual participation in the body of Christ but through strict obedience to male rulers: God, kings, bishops, deacons, and elders. When supplications, prayers, intercessions, and thanksgivings are offered for kings, "we may lead a quiet and peaceable life" (1 Tim. 2:2). All are to be "subject to rulers and authorities, to be obedient, [and] to be ready for every good work" (Titus 3:1); if they succeed at this task, they, too, might inherit eternal life. Careful obedience to rulers, elders, and God's commandments produces a healthy community, governed by honorable men who are treated with respect by their subordinates. In return, rulers demonstrate their propriety by controlling others well. The proof of their success lies in the modest comportment of their women, who marry, bear children, and remain silent, learning from their husbands at home. As masters of the house, men are masters of both their own desires and the desires of their subjects.[56]

The letter to the Colossians and the general letter known as Ephesians also stress self-control and the advantages of a well-ordered household, but, in this instance, controlled households are given a cosmological cast: the dominion and love of God justifies the dominion and love of free men, who love their wives, their slaves, and their children, even as their wives, slaves, and children honor them by obeying eagerly, without question. Desire in this instance is controlled not by the coercive discipline of free men who keep subordinates in line but by the love of men and God for their subjects. Nevertheless, Paul's own longing for androgynous, resurrection bodies—prefigured either by celibate bodies that neither marry nor are given in marriage, or by married bodies that reunite during sexual intercourse and therefore keep illicit desire at bay—has been replaced by a spiritual resurrection, already attained in the context of Christian worship. According to these later interpreters of Paul, Christian piety is to be displayed to the world by means of a quiet, well-ordered home. Paul's exhortation to the Corinthians that he wishes all could be "as I myself am" (1 Cor. 7:7) has been overlooked.

Paul, of course, was equally concerned with the control of desire. Determined to keep men from mixing their flesh with prostitutes, women other than their wives, or with one another, he portrayed same-sex pairing as an important example of Gentile sin, setting himself apart from many of his contemporaries. Yet, unlike in Colossians, Ephesians, and the Pastorals, he rejected the view that male mastery ought to be displayed in household contexts: rather than urging men to marry and women to bear children, he recommended celibacy for the strong and marriage for the weak, portraying marriage as both a temporary solution and a distraction from the "affairs of the Lord" (1 Cor. 7:32–33). In all of these letters, however, those by Paul and those written in his name, desire was a danger that had to be carefully managed. (See table 1.)

TABLE 1. A SUMMARY OF PAULINE ADVICE
REGARDING DESIRE, SEX, AND MARRIAGE

Author	Advice about Desire	Advice about Sexual Intercourse	Advice about Marriage
Paul	Should be controlled as much as possible. Out-of-control desire is a principal sign of abandonment by God.	Avoid it if possible but, if married, have sex regularly so as to avoid temptation. If one is a man, one should not submit to sexual penetration. If one is a woman, one must submit to penetration.	Avoid it unless desire is unmanageable. It is intended for the weak in faith. Those ineligible for married life are not considered and thus slaves are largely excluded from Paul's moral program.
Colossians & Ephesians	Should be controlled and managed within a hierarchical household.	No specific advice is given regarding the frequency and purpose of sexual intercourse.	Free men should love their wives, keeping them under control. Wives, children, and slaves should obey the male head of the household.

Author	Advice about Desire	Advice about Sexual Intercourse	Advice about Marriage
The Pastor	Desire is extremely dangerous, especially for women and young men.	Women must procreate if they are to be saved by God. Widows must remarry so as to avoid sexual temptation. Husbands should display their own sexual self-mastery by strictly mastering their subordinates.	Male church leaders should marry only once. Virgin "widows" must marry– celibacy is impermissible for them. Those ineligible for married life cannot be leaders in the churches.

Seven Days of Sex

The ancient Christian view that desire is a problem requiring some sort of solution fits well within other Jewish, Greek, and Roman writings from this same period, and the effort to promulgate laws capable of controlling desire in the community finds a parallel in contemporary Roman law. The biblical writings we have been considering in this chapter coincided with a Roman imperial family-values campaign in which free men were required to master not only their own desires, but also the sexual lives of their wives, children, and slaves. If they failed to do so, they could be subject to the disciplinary intervention of the Roman government. Failing to marry, they could be fined. Failing to produce three or more legitimate Roman children, they could be passed over for important government appointments. Failing to divorce adulterous wives, they could be tried in criminal court. In practice, these laws seem to have been enforced only sporadically. Nevertheless, the insistence on the part of some Christians and Jews that free men should firmly manage both their households and their desires was part of the larger complex of first- and second-century instructions. The advice offered by Paul and his later interpreters, though contradictory, expresses common assumptions about manliness, self-control, and the problems produced by sexual desire. Pauline moral teachings, then, are fully embedded within the cultural assumptions of the first-century Roman Empire. One could say the same about Reverend Young and his "sexperiment."

When Reverend Young claimed that God wants married couples to "do it" as often as possible, he departed in significant ways from the views expressed in the writings of Paul and his earliest interpreters. From the perspective of early Christians, pursuing sex for its own sake, even within the context of marriage, would have demonstrated a shameful lack of self-control. For them, the goal of God's people should be the eradication or domestication of desire within a larger household structure, not the daily enjoyment of sexual intercourse within an idealized heterosexual marriage. From the perspective of Reverend Young's audience, however, sexual intercourse within marriage should be widely celebrated. Popular books like *365 Days: A Memoir of Intimacy* or *Just Do It: How One Couple Turned Off the TV and Turned On Their Sex Lives for 101 Days (No Excuses!)* tell of the glories of heterosexual married intimacy pursued on a daily basis.[57] Jumping on this seven-days-per-week bandwagon, Reverend Young presents himself and his version of Christianity as hip, contemporary, and attractive, just as Pauline Christians once presented themselves as more capable of sexual self-mastery than their Roman and Greek neighbors. Shaping their sexual morals so that they could fit within their particular cultural contexts, Pauline Christians and Reverend Young promote sexual codes that are familiar to their audiences. They also endorse an exclusive and discriminatory version of sexual morality available to some, but not others.

Slaves could not benefit from Pauline sexual morals. Similarly, the unmarried have no real place in Reverend Young's financial and sexual recovery plan, irrespective of the reason for their unmarried state. Sexual intercourse is so important and so fundamental to intimacy with God, Reverend Young argues, that it should be undertaken on a daily basis. Single people, however, must remain celibate, since they do not benefit from the blessings of a heterosexual marriage. At best, Reverend Young concedes, they can enjoy some chocolate cake. In this account, then, celibacy is the unfortunate lot of the unmarried, not the moral and spiritual privilege of the strong, as Paul had argued. In fact, Reverend Young reverses Paul's argument for celibacy and the single life ("I wish that all were as I myself am," 1 Cor. 7:7), offering himself and his marriage as an example of God-given morality. As he promised the *Dallas Morning News,* he and his wife, Lisa, intend "to give [seven-day sex] a try."[58] Though the cultural disconnect between Paul and his followers on the one hand and Reverend Young and his flock on the other could not be more obvious, both were quite willing to employ teachings about sexual morality to exclude others from the full benefits of salvation. As we will see in the next chapter, the use of sexual morality to promote some over others is not unique to Reverend Young and Pauline Christians, but can be found in other biblical writings as well.

CHAPTER 4

Sexual Politics

God's Wife, Cursing the Canaanites, and Biblical Sex Crimes

In 2001, two days after the attacks on the World Trade Center and the Pentagon by Al Qaeda, the Reverend Jerry Falwell remarked:

> What we saw on Tuesday, as terrible as it is, could be minuscule if, in fact, God continues to lift the curtain and allow the enemies of America to give us probably what we deserve. . . . I really believe that the pagans, and the abortionists, and the feminists, and the gays and the lesbians who are actively trying to make that an alternative lifestyle, the ACLU, People for the American Way, all of them who have tried to secularize America, I point the finger in their face and say, "You helped this happen."[1]

From Mr. Falwell's perspective, then, paganism, abortion, feminism, gay and lesbian lifestyles, and secularization have no place in the America God wants. Apparently, Mr. Falwell's God is so committed to this point of view that he intentionally used members of Al Qaeda as his instruments, killing a few thousand Americans so that the nation would recognize the error of its ways and repent. Nine months later and eight months into the U.S. invasion of Afghanistan, the Reverend Jerry Vines, then pastor of the First Baptist Church of Jacksonville, Florida, offered another, rival explanation for these same events: the perpetrators were not unwitting agents of divine wrath, appropriately carried out against sinful American culture, but victims of a false, bloodthirsty God and his servant, Muhammad. He explained: "Islam was founded by a demon-possessed pedophile who had twelve wives, the last one of which was a nine-year-old girl." Moreover, "Allah is not Jehovah [i.e., Yhwh],[2] either. Jehovah is not going to turn you into a terrorist that'll try to bomb people and take the lives of thousands of people."[3] Corrupted first by their founder and then by their violent god, the terrorists expressed not the divine will, but the will of demons, or so Reverend Vines suggested.

These two explanations are entirely contradictory: one blames certain, hated insiders for bringing God's wrath upon America, while the other blames targeted outsiders, suggesting that their actions were totally foreign to the Christian God's true wishes. Nevertheless, both ministers attempted to account for the violence of September 11, 2001, by associating their enemies with false religion, sexual immorality, and divine wrath, an argumentative strategy that is also found in some biblical writings. Denigrating enemies for participation in religions that are deemed to be false and then claiming that these same enemies are sexually immoral and therefore intolerable to God, Reverend Falwell, Reverend Vines, and the biblical passages we will discuss in this chapter suggest that violence is legitimate, so long as it is directed against those whom God finds offensive.

To be clear, the list of beliefs and behaviors mentioned by Reverend Falwell and Reverend Vines find no parallel at all in biblical writings: the word "pagan" does not appear;[4] abortion is not discussed; there was no ancient "feminist" movement; "gays and lesbians" with a "lifestyle" are never mentioned; "secularism" as a concept had not yet been invented; and "pedophilia" is not talked about, let alone defined as a crime (like Muhammad, biblical patriarchs had a number of wives, some of whom may have been quite young). Whatever behaviors should or should not be identified as immoral, contemporary descriptions of the evils of American culture or the allegedly corrupt origins of Islam cannot be substantiated on the basis of biblical writings. Still, the strategy of charging enemies with religious impropriety and then linking bad religious practice to illicit sexual behavior, variously defined, is as old as the Bible.

This chapter examines charges of sexual perversion and definitions of sexual crimes put forward in a range of biblical texts. As we will see, the Bible often portrays religious misbehavior as a form of illicit sex, leading to a number of misimpressions regarding the actions, beliefs, and morals of non-Israelites and non-Christians. It is simply not the case, for example, that the Canaanites employed sacred prostitutes at their temples, a myth that was popularized by biblical scholars a century ago. Moreover, Paul and the followers of Jesus did not have to contend with sacred prostitution in the Greek city of Corinth, though some Christians today argue that they did. Characterizing the worship of gods other than Yhwh or Christ as a form of prostitution, the Bible feeds these misimpressions, making matters worse by framing biblical commandments involving sexual misbehavior with accusations against other peoples and nations. Other people do these things, the Bible states, but good Israelites or Christians avoid them, a claim that is further upheld by origin stories that represent the ancestors of the Canaanites as perverse and accursed by God. As is obvious from the Bible, however, the behaviors that are explicitly forbidden are precisely what some Israelites and Christians *were* doing.

Focusing on accusations against Canaanites and other outsiders by biblical writers, this chapter considers the unfair depiction of non-Israelite and non-Christian sexual behavior, particularly the accusation that outsiders "prostitute themselves to their gods." Charges of sacred prostitution fed charges of prostitution in general, which in turn produced stereotypical depictions of Canaanites, the inhabitants of Roman Corinth, and Gentiles. Stereotypes regarding what other nations do were then employed in biblical conquest narratives to suggest that the annihilation of these nations was both appropriate and demanded by God. The book of Leviticus furthers these stereotypes, claiming that the Canaanites, not the Israelites, engage in incest, adultery, and nonprocreative sex. Proposing the death penalty for many of these "crimes," Leviticus, like the book of Joshua, implies that those who violate its provisions deserve to be killed and displaced from their land. Apostasy, idolatry, and sexual immorality are therefore represented as a single problem, a problem that can only be overcome by divinely instigated violence.

God's Wife

The notion that Israel or the Christian church is God's "wife," familiar from interpretations of the Song of Songs, also impacted the way that "bad" Israelites were portrayed: if good Israel is God's wife, then a faithless Israel is God's whore. Comparing the exclusive allegiance due to God to the sexual fidelity owed by a wife to her husband, Israelite prophets and New Testament writers alike characterized false religion as adultery (Hebrew *n'p,* Greek *moicheia*) and prostitution (Hebrew *znh,* Greek *porneia*), representing religious infidelity as a sexual offense, apart from any actual behavior on the part of the accused.

The prophet Hosea offers a striking example of this phenomenon.[5] To him, worship of the Canaanite god Baal was by definition a form of prostitution, and so if Israel puts up altars to Baal, "she" should be regarded as a prostitute (*znh*). Encountering Israel the whore, Yhwh has no choice but to destroy her, or as Hosea puts it, to "strip her naked and expose her as in the day she was born" (Hosea 2:3), uncovering her "in the sight of her lovers" (v. 10). Likening the coming destruction of Israel to a violent rape, Hosea warns that she (the land) will be laid waste if she (the nation) does not repent and worship Yhwh alone.[6] Writing after a terrible defeat at the hands of the Babylonians (587 BCE), the prophet Ezekiel also warned that the destruction of Jerusalem and its temple would soon follow if the people did not change their ways. Employing a metaphor similar to Hosea's, he blamed the coming doom on the "prostitutions" (*znh*) of the people: "You [the city of Jerusalem] trusted in your beauty, and played the whore because of your fame, and lavished your whorings on any passer-by!"(Ezek. 16:15).[7] By worshipping other gods, the people of the city, who were supposed to be faithful wives of God, behaved like whores and so earned whatever disasters might befall them later.

Addressing Christians several centuries later, the author of the New Testament book of Revelation drew on this same prophetic figure of speech, applying the idolatry=prostitution metaphor to Christian churches as well. Upset by the teachings of a Christian prophetess with whom he disagreed, the author, John of Patmos, warned the church in

Thyatira that God plans to throw "those who commit adultery"—that is, fail to worship Christ properly on account of this woman—into great distress. "Seduced" into eating food sacrificed to other gods, the followers of Jesus in Thyatira have become idolaters, a behavior John identifies as "prostitution." He states, taking on the voice of Christ:

> You tolerate that woman Jezebel, who calls herself a prophet and is teaching and beguiling my servants [lit. "slaves"] to practice fornication [porneia, lit. "prostitution"] and to eat food sacrificed to idols. I gave her time to repent, but she refuses to repent of her fornication [porneia]. Beware, I am throwing her on a bed, and those who commit adultery with her I am throwing into great distress, unless they repent of her doings; and I will strike her children dead. (Rev. 2:20–23, NRSV, slightly altered)

As we observed in the introduction, "Jezebel" is not an innocent name. By calling this teacher "Jezebel," John recalls a biblical queen who introduced the worship of Baal to the Israelite court. The specific charge against the Jezebel of Thyatira, then, is that she and those who listen to her act like the biblical antihero Jezebel and her sympathizers, Israelites who dared to sacrifice to Baal instead of to Yhwh. Their sin has to do with idolatry, not sex, though John employs sex to discredit them.

At stake in Hosea, Ezekiel, and Revelation is the religious behavior of the people, not their sexual infidelities. To Hosea, by messing around with foreign gods, Israel invited Assyria to invade. To Ezekiel, the destruction of Jerusalem by the Babylonians was just punishment for the city's failure to remain faithful to Yhwh. And to John of Patmos, author of Revelation, eating idol meat was so offensive that it could be likened to prostitution. Still, the persistent characterization of fidelity to God as a sexual as well as a religious matter had the cumulative effect of making sex and religion appear to be one phenomenon, an impression that is intensified by the further disparagement of non-Israelite and non-Christian practices in a number of biblical writings. The view that Israel is Yhwh's "wife" or that the Christian church is the "bride of Christ"—put forward by Israelite prophets and the followers of Jesus—made the association between religious and sexual behaviors especially strong.

Prostitutes of Baal

In the Hebrew Bible, faithful Israel is depicted as God's "wife," but Israel's enemies are represented as incapable of "marriage" (proper worship). Instead, they "prostitute themselves to their gods."[8] Exodus explains:

> *You shall not make a covenant with the inhabitants of the land, for when they prostitute themselves to their gods and sacrifice to their gods, someone among them will invite you, and you will eat of the sacrifice. And you will take wives from among their daughters for your sons, and their daughters who prostitute themselves to their gods will make your sons also prostitute themselves to their gods. (Exod. 34:15–16; compare Deut. 7:1–6)*

When Israel goes off track, "she" behaves like an adulteress or prostitute, though Yhwh repeatedly offers to take her back. By contrast, according to the Bible, non-Israelite religion is never anything other than "prostitution" (*znh*). Since they are "idolaters"—that is, they do not worship Yhwh—the non-Israelite inhabitants of the land fill Canaan with prostitutes, never with wives.

Parallel arguments can also be found in the New Testament. As we observed in chapter 3, the apostle Paul presented the Gentiles—anyone who was not a Jew—as prone to out-of-control desire. Worshipping false gods, the Gentiles were abandoned by God to illicit sex, which they pursued at every opportunity, or so Paul argued. Gentile followers of Jesus were therefore instructed to break away from the bad behavior characteristic of their ancestors by adopting a strict code of sexual morality, a code in which celibacy or marriage were the only options. Only then could they prove that they had been successfully transformed by their relationship to Christ. To Paul, desire was the problem and Christ was the cure. If the Gentiles do not begin to worship the God of Israel by accepting Paul's gospel about God's Messiah, God will judge them, first by allowing them to pursue illicit sex and then by sentencing them to eternal death once Christ returns in judgment. The book of Revelation includes an even more vivid image to make a similar point. Depicting the city of Rome as a great whore, the author, John of Patmos, envisions "her" holding a golden cup "full of abominations and the impurities of her fornications [lit. "prostitution"]" (Rev. 17:4); this cup, he continues, was filled by Gentiles, who drink "the wine of the wrath of her fornication [lit. "prostitution"]" (14:8) and by Gentile rulers who "fornicate with her" (Rev. 18:3). John looks forward to a time when the city and her allies will be overthrown, burning forever, while those loyal to God look on in triumph.[9]

The Myth of Sacred Prostitution

Adopting the Bible's point of view, modern readers have often assumed that the Canaanites, the Babylonians, or the Gentiles really were engaged in sexually disgusting religious practices, practices that no true Israelite or Christian would ever consider. Most strikingly, prostitution to Baal and other gods has been interpreted as *actual* prostitution, leading to the widespread belief that there were prostitutes performing sex acts in Canaanite temples. For example, when describing the myths and rituals associated with the Canaanite goddesses Astharte and Anath, the famous biblical scholar William Foxwell Albright concluded, "the erotic aspect of their cult must have sunk to extremely sordid depths of social degradation."[10] As Exodus warned and Albright assumed, the Canaanites really did pursue the worst sorts of sexual behavior, and did so as a matter of religious obligation.[11] Ancient characterizations of Corinth as a city awash with prostitutes has led to a similar phenomenon.[12] Building on fantastical descriptions of ancient Corinth by the Greek historian Herodotus (fifth century BCE), the geographer Strabo (born ca. 64 BCE), and the humorist Athenaeus (wrote ca. 200 CE), modern interpreters imagine that the Corinthian temple of Aphrodite housed as many as one thousand slave prostitutes, dedicated to the goddess and eager to serve visitors to the city. They then argue that God sent Paul and the followers of Jesus to stamp out this problem. Some scholars have even linked the sacred prostitution in Corinth to that in Canaan, arguing that Corinth's Aphrodite was modeled on the goddess Astharte, brought to Asia Minor by early immigrants from biblical lands.[13] According to this point of view, the depraved religious-sexual practices of non-Jews and non-Christians can be traced in a genealogical line from ancient Canaan through to Roman Corinth and onward.

Yes, There Were Prostitutes, Just Not Sacred Prostitution[14]

There is, however, no material evidence to support the view that Canaanites, the Babylonians, or any other ancient Mesopotamian nation engaged in prostitution to any greater degree than those who worshipped Yhwh, let alone that sacred prostitutes dwelt in their temples. Prostitutes were marginalized members of society, which is why the charge that the idolaters "prostitute themselves to their gods" stung, but they were not identified as priestesses or sacred functionaries in nonbiblical texts. Juxtaposed with wives and honorable daughters or sons in biblical and other Mesopotamian writings, prostitutes were universally degraded and maligned, not represented as "sacred."[15] Nevertheless, their presence in Israel and elsewhere could simply be assumed. So, for example, as we observed in the introduction, when the biblical patriarch Judah encountered his daughter-in-law Tamar dressed as a prostitute, he contracted her services, offering to pay her with a kid from his flock. Only later, when he realized she was not a professional prostitute but a widow and his kin did he challenge her behavior.[16] Similarly, when the biblical hero Samson encountered a prostitute during a visit to Gaza, he "went into her" before proceeding on to the city.[17]

Toleration of prostitution as a fact of social life, accompanied by disdain for actual prostitutes, can be found in other Mesopotamian texts as well. For example, the early-second-millennium (2000–1650 BCE) Lipit-Isthtar Lawcode carefully distinguishes between a "prostitute from the street" and a wife: legally, if a wife fails to produce children for her husband, the husband may claim the children of a harlot as his own, but he must not allow the harlot to live in his house with his wife "as long as his wife is alive."[18] The status of the wife must therefore be kept distinct from the status of "prostitute," a woman who sells her body in the city, even if the husband adopts children he fathered with the prostitute as his own. A set of Assyrian laws from the twelfth century BCE promotes similar assumptions, this time by differentiating unmarried priestesses, prostitutes, concubines, and slaves from wives and married priestesses on the basis of their attire:

> Wives of a man, or [widows], or any [Assyrian] women who go out into the main thoroughfare [shall not have] their heads [bare]. Daughters of a man [. . . with] either a . . . cloth or garments or [. . .] shall be veiled. . . . A concubine who goes about in the main thoroughfare with her mistress is to be veiled. A married qaditu-woman is to be veiled . . . but an unmarried one is to leave her head bare in the main thoroughfare, she shall not veil herself. A prostitute shall not be veiled, her head shall be bare. Whoever sees a veiled prostitute shall seize her, secure witnesses and bring her to the palace entrance. . . . they shall strike her 50 blows with rods; they shall pour hot pitch over her head. . . . Slave women shall not be veiled, and he who should see a veiled slave woman shall seize her and bring her to the palace entrance; they shall cut off her ears.[19]

Forbidding veils to prostitutes, slave women, and concubines, wives and daughters were instead instructed that they must wear one, though they were not punished if they did not.[20] By contrast, harlots and slave women were severely disciplined if they dared to wear a veil—the harlot by flogging and the slave woman by having her ears cut off—since, by doing so, they took on a prerogative reserved for proper Assyrian daughters and wives. Unmarried priestesses and concubines were also prevented from veiling, though no punishment was proscribed if they disobeyed, perhaps because priestesses and concubines were able to become wives later on. Slaves and prostitutes, however, could never marry and so must never veil.

Though extrabiblical evidence for Canaanite religion is slight, what does survive also fails to support the theory that Canaanites engaged in sacred prostitution.[21] Surviving administrative tablets from Canaanite temples name religious personnel as priests and singers, not prostitutes, employing, among other terms, the title *qdsm*. In Hebrew, this word is rendered as *qedesa* or *qedesot* and has the sense of "person consecrated to a temple," perhaps as a singer of some kind.[22] English translations of the Bible, however, add to the confusion by translating this title as "temple prostitute" instead. For example, in the New Revised Standard Version (NRSV), the biblical text Deuteronomy 23:17–18 reads:

> *None of the daughters of Israel shall be a temple prostitute* (qedesa)*; none of the sons of Israel shall be a temple prostitute* (qedesot)*. You shall not bring the fee of a prostitute or the wages of a male prostitute* (lit. *"a dog"*) *into the house of the* LORD *your God in payment for any vow, for both of these are abhorrent to the* LORD *your God.*

Yet the titles *qedesa* or *qedesot* do not necessarily imply a sexual role,[23] and the slur "the wages of a dog" does not necessarily point to male prostitution. The translation of "prostitute" reflects an interpretive decision by the translators. Moreover, from the perspective of Mesopotamian sources, serving as a person consecrated to a temple (a *qdsm*) required a stringent set of marriage requirements, not ritual sex in temples.[24]

The translators who prepared the NRSV were in good company: the Revised Standard Version (RSV), the New International Version (NIV), and the King James [Authorized] Version (KJV) of the Bible all suggest in their translations that Deuteronomy was forbidding sacred prostitution.[25] In fact, the tradition of rendering "woman dedicated to a temple" (*qedesa*) or "man dedicated to a temple" (*qedesot*) as "prostitute" goes back to the first century BCE. When Deuteronomy was translated from Hebrew to Greek for the sake of Greek-speaking Jews who could no longer understand Hebrew, these verses were rendered:

> There shall be no prostitute from the daughters of Israel, and there shall be no prostitution among the sons of Israel. There shall not be a temple initiate (telesphoros) from the daughters of Israel. There shall not be an initiate (teliskomenos) from the sons of Israel. You may not offer a prostitute's payment or that which is offered to a dog to the house of your Lord God for any oath, because both are an abomination to the Lord your God. (Deut. 23:18–19, Septuagint) [26]

Ancient Greek translators therefore came up with a double solution, adding to the Hebrew text by forbidding both prostitution and initiation into the sacred rites of another god. The early-medieval Latin Vulgate, on the other hand, dropped out the religious connotations of *qedesa* and *qedesot* entirely, simply stating: "There will be no prostitute from the daughters of Israel, neither will the sons of Israel engage in prostitution." [27] The confusion between idolatry and prostitution, promoted so effectively by biblical metaphors, has left translators in a quandary for more than two thousand years.

The Temple of Aphrodite in Corinth

A similar set of possible (mis)impressions has also plagued the study of Greco-Roman Corinth. The rumors began with Herodotus, a fifth-century BCE Greek historian known for his colorful stories. Describing the worship of Aphrodite in Babylonia, not Corinth, he reported:

> Every woman who lives in that country must once in her lifetime go to the temple of Aphrodite and sit there and be lain with by a strange man. . . . Once she has lain with him, she has fulfilled her obligation to the goddess and gets to go home. [28]

Herodotus himself admits that the sources of this information are un-reliable, noting that the Phoenicians and the Persians would certainly dis-pute the information he reports about them.[29] Nevertheless, he proceeds to entertain his audiences with whatever information he could glean about the styles of dress, agricultural customs, and other rites performed by the Babylonians, the Egyptians, and other foreigners, irrespective of the reliability of his sources. It is not surprising, then, that he regularly gets it wrong.[30] Even Cicero, the first-century BCE Roman orator, belittled the accuracy of Herodotus's work: "In history the standard by which ev-erything is judged is the truth, while in poetry it is generally the pleasure one gives; however, in the works of Herodotus, the Father of History . . . one finds numerous fabulous tales."[31] Herodotus's description of the sacred sex at the temples in Babylonia ought to be read not as history but as a good, entertaining story.

Strabo, a first-century Greek writer, added fuel to the fire, applying a similar story to the ancient Greek city of Corinth, not Babylonia:

> The [Corinthian] temple of Aphrodite was so rich that it owned more than a thousand temple-slaves, courtesans, whom both men and women had dedicated to the goddess.[32]

In Strabo's account, these women are identified as courtesans (*hetai-rai*), not prostitutes (*pornai*). *Hetairai* were nonmarried female compan-ions or entertainers, not women who openly sold sex for a fee.[33] Still, the idea that they were "cult prostitutes" is furthered by his next comment:

> It was also on account of these women that the city was crowded with people and grew rich; for instance, the ship-captains freely squandered their money, and hence the proverb, "Not for every man is the voyage to Corinth."

Suggesting that everyone loves to come to Corinth to visit these women, especially sailors, Strabo implies that they performed sex acts for money.

Is Strabo's *Geography* to be believed, at least as a historical report about prostitutes dwelling at Corinth's temple of Aphrodite? Modern historians remain skeptical. As historian John Lanci puts it: "To find in [Strabo and other] sources the presence of slaves dedicated to the sexual service of the goddess of love, one has to read into the accounts something that is not there."[34] Even if Strabo's account is based in some actual historical memory, however, his description of sacred courtesans in Corinth refers to *classical* Corinth, a Corinth he had never seen, not to Corinth during Roman times. Sacked by the Romans in 146 BCE, the city was deserted, only to be refounded in 44 BCE as a Roman colony. Early religious sites were lost, including the glorious temple of Aphrodite with its numerous prostitutes, assuming these prostitutes ever existed.[35] If there was cult prostitution in Corinth, then, it had ended long before Christians entered the scene.[36]

Rumors about Corinthian prostitution continued to circulate anyway, just as they do today. Athenaeus, an early-third-century CE Greek writer from Egypt, repeated Strabo's views by suggesting that the ancient, pre-Roman Corinthians invited courtesans (*hetairai*) to join in their prayers to the goddess, allowing them to add their own supplications to those of the other women of the city.[37] Again, Athenaeus was addressing Corinth as it was long ago, not Corinth during his own times. He does so in the context of a lengthy and humorous work, not a history, designed both to entertain the reader and honor his Roman patron Larensis. *The Learned Banquet* makes a point of including a myriad of references to obscure details and fabulous tales gleaned from Larensis's large collection of Greek books.[38] As such, Athenaeus is hardly a reliable source of information regarding what was happening in Corinth during the time of Paul. He, too, enjoyed a fanciful tale, and the Corinth he described existed some two hundred years before Paul wrote letters to the followers of Jesus in that city.

Prostitution and the Christians of Corinth

Still, as we noted in chapter 3, Paul does address prostitution in Corinth. "Do you not know that your bodies are members of Christ?" Paul asked. "Should I therefore take the members of Christ and make them members of a prostitute? Never!" (1 Cor. 6:15). Placing one's "member" in the body of a prostitute, he argued, pollutes not only the body of the man doing the placing but also the whole community. Sexual intercourse with a prostitute is therefore a sexual and religious matter both. "Shun *porneia*!" ("prostitution" or "fornication"; v. 18) he commands. Paul also equates Gentile religious practices with prostitution and the worship of demons, stating, for example, "You cannot drink the cup of the Lord and the cup of demons. You cannot partake of the table of the Lord and the table of demons" (10:21). As participants in a ceremonial meal dedicated to the memory of Christ, Paul asserts, the Corinthians must avoid comparable meals dedicated to "demons," that is, to gods other than the God of Israel. He then invokes their memory of the Last Supper, the meal Jesus held with his disciples the night before he died, further encouraging religious and sexual propriety during the sacred meal.[39]

Corinth was a multicultural port city filled with inhabitants from all over the Mediterranean world. Certainly there were prostitutes there. Also, Aphrodite, the goddess of love, was the patron goddess of Corinth, and this may have influenced the character of the city as a whole. Aphrodite's name, when turned into a Greek noun or verb, meant, "to have sexual intercourse" (*aphrodisia, aphrodisiasmos, aphrodisiazein*), and she is featured in various ancient Greek love stories, where she arranges for the unification and marriage of young lovers.[40] Aphrodite's associations with sexual intercourse, beauty, and love are obvious. Still, during Paul's lifetime, the temples of Aphrodite, in Corinth and elsewhere, did not employ sanctified slave prostitutes in the context of various sacred rites. Certainly some Corinthians visited prostitutes. Some also attended the cult festivals associated with Aphrodite. But Aphrodite's significance was not limited to sex or fertility; she was worshipped as a goddess who fostered union among peoples, with her function as the goddess of love serving as only one attribute among her more important associations with fertility, abundance, and social harmony.[41] The attribution of *sacred* prostitution to Corinth, then, like the accusation that the Canaanites "prostitute themselves to their gods," appears to be a polemical argument rather than an accurate or fair report of what the devotees of Aphrodite were doing.

A similar point could be made about the Canaanites, Babylonians, and Assyrians: the law codes of these nations sought to discipline the sexual and moral behavior of their citizens, just as the Sinai covenant codes worked to define and enforce particular marriage practices, as we noted in chapter 2. Yet myths about Canaanite, Babylonian, and Corinthian sacred prostitution persist, thanks in part to the metaphorical comparison of idolatry and prostitution. If Israel is God's "wife" and the church is the "bride of Christ," then those who worship other gods can only be "whores," or so the Bible suggests. But there is more. By depicting the Canaanites and other enemies of Israel as especially prone to sexual depravity, the Bible suggests that they should be accursed and, in some cases, killed. The accusation that Canaanites and Corinthians engaged in illicit sex makes it possible for those putting the accusation forward to appear more righteous, more pious, and more deserving of God's favor. Such accusations also justified divine or divinely inspired violence.

Cursing the Canaanites

Descendants of Noah's son Ham and his grandson Canaan, the non-Israelite inhabitants of the land are introduced to the biblical narrative in Genesis shortly after the story of the flood. Already they are accused of sexual wrongdoing. After disembarking from the ark, Genesis reports, Noah planted a vineyard, drank some of the wine, and became drunk. Coming upon his father asleep and inebriated, Ham "saw the nakedness (*râ'âh 'erwat*) of his father, and told his two brothers outside." Shem and Japheth, the two righteous brothers, then entered the tent, walking backward so as to avoid looking at their father, and covered his nakedness. Genesis emphasizes this point: "Their faces were turned away, and they

did not see their father's nakedness."[42] Awaking from sleep, Noah learned
what had happened, and, in response, he cursed Ham's son Canaan and
blessed Shem and Japheth: "Cursed be Canaan; lowest of slaves shall he
be to his brothers. . . . [But] blessed by the LORD my God be Shem; and let
Canaan be his slave. May God make space for Japheth, and let him live
in the tents of Shem; and let Canaan be his slave" (Gen. 9:25–27). Apparently, viewing the nakedness of one's father was such a terrible crime that
perpetual slavery for one's descendants was an appropriate punishment,
beginning with Ham's son Canaan and continuing forever, so long as
there were Canaanites in the land.

Among other purposes, this story involving Ham, Canaan, and Noah's
nakedness likely served as a justification for the later Israelite conquest of
both the Canaanites and the Philistines: already from the time of Noah,
Genesis suggests, the descendants of Shem (the Israelites) were destined
to rule over the descendants of Ham (the Canaanites) and of Japheth
(the Philistines), but whereas the Philistines would later be tolerated (they
would live in Israel's tents), the Canaanites would not be.[43] Like their
ancestor Ham, they are beyond redemption.[44] But what was so terrible
about viewing Noah's nakedness? Such behavior hardly seems offensive,
at least initially. Moreover, why would Noah curse Canaan, Ham's son,
instead of Ham himself? Interpreters have been troubled by this odd passage for centuries, offering various solutions, some of which blame Noah
as well as Ham and, by extension, Canaan. According to the vast majority of interpretations, some sort of sexual indiscretion is in view.

Viewing Noah Naked

Reasoning that Ham must have either castrated or raped his father, late-
ancient rabbis developed an explanation of this story capable of accounting
for both the curse of Canaan rather than Ham and the severity of Noah's
reaction. Since Ham made it impossible for his father to beget further sons,
Noah appropriately denied *him* future sons, making Canaan and all his descendants into slaves rather than free men, who would be capable of pass-

ing on their property to others.[45] Alternatively, the rabbis reasoned, perhaps Ham sexually abused his father and did not castrate him, though they were not sure why this behavior would result in the curse of Canaan.[46]

Late ancient Christian readers offered a very different set of interpretations. From their perspective, Ham's sin was not so much sexual as disrespectful: Ham laughed at his father's nakedness and made fun of his father's shame in public, prefiguring the ridicule Christ would face when dying on a cross.[47] As the fourth-century bishop Methodius put it, "When overpowered by wine, [Noah] was mocked."[48] Assuming that Noah prefigured Christ, the fourth-century bishop Ambrose of Milan recalled the story to emphasize the importance of modesty: "Ham, Noah's son, brought disgrace upon himself; for he laughed when he saw his father naked, but they who covered their father received the gift of a blessing."[49] Since Christians respect Christ's flesh, like Shem and Japheth respected the flesh of their father, they, too, will be blessed. Reluctant to imagine that Noah, a savior like Christ, had been raped or castrated, Christian interpreters offered comparatively mild interpretations of this passage.[50] Still, they were also convinced that Ham—and by extension his son Canaan—were wicked and deserved the harsh punishment they received.

The Incest of Ham

Contemporary readers are more often persuaded by the theory that Ham sexually abused his father. From the perspective of Genesis, they argue, Ham must have engaged in incest. This interpretation is supported by the appearance of the Hebrew idiom "seeing his father's nakedness" in other biblical contexts. Uncovering nakedness (*galah 'ervat*) is a euphemism for illicit sexual activity in Leviticus in particular, where Israelites are instructed not to "uncover the nakedness" of their relatives. Leviticus states:

None of you shall approach anyone near of kin to uncover nakedness: *I am the LORD. You shall not* uncover the nakedness *of your father,*

which is the nakedness of your mother. . . . You shall not uncover the
nakedness of your father's wife; it is the nakedness of your father . . .
(18:6–8, emphasis added)

In Leviticus, then, inappropriate sexual activity is identified as "uncovering nakedness." In one instance, *seeing* nakedness is also used to
describe incest: "If a man takes his sister, a daughter of his father or a
daughter of his mother, and sees her nakedness, and she sees his nakedness, it is a disgrace, and they shall be cut off in the sight of their people;
he has uncovered his sister's nakedness."[51] According to the logic of Leviticus, then, by looking, one "uncovers the nakedness" of a body that is
designated for someone else: a wife's nakedness belongs to her husband;
a mother's nakedness belongs to the father, not the son; a half-sister's nakedness is identical to the nakedness of her brother (presumably since
brothers and sisters share a parent) and so should not be uncovered; and
so on. Influenced by Leviticus, perhaps readers of Genesis are to imagine
that Ham committed incest with Noah, or even raped him.[52] In any case,
"seeing nakedness" appears to have sexual overtones.

There is yet another possibility: perhaps readers are to imagine that
Ham engaged in incest not with his father but with his mother. The
nakedness of one's mother is identified as identical to the nakedness of
one's father in Leviticus ("You shall not uncover the nakedness of your
father, which is the nakedness of your mother," [18:7]). Moreover, in Deuteronomy, incest with a father's wife is described as, literally, "uncovering the father's skirt."[53] The nakedness Ham uncovered may have been
that of his mother. If so, the curse of Canaan rather than Ham becomes
somewhat more logical: Canaan can be understood as Ham's progeny
via his sexual liaison with this mother. Noah then curses the product of
their union, just as Yhwh cursed the product of David and Bathsheba's
adultery. David was also doomed to watch his son Absalom rape his concubines "in the sight of this very sun."[54] Whatever interpretation is preferred, however, Ham, the legendary son of the primeval patriarch Noah,
is depicted as engaging in some sort of shaming sexual infraction. As a
result, Genesis suggests, Canaan and his descendants were legitimately

enslaved in perpetuity.[55] But the Canaanites were not only enslaved. According to the biblical book of Joshua, they had to be systematically slaughtered at God's request.

Rahab the Prostitute and the End of the Canaanites

In Joshua, the conquest of Canaan is depicted as a violent and decisive event, undertaken at God's command. Still, the story begins not with a battle but with a legend involving a Canaanite prostitute named Rahab. Offering up a clever and faithful Canaanite prostitute as a symbol of the transformation of the land from the religiously and sexually abhorrent land of the Canaanites to the disciplined and holy land of Israel, the tale of Rahab affirms the right of the Israelites to the land and the justice of Canaanite dispossession.[56] As readers of Genesis and Exodus might have predicted, these battles had to come. The coming dispossession of the Canaanites in the promised land is acknowledged already in Genesis, when Abraham is called by God to travel from his hometown of Haran to Canaan where, God promises, his descendants will someday found a great nation.[57] Dwelling there as aliens, the patriarchs Abraham, Isaac, Jacob, and Jacob's twelve sons live among the Canaanites for four generations, avoiding their neighbors as much as possible by marrying relatives back in Haran. After moving to Egypt to escape a terrible famine, several generations later the descendants of Abraham and Sarah are led into the wilderness by Moses, setting out from there to reclaim their promised land. Finally, in the book of Joshua, the inevitable moment arrives—the Israelites take possession of Canaan. After burning Canaanite cities and killing all their inhabitants, Joshua and his generals distribute the land among the victorious tribes, founding a national confederation of Israelites, bound to one another and to the covenant given to them by God through Moses. To capture Canaan, however, they first had to depend upon the assistance of Rahab the Canaanite, who is rewarded for her good behavior with her life.

Rahab to the Rescue

At the beginning of the book, the Israelite general Joshua sends spies to scout out the land in advance of the coming attack.[58] Stopping for the night in Jericho, the spies lie with Rahab, a prostitute with a house connected to the city walls. When the king of the city hears that Israelite spies have come to Jericho in preparation for their assault, he goes to Rahab's house and demands that she turn them over. She hides them on her roof instead, helping them escape by an outer window. For this, she and her family are spared a few days later when the triumphant Israelite army kills every single inhabitant and then burns the city to the ground. Rahab and her family, the sole surviving Canaanites from Jericho, are tolerated because they took Israel's side.[59] The rest of her people were to be systematically destroyed, city by city, until none were left.

From the perspective of the book of Joshua, God demanded the total annihilation of the indigenous people of the land of Canaan. Marshalling his troops in preparation for battle with Jericho, Joshua explains God's directives: "The city and all that is in it shall be devoted to Yhwh for destruction. . . . But all silver and gold, and vessels of bronze and iron, are sacred to Yhwh; they shall go into the treasury of Yhwh." In other words, the Canaanite people and their property were so polluting that the Israelite army could not afford to enslave them or to take their livestock as booty; instead, every living creature in city was to be destroyed in a process known as *herem* or "the ban."[60] Israel was not the only Mesopotamian culture to promote this practice. A ninth-century BCE Moabite king demanded that the Moabites subject the Israelites to the same treatment:

> And [the god] Chemosh said to me, "Go, take Nebo from Israel." So I went by night and fought against it from the break of dawn until noon, taking and slaying all, seven thousand men, boys, women, girls, and maid-servants, for I had devoted them to destruction for (the god) Ashtar-Chemosh [emphasis mine].[61]

In Joshua, then, Yhwh is depicted as behaving in a manner similar to the Moabite god Chemosh, demanding that all those defeated in battle be "devoted to destruction."

Yhwh also instructs the Israelite army to "devote to destruction" the city of Ai, another Canaanite stronghold, although in this case the Israelites are permitted to preserve Canaanite livestock as their own. One by one, the Canaanite cities of Makkedah, Libnah, Lachish, Gezer, Eglon, Hebron, and Debir fall before the victorious Israelites. In each case, Joshua and his armies leave no one standing, but utterly destroy "all that breathed, as the LORD God of Israel had commanded" (10:40). From the perspective of Joshua, the land can only be occupied successfully if it is first purified of its former inhabitants. Nevertheless, the conquest is initiated with the help of a willing prostitute who dares to hide Israelite spies in her home.

Why Rahab?

The book of Joshua was written long after the nation of Israel had been founded, probably during a time when Israelite kings were ruling what was by then a well-established and independent nation.[62] By beginning the story of the conquest of Canaan with a legend involving a friendly local prostitute, the continuing presence of some Canaanites in the land could be both explained and justified. "Good Canaanites," living in Israel when Joshua was composed, should be tolerated, the story suggests. They may well be the descendants of Rahab. The story also sends another message to resident Canaanites: so long as you are cooperative like Rahab, you are free to stay. The standard of Canaanite cooperation required by this book, however, is high: according to Joshua, Rahab opened her home, her body, and her city to the invading Israelite army, and did so without protest. From an Israelite perspective, then, she represents an ideal Canaanite collaborator. Totally passive and ready to accept both Yhwh's will and the triumph of Israel, she is a traitor to her own people but a conduit of God's and Israel's desires.[63] As such, she represents both an open and compliant female body and an open and compliant land.

Yet the story of Rahab serves another function as well. By introducing the conquest narrative with a story involving a Canaanite prostitute, the Israelite audience was reminded of what they already knew, that Canaanites are prostitutes by definition, even when they are not, in fact, prostitutes. Canaanites, not good Israelites, "prostitute themselves to their gods" (Exod. 34:15). Moreover, as heirs to Noah's curse, Rahab and her kin are the descendants of a man who dared to "uncover the nakedness" of his father. As such, the Bible suggests, their bad sexual morals are genetic.[64] Leviticus confirms this impression. Prefacing a series of prohibitions against incest and nonprocreative sexual intercourse with a warning, Leviticus instructs the Israelites that they must not "do as they do in the land of Egypt" or "as they do in the land of Canaan" (18:3). After listing the prohibited behaviors, Leviticus drops the reference to the Egyptians and adds another threat: if the Israelites commit any of these abominations, defiling the land like the Canaanites did, "the land will vomit you out" (v. 28). In other words, Leviticus suggests, God arranged for the destruction of the Canaanites as a just punishment for their sexual and religious misbehavior. God is also willing to overthrow and destroy Israel, Leviticus cautions, should the nation pick up Canaanite habits. Reading Joshua and Leviticus, therefore, leads readers to the conclusion that the Canaanites deserve to be displaced and killed, a point that is further reiterated by making a prostitute the only heroic Canaanite in the conquest narrative.

But How Pure Were the Israelites Really?

Nevertheless, there is still another way to read this story. By casting Rahab in the role of a heroine, the book of Joshua doesn't simply confirm Israel's unquestionable right to Canaan. The story also challenges the notion that the Israelites actually deserved what God wanted for them: a land devoid of Canaanites and purified of sexual and religious wrongdoing. Rahab comes across as significantly more faithful to Yhwh's directives than do Joshua's Israelite spies. Sent out to spy on the land of Canaan, instead they stop at the house of a local prostitute, "sleeping there." (In Hebrew, the verb employed for "sleeping" [*skb*] highlights just the kind of "sleeping" they were [or were not] doing.[65]) They then spend their entire mission hiding out, only to return to Joshua and the Israelite camp with information they did not gather themselves.

Of course, as we have seen, from the perspective of the Hebrew Bible there was nothing inherently wrong with visiting a prostitute. Still, these spies first risk the success of their mission by spending their night out "sleeping," and then they abandon their assignment altogether. Sneaking out of the city with Rahab's help, they hide in the hill country above the city until men sent by the king of Jericho to find them give up the search. The spies then return to Joshua, offering him falsified information: "Truly the LORD has given all the land into our hands," they report, continuing, "all the inhabitants of the land melt in fear before us" (Josh. 2:24). At this point, however, the only people who have displayed fear are the spies, who hid under stalks of flax on Rahab's roof and then in the countryside. In fact, it is Rahab whom the spies quote to Joshua. She has already predicted that the Canaanites will "melt in fear" before Israel, which is why she decided to assist them. Recognizing the inevitable defeat of her people by God's army, she has more faith in Yhwh than the spies do.[66] At the beginning of Joshua's narrative is a story capable of undermining the central claim of the book, that the Israelites are better than the Canaanites and more deserving of the land than they are.

Still, as far as much of the Bible is concerned, the native people of Canaan remained a serious threat. Their religious practices and their gods were so dangerous, the book of Deuteronomy warns, that Yhwh cannot tolerate their continuing presence in the land. Anticipating the coming conquest, Deuteronomy presents Moses offering a set of anti-Canaanite policies and procedures: all their altars must be broken, their sacred poles must be burned, their idols must be hewn to pieces, and their sacred rites must not be performed or even recalled. In fact, these people and their gods are so abhorrent to Yhwh that any Israelite who consorts with them

must be executed: "Stone them to death" (Lev. 20:2), Moses insists, and
raze any Israelite city that dares to establish an idolatrous shrine.

In the end, the book of Joshua offers a similar perspective. When
some Israelite soldiers fail to carry out God's explicit order that Canaanites be subject to the ban (*herem*), the entire army begins to lose battles
they should have won. Only by identifying and then stoning the culprits
to death are Israel's victories once again assured. Condemning the religious practices of the indigenous people of the land, linking their gods
with prostitution, and tolerating them only when they behave like the
good prostitute Rahab, the books of Joshua, Leviticus, and Deuteronomy
imply that the Israelites and the Canaanites are totally different. Their
morals are different, their gods are different, and their peoples are different. All they share in common is a claim to the same land. Yet, as we shall
see, they likely shared much more than this. Israel and Canaan were not
as different as the Bible makes them out to be.

Yhwh and His Asherah

Over the last century, archaeologists and Bible scholars have been surprised to discover that Canaanites and Israelites cannot easily be distinguished, despite the Bible's stories. The cultural melting pot of Canaan
during the twelfth and eleventh centuries BCE included Canaanites, Israelites, and others living in a small piece of land between the Mediterranean Sea and the Arabian desert (called the "Levant" by scholars), and,
for all practical purposes, they were neighbors, not different nations.[67]
Israel is first mentioned as a distinct people in a victory stele of the Egyptian king Merneptah (1207 BCE), where Merneptah reports, "Israel is laid
waste; its seed is not."[68] This stele, a stone monument put up to commem-
orate Merneptah's triumphs, suggests that Israel was viewed as a group
of people dwelling in Canaan among other Canaanite peoples, who are
also listed among Merneptah's conquests. The Hebrew language further
affirms Merneptah's point of view: Hebrew is identified by scholars as a
Canaanite language that is related to Moabite, Ammonite, Edomite, and

Phoenician, other languages associated with peoples dwelling in the land at the same time.[69] Israelites were distinctive for their role as a pastoral peoples living in the highlands around Ai, Bethel, Shiloh, and Raddana, not for their distinct language, religion, and culture.[70] Many scholars today would challenge the notion that there were "Canaanites" at all, if by "Canaanite" we mean to refer to people dwelling in Israel/the land of Canaan who did not mix with the Israelites.[71] If archaeological evidence is to be believed, Israelite culture and Canaanite culture overlapped for centuries, suggesting not a sudden and decisive conquest but gradual occupation and assimilation of Israel to Canaan and Canaan to Israel.

The intertwining of Canaanite and Israelite gods, identities, and peoples was strikingly confirmed in the twentieth century by the discovery of an eighth-century BCE inscription from outside of Jerusalem:

Blessed be Uriyahu by Yhwh . . . for from his enemies by his [Yhwh's] asherah he [Yhwh] saved him. [Written by] Oniyahu and by his asherah.[72]

Uriyahu, it would appear, considered both Yhwh and Yhwh's asherah to be his divine patrons, implying that he worshipped both the biblical god and a goddess associated with him. Other similar inscriptions have led many scholars to reach a surprising conclusion: in many parts of Israel, both North and South, Yhwh and his consort Asherah were worshipped as a pair, even during the period of the Israelite monarchy.[73] Polemical arguments against Asherah in the Bible, therefore, represent infighting among Israelites over proper forms of worship. They do not describe the polluting influence of Canaanites. Asherah was a native goddess of the people of Israel. When the biblical book of Judges complains, "The Israelites did what was evil in the sight of the Lord, forgetting the Lord their God, and worshipping the Baals and the Asherahs" (3:7), the writers are actually acknowledging the truth of the matter: that not every Israelite thought that Yhwh should be worshipped exclusively. Even Baal, who competed with Yhwh for status as the sole male God of Israel among the people living in the region, was depicted in ways similar to his rival. Both Yhwh and Baal are described as storm gods, both Baal and Yhwh dwell on mountains, and both Baal and Yhwh are portrayed as killing a sea monster known as the Leviathan.[74] Once one looks beyond biblical writings to include archaeological and other evidence, one finds not clear differences between Israelites and Canaanites, but a shared religious and cultural milieu.

If this modern account of ancient Canaan is correct, then the charge that Canaanites "prostitute themselves after their gods" may well have been directed at Israelites, not at outsider Canaanites. The problem in Israel was not that foreigners polluted land but that insiders in the community had differing perspectives regarding which religious practices should be regarded as worthy of God. The biblical image of radical differences between the peoples of Canaan and the people of Israel appears to have been manufactured by biblical writers who wanted to promote the cult of Yhwh over all other forms of worship.[75] Convincing fellow Israelites to go along with this plan was, apparently, a difficult task. Again and again, Israelites are warned against worshipping Baal, Asherah, and the other gods and goddesses they shared with their neighbors. Whatever Joshua's conquest narrative might suggest, Canaanites and Israelites remained close neighbors and coreligionists for centuries.[76] Still, in the Bible sexual offenses continued to be depicted as particularly Canaanite in character.

Biblical Sex Crimes

In 1961, Jean Thorson Chadwell, my grandmother, obtained what was by then her second divorce from my grandfather, John B. Chadwell. Grandpa John, a dashingly handsome California businessman, married my grandma when they were both nineteen. After a few years of marital bliss and the birth of two wonderful daughters, my mother and my aunt, he began a series of extramarital affairs, usually with secretaries at his firm. Grandma Jean, a redhead so lovely that she was once recruited to audition as a "Breck Girl," was not about to put up with it. A pious Lutheran and former farm girl from Iowa, her values did not include tolerating adultery. After much misery and broken promises on all sides, they finally split, my grandfather going on to marry Donnelda, "Grandma Donnie" to me, and Grandma Jean marrying Sherman Nash, otherwise known as Grandpa Sherman. A lucky child, I had three sets of grandparents growing up: Grandma Donnie and Grandpa John, Grandma Jean and Grandpa Sherman, and, on my father's side, Grandma Billie and Grandpa Tim. I only just lost Grandma Donnie this year and Grandpa Sherman, I am pleased to say, is still alive.

Now let's imagine that my grandparents lived in ancient Israel. Assuming that biblical laws were actually enforced, Grandpa John would either have been stoned to death or, if his paramours were unmarried, he could have taken them on as wives, slaves, and concubines. Then I would have had the privilege of knowing not only Grandma Donnie, but all the other women with whom my grandfather was involved. Grandma Jean would have been stuck living as one wife among many, and Grandpa Sherman could never have wooed the woman who eventually became his beloved Jean. Alternatively, if one of Grandpa John's mistresses was married and he was caught in the act of violating another man's wife—a not altogether unlikely scenario given the lack of caution he displayed by leaving incriminating evidence in the back of the family car—he and his lover would have been executed. Or so I imagine. Yet family and sexual laws are irregularly enforced and subject to constant revision, both in America and in the Bible. It is actually quite difficult to know how the case of John and Jean Chadwell (née Thorson, later Nash) would have been handled, since sexual behavior labeled objectionable is tolerated in one biblical book and even promoted by the next. A straightforward application of biblical law, even to the sexual behavior of my own family members, would be difficult indeed. Biblical books disagree regarding which behaviors ought to be regarded as criminal.

Nevertheless, the book of Leviticus does single out particular sexual acts for censure, and, not surprisingly, Canaanites are said to be especially prone to bad behavior. In the United States, one might credit the lax morals of the state of California for leading my grandpa John into sin.[77] In Israel, it was the Canaanites who were regarded as both morally objectionable and destined for destruction, along with anyone else who emulated them. When the writers of Leviticus asserted that incest, adultery, and nonprocreative sex would lead Israelites to become Canaanites, they were also suggesting that Yhwh would have no choice but to expel both people from their land. Identifying illicit sex with Canaanites, Leviticus used sex as a weapon, insulting the Canaanite nations and accusing Israel's royal family of corruption.

The Holiness of Israel

Identified by scholars as "the holiness code," Leviticus 17–26 repeatedly asserts "you shall be holy," a declaration that knits this half of Leviticus together while also affirming the book's central purpose: the cultivation of a distinct "holy" identity among the people of Israel. To Leviticus, holiness involves the proper observance of sacrificial rites, the keeping of festivals and holy days, and the maintenance of purity in eating, sexual relations, and worship, among other practices.[78] Including commandments about sex within a larger set of cultic and community provisions, Leviticus is most concerned about preserving boundaries between Israel and other nations, between various categories of Israelites (man/woman, priest/layperson, family member/appropriate sexual object), and between sacred and profane space and time (the Temple and the land of Israel/ everywhere else).[79] In terms of sexuality, Israel must distinguish between appropriate and inappropriate sexual objects, Leviticus argues, avoiding sexual unions between members of the same household and maintaining clear distinctions between man and woman, animal and human.[80] Elaborating a series of laws that blame both the Canaanites and fellow Israelites for bad behavior, the holiness code suggests that Israel's problems are rooted in illicit sex.

Incest

Using the formula "you shall not uncover the nakedness . . ." and addressing Israelite men, the sexual prohibitions of Leviticus begin with a general provision: do not uncover the nakedness of your kin.[81] Following this broad instruction, the following relatives are singled out as forbidden sexual objects:

1. a mother (18:7)

2. a father's wife (18:8)

3. a half-sister (18:9)

4. a granddaughter (18:10)

5. a sister, half-sister, or stepsister (18:11)

6. a paternal aunt (18:12)

7. a maternal aunt (18:13)

8. a daughter-in-law (18:15)

9. a brother's wife (18:16)

10. a mother and a daughter (18:17)

11. a step-granddaughter (18:17)

12. a sister of a current wife (18:18)

Some of these same prohibitions are reiterated in Leviticus 20, this time with a punishment specified for each type of infraction:

1. a father's wife: "both of them shall be put to death; their blood is upon them." (20:11)

2. a daughter-in-law: "both of them shall be put to death; they have committed perversion, their blood is upon them." (20:12)

3. a half-sister: "they shall be cut off in the sight of their people." (20:17)

4. a paternal or maternal aunt: "they shall be subject to punishment." (20:19)

5. an uncle's wife: "they shall be subject to punishment; they shall die childless." (20:20)

6. a brother's wife: "they shall be childless." (20:21)

As in Leviticus 18, the commandments in Leviticus 20 conclude with a reminder about the indigenous people of Canaan: "You shall not follow the practices of the nation that I am driving out before you. Because they did these things, I abhorred them" (v. 23). In other words, Leviticus claims, Canaanites are known for their incestuous practices, but Israel must be holy.

This assertion is belied, however, by a number of other biblical passages. According to Genesis, Exodus, 2 Samuel, and 1 Chronicles, Israelites engaged in the very practices forbidden in Leviticus, both before and after they entered the land. Abraham married Sarah, a half-sister on his father's side, an infraction that should have led to his being cut off from the people. Jacob married a second sister while the first sister was still living. Mistaking his daughter-in-law for a prostitute, Judah had intercourse with her, an activity that should have led to their deaths. Reuben, Judah's brother, had sexual relations with his father's concubine while his father was still alive, also a capital offense. Even Moses, the ostensible author of this text, was fathered by a man and his aunt, although liaisons between a nephew and his aunt were supposed to remain childless. Then, after Israel entered the land, David married his half-sister Abigail, Absalom slept with his father's concubines, and Amnon raped his half-sister Tamar. Incest, as Leviticus defines it, was certainly not limited to the Egyptians or the Canaanites, but included such biblical luminaries as Abraham, Moses, and King David. But perhaps this is why the writers of Leviticus identify incest as a crime to begin with. Written by priests, not rulers, Leviticus holds the Israelite monarchy responsible for behaving "like Canaanites."

As the priestly writers would have known, technically, only David and his heirs were responsible to uphold the holiness code they were promulgating, because only they dwelt in the land after the Mosaic covenant had gone into effect.[82] The marriages of Abraham to Sarah, Jacob to Rachel and Leah, and the incestuous marriage that produced Moses were therefore not accountable to the laws of Leviticus. By contrast, David's marriage to Abigail, Absalom's intercourse with David's concubines, and Amnon's rape of Tamar could be understood as serious violations of God's requirements, so serious that Israel might well be "vomited out of the land."[83] As biblical scholar Tirzah Meacham has argued: "[I]t seems that the incest code is also a polemic—not against Egypt or Canaan, but rather against one of Israel's most charismatic leaders [David]."[84] Preaching to the exiles after the fall of the monarchy to Babylon, the prophet Ezekiel made exactly this point:

> *The princes of Israel in you [the land of Judah], everyone according to his power, have been bent on shedding blood. . . . In you they uncover their father's nakedness; in you they violate women in their menstrual periods. One commits abomination with his neighbor's wife; another lewdly defiles his daughter-in-law; another in you defiles his sister, his father's daughter. . . . You have forgotten me, says the Lord GOD. (Ezek. 22:6, 10–12)*

By the time Ezekiel was writing, many in the land had been "vomited up," and, Ezekiel explains, the kings of Judah should be blamed. Repeating the commandments of Leviticus in almost exactly the same order as is found in the holiness code, Ezekiel claims that the kings of Judah were "Canaanites," and so, like Canaan, they had to be destroyed. Framing the laws about sex with a mischaracterization of Canaanites and Egyptians therefore helped the priestly writers of Leviticus disguise their true target—David and his heirs—even as they continued to argue that Israel was better than her neighbors.[85] The princes of Judah—Leviticus and then Ezekiel complain—act *like* the Canaanites, a charge that serves to disparage the Canaanites and rulers like David and his heirs all at the same time.

Fathers and Daughters

Yet how bad were the Canaanites really? A comparison of the list of forbidden unions in Leviticus to those found in other Mesopotamian law codes demonstrates just how similar the holiness codes could be to these earlier laws. Strikingly, though, while other Mesopotamian codes explicitly forbid father-daughter incest, Leviticus leaves this particular provision out. The Laws of Hammurabi state:

> *If a man should carnally know his daughter, they shall banish that man from the city. If a man selects a bride for his son and his son carnally knows her, after which he himself then lies with her and they seize him in the act, they shall bind that man and cast him into the water. . . . If a man, after his father's death, should lie with his mother, they shall burn them both. If a man, after his father's death, should be discovered in the lap of his (the father's) principal wife who had borne children, that man shall be disinherited from the paternal estate. (Laws of Hammurabi 154–56, 158)*[86]

According to old Babylonian law, the wives of sons, mothers, and foster mothers were off-limits, just as in Leviticus. Incest with a daughter is specifically listed, with such behavior leading to expulsion from the city. The Hittites also forbade sex with a mother, with a father's wife during his lifetime, with a brother's wife during his lifetime, with a sister of a current wife during her lifetime, and with a mother and a daughter at the same time, a list that is similar to that in the holiness code.[87] Unlike Leviticus, however, Hittite laws, like the Laws of Hammurabi, explicitly outlawed father-daughter relationships, punishing these unions severely.

The omission of a direct prohibition against father-daughter incest in

Leviticus has troubled many commentators. Was father-daughter incest tolerated in ancient Israel? Or, worse, was it accepted as moral behavior? Rabbinic literature was careful to indicate that father-daughter incest was forbidden, whatever Leviticus may or may not say.[88] Modern interpreters have also resisted the conclusion that such behavior was permitted by biblical writers. Jonathan Ziskind, for example, argues that the holiness code neglected to include daughters in their list out of respect for the father's authority within the family. This does not mean, however, that they believed father-daughter incest was permissible, or so Ziskind argues.[89] Judith Romney Wegner offers a similar solution: Since an unmarried Israelite girl's sexuality belongs to her father, Leviticus did not need to include her in this list. After all, it was in the father's self-interest to avoid sex with his daughter. If he did not, he would have failed to preserve his daughter's virginity for her husband, "at which point his ownership of the daughter's virginity accrues to the father in the form of a bride-price."[90] In other words, a daughter's virginity was valuable to her father. If he broke her hymen himself, at the very least he would suffer a financial penalty. At worst, if she was found guilty of "playing the harlot" prior to marriage, he would be forced to witness her stoning. Still, perhaps the general command in Leviticus 18:6, "None of you shall approach anyone near of kin to uncover nakedness," was meant to include daughters as well as sons, neither of whom are mentioned.[91]

The incest provisions, then, are problematic on two fronts: they were never actually obeyed by Israelites, either before or after the conquest of Canaan, and they do not explicitly outlaw what is by far the most common form of incest today, that between a father and his daughter. Later interpreters may well be correct. Perhaps Leviticus intended to legislate against father-daughter incest by subsuming this behavior under a general provision regarding "uncovering the nakedness" of close kin. Moreover, perhaps the disadvantages of father-daughter incest were so obvious to ancient Israelite men that there was no need to specifically forbid it. Nevertheless, it is disturbing that the holiness code omitted what other Mesopotamian codes include, especially since the incest laws are presented as distinctive to Israel. A proof of Israelite holiness, the avoidance of incest is portrayed in Leviticus 18–20 as something Israelites can manage but other nations cannot.

Illicit Sexual Unions

A second set of sexual prohibitions follows the laws regarding incest, laws that forbid intercourse with particular persons at particular times or in particular ways. Though it is difficult to discern what these laws share in common—and Leviticus offers no rationale for the instructions given—the requirement that semen be emitted only in an appropriate receptacle may offer an interpretive key. If the vessel is "unclean," the property of another man, or incapable of producing children, then sexual intercourse is not permissible.[92] Semen was regarded as too important to procreation to be spilled into a container that could not become pregnant or that might produce an illegitimate child. The seed of an Israelite man must not be wasted. With this criterion in mind, the Levitical laws bar:

1. intercourse with a menstruating woman (18:19)

2. intercourse with the wife of a relative (18:20)

3. lying with a man in the manner of a woman (18:22)

4. bestiality (18:23)

The same laws are reiterated in Leviticus 20, in slightly altered form and accompanied by specified punishments:

1. adultery with the wife of a neighbor: "both the adulterer and the adulteress shall be put to death." (20:10)

2. lying with a man in the manner of a woman: "both of them have committed an abomination; they shall be put to death" (20:13)

3. bestiality: "[the man] shall be put to death; and you shall kill the animal . . . you shall kill the woman and the animal; they shall be put to death." (20:15–16)

There will be more to say about menstruation in chapter 6. For now it is important to note that intercourse with a menstruating woman involves an inappropriate emission of semen, probably because, by doing so, a man has ejaculated within the body of a woman who cannot become pregnant. Intercourse with a menstruating woman wastes semen.

As in the Sinai covenant codes, adultery is once again identified as a crime punishable by death in this section of Leviticus, despite the adulterous liaisons of various biblical heroes. As we observed in chapter 2, an Israelite wife was viewed as the property of her husband and was therefore forbidden to other Israelite men. A man who violates another man's wife steals that man's property and uncovers that man's nakedness. Moreover, from the perspective of Leviticus, placing semen within another man's wife can lead both to unwanted progeny and to the mixing of the semen of one man with that of another, activities that should be avoided. The remaining two prohibitions—"lying with a man as with a woman" and bestiality—also involve the inappropriate emission of semen. In the first instance, semen is emitted in the body of one man by another. In the second, either human semen is emitted in the body of an animal or animal semen is emitted in the body of a woman. In both cases, however, boundaries are crossed and bodily fluids mixed in a way that the priestly writers found abhorrent.

The Lying Down of a Woman

Given the current obsession with the holiness code's prohibition against "lying with a man as with a woman," it is worth noting that there are no other such laws in the Hebrew Bible. Though one can find biblical commandments forbidding incest, adultery, and bestiality elsewhere, there is no comparable prohibition in any other biblical book. Bestiality, for example, is also condemned in Exodus and Deuteronomy, incest is forbidden in Deuteronomy and Ezekiel, and adultery is addressed in Exodus, Deuteronomy, and Numbers.[93] These two references to "lying with a man as with a woman" are therefore entirely exceptional.

Since these passages are repeated nowhere else, they are difficult to translate. The Hebrew words rendered in many English translations as "lying with a man as with a woman" (*miskeba issa*) is actually an interpretive guess, not a literal translation. The closest parallel to the saying is the phrase *miskab zakar,* which, Saul Olyan suggests, means "the lying down of a male," with the sense of "to be penetrated by a penis."[94] With this in mind, Olyan proposes that the phrase in Leviticus must mean something like "the act or condition of the woman's being penetrated," or "vaginal receptivity."[95] Thus, the interdiction in Leviticus is addressed specifically to the insertive partner in the sex act, not the receptive partner. It is the penetrator who is instructed not to engage in the "lying down of the woman" with a man.

But why, from the perspective of Leviticus, must a man not engage in the "lying down of the woman" with another man? As we observed in chapter 3, in Greek and Roman culture, criticism of male-male sex acts was largely reserved for adult free men who desired penetration, not for the man doing the penetration. Men were expected to desire to penetrate beautiful younger men and to act on those desires. The opposite appears to be true in Leviticus: it is the penetrator who is addressed, as was the case in the incest provisions as well. With one exception, the Leviticus codes are addressed to men who penetrate others, not to their partners, and it is these men who are told they should be "holy." Only in the case of animal-woman bestiality is someone other than the penetrator considered, though the punishment prescribed for both the woman and the animal is to be carried out by Israelite men, the "you" in the commandment "you shall kill the woman and the animal; they shall be put to death."

The rationale given for the prohibition against penetration of another man is that "it is an abomination" (*to'eba*). A related claim is made about bestiality:

You shall not have sexual relations with any animal and defile yourself
with it, nor shall any woman give herself to an animal to have sexual
relations with it: it is a perversion (tebhel). *(Lev. 18:23)*[96]

The basic meaning of the rare Hebrew word *tebhel*, translated here
as "perversion," is that it involves the combination of things that ought
not to be combined. The problem with bestiality is that it involves the
mixing of humankind with animals. Or, more specifically, the placement
of human semen in an animal body or animal semen in a human body.
The problem with "lying with a man as with a woman," then, is that it
involves the confusion of appropriate gender roles, as Leviticus defines
them, while also spilling semen in a situation where pregnancy cannot
take place.

As scholar Daniel Boyarin has suggested, inappropriate mixing may
be Leviticus's main concern when it comes to forbidding male-male sex.
The one who is penetrated, Boyarin points out, becomes subject to the
"mixing" or "confusion" (*tebhel*) of being receptive to another man's
penis. Deuteronomy applies this same principle to forbid cross-dressing:

A woman shall not wear a man's apparel, nor shall a man put on a
woman's garment; for whoever does such things is abhorrent (to'eba) *to*
the LORD *your God. (22:5)*[97]

So, Boyarin explains, "when one man 'uses' another man as a female,
he causes a transgression of the borders between male and female."[98] The
maintenance of clear distinctions was an important concern to those who
wrote Leviticus, a concern that appears to have influenced these commandments as well.[99] The mixing that Leviticus seeks to avoid in this
instance is the act of gender-crossing, in which the receptive partner is
assimilated to the category of "woman" by being anally penetrated. Other
male-male sexual behaviors, however, are not forbidden, or even mentioned. The sole target of this commandment is an Israelite man who
anally penetrates another Israelite man with his penis and ejaculates
within his partner's body.

Interestingly, there is at least one Israelite man who may have been guilty of precisely this offense: King David. According to 1 Samuel, the love of Jonathan for David surpassed his love of women, and it was Jonathan who shamed himself and his "mother's nakedness" (1 Sam. 20:30) by choosing David as his partner. As scholar Susan Ackerman has shown, this vocabulary implies that Jonathan was the receptive partner in their sexual relationship and, as such, was beloved by David as a "wife." David's ascendancy was just, the book 2 Samuel implies, because he was the "man" to Jonathan's "woman," even if Jonathan was King Saul's son and therefore the obvious heir to the throne.[100] To the writers of 1 and 2 Samuel, this argument made sense, yet the priestly writers of Leviticus seem to be rejecting their point of view. David's affair with Jonathan did not legitimate his rule, they suggest. Instead, it undermined it, assimilating him to the category "Canaanite" and justifying the tragedies that later befell both David's heirs and the people as a whole. Once again, the holiness code can be read as an explicit critique of Canaanites and an implicit attack on the Israelite monarchy, which is blamed for turning Israel into "Canaan."

The Bible's Sexual Politics

According to Leviticus, sexual immorality is characteristic of others, not Israelites. But, as we have seen, this claim can easily be overturned. Even the patriarch Abraham, the prophet Moses, and the Davidic royal family failed to observe the standards of sexual morality outlined by the writers of the holiness code. According to Genesis, the descendants of Canaan were tainted by the shameful behavior of their ancestor Ham, behavior that is alluded to in Joshua in the story of Rahab, the only Canaanite, with her family, to survive the advance of Israel's armies. According to Exodus, Deuteronomy, Judges, and other biblical books, the national gods of these other peoples enforce a form of worship on their devotees that makes them behave like prostitutes. Thus, they "prostitute themselves to their gods," a charge that gets recycled by the New

Testament authors Paul and John of Patmos. By contrast, according to the biblical prophets and the New Testament writers, Israel is God's "wife," and, as such, she must avoid behaving like an adulteress by committing idolatry. These biblical passages therefore associate illicit religion with illicit sex, with both sins described as typical of outsiders. Religious-sexual sins were offered as an explanation for the suffering inflicted on those who participate in them, be they Canaanites, who were to be annihilated, or Israelites, who were to be "vomited" out of their land, or the Romans, who, according to John of Patmos, would watch their city burn for eternity.

Sound familiar? Blaming the violence experienced on September 11, 2001, on "pagans," "abortionists," "feminists," and "gays and lesbians" with a "lifestyle," Reverend Falwell implied that, from God's perspective, certain Americans deserve to die. Blaming this same violence on Muslims, Reverend Vines implied that violence is perpetrated only by those who do not worship the Christian God, though the United States was at war with Afghanistan at the time. Violence, they assume, is either something God does to punish enemies or that enemies do, probably after they have first enjoyed illicit sex at the behest of their demonic gods. Yet, as this chapter demonstrates, these sorts of charges point to the fantasies and concerns of particular writers, not to acts and beliefs characteristic of particular peoples. Likening unwanted religious beliefs to illicit sex denigrates targeted enemies without proving much of anything about what those enemies are doing. At the same time, behaviors identified as immoral remain inconsistent. Incest is defined differently in Genesis and Leviticus. The worship of both Yhwh and Asherah could be regarded as appropriate among Israelites, despite arguments to the contrary in Deuteronomy, Judges, and elsewhere. And Christians could disagree about whether the meat sold at a local Greek market was demonic idol meat, the consumption of which was tantamount to "prostitution," or a practical problem that could easily be solved with a "don't ask, don't tell" policy.

Nevertheless, preserving and defending particular versions of sexual-religious morality was a deeply important priority to many biblical writers, whether they based their instructions in an abhorrence of illegitimate mixing or a desire to manufacture Israelite-Canaanite differences. As we will see in the next chapter, these concerns were extended to include unions with foreign women and intercourse between human beings and angels. Since non-Israelites worship other gods, Exodus warned, taking wives from among them can also lead Israelite sons to prostitute themselves to the gods of their wives. Since dangerous foreign women employ, as Proverbs puts it, a "smooth tongue," "smooth words," and "smooth lips" to lead otherwise righteous men astray, they must be avoided at all costs.[101] Following the return from the Babylonian exile in the sixth century BCE, the prevention of mixed marriages became a distinct Israelite policy, promoted in particular by Ezra, who demanded that Israelite men divorce their foreign wives, and do so immediately.

But, as the next chapter shows, mixing with foreign women was not the only or even the most important danger. According to Genesis, intercourse between humans and angels was also deeply abhorrent to Yhwh, a tradition that was elaborated on by New Testament writers. According to Genesis, when the "sons of God" went into the "daughters of men" (Gen. 6:4), God responded with a flood, killing the products of human/angel intercourse as well as every other human inhabitant of the world, with the exception of Noah and his family. When the Canaanite residents of Sodom and Gomorrah wanted to rape angels, God's response was similar: he quickly and decisively burned Sodom and Gomorrah to the ground. These stories were recalled with great urgency by Paul and other New Testament writers, convinced as they were that human-angel sexual mixing was one of the worst sins imaginable.

CHAPTER 5

Strange Flesh

The Sons of God and the Daughters of Men

Walking by a storm-swept sea in 1912, poet Rainer Maria Rilke wondered, "Who, if I cried, would hear me among the angelic orders?" Would the angels hear, let alone God? He continued, "And even if one of them suddenly pressed me against his heart, I should fade in the strength of his stronger existence."[1] Imagining himself wrapped in an erotic angelic embrace, Rilke concluded that such an encounter could only lead to his destruction:

For Beauty's nothing
but beginning of Terror we're still just able to bear,
and why we adore it so is because it serenely
disdains to destroy us. Each single angel is terrible.[2]

In Rilke's *Duino Elegies,* the longing for the touch of angels serves as a symbol for the attempt of the human person to reach beyond, into a consciousness where the self is surpassed and individual human limits give way. If only we could embrace angels, perhaps we could touch God.[3] Imagining angelic-human intimacy as a risky and yet desired crossing of the divine and human realms, in the *Elegies* and other poems Rilke recalled biblical events like Jacob's wrestling with an angel or Gabriel's visiting the Virgin Mary to play with the possibility of divine encoun-

ter, likening human and angelic desire.[4] Evoking not only the visits of
angelic messengers but also the longings of angels for human touch, the
poet indirectly built upon a tradition that goes back to the Bible. Biblical writers also imagined that there could be an erotic charge between
humans and angels, but, to them, sex with angels could lead to only one
result: disaster.

Narratives involving sex with angels and other forbidden forms of
sexual congress will occupy our attention throughout this chapter. We
have considered other prohibited unions already, but we have yet to discuss two equally important biblical themes: sex with angels and sex with
foreigners, especially with foreign women. Certainly these were not the
only forms of forbidden sex; neither were they the only forbidden forms of
sex that were also enjoyed by various biblical characters. As we observed
in chapter 2, legally speaking at least, adultery was supposed to lead to the
death penalty. Still, the adulterous liaison of King David with Bathsheba
resulted not in death but, ultimately, in the birth of King Solomon. As we
observed in chapter 4, the book of Leviticus insisted that incest, bestiality,
and "lying with a man as with a woman" were also supposed to lead to
death or exile, yet incest regularly went unpunished, and, on a few occasions, a child of incest went on to be a great hero of Israel. Moreover, as we
observed in chapter 1, the erotic attachment of David and Jonathan led to
the elevation of David to the throne. As we will see in this chapter, sex with
angels was also both condemned and practiced, as was sex with foreign
women.[5] The comingling of different kinds of flesh—human and angel
or Israelite and Gentile—was not to be tolerated, at least in theory. Crossing the angel-human boundary or the Israel-Gentile boundary in an erotic
embrace threatened the very existence of both the people and the nation.

The Sons of God and the Daughters of Men

Early in the book of Genesis, just before the flood, there is an enigmatic
story involving "sons of God" who are attracted to human women and
"go into" them:

When people began to multiply on the face of the ground, and daughters were born to them, the sons of God saw that they were fair; and they took wives for themselves of all that they chose. (6:1–2)

This event is so disturbing that God must respond. He rules that the offspring of these divine-human liaisons must not enjoy the privilege of immortality. Speaking to the divine court, God states, "My spirit shall not abide in mortals forever, for they are flesh; their days shall be one hundred and twenty years" (v. 3). But divine-human hybrids were produced nonetheless, filling the earth with "warriors of renown":

The Nephilim were on the earth in those days—and also afterward— when the sons of God went in to the daughters of humans, who bore children to them. These were the heroes that were of old, warriors of renown. (v. 4)

The Nephilim, described elsewhere in the Bible as frightening giants, could not be tolerated. Yhwh determines to put an end not only to the Nephilim but to all of humanity, preserving only Noah and his family: "I will blot out from the earth the human beings I have created . . . for I am sorry that I have made them" (v. 7).[6] Since all human flesh had "corrupted its ways upon the earth" (v. 12), the only choice was destruction. The Nephilim, their descendants, and all other living creatures were drowned in a deluge, renewing both the earth and Yhwh's commitment to his creation. "I will never again curse the ground because of humankind" (8:21), God resolves, sealing the promise with a rainbow.

Whatever this story might have meant when it was first told, among later Jews and Christians, the episode of the "sons of God" who had intercourse with human women could only mean one thing: angels had breached the divine realm in order to sate their illicit sexual desires. Genesis 6, elaborated and expanded in other writings, became a principal explanation for the introduction of evil into the world. If angels had never lusted after women, human beings would not have learned wickedness, many Jews and Christians argued. Though largely forgot-

ten, books containing these stories were often regarded as sacred revelation in the first century, particularly a book now known as 1 Enoch.
Rewriting Genesis 6, new explanations for the bad behavior of angels
were developed, pointing out just how devastating the consequences of
angelic lust could be.

The Visions of Enoch

A seemingly minor character in Genesis, the biblical patriarch Enoch
was identified as the author of several books in antiquity. Since he "walked
with God" and was then "no more, because God took him" (5:24), Enoch
could be invoked as a seer with privileged access to heavenly secrets. The
earliest book attributed to him, the Book of the Watchers, was probably
written in the second century BCE, even before the composition of the
biblical book Daniel.[7] Now contained in a later, longer book known as 1
Enoch, fragments of the Book of the Watchers have been found among
the Dead Sea Scrolls, attesting to its popularity at the time. This cache
of ancient Jewish writings was the prize possession of a group of Jews
living in the desert outside of Jerusalem, in an area known as Qumran.
Dwelling there from the second century BCE to the first century CE, these
Jews copied and preserved a number of biblical and other books, including the Book of the Watchers. They also wrote commentaries that quote
1 Enoch, further demonstrating their high regard for the work.[8] But the
Jews of Qumran were not the only group that viewed Enoch as a prophet
and his books as sacred; the Book of the Watchers was also cited as a
sacred text by the author of the New Testament letter Jude.

Decrying the bad behavior of false Christian teachers and promis-
ing that these teachers would be punished, Jude tells his audience that
Enoch predicted they would come, and also that they would be judged.
He states:

*It was also about these [false teachers] that Enoch, in the seventh gen-
eration from Adam, prophesied, saying, "See, the Lord is coming with*

ten thousands of his holy ones, to execute judgment on all, and to con-
vict everyone of all the deeds of ungodliness that they have committed
in such an ungodly way, and of all the harsh things that ungodly sinners
have spoken against him." (Jude 14–15; 1 Enoch 1:9)

Directly quoting the Book of Watchers, Jude shows that he regards
1 Enoch as a source of prophecy, applicable to his own time.[9] In other
words, the book was so well known that both Jude and the Jews who produced the Dead Sea Scrolls scour it for information about how to understand divine secrets.[10] Among other bits of heavenly lore, the main subject
of this book is a vision of Enoch regarding the sons of God who lusted
after the daughters of men. These are the Watchers, a band of rebellious
angels who introduced evil to the earth.

Beware of the Watchers

Prior to the flood, the Book of the Watchers explains to the patriarch Enoch, two hundred angels descended to earth, taking wives for
themselves and impregnating them.[11] Swearing an oath that they would
accept whatever consequences God might impose, they fornicated with
human wives, producing gruesome, violent offspring. Guilty of a number
of crimes, the Watchers taught humanity how to make weapons of war,
introduced vanity to women in the form of jewelry and cosmetics, and
instructed their human victims in the magic arts:

[The wicked angel] Asael taught men to make swords of iron and breast-
plates of bronze and every weapon for war. . . . He instructed them
about antimony, and eye-shadow and all manner of precious stones and
about dyes and varieties of adornments . . . Semhazah [the angel] taught
spell-binding and the cutting of roots; Hermoni [the angel] taught the
loosing of spells, magic, sorcery and sophistry. . . . Then the giants began
to devour the flesh of men. (1 Enoch 8)[12]

In other words, the fallen angels, their wives, and their offspring were responsible for introducing every kind of wickedness to the earth, including war, greed, pride, sorcery, false wisdom, and cannibalism.

Appalled by these terrible events, the righteous angels Michael, Sariel, Raphael, and Gabriel appealed to God for assistance, leading to the deluge. God resolved:

> *I shall destroy all the spirits of the bastard offspring of the Watchers, because they wrong mankind. I shall destroy all iniquity from upon the face of the earth, and every evil work shall come to an end. . . . And the whole earth shall be freed from all defilement and from all uncleanness, and wrath and castigation. (1 Enoch 10)*[13]

God then sent each of the four righteous angels on a cleansing mission: Michael bound the angels in a pit, where they await the end of time; Sariel informed Noah of God's plan to flood the earth; Raphael imprisoned the chief Watcher, Asael, until such time as God was ready to immolate him eternally in divine fire; and Gabriel led the giants (Nephilim) into war, bringing on their extermination.

Though there are alternative versions of this story, its basic elements can be found in many later Jewish and Christian works, whether or not 1 Enoch is explicitly cited. According to Jubilees, a second-century BCE retelling of Genesis, the fallen angels are bound underground, awaiting immolation in a fiery abyss.[14] According to the First Sibylline Oracle, a first-century prophecy book, the Watchers taught astrology and magic to humanity, bringing further corruption upon the earth.[15] According to the Testament of Naphtali, a Jewish-Christian book purporting to preserve the last words of the patriarch Naphtali to his sons, the Watchers violated nature by sleeping with women and so were accursed.[16] Jubilees offers a particularly memorable version of these events, emphasizing the cross-species nature of the sex involved:

> *And lawlessness increased on the earth and all flesh corrupted its way, alike men and cattle and beasts and birds and everything that walks on*

the earth—all of them corrupted their ways and their orders, and they began to devour each other, and lawlessness increased on the earth and every imagination of the thoughts of all men (was) thus evil continually. (Jubilees 5.2–3) [17]

The second-century CE Jewish work 2 Baruch also presents a particularly vivid retelling:

For [the angels] possessed freedom in that time in which they were created. And some of them came down and mingled themselves with women. At that time they who acted like this were tormented in chains. But the rest of the multitude of angels, who have no number, restrained themselves. And those living on earth perished together through the waters of the flood. (2 Bar. 56.12–16) [18]

In other words, sex with angels leads inexorably to divine punishment. The angels, their human consorts, and their monstrous offspring had to be wiped out or imprisoned. Longing for an angelic embrace was therefore a dangerous proposition, whatever the German poet Rilke may have suggested in 1912. Given this fear, it is not surprising that the apostle Paul sought to protect women from the gaze of angels. Angels—created by God and yet not human—were supposed to keep to heaven, their own realm, unless specifically sent to earth by God. Thanks to the revelation Christ brought, however, the boundary between heaven and earth was significantly more permeable, or so the New Testament writers believed. Under these new circumstances, the maintenance of the human-angel divide became even more pressing.

On Account of the Angels

Interrupting a discussion of proper behavior during worship in his first letter to the Corinthians, Paul introduces a surprising principle: women ought to wear a veil (*lit.* "an authority") on their head "on account of the angels" (11:10). It is difficult to know precisely what Paul could mean by this statement, but the tradition of the Watchers offers one obvious possibility. As we observed in chapter 3, Paul was highly concerned both with the problem of desire and with the strict observance of gender roles. From his perspective, celibacy was ideal, marriage was for the weak, and sex outside of marriage was deserving of death. In this passage, he also argues that there is a natural hierarchy of man and woman, enacted in their clothing, hairstyles, and appearance: Since man is the source and head of woman (after all, she was made from Adam's rib), and since man is the image of God, but woman is the image of man (he was made first and she was made from him), it would be shameful for a woman to neglect to cover her head, a point Paul makes with a rhetorical question: "Judge for yourselves, is it proper for a woman to pray to God with her head unveiled?" (v. 13). From his perspective, the obvious answer is no. Women must keep their hair long and must cover their hair during worship. The comment about angels serves as the linchpin of the argument. Women, Paul insists as emphatically as he can, must wear a covering over their heads if they are to avoid disgrace, preserve the order of creation, exhibit their "nature," and, above all, protect themselves from angels.

Likely familiar with the notion that angels could desire human women—as a first-century Jew he may well have known some version of the story of the Watchers—Paul appears to have viewed sexual congress with angels as an especially threatening possibility. Given the worship practices of his community, his concerns make sense. As beneficiaries of the more permeable boundary between earth and heaven, the Christians in Corinth spoke angelic languages, otherwise known as glossolalia, when praying and prophesying. Discernible with the help of the spirit, glossolalia was a sign of the spiritual blessings to come, given by God to show that the divide between earth and heaven had been partially breached. A reference to angelic languages in the Testament of Job, a Jewish book written around the same time as 1 Corinthians, offers a helpful comparison.[19] At the end of the book, Job's daughters are given a special gift by their father, miraculous sashes that enable them to speak in a heavenly dialect:

When one [daughter] called Hemera arose, she wrapped her own string just as her father said. And she took on another heart—no longer minded toward earthly things—and she spoke ecstatically in the angelic dialect, sending up a hymn to God in accord with the hymnic style of the angels. And as she spoke ecstatically, she allowed "The Spirit" to be inscribed on her garment.[20]

Job's two other daughters also don the sashes given to them, and they, too, are able to speak in the languages of the heavenly beings. Glossolalia, then, was understood to be a sign of spiritual blessing and privilege among Jews during Paul's time. Like the followers of Jesus in Corinth, the daughters received a spiritual gift that enabled them to participate in heavenly worship with the angels. The followers of Jesus could also participate in a divine liturgy, joining with the angels who worshipped God perpetually. Paul himself spoke these languages, or so he boasted in 1 Corinthians, "I speak in tongues more than all of you" (14:18). By speaking in tongues, participants crossed the divide between earth and heaven.

With the community speaking angelic languages so well, however, a danger arose—angels might take particular notice of Corinthian women. It was therefore especially important for women to guard against angelic desire. Women ought to wear veils over their heads when praying and prophesying, Paul insisted, and not only because praying with head uncovered is shameful. The angels might be watching. What if an angel, attracted by the heavenly liturgy celebrated in Corinth, were to look down and desire Corinthian Christians, just as the Watchers had once desired the daughters of men? The late-second-century North African Christian Tertullian made this point explicit, linking the story of the Watchers to Paul's insistence that women ought to veil:

Therefore, a face which is so dangerous and which has cast scandals from here to heaven, ought to be shaded . . . so much more the virgins ought to be veiled 'on account of the angels,' as the sin of the angels would have been greater on account of [them being] virgins. . . . [But] a man may not veil his head . . . because it was not on account of him that the angels deviated.[21]

To Tertullian, a virgin's face was so dangerous that it "cast scandals from here to heaven," tempting angels to illegitimate intercourse, a point he made by citing both Genesis 6 and Paul's letter to the Corinthians. Paul's advice is not as clear as Tertullian's. Still, he also wanted women to veil "on account of the angels," hiding their beauty and thereby protecting both the women and the angels from illicit desire. Operating within a logic fully recognizable in his own time, Paul's concerns were warranted. The last time angels slept with women, the earth was corrupted and God had to destroy it. Crossing to the divine realm from the human realm, and vice versa, was both deeply attractive and profoundly dangerous. And, as early Christians knew, there was another frightening example of (near) human-angel sexual congress in the Bible, and it, too, had devastating results. This is the story of Sodom and Gomorrah.

The Watchers and the Men of Sodom

Though the Sodom episode is seldom read this way today, among New Testament and early Christian authors, the sin of the Sodomites was horrific not because the men of Sodom sought to rape *men* but because they wanted to rape *angels*. In a reversal of the Watchers incident, the men of Sodom pursued unnatural, cross-species desire by lusting after angels. The Epistle of Jude explains:

And the angels who did not keep their own rule, but left their proper dwelling behind, he has kept in eternal chains in deepest darkness for the judgment of the great day. Similarly, Sodom and Gomorrah and the surrounding cities, in the same manner as [the angels], indulged in fornication and went after strange flesh. These serve as an example by undergoing a punishment of eternal fire. (vv. 6–7)[22]

Thus, as Jude saw it, fearful punishment necessarily awaits those who go after a different order of flesh, be they angels or men. To Jude, the sins of these two groups are strikingly similar: in the first case, angels fornicated with women, and, in the second, men sought to rape angels. Linked by the type of sin committed, the angels and the men of Sodom were also linked by the type of punishment they would endure, either during their own lifetimes or at the judgment to come. Sodom had already been annihilated by divine fire. At the end of time, the angels will also be burned eternally. If this is how God treats those who disobey him, Jude declares, the false teachers troubling the Christians during his own time do not stand a chance.[23]

The author of 2 Peter elaborated on this same theme, combining the two stories about sex with angels in order to argue that anyone who engages in defiling sex can expect divine punishment. The letter states:

> *If God did not spare the angels when they sinned, but cast them into hell and committed them to chains of deepest darkness to be kept until the judgment . . . and if by turning the cities of Sodom and Gomorrah to ashes he condemned them to extinction and made them an example of what is coming to the ungodly . . . then the Lord knows how to rescue the godly from trial, and to keep the unrighteous under punishment until the day of judgment —especially those who indulge their flesh in depraved lust, and who despise authority. (2:4–10)*

Since God punished both the sinning angels and the sinners of Sodom for lusting after a different kind of flesh, the followers of Jesus, 2 Peter states, can rest assured that those who indulge in sexual depravity will also be judged.[24] Given interpretations of the Sodom story today, which commonly regard the sins of the Sodomites as having to do with "homosexuality," this emphasis on angels in Jude and 2 Peter may seem startling. Nevertheless, as we shall see, Sodom has very little to do with "sodomy," as this English word is commonly understood.

Inventing Sodom

In 1986, Cardinal Joseph Ratzinger, now Pope Benedict XVI, sent a letter on behalf of the Vatican's Congregation for the Doctrine of the Faith to the Catholic Bishops explaining church policy regarding the "pastoral care of homosexual persons."[25] While it is "deplorable that homosexual persons have been and are the object of violent malice in speech or in action," he argued, and essential for the bishops to "provide pastoral care in full accord with the teaching of the Church," homosexuality must nevertheless be regarded as immoral; it is a symptom of original sin. He explained:

> In Genesis 3, we find that this truth about persons being an image of God has been obscured by original sin. There inevitably follows a loss of awareness of the covenantal character of the union these persons had with God and with each other. . . . Thus, in Genesis 19:1–11, the deterioration due to sin continues in the story of the men of Sodom. There can be no doubt of the moral judgment made there against homosexual relations.[26]

Invoking the destruction of Sodom and Gomorrah to support his conclusion, the cardinal suggested that God finds homosexuality to be both objectionable and worthy of judgment. After all, Sodom and Gomorrah were utterly annihilated in a rain of divinely given fire. From the cardinal's perspective, then, homosexuality is such a grievous sin that God obliterated a city to prove it.

From a biblical perspective, however, Cardinal Ratzinger's argument is seriously flawed. The notion that the story of Sodom involves a moral judgment against homosexuality is not the least bit obvious. As we have already seen, the authors of Jude and 2 Peter thought that the problem with Sodom had to do with the determination of the men of the city to go after "different flesh," that is, the flesh of angels, not their "homosexuality." These New Testament letters express no concern for the gender of the angels involved. Instead they are concerned about the mixing of two different kinds of flesh, angelic and human. Moreover, "sodomy" as a euphemism for homosexual (anal) sex occurs only in later Latin and English writings and cannot be found in the Bible, despite misleading translations. Simply put, English translations that employ the word "sodomy" are incorrect since, as Mark Jordan has shown, the identification of "sodomy" (Latin, *sodomia*) with same-sex intercourse or, more specifically, with anal sex between men does not appear before the eleventh century.[27]

Unfortunately, contemporary English versions confuse readers further, employing the words "sodomy" or "sodomites" to translate one or more words in various New Testament vice lists, particularly those found in 1 Corinthians 6:9 and 1 Timothy 1:10. A quick survey of the original Greek, however, demonstrates just how misleading these translations are. In 1 Corinthians, Paul suggests that "neither *malakoi* nor *arsenokoitai*" will inherit the kingdom of God. In 1 Timothy, the author states that the law was given for the sake of "*pornoi, arsenokoitai*, slave traders" and others, but not for the innocent. The word "sodomite" simply does not appear, and there is no reference, implicit or explicit, to the story of Sodom. Instead, words meaning "soft" or "cowardly" (*malakoi*), "man-beds" or perhaps "lying with men" (*arsenokoitai*), and "fornicators" or "male prostitutes" (*pornoi*) are used. *Arsenokoitai* may refer to male-male sex, but all of the other words are much more general, and not a one carries the meaning "sodomite" as this term is commonly understood today. The choice to employ "sodomite," then, imports later European ideas and words into the biblical text.

Popularized first in medieval Latin sermons and then in early English Bible translations, the transformation of the Sodom episode into a story about (attempted) anal sex took centuries to accomplish. In fact, the flattening of the Sodom story into a shorthand condemnation of same-sex desire can be traced rather precisely to the writings of Peter Damian, an eleventh-century reformer who, among other works, wrote a highly polemical treatise titled the *Book of Gomorrah*.[28] It is not that no one had ever associated Sodom with sexual immorality prior to Peter Damian—the first-century Jew Philo of Alexandria had already linked Sodom with sexual deviance[29]—but the idea that the Sodom story is exclusively about a certain form of sex is a recent development, no matter how often the word "sodomy" appears today. Biblical authors employed the Sodom story to other ends, most often as a proof of the swiftness of divine punishment.

The Sodomites and the Bible

Though the Bible knows nothing of this later identification of Sodom with sex between men, the story was cited for other reasons. The prophets of Israel, for example, regarded Sodom's misdeeds as economic, not sexual: from their perspective, God destroyed Sodom and Gomorrah because the people had become selfish and corrupt, not because they were sexually depraved. Thus, in an oracle condemning Judah's rulers, the prophet Isaiah compared the men of Judah to the rulers of Sodom, arguing that God's punishment necessarily descends upon those who mistreat widows and orphans:

> Hear the word of the LORD, you rulers of Sodom! Listen to the teaching of our God, you people of Gomorrah! What to me is the multitude of your sacrifices? says the LORD. . . . Wash yourselves; make yourselves clean; remove the evil of your doings from before my eyes; cease to do evil, learn to do good; seek justice, rescue the oppressed, defend the orphan, plead for the widow. (Isa. 1:10–11, 16–17; compare Isa. 3:9)

In other words, to Isaiah the Sodom incident proves that injustice against the poor leads inexorably to divine punishment, a sentiment repeated by the prophet Ezekiel some time later.

Responding to the destruction of Jerusalem by the Babylonians, Ezekiel blamed the greed of selfish Judeans for bringing disaster upon the city, accusing them of behaving like Sodomites. Despite the abundant pride, food, and ease enjoyed by prosperous citizens, they had refused to aid the poor and needy, and so God had no choice but to punish them:

This was the guilt of your sister Sodom: she and her daughters had pride,
excess of food, and prosperous ease, but did not aid the poor and needy.
They were haughty, and did abominable things before me; therefore I
removed them when I saw it. (16:49–50)

As Isaiah and Ezekiel saw it, then, God destroyed Sodom and Gomorrah for refusing to be generous to the poor. Sex had nothing to do with it.

In biblical contexts, Sodom was also frequently raised to remind readers of the speedy, devastating punishment that awaits sinners. The book
of Deuteronomy applied this interpretation to the dangers of idolatry.
Those who worship the "detestable things" of the Canaanites, the "filthy
idols of wood and stone, of silver and gold," Deuteronomy warns, God
will "single . . . out for . . . calamity" by being "burned out by sulfur and
salt . . . like the destruction of Sodom and Gomorrah" (Deut. 29:17–23).
The prophet Amos also threatened Israel with Sodom's example, re-
marking, "I overthrew some of you, as when God overthrew Sodom and
Gomorrah" (4:11). Mourning the loss of Jerusalem to the Babylonians,
the book of Lamentations compared the suffering of the two cities, "For
the chastisement of my people has been greater than the punishment of
Sodom, which was overthrown in a moment, though no hand was laid
on it" (4:6). The Gospel of Matthew offered a similar interpretation, suggesting that those who failed to welcome Jesus's disciples would be wiped
out. "Truly I tell you," Matthew predicts, "it will be more tolerable for
the land of Sodom and Gomorrah on the day of judgment than for that
town" (10:15). For many biblical writers, then, Sodom was a paradigmatic example of the punishment that awaits those who are selfish, in-
hospitable, or generally disobedient. The destruction of the city, however,
did not imply a judgment against "homosexuality." In every case, the emphasis was on the inevitability of divine vengeance. Still, the story does
involve an attempted rape of angels. Given the risks of mixing human
and angel flesh, this was a dangerous proposition.

Sodom and the Rape of Angels

The story of Sodom, Gomorrah, and the angels appears in Genesis, as part of a larger cycle of stories about Abraham and his nephew Lot.[30] Prior to visiting Lot, Genesis states, three angels disguised as men visited Abraham and his wife, Sarah. Displaying proper ancient Hebrew hospitality, Abraham immediately welcomed the angels into his tent, presenting them with a large meal.[31] While Abraham slaughtered and prepared his best calf, Sarah baked cakes. After the meal, the three angels/men predicted to Abraham that Sarah would bear a son before their next visit, a promise that Abraham had been anticipating for some time. Two of the angels/men then set out for Sodom, while Abraham stayed behind. Upon arrival in the city they were met by Lot, who offered them a meal and a place to stay. Persuaded to spend the night in Lot's home, the angels shared bread with their host and began to lie down to rest. But then the story takes a sinister turn.

During the night, the men of Sodom surrounded the house. "Where are the men who came to you tonight?" they demanded. "Bring them out to us, so that we may know them!" (19:5). Shocked, Lot refused, offering them his virgin daughters instead. Rejecting Lot's offer, the men attempted to enter the house (and the angels/men) by force, so the angels blinded them, escaping the intended assault. Warning Lot to take his family and run from the city, they urged him, "Flee for your life; do not look back or stop anywhere in the Plain; flee to the hills, or else you will be consumed!" (v. 17). As they were running away, God rained sulfur and fire from heaven onto the cities, condemning everything to total destruction. The next day, Abraham observed the massacre, seeing "the smoke of the land going up like the smoke of a furnace" (v. 28).

It's About Hospitality

Though popularly invoked to prove God's hatred of homosexuality, among biblical scholars today this story is thought to teach something else entirely: the importance of showing hospitality to strangers. There were no hotels in biblical times, and travelers had to seek lodging with local residents, not at public inns. Hospitality to strangers was therefore a key value in ancient Near Eastern and Mediterranean cultures, a value biblical writers shared. Drawing a clear contrast between the hospitality offered by Abraham, Sarah, and Lot, on the one hand, and the violent attack attempted by the men of Sodom and Gomorrah on the other, biblical writers made a point of emphasizing the importance of welcoming strangers into one's home and protecting them throughout their visit.[32] While Abraham and Sarah gave their angelic guests the best they had to offer and Lot willingly presented the angels with food and shelter, the men of Sodom demanded to "know" the strangers in their midst, going so far as seeking to rape them.[33] As such, the Sodomites violated ancient cultural customs in the worst way, attempting to harm the strangers in their midst rather than extending them protection, food, and shelter. The men did not need to know that they were seeking to rape angels. Their attempt to violate guests was bad enough.

Read as a story about hospitality, the destruction of Sodom can be fruitfully compared to a parallel story in Judges, the story of the Levite's concubine. This story also presents a terrible violation of the principle of hospitality, illustrating the devastating results of such a violent affront to the social fabric, though in this case it is Israelites themselves who refuse to welcome the stranger. Thematically and structurally similar, the two stories are clearly linked.[34] And, as in the story of Sodom, irregular sexual intercourse between men is not the relevant narrative detail. No same-sex intercourse takes place. Instead, violence against an Israelite stranger is offered as a proof of the chaos of living in a world without kings.

The Levite's Concubine

According to Judges 19, after the founding of the nation of Israel but before there was a king to control the land, a descendant of Levi, one of the sons of Jacob, took a concubine from the town of Bethlehem to live

with him.[35] Becoming displeased with her husband, she returned to her father's house, though the Levite soon followed after her, hoping to persuade
her to return. After staying at his father-in-law's house for nearly a week,
eating and drinking and enjoying himself, the Levite took his concubine
with him and began the journey to his home territory, knowing he would
need to stop on the way. Arriving in Gibeah, a town belonging to the
descendants of Benjamin, another son of Jacob, the tired party searched
in the city square for someone who might be willing to host them for the
night. They were finally approached by an old man, who welcomed them
into his home, offering them shelter and a meal. But then, as in the story
of Sodom, at nightfall circumstances took a turn for the worse.

Surrounding the old man's house, the Benjaminites of Gibeah demanded that he send the Levite outside so that they might "know" (rape)
him. Rather than succumb to their demands, the old man offered his
virgin daughter and the Levite's concubine as acceptable substitutes. In
the end, the Levite himself threw his concubine out of the house, and
the men raped her all night long. Finding her battered body on the doorstep in the morning, the Levite draped her over his donkey and returned
home. When he arrived, he cut her body into twelve pieces, severing her
"limb by limb," and sending out a gruesome call to arms. He dispatched
segments of her dismembered body to the leaders of Israel, demanding,
"Has such a thing ever happened since the day that the Israelites came up
from the land of Egypt until this day?" (v. 30). Responding to his message, the people of Israel went to war against their relatives, the descendants of Benjamin. An attempted rape of the Levite by the Benjaminites,
followed by the actual rape of the Levite's Israelite property, his concubine, ultimately led to a civil war.

The story of Sodom and the story of the Levite's concubine share a
number of key features: both stories involve strangers seeking hospitality
for the night; both offer examples of what a hospitable welcome should
look like; both involve a demand by the men of the city that they be
given access to the strangers in the house; both portray the righteousness
of a host who is willing to turn over a female substitute to fill in for his
male guests; and, in both cases, the men fail to gain sexual access to their

desired object(s). The willingness of Lot to give his virgin daughters to the men of Sodom in place of the angels earned him the epitaph "righteous Lot" in later writings.[36] The willingness of the old man of Gibeah to hand over both his virgin daughter and the Levite's concubine to the rapists outside was also positively evaluated.[37] By going to such extraordinary lengths to guard the honor of their guests, the bloodshed that followed was depicted as fully justified. Sodom and Gomorrah had to be destroyed by God, and the Benjaminites had to be decimated by their kinsmen. When hospitality codes are violated so drastically, violence and chaos inevitably follow.[38]

Putting an End to Sodom

As our survey of biblical responses to the story of Sodom and Gomorrah has demonstrated, from the perspective of ancient writers, this story could have a number of possible resonances, but none had to do with sex between men. When compared to the rape of the Levite's concubine, the story appears to emphasize the critical importance of extending hospitality to strangers. Any violation of hospitality, symbolized most vividly by the attempted rape of honored male or angelic guests, results in social upheaval and so must be decisively stamped out.[39] Read in the overall context in the book of Judges, the rape of the Levite's concubine also demonstrates the political instability of Israel under the tribal rule. If a king had been in power, Judges implies, then the Benjaminites would not have tried to rape the Levite, and the Levite, a member of the clan of Israelite priests, would not have used his sacrificial knife to slaughter and dismember his own Israelite concubine.[40] The Levite, the Benjaminites, and the men of Gibeah are all negatively portrayed in these stories, with only the old man emerging unambiguously as a hero. In none of these stories, however, is the bodily integrity of women something worthy of protection. When faced with a choice between protecting one's guests and protecting the women in one's household, the guests are supposed to come first.

Interpreted by biblical prophets, the story of Sodom offered a lesson about the dangers of selfishness. The men of Sodom should have welcomed Lot and his family. They should have willingly shared resources, food, and land with not only Lot, but with Lot's angelic visitors. Instead they aggressively assaulted Lot, his family, his property, and his visitors. As such, their behavior could be invoked to shame and threaten Israelites who refused generosity to the poor, the widow, or the orphan. God had no choice but to destroy such people, they argued, a point the writers of Genesis also emphasized in the context of an argument between Yhwh and Abraham:

> *Abraham came near [to God] and said, "Will you indeed sweep away the righteous with the wicked? Suppose there are fifty righteous within [Sodom]; will you then sweep away the place and not forgive it for the fifty righteous who are in it? Far be it from you to do such a thing, to slay the righteous with the wicked, so that the righteous fare as the wicked! Far be that from you! Shall not the Judge of all the earth do what is just?" And the* LORD *said, "If I find at Sodom fifty righteous in the city, I will forgive the whole place for their sake." (18:23–26)*

Pleading for mercy for the city, Abraham argued that God should preserve Sodom if even a small number of righteous people could be found. But since only Lot and his family treated the angels properly, only Lot and his family were saved. Viewed from this perspective, the wickedness of the city was indisputable.

Of all biblical interpreters, only Jude and 2 Peter understood the wickedness of Sodom to be sexual in nature. Still, to these writers, the illicit sex in question had to do with the desire of the Sodomites to penetrate the flesh of angels, not men. Like other Jews and Christians of their generation, these authors were acutely anxious about the results of angelic-human sexual mingling. Eager to avoid the fate of humanity before the deluge and the angels who lusted after women, Jude and 2 Peter placed the Sodom story firmly within the tradition of the Watchers, interpreting both stories as a warning against forbidden desires. At the same time, they, too, longed to cross the divine between earth and heaven so that they could participate in the angelic liturgy. That's why both the Watchers and the Sodomites were so dangerous—these men/angels took the desire for divine-human union too far. The notion that the story of Sodom illustrates God's attitude toward homosexuality is therefore a modern invention, expressive of modern anxieties. Such anxieties simply cannot be supported on the basis of biblical teachings.

Ancient writers were concerned about sexual boundary crossings, but the crossings they feared were different from those expressed by Cardinal Ratzinger and the Congregation for the Doctrine of the Faith. To them, the possibility of an erotic relationship across the gulf between heaven and earth was so upsetting that it could be invoked to explain the origins of evil. When one violates the boundary between what is human and what is divine, one plays with fire, biblical writers suggested, and sometimes one gets burned.

Emerging from exile in the fifth century BCE and living under the shadow of first the Persian and then the Macedonian Greek and Roman empires, biblical writers came to view another sort of sexual mingling as equally dangerous: sex with foreigners. Breaches of the angel-human divide threatened to create monstrous half-breeds like the Nephilim. Breaches of the Gentile-Israel divide called Israelite identity into question, especially since Israelites, now known as "Judeans," were so thoroughly surrounded by outsiders they called the "peoples of the land."

The Holy Seed of Israel

Returning to the land of Israel after exile in Babylon, Ezra the scribe was profoundly disturbed to learn that Israelite men had married local women. These "peoples of the lands with their abominations" threatened to overtake the newly arrived former exiles, corrupting them with their foreign ways, or so Ezra argued.[41] When he heard this, he tore his garments, pulled his hair, and "sat appalled." With Jerusalem already dangerously polluted by intermarriage, he then pleaded with God for mercy:

After all that has come upon us for our evil deeds and for our great guilt, seeing that you, our God, have punished us less than our iniquities deserved . . . shall we break your commandments again and inter-marry with the peoples who practice these abominations? Would you not be angry with us until you destroy us without remnant or savior? (9:13–14; compare Neh. 13:23–30)

According to the biblical books of Ezra and Nehemiah, then, sexual congress with Gentiles would certainly lead to immediate expulsion from land the exiles had just recently regained. The only possible solution was divorce. Family by family and town by town, Ezra and officials he appointed visited each of the returned exiles, making sure that the foreign women and their children were sent away. One hundred and eleven affected families—husbands, wives, and children—are listed at the end of the book, verifying the success of the operation. Still, with a population of around twenty thousand people dwelling in postexilic Judea, Ezra's reform would have had little practical impact.[42] The expulsion of the foreign wives and their children from a newly reconstituted Judean homeland, as depicted in Ezra and Nehemiah, appears to have been largely rhetorical.

Nevertheless, the rhetoric of these two books still represents a dramatic departure from earlier Israelite practice, despite the presentation of these events as "tradition." Earlier law directed at preexilic Israel and Judah prohibited intermarriage with the seven Canaanite nations—the Hittites, the Girgashites, the Amorites, the Canaanites, the Perizzites, the Hivites, and the Jebusites—but not with other peoples.[43] So, for example, Moses married a Midianite, David's ancestor Boaz married the Moabite Ruth, and, in order to restore a depleted tribe of Benjamin after the civil war brought on by the rape of the Levite's concubine, four hundred virgins of Jabesh-gilead were captured as war booty and given as wives to the Benjaminites, all without violating the Sinai covenant.[44] Radically reinterpreting and expanding the Sinai covenant in order to develop a new, more general decree, the version of the law put forward in Ezra and Nehemiah responded to the exile by redefining Judean identity in terms of genealogy.[45] Living in a world where the hold on the territory of Judea was tenuous at best, marriage reform sought to succeed where the Sinai covenant had failed.

The Rape of Dinah

Ezra's action was unprecedented. Still, the notion that intermarriage with outsiders could be threatening, if not downright defiling, can be found in earlier biblical writings. In Genesis, for example, the favored genealogical line from Abraham to Joseph was largely produced by means of marriages within the group. Not yet bound to the Mosaic covenant—and therefore to commandments forbidding sexual congress with Canaanites—the patriarch Abraham was nevertheless depicted as going to great lengths to ensure that his son Isaac married within the family. Loyal to God's preference for in-group marriage, Abraham sent for a wife for his son from an uncle back home. Isaac's sons Jacob and Esau were also evaluated by biblical writers, in part, on the basis of their marriage choices: Esau married Canaanite women and became the ancestor of Moab, but Jacob married his cousins, maintaining the genealogical line of Israel and staying away from sexual mixing with Canaanites. A generation later, two of Jacob's sons did marry Canaanites. Still, they enforced in-group marriage nonetheless, at least when it came to their sister Dinah. Dinah's brothers are represented as so determined to keep Dinah from intermingling with the Hivvites of Shechem that they killed all the male Shechemites when intermarriage was proposed.[46]

Arriving back in Canaan after his sojourn with his uncle Laban, Jacob settled in Shechem, purchasing a plot of land from Hamor, the king of the city. His daughter Dinah set out to visit her new neighbors, the women in the region, only to be assaulted during her travels by Prince Shechem, son of Hamor. First kidnapped and then raped, Dinah found herself the love object of her rapist: "he loved the girl and spoke tenderly to her" (Gen. 34:3).[47] Resolving to marry her—a satisfactory resolution from the perspective of later biblical law[48]—Shechem sent his father, Hamor, to Jacob to pay the bride-price and arrange the marriage, offering to incorporate Jacob and his family into the city:

Make marriages with us; give your daughters to us, and take our daughters to yourselves. You shall live with us; and the land shall be open to you; live and trade in it; and get property in it. (vv. 9–10)

Jacob's sons, however, refused the offer, concluding, "such a thing ought not to be done" (v. 7)—no foreigner should be allowed access to a daughter of Jacob. They then concocted a terrible ruse capable of protecting their family honor and "saving" their sister Dinah.

Pretending to acquiesce to the proposal of intermarriage, the sons of Jacob requested that all the men in the city submit to circumcision in preparation for a full integration of the Israelites with the Hivvites. "But if you will not listen to us and be circumcised," they warned, "we will take our daughter and be gone" (v. 17). Anticipating the advantages of such a propitious marital-political alliance, the men of Shechem accepted this condition, only to be attacked while still recovering from the pain of the operation. Taking them by surprise, Jacob's sons Simeon and Levi slaughtered all the men of the city during their convalescence, recapturing Dinah and confiscating the flocks, wives, and children that had once belonged to them. When challenged for their (over)reaction by their father, Jacob, the brothers retorted, "Should our sister be treated like a whore?" (v. 31). Forced to flee to another region of Canaan, Jacob and his family set up a new altar to Yhwh at Bethel, where Yhwh reaffirmed his promise, "The land that I gave to Abraham and Isaac I will give to you" (35:12). With Israel's genealogical line preserved, Dinah was never mentioned again.

The rape of Dinah is a complex story and has been interpreted in a number of ways. Still, at least one meaning seems plain: if Jacob and his descendants were to retain a separate identity from the Hivvites, they could not agree to Shechem's terms. The biblical writers make this point in the context of a speech supposedly delivered by Hamor to the men of Shechem: "Will not their livestock, their property, and all their animals be ours? Only let us agree with them, and they will live among us" (34:23). At stake, then, was not only Dinah's honor as a marriageable Israelite girl but the distinctiveness of the (male) descendants of Abraham, Isaac, and Jacob. The Shechemites did not mind circumcising themselves, but they did so as Shechemites, not Israelites. Intermarrying with the Hivvites would therefore mean becoming a kind of Canaanite and, as such, their proposal had to be rejected.[49] In this way, the action of the brothers prefigured commandments that would later be included in the covenant of Moses. Widespread intermarriage, such as was proposed by Hamor and Shechem, would have led to the assimilation of Israel into the "peoples of the land" even before they could be led by Moses out of slavery in Egypt and into Canaan, a horrific possibility from the perspective of biblical writers. Marriage within the family therefore preserved Israelite distinctiveness until such time as the nation could be founded and the Canaanite nations overthrown.[50] Just as Ezra would later declare the "peoples of the land" to be off-limits, biblical writers living during the Israelite monarchy could not mingle with their own cousins, the Canaanites.

The Problem of Foreign Women

Genesis 34 taught that marriages between a daughter of Israel and a Canaanite man should be avoided, especially if the integration of the Israelites into the Hivvites was the intended result. Nevertheless, marriage between Israelite *men* and Canaanite or other foreign *women* appears to have occurred on a regular basis, and not only among the patriarchs. As property, the accumulation of wives, foreign or otherwise, did not threaten the genealogy of Israel, which passed exclusively through the male line well into the second century CE.[51] Thus, the kings of Israel were quite content to form alliances with their non-Israelite neighbors by way of marriage. And sometimes kings simply took as wives whatever foreign women happened to please them, as David did when he married Bathsheba. King Solomon, ruling at the height of the Israelite monarchy, was said to have married seven hundred foreign princesses. From the perspective of some biblical writers, however, this sort of behavior was precisely the cause of Israel's downfall.

Reflecting on the reigns of David and Solomon during the reign of the much later king Josiah (641–609 BCE), the writers of Deuteronomy insisted that Israel's kings should have abstained from taking so many wives. Because of this, the Deuteronomist insisted, "a king's heart will turn away" and allow idolatry to be promoted in the land.[52] Telling the story of Solomon's glory long after it was over, the writers of 1 Kings expressed a similar point of view. As they put it:

Among [Solomon's] wives were seven hundred princesses and three hundred concubines; and his wives turned away his heart. For when Solomon was old, his wives turned away his heart after other gods. . . . For Solomon followed Astarte the goddess of the Sidonians, and Milcom the abomination of the Ammonites. So Solomon did what was evil in the sight of the LORD, and did not completely follow the LORD, as his father David had done. (11:3–7)

Though Solomon did not marry Canaanites, the one forbidden group, he nevertheless succumbed to the wiles of his foreign wives and their gods, allowing idolatrous worship to take place. Is it any wonder, biblical writers implied, that the kings after Solomon never achieved the same level of success? By subverting Deuteronomy's laws, 1 Kings observed ominously, the seeds of collapse had already been sown. The fall of Israel, then, first to foreign gods and then to foreign nations, was only a matter of time.[53]

Observed from the perspective of the Babylonian exile, marriage to foreign princesses appeared even more threatening. These women and the men who married them were a significant cause of the nation's destruction, or so it was argued. With idolatry rampant and the land polluted, Yhwh had no choice but to permit the destruction of first Israel (the nation to the north) and then Judah (the nation to the south). Reflecting on these tragedies and adopting the voice of Yhwh, the exilic prophet

Ezekiel declared:

> *When the house of Israel lived on their own soil, they defiled it with their ways and their deeds; their conduct in my sight was like the uncleanness of a woman in her menstrual period. So I poured my wrath upon them for the blood that they had shed upon the land, and for the idols with which they had defiled it. I scattered them among the nations, and they were dispersed through the countries; in accordance with their conduct and their deeds I judged them. (36:17–19)*

Blaming the downfall of Judah and the destruction of Solomon's temple, at least in part, on sexual defilement, Ezekiel compared Israelite men to menstruating women who had made themselves unclean before God. God's "wife"—that is, the men of Israel—had been unfaithful, and, as such, they ("she") had become disastrously unclean. Deserving of God's wrath, these men inevitably lost the land. Their dispersion throughout the nations was their own fault.[54] A century later, when finally allowed to return to their homeland, Ezra and Nehemiah applied this perspective to the exiles, seeking to solve the problem of foreign wives for good.

The Menstruous Land

In 539 BCE, Cyrus the king of Persia defeated the Babylonian Empire and permitted the Judeans to return to their homeland. Over the course of about a century and with the assistance of the Persian kings, the exiled Judeans went home, rebuilding the capital city of Jerusalem and then the temple. The residents of the land, however, were not the least bit enthusiastic about this reestablishment of the exiles, despite the fact that some of the people dwelling there may well have been Judean kinsmen left behind a century before. Appealing to Cyrus's successors, these "peoples of the land" attempted to block the rebuilding projects of the exiles, and, though the exiles ultimately prevailed, Ezra and his allies were not amused. They came to identify local, native residents with foreigners, likening them to the Canaanites of old while claiming Judean ancestry for themselves alone. Declaring a crisis of both sexual and religious immorality, Ezra argued that the Jews could not afford to intermarry these "Canaanites." From his perspective, sexual mingling was tantamount to treason.

Reinterpreting earlier biblical law, Ezra picked up on Ezekiel's metaphor of the menstruous men of Israel, transferring the metaphor to women dwelling in the land. From his perspective, Judea had become totally polluted while the exiles were away. Male exiles, then, must not place their "holy seed" in such dirty vessels. He puts this teaching forward in a newly invented commandment:[55]

> We have forsaken your commandments, which you commanded by her servants the prophets, saying, "The land that you are entering to possess is a land unclean (lit. a menstruous land) with the pollutions (lit. the menstruations) of the peoples of the lands, with their abominations. . . . Therefore, do not give your daughters to their sons, neither take their daughters for your sons, and never seek their peace or prosperity." (9:10–12)[56]

This commandment is not included in any known copy of earlier biblical law. Still, likening the people dwelling in Judea to a woman during her period, Ezra recalled Leviticus's prohibitions against having sexual intercourse with a menstruating woman—"You shall not approach a woman to uncover her nakedness while she is in her menstrual uncleanness" (18:19)—in order to prohibit any and all sexual intercourse between the returned exiles and native women. Since "the people of the land" were permanent menstruants, figuratively at least, their nakedness should never be uncovered.[57] To Ezra, native women and their children were permanently defiled. Nehemiah recalled the lesson of King Solomon to make the same point:

> Did not King Solomon of Israel sin on account of such women? Among the many nations there was no king like him, and he was beloved by

his God, and God made him king over all Israel; nevertheless foreign
women made even him to sin. (Neh. 13:26)

Reenvisioning Israel's boundaries as a matter of birth rather than territory, Ezra and Nehemiah warned that sexual congress with foreigners
would, in fact, destroy the nation.

Written or edited at approximately the same moment in Judea's history, warnings against the dangers of the strange woman in the book of
Proverbs reinforced this same theme.[58] Developing a portrait of a stereotypical foreigner, Proverbs describes this woman as "loud and wayward"
(7:11). An adulteress or prostitute, she decks her couch with Egyptian
linen and persuades vulnerable Judeans with her smooth talk. An idol-
ater, she sits at her window, calling to those who pass by. Attributed
to Solomon, perhaps this section of Proverbs was intended to teach the
exiles a hard lesson on the basis of the famous king's own bitter experience—stay away from seductive foreign women, "Solomon" cautioned.[59]
At the very least, in the context of postexilic Judea, this representation of
the strange woman reemphasized the dangerous threat of assimilation:
succumbing to women outside the group endangered not only the man
seduced but Judea as a whole.[60] Projecting anxieties about their lack of
control of the newly restored territory of Judea onto foreign women,
both Ezra and Proverbs posited that mixing with foreign flesh results in
personal and national disaster. Reflecting on these same concerns under
Macedonian Greek and then Roman rule, later writings adopted a similar strategy, insisting that Jewish men must not marry foreign women,
whoever they may be.[61]

Telling a story involving the simultaneous translation of the Hebrew
Bible by seventy revered Jewish elders, the second-century BCE treatise
the Letter of Aristeas sought to explain and defend the making of the
Septuagint, the most widely known Greek version of the Hebrew Bible.
Written in Greek and for Greek audiences, all to defend the Greek version of the Hebrew Bible, this author also insisted that intermarriage
with outsiders was impermissible for Jews:

In his wisdom the legislator [Moses] . . . surrounded [Jews] with unbro-
ken palisades and iron walls to prevent our mixing with any of the other
peoples in any matter. Being thus kept pure in body and soul we were
preserved from false beliefs, and worshipped the only God omnipotent
over all creation." [62]

From the perspective of Aristeas, then, sexual mixing had already
been forbidden by Moses. And not only this: Jews had obeyed this commandment so thoroughly that they were (figuratively) surrounded by
iron walls. The author of Jubilees, a retelling of Genesis written at about
the same time, made a similar claim:

And if there is any man in Israel who wishes to give his daughter or his
sister to any man who is from the seed of the Gentiles, let him surely die,
and let him be stoned because he has caused shame in Israel. . . . And
let any man who causes defilement surely die, and let him be stoned
because thus it is decreed and written in the heavenly tablets concerning
all of the seed of Israel, "Let anyone who causes defilement surely die.
And let him be stoned." [63]

Arguing that intermarriage with any non-Israelite should be punishable by death, Jubilees drastically revised earlier biblical precedent, just
as Ezra had before him.[64] With their own territory ruled by one empire
after another and so many Jews living outside of Judea proper, sexual
congress with the Gentiles was widely depicted as the worst thing that
could happen.[65]

Demons and Jews

Writing in Rome in the mid-second century CE, the Christian writer
Justin Martyr recalled the story of the Watchers once again, but offered
his own unique twist—the children of the Watchers and their wives, he
claimed, were the gods of the Greeks and Romans. As earlier writers had

claimed, these angels were understood to have transgressed the heavenly order. "Captivated by the love of women," they produced monstrous offspring. To Justin, however, the children of the women and angels were the very same gods-demons who continued to demand the sacrifices, incense, and libations offered in Roman temples in his own day. To make matters worse, the famous poets sang of their deeds, enslaving the gullible and the ignorant to the very demons God had rejected:

> *Poets and mythographers, since they were ignorant that it was the angels and the demons which had been begotten by them that did such things to men and women and cities and nations, ascribed to God himself the things they related.*[66]

Yet, despite this disastrous state of affairs, God has chosen to spare the world for the time being for the sake of the Christians. Since there is still a chance for Gentiles enslaved to the demons/offspring of the Watchers to recognize the true reason of the Christ, they might also escape the coming punishment. Poised like Sodom before the rain of fire, they still have a chance. Soon, however, God will rain down judgment upon all, and those who follow the Watchers' children (that is, the Greek and Roman gods), like the Watchers themselves, will suffer eternally for what they have done.[67]

Concerned not only about sex-crazed demons but also about the sexual purity of Christians, Justin presented Christian marriage practices as exceptionally strict, even more rigorous than those of Jews. Those Christians who married were chaste nonetheless, remaining faithful to their spouses. Many of those who follow Christ, Justin claimed, adopt an even stricter path, choosing celibacy over marriage. These Christians "have preserved their purity at the age of sixty or seventy years," irrespective of their nation of origin.[68] As such, Gentiles in Christ have outpaced the people of Israel with their sexual self-control, replacing the genealogical line of Israel with a true, spiritual line:

> *We have been led to God through this crucified Christ, and we are the true spiritual Israel, and the descendants of Judah, Jacob, Isaac and*

Abraham, who, though uncircumcised, was approved and blessed by
God because of his faith and was called the father of many nations [i.e.,
the Gentiles].[69]

The genealogical line of the Jews, preserved so carefully from Abraham to Jesus Christ, has been replaced by a new nation with a new genealogy: the Christians.

Justin's arguments, put forward at a time when Christians and Jews were so closely related that they were nearly indistinguishable, built on postexilic Jewish arguments about Israel's "holy seed" to argue that the "holy seed" belonged to the Christians, not the Jews. As such, Justin reinterpreted "holy seed" arguments also found among New Testament writings like 1 Peter and Paul's letter to the Galatians to claim special genealogical privileges for Gentiles in Christ.[70] Still, sexual mixing with outsiders, if not with angels, clearly took place. Christians debated the relative merits of staying married to unbelievers, with some deciding that such marriages should continue and others determining that divorce was the only option.[71] Later rabbinic Jews also continued to debate the complexity of intermarriages, wondering, for example, if a man of mixed heritage might marry the widow of a priest.[72] Jews sometimes married non-Jews, and Christians sometimes married non-Christians. To assume otherwise would be a mistake.[73] The problem with strange flesh is that this flesh was so readily available and so very attractive.

Worries about sex with angels and sex with Gentiles, then, acknowledge just how close these categories of foreign flesh were perceived to be. The "peoples of the land" were likely to have been former residents of Judah left behind by the Babylonians. The Shechemites were likely encountered by and familiar to Israelites both before and after the monarchy. The men of Gibeah who dared to abuse the Levite's concubine were always part of the group—they were Benjaminites. Even the Watchers, when looked at from the perspective of Jews and Christians living under Greek and Roman rule, could be perceived as "one of us." Crossing the divide between the human and divine realms, the Watchers fulfilled the fantasies of Jews and Christians who also longed to journey into heaven, bridging what seemed to be an insurmountable gap. As it turns out, strange flesh is all too familiar.

Sex with Strangers

Israelites, Judeans, and Christians were not the first groups to attempt to create community boundaries by manufacturing a sex panic, and they will not be the last. From American antimiscegenation laws to rhetoric about the "racial degeneration" that occurs when the "blood" of one group is combined with another, anxieties about crumbling social divisions are regularly represented as sexual crises, especially when resources, land, and labor are at stake. So, for example, when Australia gained its independence in 1901, offspring produced by white men and Aboriginal women, once tolerated as inevitable products of colonial expansion, came to be regarded as a "half-caste menace" requiring systematic state response. Children who appeared to be less than 51 percent Aborigine were forcibly removed from reservations and sent to institutions where they would be trained in "acting white," and then allowed to relocate among the lower echelons of white society, a policy that was abandoned only in 1967.[74] In the United States, discriminatory laws sorting among whites, Native Americans, African Americans, Asian Americans, and their children served as a bulwark of white privilege for more than two centuries. Accompanied by a racist rhetoric as venomous as anything 1 Enoch could say about wicked angels or Justin Martyr about Jews, laws against intermarriage presented the white race as "civilized" even as nonwhite labor was ruthlessly exploited and nonwhite bodies were systematically disenfranchised.[75] To offer just one example, in 1824 when the highly educated Cherokee John Ridge married Sarah Northrup, the genteel daughter of a Connecticut aristocrat, the local paper declared that "the girl ought to be publicly whipped, the Indian hung and the mother drowned."[76] Whether expressed as a crisis of seed or of blood, the stranger within refuses to stay strange for long. And that is precisely the problem.

The next chapter turns to biblical discussions of actual flesh—its parts, its fluids, and its functions. Sexual intercourse was, biblical writers warned, a passageway through which inappropriate mixing between different kinds of flesh could take place, threatening the viability of the nation or the community. Foreskins, semen, and menstrual blood were also employed as key symbols of difference in biblical literature. Over time, the presence or absence of a foreskin became the central sign of Israelite identity, so much so that the apostle Paul could call Jews "the circumcised" and Gentiles "the foreskinned." The handling of semen and menstruation was also taken as a proof of the community's special relationship to Yhwh. Keeping genital discharges away from the sanctuary marked God's house as a sacred precinct, separate from the mundane pollutions of daily living. When the Romans destroyed the Jerusalem temple in 70 CE, concerns about contact with semen and vaginal blood were transformed, but not eliminated. Later Jews and Christians, for example, continued to wonder if menstruating women ought to visit the synagogue or the church, with some ruling that they should and others ruling that they should not. Approaches to the human body—particularly the sexed human body—could convey a great deal about what it might mean to be Israelite, Jewish, or Christian.

CHAPTER 6

Bodily Parts

Circumcision, Semen, and the Products of a Woman's Womb

On July 5, 2002, famed left fielder for the Boston Red Sox Ted Williams died at the age of eighty-three. A beloved all-star player with one of the best batting averages of all time, Mr. Williams left behind millions of devoted fans. He also left behind his frozen body, ready for future reanimation. In a controversial decision, contested by his daughter but supported by his son, Ted Williams's body was placed in a deep freeze at an Arizona cryonics laboratory called the Alcor Life Extension Foundation.[1] Joining several others with similar dreams, the Boston slugger froze his body in anticipation of a time when nanotechnology will make it possible for humanity to achieve an endless physical life.[2] As such, cryonics turns to science to accomplish something ancient Jews and Christians once thought God alone could bring about: immortal life in a physical body free from illness and pain. Yet the modern assumption that science can explain and often control both life and death, brought to such controversial extremes by cryonics, would have made no sense at all to biblical writers—they turned to God, not science, to solve their health problems. As we will see, a drastic disconnect between ancient and modern ideas about the physical body extends not only to beliefs about immortality but to beliefs about sex as well.

In this chapter we consider biblical statements about bodies, bodily fluids, and flesh, particularly those pertaining to sex and desire. Ancient Christians, Hellenistic Jews, and Ted Williams may have all longed for a return to their individual, unique physical bodies, but they certainly would not agree about the method for achieving their goal. To biblical writers and ancient interpreters of biblical texts, the desire for an everlasting human body was to be met by God. Not surprisingly, then, biblical statements about genitalia, menstruation, semen, and blood were also expressed in social or theological, not scientific, terms. Whereas today medical doctors might debate the relative merits of circumcision by conducting empirical studies addressing, for example, the impact of circumcision on the spread of sexually transmitted diseases,[3] among biblical writers circumcision was interpreted as a sign of membership in God's community, written on the male member. The impact of circumcision on disease, sexual pleasure, or sexual functioning was simply not addressed. Similarly, whereas nowadays menstruation is often presented as a hormonally governed inconvenience to be managed with tampons, maxi pads, and medicine for PMS, biblical writers were not the least bit interested in "feminine-hygiene products" or the impact of estrogen on a woman's cycle.[4] Instead, they were concerned with the theological and practical impact of vaginal bleeding on God's sanctuary and the fertility of a menstruant. Finally, though semen remains as precious a fluid today as it was in antiquity—if it were not so precious, why would we need sperm banks, fertility clinics, and scientific studies of sperm counts?—biblical writers had no way to ensure that male seed would be protected. To them, the preservation of semen required bodily and social, not medical, solutions, and both semen and menses were sources of pollution that needed to be carefully managed. Bodily parts and fluids signified one's place in a divine-human economy that extended into eternity, and no amount of human ingenuity could solve the problem of death.

Still, biblical attitudes toward bodies and death changed, and attitudes toward sex changed with them. As far as can be detected from the Hebrew Bible, ancient Israelites had no hope of eternal life, either in their bodies or in heaven. They thought that their bodies would simply decay, and if souls lived on at all, they survived as "shades" (*rephaim*) dwelling in an unpleasant underground abode of the dead called Sheol. As Psalms puts it, the days of mortals "are like grass; they flourish like a flower of the field; for the wind passes over it, and it is gone, and its place knows it no more" (103:15–16). Continuity was therefore achieved through faithful children, "who keep [God's] covenant and remember to do his commandments" (v. 17).[5] Since the descendants of Abraham believed that they would live on through their progeny alone, the successful production of children was a matter of the utmost significance. A failure to produce descendants, the very problem faced by Abraham, Sarah, and many other biblical heroes and heroines, was a grave misfortune—anything that could both encourage fertility and keep the family line intact was to be recommended. Productive sex had eternal implications: if one failed to reproduce, one failed to live.

We have noted the importance of fertility and family continuity to biblical writers already in earlier chapters. According to the custom of Levirate marriage, childless widows were supposed to be remarried to a brother-in-law or another near male kinsman so that children could be borne for the family, a strategy that drives Ruth's seduction of Boaz and Tamar's attempt to conceive a son by means of her father-in-law, Judah. Sex acts incapable of producing legitimate children for their families were to be discouraged, since these acts wasted precious Israelite semen on barren ground. The sex acts forbidden in Leviticus are linked by this principle—sex with a menstruant, an Israelite man, the wife of another Israelite, or with an animal cannot result in progeny capable of ensuring eternal life through a male descendant. Therefore such sex is described as illegal and wrong. With immortality achieved through children, divine intervention in the fertility process served as a clear sign of God's favor. The miraculous conception of Isaac by Sarah, predicted by an angelic visit to Abraham, serves as a paradigmatic example of this point of view. Prior to the births of first Ishmael, son of Abraham and Sarah's slave Hagar, and then Isaac, Abraham was destined to remain forever dead, with no heirs to regard him as ancestor. Then, once Abraham secured a covenant with Yhwh, his fortunes were reversed: in return for making Yhwh his only god, Abraham's descendants would become as numerous as the stars. With God's intervention in the intimate relations between Abraham and Sarah, Abraham could live forever.

Beginning in the Hellenistic period, however, after the Macedonian king Alexander the Great conquered the lands of the eastern Mediterranean (323 BCE) and Judea was ruled by one intrusive foreign power after another, some Jews came to understand the afterlife quite differently: immortality was no longer a matter of progeny but of righteousness expressed in part through a new understanding of marriage and procreation. Given the terrible state of injustice in the world, these Jews argued, God would certainly bring both the nation and the faithful back to life to put things right, granting restoration to those who held steadfast to their covenantal obligations. These faithful would someday live in their own, redeemed physical bodies within a restored nation of Israel, a "kingdom of God" or a "kingdom of heaven." Widely held, this belief in the restoration of the bodies and lives of the faithful was promoted by Jesus and other contemporary Jews as well, including the authors of the Dead Sea Scrolls, members of a first-century Jewish sect known as the Pharisees, and, above all, by the New Testament writers.[6] Once beliefs about eternal physical life had shifted, sexual morals shifted as well. With the drive to produce actual descendants of Abraham no longer quite so pressing, monogamy became the recommended norm among Jews and Christians alike, and Jews like Paul and the author of Matthew advocated for celibacy over marriage. Circumcision, once designed to prepare Israelite male members for the fruitful penetration of a fertile woman, became a sign of Judean identity first, though the sexual implications of the practice were never lost. Finally, anxieties about sex with an infertile menstruant or the wasting of Israelite seed, already extended by the authors of Leviticus to include concerns about protecting God's sanctuary from pollution, contributed to the identification of menstrual blood as a principal sign of both moral and physical impurity. Bodies, including their sexual parts and products, were reinterpreted in light of the circumstances and concerns first of biblical writers and then of those who held these writings sacred. In the process, Israelites, Jews, and Christians infused bodily parts with eternal significance.

The Difference a Foreskin Makes

Initially, circumcision was not so much an Israelite as a Canaanite practice, in the sense that people living in the region of Canaan often circumcised, irrespective of the particular god they worshipped. In fact,
circumcision was so widely practiced that the failure of the Philistines
(enemies of Israel who dwelt along the shore of the Mediterranean) to
remove their foreskins earned them their biblical nickname, "the foreskinned."[7] As oddities, the Philistines could be compared to everyone
else, who, like the sons of Abraham, Isaac, and Jacob, also circumcised.
The story of the rape of Dinah paradoxically confirms this shared Canaanite attitude: the men of Shechem did not hesitate to circumcise when
asked, nor did they identify circumcision as particular to Jacob and his
sons. "Will not [Israelite] livestock, their property, and all their animals
be ours?" they concluded. "Only let us agree with them, and they will
live among us" (Gen. 34:23). The implication of this statement is that
Jacob, his sons, and the Shechemites would live together as circumcised
Canaanites, not as Israelites. Foreskin free, they would live together and
intermarry irrespective of their relationship to the god Yhwh.

The curious two-step account of the covenant between Abraham and
Yhwh further suggests that circumcision was not always quite so distinctive to Israel. In Genesis, Abraham is depicted as receiving the covenant
with Yhwh not once but twice, and only in the second story does circumcision play a role. First, in Genesis 15, God promises Abram that his
descendants shall be as numerous as the stars, sealing the promise in a
mysterious ceremony involving the sacrifice of a heifer, a female goat, a
ram, a turtle dove, and a pigeon, all cut in half and placed side by side.
In this way Abram "cuts a covenant," the Hebrew expression for establishing a covenantal relationship between two parties, but the cut that
seals the deal is made to the animals, not to Abram's foreskin. Then,
in Genesis 17, God makes the same promise once again, only this time
Abram is renamed Abraham and God orders the patriarch to circumcise both himself and all the males in his household. The cut here is to
the foreskins not only of Abraham but of all his male descendants for-

ever. Indeed, circumcision is so central to this version of the story that the practice is invested with three separate meanings: it is a visible sign that reminds both God and Abraham of their promise to each other; it is an obligation incumbent on Israelite men in perpetuity; and it is identical to the covenant itself.[8] A few verses later, the ninety-nine-year-old Abraham removes first his own foreskin and then the foreskins of Ishmael, the slaves born in his house, and the foreign slaves he had purchased, an act that sets the stage for the birth of Isaac. In the second Genesis story, then, Abraham has become the very model of the good circumcised and circumcising Israelite patriarch. Thanks to his bold actions, his fertility is restored and, as promised, Sarah becomes pregnant.

Among contemporary biblical scholars, the repetition of God's promise first to Abram and then to Abraham is best explained as a result of the long process of transmission and reception of the Hebrew Bible. From this perspective, Genesis was written not by one author—traditionally, Moses is thought to be the author of the first five books of the Hebrew Bible—but by a whole series of writers and editors who revised the book over time in light of their own concerns. The first story, with its unusual cutting sacrifice, is therefore a product of an earlier group of storytellers who believed that God's covenant with Israel was best sealed by a dramatic sacrifice, not by Abram's foreskin. The second story, however, represents a later development in Israelite thinking. The product of a writer or writers who equated Israelite distinctiveness with the cutting away of foreskins, these editors wrote the circumcision rite back into the covenant at some point after it had become a central Israelite practice. Traces of this editorial reworking are especially evident in the specific details given to Abraham regarding the rite: Circumcise baby boys on the eighth day, Yhwh commands Abraham, an instruction that establishes a key provision for the ritual itself. This same instruction is also found in Leviticus 12, a book that was likely composed by the same priests who edited Genesis (among scholars, these writers are known as the "Priestly" or "P Source"). In this way, the actions of Israel's legendary progenitor came to reinforce the central importance of the rite of circumcision to the national character, offering further support to this writer's point of view.[9]

Oops, We Forgot

Shifts in Israelite practice can also be detected in the context of an odd story from the book of Joshua. Many Israelites were not circumcised at all, Joshua reports, even though they lived long after the covenant between Abraham and Yhwh had been sealed with the family foreskins. Just after entering Canaan, but before celebrating their first Passover in the promised land, a problem involving male foreskins needed to be corrected:

> At that time the LORD said to Joshua, "Make flint knives and circumcise the Israelites a second time." So Joshua made flint knives, and circumcised the Israelites at Gibeath-haaraloth (that is, the "hill of the foreskins"). (5:2–3)

It appears that some Israelites were either not satisfactorily circumcised or perhaps not circumcised at all, and so many foreskins had to be sliced off. Rather than clarifying the state of these foreskins, however, the next few verses add to the confusion:

> This is the reason why Joshua circumcised them: all the males of the people who came out of Egypt, all the warriors, had died during the journey through the wilderness after they had come out of Egypt. Although all the people who came out had been circumcised, yet all the people born on the journey through the wilderness after they had come out of Egypt had not been circumcised. . . . So it was their children, whom he raised up in their place, that Joshua circumcised; for they were uncircumcised, because they had not been circumcised on the way. (vv. 4–7)

In other words, the problem involved both circumcision and second circumcision: The warriors born in Egypt had been circumcised, but they died. Wandering in the wilderness for a generation, however, circumcision was neglected, and so these Israelite boys—now men—still needed to have their foreskins removed.[10] But in what sense, then, would this be a second circumcision? Had some of the boys been circumcised, but improperly? Had some of the circumcised warriors survived to fight in Canaan, but their circumcisions were no longer adequate? The text does not answer these questions. Still, one thing is clear: the writers of Joshua were at pains to argue for the value of circumcision in a situation where it had not been consistently practiced. Interestingly, the Egyptians were also known for circumcising. Had the Israelite warriors adopted the practice from their Egyptian counterparts? The ancient Greek historian Herodotus implies that they did.[11] Perhaps, then, the first circumcisions of the warriors were Egyptian rather than Israelite in character, and so needed to be redone. Again, the text provides no answer.

An equally awkward story in the book of Exodus also belies the notion that circumcision was always both practiced and distinctive to Israel. The warriors of Israel appear to have forgotten the necessity of circumcision. So, apparently, did Moses. Returning to Egypt from Midian after being appointed by God to lead the Hebrew people out of slavery, Moses, his wife Zipporah and their son stopped for the night. Then, "the Lord met him and tried to kill him" (Exod. 4:10). Whomever the Lord was threatening (Moses? their son?) Zipporah solved the problem. She "took a flint and cut off her son's foreskin, and touched Moses's feet with it, and said, 'Truly you are a bridegroom of blood to me!'" The Lord then let "him" (Moses?) alone and Zipporah declares, "A bridegroom of blood by circumcision." This enigmatic story has puzzled interpreters for centuries. Who was the Lord threatening, Moses or his son? Why? And in what sense does circumcision make Moses a "bridegroom of blood"? Why is Zipporah, a Midianite woman, doing the circumcising? Moreover, if circumcision was so important, why wasn't Moses's son circumcised already? And why would Zipporah touch Moses's "feet," that is, his genitals, with her son's foreskin, making him a "bridegroom of blood"?[12] As scholar Shaye Cohen concludes, "Perhaps the only thing that is clear in the story is the protective power of circumcision."[13] Something about that dramatic, emergency circumcision performed by the Midianite Zipporah protected Moses and/or his son from the torment by the Lord. Just as, by cutting away their foreskins for the first or the second time, Joshua and his companions sealed their special relationship to Yhwh, so, too, Moses needed to be protected by the removal of his son's foreskin. Still, as Genesis would have it, they should have been circumcising all along.

The identification of circumcision with Israel is therefore not as straightforward as it eventually became. Canaanites also circumcised, circumcision only gradually became associated with the covenant with Abraham, and Abraham's descendants did not always remember that they were supposed to circumcise. The foreskin of Moses's son had to be removed in an emergency, as did the foreskins of the Israelite warriors, and the early version of Abram's covenant interpreted animal sacrifice, not circumcision, as the cut that mattered. Still, the removal of the male foreskin did eventually become an established sign of community membership. In the final version of Genesis, Abraham undertook circumcision on the very day of his encounter with Yhwh, marking his new status as God's chosen patriarch with particular determination. Offering instructions to the nation of Israel after it was established, Exodus made circumcision a requirement, and not only for the descendants of Abraham but also for foreigners residing in the land. If immigrants are circumcised, Exodus instructs, then they, too, can join in the Passover celebration (see Exod. 12:47–49). To the writers of Deuteronomy, circumcision was such a badge of Israelite status that it could be employed as a metaphor. "Circumcise the foreskin of your hearts," the author exhorts, bringing the heart into harmony with the marked penis.[14] The prophets also employed this metaphor. "Circumcise yourselves to the LORD," Jeremiah pleaded, removing "the foreskin of your hearts" as well as the foreskin of your penis (Jer. 4:4). The overall impression left by the Hebrew Bible in its final, canonical form is that to be an Israelite man is to be circumcised.

Being Circumcised, Being Judean

Once circumcision had been identified as a key indicator of Israelite ancestry, it could then be employed to summarize first Israelite and then Judean identity, particularly in contexts where the practice was distinctive. Israelites and their neighbors traded insults on the basis of the appearance of their respective penises, with Israelites regarding uncircumcised men as disgusting and unfriendly outsiders employing circumcision to summarize Israel's alleged barbarism. Writing just before the fall of the kingdom of Judah to the Babylonians (587 BCE), for example, the prophet Jeremiah lumped non-Israelites together, identifying all of them as "the foreskinned" (*orlim*).[15] The exilic prophet Ezekiel employed this same term to abuse his non-Israelite targets, suggesting that the *orlim* are destined for dishonor. Subject to God's wrath, warriors from the uncircumcised nations of Tyre and Egypt will die in ignominy, the prophet warned, buried with others who have been subject to disgrace and shame.[16]

After the Israelites returned from exile and lived first under Persian and then Greek rule, circumcision became increasingly emblematic of Judean difference, especially since the Greeks did not participate in the practice. Already in the fifth century BCE, Greeks were identifying the removal of the foreskin as barbaric, associating it with foreign nations like Egypt, Phoenicia, and Syria. From the perspective of Greek authors like Diodorus (first century BCE) and Strabo (first century CE), circumcision was tantamount to genital mutilation.[17] It is perhaps not surprising, then, that some Judeans, interested in improving relations with their Greek rulers, attempted to remove the marks of their circumcisions, drawing down any remaining foreskin to disguise the surgery.[18] When Antiochus IV Epiphanes, the Syrian Greek king who ruled Syria and Judea from 175 to 164 BCE, forbade circumcision in his lands, he may have been building on a trend already begun by Judeans themselves. Still, some Judean mothers circumcised their baby boys anyway, in defiance of both Antiochus and the Judeans who agreed with him. In response, the king killed both the mothers and their babies, hanging the infants around their mothers' necks (see 1 Macc. 1:60–61).

From the perspective of 1 Maccabees, the first-century BCE account of these events, circumcision was both a central sign of Judean identity and an important source of the conflict between Antiochus and the Judeans.

The Maccabees, a set of zealous Judean brothers determined to prevent the king from forcing Greek customs upon the land, led a successful revolt against the Syrian king, establishing a quasi-independent nation ruled by their descendants, the Hasmoneans. Among other policy changes, they made circumcision a state requirement. 1 Maccabees explains:

Mattathias [the Maccabee] and his friends went around and tore down the altars [dedicated to other gods]; they forcibly circumcised all the uncircumcised boys that they found within the borders of Israel. They hunted down the arrogant, and the work prospered in their hands. They rescued the law out of the hands of the Gentiles and kings, and they never let the sinner gain the upper hand. (2:45–48)

Thus, all the boys living within their territories had no choice but to be circumcised. According to the Jewish historian Josephus (first century CE), the Hasmoneans continued this policy when they captured the neighboring region of Idumaea, identifying circumcision with loyalty to their Judean state. Adding Idumaea to their territories, they made the Idumaeans "Jewish" by forcing them to be circumcised.[19] In this way the Idumaeans became Judeans, or, as Josephus puts it "they were hereafter no other than Judeans."[20] From the perspective of the Hamoneans, to circumcise was to be Jewish and to be Jewish was to circumcise.

In 63 BCE, the Roman general Pompey marched Roman troops into Jerusalem and entered the city's famous temple to Yhwh, effectively putting an end to Hasmonean rule. The Idumaean-Jewish general Herod was later installed as king of the region, and Judea became a vassal state of Rome. To the Romans, circumcision was an unfortunate but undeniable sign of Judean identity, a practice to be tolerated on the basis of its antiquity but disdained for its barbarism. So, for example, the insulting Latin word *apella* (for *sine pelle*, "without a foreskin") was employed to discredit Jews as early as the third century BCE, reappearing again in the satires of Horace, a contemporary of Pompey.[21] Ridiculing Jews both for their superstitious religion and their strange habits, Horace contrasted himself to "the Jew Apella" (*lit.* the Unforeskinned Jew), who might believe some superstitious nonsense, and promised not to insult some "clipped Jew" (*curtis Iudaeis*) by violating their odd religious festivals.[22] Such crude jokes depend upon a Roman knowledge of Jewish circumcision as well as a racist disregard for Jews and their customs.

Later Roman authors like Tacitus and Juvenal continued to mock Jewish circumcision, making fun of Romans who behaved like pseudo-Jews by observing Sabbath, refusing to revere cult statues, abstaining from pork, and going so far as to "take to circumcision."[23] After the Jewish Wars (66–73 CE), when the Romans forced Jews to pay a special tax known as the *fiscus Iudaicus*, Roman officials particularly eager to increase their tax yield checked for Jewish identity by examining penises. The second-century Roman historian Suetonius describes the Emperor Domitian's (ruled 96 CE) vigorous pursuit of the tax:

> *Besides other taxes, that on the Jews was levied with utmost rigour, and those were prosecuted who without publicly acknowledging that faith yet lived as Jews. . . . I recall being present in my youth when a person of a man ninety years old was examined before the procurator and a very crowded court, to see whether he was circumcised.*[24]

One strategy of identifying Jews, then, was to expose their penises, checking for the absence of a foreskin. In a Roman context, a circumcised penis made Jewish difference visible to all and, in some cases, this visible difference brought about abuse, persecution, or even death.[25]

The act of circumcision, once a shared practice, had, by the Roman period, become a clear sign of Jewish difference, acknowledged by Judeans and non-Judeans alike. As such, the absence of a foreskin could symbolize everything that was right with the people of Israel—their special status before Yhwh, the righteousness of their "circumcised hearts," and their fidelity to their national god. Alternatively, the "clipped" penises of faithful Jews could, from the perspective of critical outsiders, sum up everything that was supposedly wrong with this curious people—their strange customs, their misanthropic attitude, and their superstitious religion. And yet there really was no other way to tell Jews from their neighbors, so long as men remained clothed. Ra'anan Boustan explains, "neither their names, nor their accents, nor their professions, nor their clothing, nor many other aspects of their daily lives served as reliable signs of [Jewish] ethnic or religious difference in Greco-Roman antiquity."[26] A highly charged issue, circumcision became a source of both interest and anxiety among Judeans and non-Judeans alike. To many Jews, circumcision remained a badge of covenant loyalty to be defended and explained, even when a missing foreskin could lead to disadvantage or death. To many ancient Christians, however, circumcision eventually became a source of embarrassment, particularly as they sought to disassociate themselves from their Jewish origins. According to the Gospel of Luke, Jesus's family met their covenantal obligations as Jews, circumcising the baby Savior on the eighth day and presenting the appropriate sacrifice on his behalf (see Luke 2:21–24). According to Paul, his own circumcision on the eighth day was a sign of the advantage he, as a Jew, appropriately enjoyed (see Phil. 3:5). Nevertheless, among later Christians, a practice that had once been interpreted as honorable and essential came to be regarded with scorn.

The Productive Penis of the Patriarch

Explaining the covenant of circumcision in the mid-first century CE, the highly educated Greek-speaking Jew Philo of Alexandria offered a sustained defense of the practice, which he regarded as wise, a sign of Jewish morality, medically advantageous, and symbolically significant. First of all, Philo argued, circumcision checks the pride of the man, who, as the one who contributes the most to procreation, might be tempted to lord it over the woman. She offers only her menstrual fluids to the generative process, but he is the "skill and the cause" behind their fruitful encounter. Next he offers a medical rationale: circumcision is commonly adopted by persons living in warm southern climates, for it guards against infection and disease of the male member. Moreover, circumcision aids in fertility, ensuring that the semen reaches its proper destination instead of getting stuck in the folds of the foreskin. Finally, circumcision symbolizes the importance of sexual self-control: by shedding foreskins, God intends the men of Israel to cut themselves off from excessive desire. Thus, though other nations also circumcise, Moses, in his wisdom, added a requirement unique to Jews, imposing circumcision on the eighth day, long before the impulse for sexual intercourse even arises.[27]

In *On the Special Laws,* a reconsideration of the Sinai covenant designed for those educated in Greek philosophy, Philo prefaces the discussion with yet another defense of circumcision.[28] There are four principal reasons for the practice, he explains, "handed down to us from the old-time studies of divinely gifted men": it prevents infection, promotes cleanliness, generates wisdom, and encourages fertility. Of these, the last is most important: "we are told that [circumcision] causes the semen to travel aright without being scattered or dropped into the folds of the foreskin, and therefore the circumcised nations appear to be the most prolific and populous."[29] The Jews are therefore among the most fertile of peoples and also the most self-disciplined. By excising the foreskin, they symbolically excise "excessive and superfluous pleasure," cutting away the most imperious desire of all, the desire of a man to mate with a woman.

Philo's particular interpretation of Jewish circumcision was appropriate to his larger cultural context. As we observed in chapter 3, Greek and Roman philosophers regularly taught that desire should be suppressed, even as they underscored the importance of fathering legitimate children.[30] Philo's interpretation of the role of men and women in conception is also in accord with medical assumptions of the time, though no Greek or Roman medical doctor recommended circumcision as a healthy choice. The second-century Greek physicians Soranus (ca. 98–138 CE) and Galen (ca. 129?–216 CE), for example, also discussed the nutritive functions of menstruation and the superior role of semen in producing the fetus.[31] To Galen, however, the foreskin was a valuable ornament, not a threat to men of the warmer climes, serving as a parallel to the woman's labia.[32] The connection Philo drew between fertility and circumcision, however, seems to have been adapted from biblical literature, not practical philosophy, yet in the Bible the link is implied rather than stated.

Fruit from the Tree

Circumcision, Philo asserted, prepares the penis for the successful, fruitful emission of seed. The priestly writers of Genesis and Leviticus would agree. In Genesis, for example, Abraham's circumcision leads directly to his newfound success at fathering Isaac. Immediately after the encounter with Yhwh and the circumcision of the males in his household, messengers from God are sent to inform Abraham that Sarah will become pregnant, at which point Sarah laughs, "After I have grown old, and my husband is old, shall I have pleasure?" (18:12). But, of course, she does become pregnant: her husband's newly naked penis allows his seed to hit its intended mark.[33]

A connection between fertility and the removal of the foreskin is also made in the context of a set of agricultural commandments found in Leviticus. Offering instructions on how to cultivate fruit trees in the land of Israel, Leviticus labels forbidden fruit "foreskins":

When you come into the land and plant all kind of trees for food, then you shall regard their fruit as their foreskin; three years it shall be as a foreskin to you; it must not be eaten. In the fourth year all their fruit shall be set apart for your rejoicing in the LORD. But in the fifth year you may eat of their fruit, that their yield may be increased for you. (19:23–25, adapted from the NRSV).

In other words, fruit may be harvested and eaten only after three years of discarding the "foreskins," the fruit that must not be eaten.[34] Pruning trees and waiting for the fruit to mature, like pruning away the foreskin from the penis, increases the fertility in the land, bringing forth both fruitful fruit trees and fruitful men.

Several centuries later, Philo and then the rabbis of Palestine made similar connections between circumcision and agricultural cultivation. Philo applied an agricultural metaphor to the necessity of circumcising the slaves kept in Israelite households:

There is need for both [the home-born and bought male slaves] to be purified and trimmed like plants, both those which are natural and genuine and those which are able to bear fruit constantly; for well-grown [plants] produce many superfluous [fruits] because of their fertility, which it is useful to cut off.[35]

Like plants, slaves should be pruned to increase their yield. The early-fifth-century rabbinic text *Genesis Rabbah* also drew an analogy between trees and penises, comparing Abraham's newly circumcised phallus to a well-cultivated cinnamon tree. "Just as the cinnamon tree yields fruit as long as you manure and hoe around it," Rabbi Simeon b. Lakish taught, appropriately cultivated, Abraham's penis became productive once again.[36] "Hoeing" around Abraham's phallus awoke its procreative potential, making it possible for him to father Isaac in his old age. In this way, Leviticus, Philo, and Rabbi Simeon presented circumcision as an agricultural method leading to a more productive "tree," that is, a more productive phallus.[37]

From an ancient Jewish perspective, circumcision transformed the penis into a more potent organ of reproduction. But, as the rabbis saw it, circumcision had an even more important function: removal of the foreskin readied Jewish men to enter the divine presence.[38] Playing on the notion of Israel as God's wife, a popular metaphor we have already discussed at some length, the rabbis compared the act of circumcision to the beautification rituals undertaken by a woman eager to make herself more attractive for her man. Those who circumcise their foreskins, Rabbi Levi explained, are like a princess preparing to receive her king and worried about her possible defects:

Said the king to her, "You have no defect, but that nail of your little finger is slightly too long; pare it and the defect will be gone." Similarly, God said to Abraham, "You have no other defect but this foreskin: remove it and the defect will be gone."[39]

Just as the princess cut away an overly long little fingernail, Abraham cut away his foreskin, making himself fully pleasing to God and ready to receive Him.[40] Outsiders were also impressed by his beautifully trimmed member: "Abraham said, 'After I circumcised myself, many proselytes came to attach themselves to this sign [of the covenant].'"[41] Romans may have asserted that circumcision was a form of genital mutilation, rendering the Jewish male body ugly, but the rabbis countered with the opposite point of view—circumcision made their bodies beautiful.

Spiritual Circumcision

Late antique rabbinic interpretation, in harmony with earlier Judean ideas, emphasized the importance of the rite of circumcision, both as an aid to fertility and as a minor surgery capable of making Jewish men more comely to God. By contrast, late-antique Christian interpretation largely repudiated the practice, blaming Jews for their insistence that circumcision remain "fleshly," a matter of removing actual foreskins. Already in the early second century, a letter attributed to Barnabas, a companion of the apostle Paul, declared that circumcision had been nullified, "For he [God] has said that circumcision is not a matter of flesh. But they violated his law, because an evil angel instructed them."[42] Attributing fleshly circumcision to the misguidance of an evil angel, Barnabas concluded that the only way to interpret earlier biblical references to circumcision was as a sign of the coming of Jesus. "For Abraham, the first to perform circumcision," Barnabas claimed, "was looking ahead in the Spirit to Jesus when he circumcised." The author proves the point by introducing a fanciful interpretation of the number eighteen, supposedly the number of men Abraham circumcised on the day he received the covenant: "The number eighteen consists of an Iota [J], ten, and an Eta [E], eight. There you have Jesus."[43] Of course, this creative number crunching only works in Greek, where the letter iota doubles as the symbol for the number ten and the letter eta for the number eight, while also forming the first two letters of Jesus's name. Moreover, the detail involving the number of men circumcised does not actually appear in Genesis 17. Still, from Barnabas's perspective, the point is clear: God never intended to instruct Israel to cut away actual foreskins. Any cutting was either a spiritual requirement or a symbolic road sign designed to point toward the coming of Christ.

A few decades later, the Samaritan Christian Justin Martyr went further, claiming that circumcision was neither a positive symbol nor a spiritual sign, but given by God so that Jews could be more easily punished:

> *The purpose of [circumcision] was that you [Israelites] and only you might suffer the afflictions that are now justly yours; that only your land be desolate, and your cities ruined by fire; that the fruits of your land be eaten by strangers before your very eyes; that not one of you be permitted to enter your city of Jerusalem.*[44]

Referring to the devastation of Judea following the Second Jewish Revolt (132–135 CE),[45] Justin implies that the Romans were correct to investigate Jewishness by examining suspect penises. Exposing Jewish male members or destroying Judean lands, the Romans were carrying out God's wrath, not God's blessing. And yet, as Justin well knew, there were also circumcised Christians in his own community. In the very same treatise, he concedes their existence, accepting them as brothers, so long as they do not attempt to spread their outdated practices more widely.[46] Seeking to draw a boundary between Christians and Jews at a time when any distinction between them was far from clear, Justin turned to circumcision—already a source of contempt among Greek and Roman writers—to further disparage his non-Christian, Jewish opponents.[47] Such an interpretation of circumcision, however, departs significantly from New Testament teachings. Whatever second-century Christians may have taught, the followers of Jesus did not reject circumcision. Instead, they employed it as a key sign of Jewishness, an identity that they also claimed for themselves.

Bringing in the Foreskins

Like many other first-century Jews, the apostle Paul divided the world into two groups: those with foreskins and those without. The fore-skinned (*akrobystiai*) were the Gentiles, those who could not count on a covenantal relationship with Yhwh, and the circumcised (*peritomai*) were the Jews, blessed through Abraham and Moses both. Like the writers of Deuteronomy and the prophet Jeremiah, Paul argued that true circumcision changed the heart, not the penis: "a person is a Jew who is one inwardly, and real circumcision is a matter of the heart—it is spiritual and not literal" (Rom. 2:29). Nevertheless, he did not necessarily reject circumcision of the flesh, at least for Jews. Jews, he insisted, are the heirs to the covenant and enjoy the distinction of sharing the same "flesh," that is, the same material stuff, as the Messiah. "They are the Israelites," he declared, and as such they possess "the adoption, the glory, the covenant, the giving of the law, the worship and the promises." They are descended from the patriarchs, as was the Messiah, "who is above all of them" (Rom. 9:3–5, my translation). And yet, by placing a higher value on spirit than flesh, it can seem that Paul was not particularly interested in ensuring the continuation of the practice among Jews either. After all, though proud of his own fleshly heritage—"circumcised on the eighth day, a member of the people of Israel, of the tribe of Benjamin, a Hebrew born of Hebrews, as to the law, a Pharisee"—he was nevertheless willing to count all these blessings a loss if they kept him from honoring Christ (Phil. 3:4).

Over the last few decades, Paul's attitude regarding circumcision has become a subject of considerable dispute among biblical scholars. Traditionally, Paul was thought to reject circumcision altogether, not only for Gentile Christians but for Jews as well. Circumcision is an unnecessary, fleshly practice, interpreters of Paul have insisted, irrelevant to faith in Christ and, when improperly understood, a hindrance to the unity of the church. Such an interpretation of Paul is not only traditional, but also defensible. As Daniel Boyarin has persuasively argued, Paul regularly values spirit over flesh, and in such a way that the fleshly practices of Israel are seriously undermined.[48] Paul's argument in Romans offers a case in point: if one breaks the law, Paul argues, one becomes "foreskinned," whether or not the foreskin has been removed (see Rom. 2:25–26). Actual foreskins are irrelevant to the distinction. Similarly, both the circumcised and the foreskinned are made righteous exclusively on the grounds of faith, not on the basis of the appearance of their penises.[49] Even more important, Abraham received the covenant and the promises because of his faith, not because of his circumcision (see Rom. 4:11–12). Obeying God *before* receiving the covenant of circumcision, he was made righteous on the basis of his loyalty to Yhwh, not by the removal of his foreskin. Thus, Abraham is the appropriate progenitor of Israel and Gentiles alike, who may approach God in faith together. Such an argument clearly devalues the importance of literal circumcision, even as it repeatedly invokes foreskins as the key symbol of Gentile and Jewish difference.

More recently, however, scholars have been reading Paul's letters in other ways, suggesting that the apostle regarded circumcision as an enduring sign of Israelite blessing, even as he denied this particular blessing to Gentiles. Operating out of a prophetic framework in which the Gentiles must worship Israel's God *as Gentiles* for the resurrection of the righteous to occur, Paul would not allow Gentile followers of Jesus to participate in what was for him the central symbol of Israel's identity: the removal of the foreskin. Circumcision was intended by God to remain distinctive to Jews alone. As he explains at the very beginning of Romans, salvation is available to everyone who has faith, "the Jew first and also . . . the Greek" (1:16). Salvation is therefore sequential: Jews had it first, and then Greeks were added through faith, but not through the covenant of circumcision. Gentiles must keep their foreskins on, approaching the God of Israel as Gentiles, not as pseudo-Jews. If they do not, their identity as Gentiles is undermined and God's prophecies cannot be fulfilled.

According to the prophet Isaiah, someday God would raise up the tribes of Jacob and restore the survivors of Israel, making the nation "a light to the Gentiles" and bringing salvation to the end of the earth (Isa. 49:6). In Paul's understanding, this moment had finally arrived: with the advent of the Messiah, the Gentiles could be adopted into the family of God's people by obeying the law of Christ, not the law of Moses, and being incorporated as faithful Gentiles, not as Jews. He explains, offering a novel interpretation of Genesis 17:

> [Abraham] received the sign of circumcision as a mark of the righteous-
> ness of faith while he was still foreskinned [akrobystia] in order that
> he might be father of the those who are faithful while foreskinned [ak-
> robystias], so that righteousness might be accounted to them. And [he
> is also] father of the circumcision [peritomês], to those not only from
> the circumcision but also to those who follow in the footprints of the
> faithfulness of our father Abraham, while [he was] foreskinned. (Rom.
> 4:11–12, my translation)

Both groups are therefore descendants of Abraham, irrespective of the appearance of their penises: Gentiles join the family by adoption through faith and Jews by both faith and descent in the flesh.[50]

Circumcision Belongs to Jews

If this reading of Paul is correct, he does not so much devalue circumcision as protect its exclusivity—it is intended for Jews alone. From
his perspective, Gentile circumcision is unnecessary, even harmful, for it
implies that "the nations" can become participants in a set of covenant
relationships that are inappropriate to them. Even worse, circumcision
undermines the apostle's understanding of what the Messiah has accomplished. If Gentiles become circumcised, they are attempting to enter
God's community as fake Jews instead of as Gentiles who, the prophets predicted, would one day prostrate themselves before Israel's God. As
such, they are denying the validity of the Messiah's death on the cross.
Paul explains:

> All who rely on the works of the law are under a curse; for it is written,
> "Cursed is everyone who does not observe and obey all the things writ-
> ten in the book of the law." . . . Christ redeemed us from the curse of

the law by becoming a curse for us, for it is written "Cursed is everyone who hangs on a tree"—in order that in Christ Jesus the blessing of Abraham might come to the Gentiles, so that we might receive the promise of the Spirit through faith. (Gal. 3:10–14)

If Paul is addressing Gentile followers of Jesus exclusively, which appears to be the case in his letter to the Galatians, then this passage might be clarified to mean: "For all [Gentiles] who rely on the works of the law [specified in God's covenant with Israel] are under a curse" since the law curses them by placing them outside of God's community. Their accursed situation—the curse of being Gentiles with foreskins, false gods, and bad morals—was lifted when God's Messiah became a curse for them by "hanging on a tree," that is, by being crucified. As such, their curse cannot be lifted by pretending to be Jewish, removing their foreskins, and keeping the commandments specific to Israel, but only by adopting their new role as Gentiles who follow God's Messiah, crucified for them. By contrast, Jews should continue to circumcise. God gave this practice to them as their special heritage, and they should continue to honor God's command, though they, too, must circumcise their hearts.

Whatever Paul intended to indicate in these lengthy discussions of Abraham, circumcision, and faith, however, one thing is clear: to him, Jewish and Gentile identity could be summarized by the presence or absence of a foreskin. And yet, by bringing uncircumcised Gentiles into a movement designed to honor Yhwh, the God of Israel—a God known for demanding circumcision from his people—Paul created a whole host of problems for later Christians. As we have already seen, both the Hasmoneans and the historian Josephus understood circumcision to be the single, certain mechanism whereby one can become Judean. The book of Judith, a Jewish text also from the Hasmonean period, offers another example of this point of view. According to Judith, one Achior the Ammonite entered the Judean community in a two-step process, first by faith and then by circumcision; Achior, "believed firmly in God. So he was circumcised, and joined the house of Israel, remaining so to this day."[51] From the perspective of these authors at least, becoming fully Jewish en-

tailed circumcision, an assumption shared by many Gentile followers of
Jesus as well. In fact, Paul's most significant enemies, the "circumcision
faction," were actually Gentiles, not Jews. These Gentiles, seeking full
assimilation into a community of Judeans who worshipped the God of
Israel and his Messiah, Jesus, circumcised themselves and then preached
circumcision to others. Logically, their argument made sense: if Gentiles
were attaching themselves to the God of Israel, then why wouldn't they
circumcise? As everyone knew, circumcision is what Judeans did. Moreover, if circumcision was a sign of Jewish sexual self-control, as Philo had
argued, why wouldn't Gentiles want to adopt the practice? Paul himself
claimed that celibacy and self-control were distinctive characteristics of
those who followed Christ.

By insisting that Gentiles keep their foreskins, Paul left Gentile Christian identity disturbingly unresolved, particularly since the general resurrection of the righteous did not take place as he had expected.

A Set of Minimum Requirements

Some fifty years after Paul wrote his letters, the author of the Gospel
of Luke and the Acts of the Apostles revisited the question of Gentile circumcision in the context of his two-volume work. Addressing first the life
of Jesus and then the history of the church, Luke-Acts tells the story of
the spread of the Jesus movement from Galilee to Jerusalem and, finally,
to Rome. Agreeing with Paul, this writer also sorts Gentiles and Jews
on the basis of their foreskins, viewing circumcision as a central sign of
Jewish identity. Eager to present Jesus, Jesus's family, and his first followers as pious Jews, he narrates the circumcisions of both Jesus and Jesus's
cousin John the Baptist, the only gospel writer to include these stories (see
Luke 1:59; 2:21). John and Jesus, Luke emphasizes, were properly initiated into the ranks of circumcised Jewish males. Gentiles, however, ought
not to be circumcised, a point the author makes quite emphatically in his
second volume. Unlike Paul, however, he blames Jews, not overly zealous
Gentiles, for seeking to impose circumcision on the faithful. And, even

more than Paul, he acknowledges the complexity of sorting identity on the basis of the presence or absence of a foreskin even as he insists that Gentiles, like Jews, must avoid fornication.

Throughout the first several chapters of Acts, "the faithful from the circumcision" (i.e., Jesus-following Jews) raise objections whenever Gentiles seek incorporation into the Jesus movement. Can a foreskinned Gentile receive the gifts of the Holy Sprit, some "from the circumcision" (*ek peritomes*) demand after observing the Gentiles speaking in tongues and praising God (see Acts 10:45). Then, when Peter eats with "the foreskinned" (*akrobystiai*), those "from the circumcision" complain, asking how he can eat with foreskinned men (11:2–3). The crisis reaches its peak when some Jesus-believing Pharisees insist that Gentiles "be circumcised and ordered to keep the law of Moses" (15:4). Repudiating their claim, the author of Acts presents James, the brother of Jesus, as settling the matter. James states, "We should not trouble those Gentiles who are turning to God [with circumcision], but we should write to them to abstain only from things polluted by idols and from fornication and from whatever has been strangled and from blood" (vv. 19–20). Gentiles, then, are to be held to a minimum set of requirements involving food, sexual morals, and idol worship, but they are not to be circumcised, a policy that is to be disseminated among all the churches.

Still, the situation Acts describes is not nearly as tidy as James's pronouncement might suggest. Just a few verses later, Acts tells a story that seems to reverse the policy. Traveling to Derbe and Lystra, two cities in Asia Minor, Paul brings along a disciple named Timothy. Son of a Jewish mother and a Greek father, Timothy was uncircumcised, in line with the ethnic identity of his father, as both Jews and Greeks would expect. The apostle Paul, however, rectified the situation, circumcising him anyway: "[Paul] took him and had him circumcised because of the Jews who were in those places, for they all knew that his father was a Greek" (16:3). Did Paul violate James's decree as a concession to the Jews of Lystra and Derbe? But why would he, especially since the Jews they would be visiting knew that Timothy's father was Greek? From the perspective of first-century Jews, ancestry passed through the male, not the female line.[52]

"Jews in those places" were unlikely to have regarded Timothy as Jewish by birth, though they might have welcomed his circumcision as a sign of his full acknowledgment of a Jewish identity. When Paul circumcised him, Timothy was a Gentile. Once circumcised, he was a Jew.

Why Was Timothy Circumcised?

The choice to circumcise Timothy, then, is an apparent contradiction of the ruling of the disciples a few verses earlier, which, in the context of Luke-Acts, makes little sense. Since apostolic harmony is an important narrative theme throughout the Acts of the Apostles, it is highly unlikely that the author would portray Paul in direct opposition not only to James but to a widely accepted apostolic decree. Some other message must have been intended. The fifth-century Christian interpreter Augustine offered a novel solution: by including this story, Acts shows that Christians do not detest circumcision per se, only circumcision for Gentiles, for whom it was not commanded.[53] If Augustine is right, then Timothy's circumcision was intended as a proof of Paul's scrupulous attitude toward Judean and Gentile identity both. When it comes to marginal cases like Timothy, who had at least a partial claim to Jewish ancestry, circumcision could be regarded as permissible since, as James and the rest of the apostles knew, God intended circumcision as a blessing for Jews. Moreover, as the author of Luke-Acts knew, Timothy's identity as a Jew could be supported on the basis of Roman law, if not Jewish or Greek customs, though technically Roman attitudes would not apply to his case.[54]

According to Roman law, the offspring of mixed marriages were not regarded as the legitimate children of their fathers; instead, they followed the legal status of their mothers. Thus, the children of slave women were enslaved, the children of freedwomen were free, and the children of non-Roman provincials were non-Roman, even if they were fathered by Roman citizens.[55] The specific Roman legal principle in play was that of *conubium,* the right to contract a legal marriage. When there was no *conubium,* the child retained the status of the mother, irrespective of her relationship to the child's father.[56] If one applies a Roman sensibility to Timothy's circumstances, then, he could be regarded as "Jewish," though, from a Jewish perspective, he was "Greek." By applying Roman logic to the half-Jewish, half-Greek Timothy, Acts demonstrates the open attitude of both Paul and Christians in general to circumcision. The apostles might have rejected circumcision for those of Gentile ancestry, but, if even one parent was Jewish, circumcision was not only acceptable but was required. Or so Paul's action suggested. The confusing status of Timothy, then, provided an opportunity for the author of Acts to make a polemical point about Christian versus Jewish attitudes. Prior to James's ruling, Jewish Christians were pushing circumcision on those who did not want it. After James's ruling, the question had been settled—Gentiles ought not to circumcise—but this decision did not mean that Christians were unreasonable. Paul, the principal hero of Acts and, from the perspective of Acts anyway, a Roman citizen, was quite willing to circumcise half-Jews, even if they were Jewish from a Roman, not a Jewish, perspective.

Who Is a Gentile? Who Is a Jew?

For both Paul and the author of Luke-Acts, then, foreskins served as a borderline around which Jewish-Gentile and then Jewish-Christian identity could be negotiated. Yet, as their writings also reveal, there was no firm agreement regarding the proper approach to Gentile foreskins. To some, Gentile circumcision seemed appropriate; to others, Gentile circumcision must be avoided. Yet to all, the circumcision of Judeans could simply be assumed. Ignatius of Antioch, a near contemporary of the author of Luke-Acts, offers a further example. "If someone should speak about Judaism to you," he advised the Christians of Philadelphia, "do not listen to him, for it is better to hear about Christianity from a man having a circumcision than Judaism from a man who has a foreskin."[57] In other words, a Jew (a man having a circumcision) can be a good teacher of Christianity, but a Gentile (a man with a foreskin) is a lousy teacher of Judaism. Gentile Christians are therefore to keep to their own area of expertise: being Gentile Christians. By contrast, circumcised Christians, that is, Jews, can be good teachers of Christianity, so long as they follow Jesus Christ. If they don't, they are "burial stones and funerals for the dead" and should in any case be avoided.[58] Yet, it is important to note, all the men Ignatius imagines are followers of Jesus, though not all have foreskins and only the nonforeskinned type are qualified to teach Judaism. As Justin Martyr would also admit much later, circumcised and uncircumcised Christians continued to worship together for quite some time.

The exceptional case of Timothy, Ignatius's concerns about foreskins, and Justin's anti-Jewish reinterpretation of circumcision in the late second century point to the continuing problem of determining who is who in a mixed group that, as we have already observed, practiced intermarriage, intentionally encouraged non-Jews to join up, and promoted worship of the God of Israel but apart from the customs that were by then recognizably "Jewish." It is no wonder that foreskins became such a point of controversy. When later Christians increasingly came to see themselves as something other than Jewish, arguing that they were somehow both "true Israel" and yet not actually Jews, Christian theories of circumcision became even more elaborate. For the first time, Jesus's circumcision was a problem. If, as many came to believe, Christians were strictly enjoined *not* to circumcise, why would the founder and very center of their faith allow his own foreskin to be removed? As heirs to the teachings of the Gospel of Luke, the very public circumcision of Jesus could not be denied. It could, however, be radically reinterpreted.

Jesus's Foreskin

In the context of Luke-Acts, Jesus's circumcision serves as proof of the piety of both the Savior and the holy family—Mary, Joseph, and Jesus were strictly observant Jews. To Justin Martyr, however, Jesus's circumcision fulfills another role entirely—it ends the requirement of circumcision forever. Jesus did not submit to circumcision and the other requirements of his Jewish identity "as if he was made righteous through them," Justin claimed, but in order to bring to completion "the order of things which his father had established." In the case of Jesus, then, circumcision is not a punishment, as it was for Jews, but a form of suffering he willingly undertook, just as he also "submitted to death by crucifixion, and to becoming human and to suffering all such things which [were] arranged for him."[59] Circumcision, then, was something one suffered, not something one practiced with pride.

Origen of Alexandria, offering a creative interpretation of the story of Zipporah's emergency circumcision of Moses's son, offered a slightly different point of view. To Origen, Jesus ended the protective power of circumcision by permitting his own body to be subjected to the rite: Before the advent of Christ, circumcision guarded God's people against the malicious intervention of angels, including the angel who contended with Moses until Zipporah's crucial action. After Jesus's circumcision, however, the power of both circumcision and contending angels was overturned.[60] Circumcision was useful prior to Christ but, once Jesus submitted to the rite, its utility was ended. Among Latin-speaking Christians, another tradition developed: Jesus was circumcised not to fulfill and therefore end the practice but so he would be perceived as more convincing to Jews during his own lifetime. As the fourth-century bishop Ambrose of Milan put it, "[His body] was fashioned under the Law so that he might win those who were under the Law."[61] To Ambrose, Jesus did not so much endorse circumcision as tolerate it for the sake of Jews who didn't know any better and Christians who would someday become the full beneficiaries of his mercy. As late-antique Christians saw it, from the time of Jesus onward, circumcision was a painful disadvantage that was first accepted and then ended by Christ. Removal of actual foreskins could play no real role in Christian life.

But the story of Christian circumcision did not end in late antiquity. Though Christians would no longer circumcise, at least in theory, their fascination with circumcision as a sign of God's mercy never waned. Besides being willing to suffer the torments of the cross, through the cut of a knife on his vulnerable infant member, Christians argued, Christ bore the pain of circumcision and opened God's mercy to those ready to receive it. With Jesus no longer imagined as "Jewish," his circumcision could be invoked as a tangible proof of the willingness of God to take on even the most humiliating fleshly procedures. In the medieval period, interest in Jesus's Christian circumcision reached new heights, leading to a popular feast day and widespread interest in one of the few lingering bits of flesh Jesus had left behind, his foreskin.

First attested in the eleventh century, the Cult of the Holy Foreskin brought with it relics of the precious remnant of Jesus's member, a holiday on which Christ's merciful act could be recalled (January 1), and a philosophical discussion regarding the possibility that some fragment of Christ's flesh could remain. Since, as Christian tradition universally acknowledged, Christ rose bodily from the dead and then ascended into heaven, the only portions of Jesus's flesh that could possibly exist on earth were those that he discarded over the course of his lifetime: his blood, umbilical cord, and foreskin. According to legend, Holy Roman Emperor Charlemagne received both Christ's foreskin and his umbilical cord as gifts from the Savior himself, bringing the precious objects back to the Frankish kingdom from Jerusalem sometime later.[62] Now preserved at the Abbey of Charroux, as well as in other locations, the foreskin became an object of veneration too precious to deny. So, when a series of twelfth- to fourteenth-century theologians contemplated whether or not all of Christ's fleshly remains—including his foreskin—would have been incorporated into his resurrected body, the possibility that the foreskin was miraculously left behind was explicitly defended. As Pope Innocent III (pope 1198–1216) put it, "But what is to be said of [the foreskin] believed [to be] preserved in the Lateran Basilica? . . . It is better to commit such questions entirely to God than to define rash and overconfident answers."[63] Christians may have stopped circumcising, but foreskins remained central to medieval Christian theology and practice.

The Sin of Onan

Today, Christians who practice circumcision usually justify it on scientific rather than religious grounds. Still, Christian biblical interpretation left its mark on contemporary practice as well. Deeply concerned by the ill effects of "onanism," a euphemism for masturbation invented in the eighteenth-century, physicians of the time proposed a variety of solutions to a practice they considered both a social scourge and a serious danger to health. The rejection of onanism appealed to the biblical story of Onan, a son of Judah who "spilled his seed on the ground" rather than impregnating his brother's former wife when, in obedience to Levirate marriage laws, his father Judah forced him to take the widow into his own household (see Gen. 38:8–9). On its surface, the story appears to be about *coitus interruptus,* not masturbation—Onan's sin was that he refused to impregnate his brother's widow, not that he pleasured himself—but in eighteenth-century moralizing discourse, Onan's sin was reduced to his pursuit of nonprocreative sexual pleasure.[64] Onan, then, was imagined to be the paradigmatic masturbator, entertaining a habit that, famous doctors like Simon-Andre Tissot argued, could lead to rheumatism, blurred vision, gout, headaches, and other diseases, large and small.[65] Alluding to Christian morality even as they enforced "scientific" solutions, Tissot and the physicians of his generation sought relief for onanism in a number of devices, including restrictive underwear and a toothed urethral ring. In the late nineteenth century, however, another, more permanent solution was discovered: circumcision.

In 1870, puzzled by a case of paralysis plaguing a young Wisconsin boy, Dr. James Sims discovered that an overly tight foreskin was the cause of the problem. The irritated and enclosed glans of the boy was puffed and swollen, causing him to experience painful erections at the slightest touch. Once the foreskin was removed, however, all of his symptoms abated, including his paralysis. The rush to promote circumcision as a cure not only to paralysis but to epilepsy, hernias, and other disorders was on.[66] Soon the surgery was being recommended as a preventative device, a conservative intervention capable of removing a potential source of irritation from "an exquisitely sensitive organ,"[67] and thereby curing a whole host of diseases and disorders, especially those related to masturbation. As Dr. E. J. Spratling explained in 1895, in the case of masturbation "circumcision is undoubtedly the physician's closest friend and ally."[68] A year later, in 1896, a popular baby-care book advised mothers to circumcise their sons if they wanted to spare them the development of the "vile habit."[69] Popularizing recommendations regarding circumcision had come full circle. No longer justified on the basis of Genesis 17 and the covenant with Abraham but instead on the basis of a reinterpreted sin of Onan, medical doctors found in circumcision a cure for multiple evils. Medically and morally beneficial, circumcision, it was argued, reformed both the body and the soul.

Foreskins Make All the Difference

From biblical Canaan to modern America, from first-century Judea to the Cult of the Holy Foreskin, alterations to the male member have been justified, admired, or critiqued on any number of grounds. Those who value circumcision have promoted it as a sign of difference, a preparatory fertility rite, a beautification technique, or a cure for any number of real or imagined medical and social ills, often turning to the Bible to explain their perspectives. Those who reject it have appealed to nature, theology, biology, fear, and racism to defend their views, arguing that the Bible is outmoded, obsolete, or irrelevant. As both a metaphor and a practice, circumcisions are therefore capable of symbolizing multiple cultural and religious values. Socially and culturally entrenched, religiously significant, contested and yet enduring, circumcision has interested biblical interpreters at least since the priestly writers added their own perspective to Genesis. These same writers also turned their attention to other bodily products, especially vaginal blood and semen. Circumcision may signify a man's exclusive devotion to Yhwh, but man's treatment of blood and semen demonstrates his respect for God. And here Israelite women can also play a role. Though biblical commandments are largely directed

at men and circumcision applies exclusively to them, both Israelite men
and women were held responsible for handling genital emissions appropriately. Yet attitudes toward menstruation and semen changed as well,
once again showing that the body never carries a constant and divinely
given meaning.

Approaching Yhwh's Sanctuary

In addition to commandments involving sexual activities, the book of
Leviticus offers a series of instructions regarding the proper approach to
genital discharges. If a man has a seminal emission, Leviticus instructs,
he must take a bath and be regarded as unclean until the evening, washing any cloth or skin that has come in contact with the semen (see 15:1–
17). If he has another kind of discharge from his member, his degree of
uncleanliness is more severe. Every bed or seat upon which he has rested
is unclean and anyone who touches items he has touched must wash both
body and clothing, remaining impure until the evening. Once his discharge has ended, he must wait seven days before he may be treated as
clean again, after he takes a bath and washes his clothes. On the eighth
day, cleaned of his discharge, he is to offer a sacrifice to God, visiting the
Lord's sanctuary and giving the sacrifices to the priest.

A similar set of principles is applied to vaginal discharges. If a woman
has had sexual intercourse with a man, she must take a bath and be regarded as unclean until the evening (see vv. 18–30). During her time
of menstruation, which Leviticus considers to last for seven days, she is
impure, as is her bed, the places where she sits, and the clothes she wears.
Anyone who has contact with her during this time is also impure and
must take a bath, waiting until the following evening before approaching God's sanctuary. Though sexual intercourse with a menstruating
woman is explicitly forbidden a few chapters later, here Leviticus rules
that any man who lies with a menstruant will be unclean for seven days,
the duration of her period. If the woman has a vaginal discharge at a time
other than her monthly period, she, like a man with an unusual seminal

discharge, is to be regarded as unclean, as are the clothes she touches and the bed on which she sleeps. According to Leviticus, all this careful washing is necessary to protect God's house: "Thus you shall keep the people of Israel separate from their uncleanness, so that they do not die in their uncleanness by defiling my tabernacle that is in their midst" (v. 31).

By protecting God's tabernacle from bodily discharges, the writers of Leviticus seek to make God's space separate, holy, and distinct—the place where one offers sacrifice to God is not the same as a home or a roadside or a field, where regular contact with semen and vaginal blood are to be expected. The fluids and substances that render one unclean in Leviticus are commonly encountered in everyday human life, be they genital discharges, the residues of various skin diseases, human corpses, or animal carcasses. The problem with these substances, if there is a problem, is that they are unwelcome at God's house, not that they are unwelcome in any number of other settings. As Jonathan Klawans has pointed out, "ritual impurity," the type addressed in Leviticus 15, is conveyed by materials that are entirely natural; therefore contact with them is not sinful and the contagion they convey is only temporary.[70] The point of these laws is to set God's sanctuary, and the procedures that take place within it, apart from the spaces and moments of everyday living. Unavoidable fluids like menstrual blood and semen are particularly suited to making such a point, since it is virtually impossible to avoid coming into contact with them, either directly or via contact with someone else who has recently touched them. They are also convenient opposites to the animal blood poured out during sacrifice, another important concern of Leviticus.[71]

Prior to the instructions regarding ritual purity, Leviticus describes the various sacrifices that are to be offered to Yhwh, indicating which objects should be offered on which occasions, the methods to be employed when making these offerings, and the function of various kinds of sacrifices (see Lev. 1–7). To Leviticus, sacrifice and sexual discharges are to be regarded as opposite to each other, though the biblical writers themselves do not present the reason for this contrast. Why, among all the possibly defiling human products, are genital emissions singled out for special concern, especially since the priestly writers encourage reproduction in other contexts? Klawans has offered one persuasive hypothesis: Unlike menstruation and ejaculation, which are uncontrolled and uncontrollable processes leading to bloodletting and fluid release, the sacrifice of animals in God's sanctuary is controlled, regulated, and carefully administered, in part by the priestly handbook Leviticus. As such, Israel's priests imitated God's own behavior: "God, too, selects, kills, looks inside things, and appears on earth as a consuming fire."[72] By contrast, semen and menstruation are uniquely human products associated with a uniquely human activity: sex. Sex is therefore the very opposite of sacrifice, and, as such, its products are not welcome in God's home, though they are very much welcome in the places where human persons dwell.

Klawans's theory can be complemented by the observations of anthropologist Nancy Jay, who famously observed that, when it comes to the performance of blood sacrifice, women and their sexual products are rarely welcome. Semen is defiling and menstrual blood is defiling, and so, she points out, is the blood spilled during childbirth. As Leviticus instructs, a woman who bears a male child is ritually unclean until her son's circumcision on the eighth day, a period of time identical to that of her menstrual discharge. She is not to enter God's sanctuary for thirty-three days, after which she should return, making a sacrifice of a lamb and a small bird. If she bears a female child, she is ritually impure for two weeks and is not to enter the sanctuary for sixty-six days (see 12:1–8). The initial period of impurity appears to be governed by the same principle as the provisions regarding menstruation—she is impure because she has had a vaginal discharge. The second period of impurity, after which she is instructed to offer a sacrifice, appears to be a direct consequence of her childbearing activity. But why would childbearing pollute? After all, Israelite men and women were commanded by God to bear children and, as we observed earlier in this chapter, children were understood to be great blessings, the only available guarantors of immortality. Why would Israel's God object to the presence of new mothers in his house? According to Jay, the answer is obvious: because ensuring that inheritance would pass through the male line was one of the central functions of Israel's cult.

Born from a Woman

Before the advent of DNA testing, establishing paternity was not an easy task. Hence, if inheritance was to pass from father to son, various mechanisms were required to guarantee that women's reproductive capacities could be safely controlled. We have already encountered some of these regulatory mechanisms, including procedures designed to ensure that a woman be a virgin at marriage and laws intended to discourage adultery. Even these procedures were not sufficient to determine which father-son relationships would be regarded as legitimate for the purposes of inheritance, however, as the story of Ishmael indicates. Though Ishmael was circumcised and, as Yhwh promised, he, too, became the father of nations, only Isaac was to be regarded as Israel's true ancestor, as was established when Abraham nearly sacrificed him at Yhwh's request. "Because you have done this, and have not withheld your son, your only son," Yhwh declared, "I will indeed bless you, and I will make your offspring as numerous as the stars" (Gen. 22:16–17). Sacrificing publicly establishes paternity—men who sacrifice together stay together. As Jay explains:

> The only action that is as serious as giving birth, which can act as a counterbalance to it, is killing. . . . [And] unlike childbirth, sacrificial killing is deliberate, purposeful, "rational" action, under perfect control.[73]

Offered by male priests, attended by fathers and sons, and unavailable to women who have recently undergone childbirth, sacrifice incorporates women's children into a male-centered kin group dominated by men who "own" women and their offspring. In such a setting, menstruation and the products of childbearing can have no place. So, unlike semen, which pollutes only for one day, menstruation pollutes for a week and is contagious as well—anyone who touches a menstruant is also polluted. Sacrifice, Jay suggests, is the "remedy for having been born a woman."[74]

Jay's approach to sacrifice receives further support when Leviticus's instructions regarding childbirth are compared to instructions regarding circumcision. After bearing a male child, the mother is impure for seven days; the impurity is lifted on the eighth day when "the flesh of [the baby boy's] foreskin" is circumcised. With no circumcision ritual available to end it, the duration of her impurity is twice as long if she bears a female child. As Shaye Cohen observes, the wording of these instructions is quite similar to instructions regarding the breeding and sacrifice of Israel's livestock: "When an ox or a sheep or a goat is born, it shall remain seven days with its mother, and from the eighth day on it shall be acceptable as the LORD's offering by fire" (Lev. 22:27). In other words, just as a baby boy is circumcised on the eighth day, so, too, a baby animal may be sacrificed on that day, offered to Yhwh. Cohen concludes, "Circumcision is analogous to, and a surrogate for, sacrifice."[75] Since circumcision is available only to men and sacrifice is a ritual properly performed by men, mothers and daughters are written out of full participation in ancient Israelite religion, while men are given a privileged place as keepers of the covenant and its obligations.

Still, the exclusion of women from the Israelite sacrificial system is not as absolute as Jay's analysis suggests. As Charlotte Elisheva Fonrobert has pointed out, the priestly writers of Leviticus posit a basic symmetry between men, women, and their discharges, addressing seminal emissions and vaginal blood in parallel ways, even if women bear their disabilities for a greater length of time.[76] Structurally, Leviticus addresses men with unusual seminal discharges, men with regular seminal emissions, women with irregular vaginal discharges, and, finally, women with regular menstrual periods, in that order, legislating the proper approach to each condition. The bodily products of men and women are treated as equivalent. Moreover, "men's bodily fluids transfer a status of impurity to anyone, including the woman who has sexual relations with him (Lev. 15:7), just as women's bodily fluids transfer a status of impurity to anyone, including the man who has sexual relations with her."[77] As such, men, women, and their fluids are equally polluting and equally susceptible to purification. After taking a bath, both men and women are welcome at God's tabernacle. Indeed, Leviticus commands them to go, instructing those with irregular discharges to offer sacrifice to Yhwh once their impurity has come to an end. Interestingly, the Gospels suggest that Jesus shared these assumptions. On the few occasions when Jesus addresses ritual impurity and vaginal bleeding, he, too, assumes that persons with bodily discharges should avoid the temple.

Jesus and the Bleeding Woman

Early in the Gospel of Mark, Jesus encounters two women, one young, one old, and both endangered by illness. The first, a young girl of twelve, is the daughter of a local synagogue leader. Urgently seeking Jesus out, her father, Jairus, asks that the Savior visit his home to heal his beloved daughter. On the way, however, Jesus encounters another woman, significantly older and very sick. She had been bleeding for twelve years, spending all her resources on physicians who failed to cure her. Creeping up behind Jesus, she touches his cloak and is instantly healed. Sensing that his power has been tapped, Jesus then turns around and demands, "Who touched my clothes?" (Mark 5:30). Falling down before him, the woman confesses her bold action, to which Jesus responds, "Daughter, your faith has made you well; go in peace, and be healed of your disease" (v. 34). In the meantime, however, Jairus's daughter has died. Arriving at the house, Jesus interrupts the mourning outside, claiming that the girl is "not dead, but sleeping" (v. 39). Taking three of his disciples and the child's parents into the house with him, he raises her from the dead.

The author of Mark clearly intends these stories to be read together. He inserts the story of the bleeding woman within the story of the raising of Jairus's daughter, a literary technique designed to clue in the reader that one story ought to be interpreted in light of the other. He also draws several direct parallels between the two women: the woman has been bleeding for twelve years and the daughter is twelve years old; both the woman and the girl are miraculously healed by the touch of Jesus as the result of faith; neither woman speaks, at least in the context of the narrative, though offstage the bleeding woman "told him the whole truth"

(v. 33); finally, Jesus calls the woman "daughter," proclaiming, "Daughter, your faith has made you well," just as the little girl is identified as the daughter of Jairus, leader of the local synagogue. As such, a comparison is drawn between a girl at the age when her menstruation was about to begin and a woman who has been bleeding too much, likely from her womb. One woman is troubled nearly to the point of death by an inappropriately open womb, the other by one that is tragically closed, just before it was ripe for opening since, according to both Roman law and later rabbinic teaching, twelve was precisely the age when a girl became eligible for marriage.[78]

Touching Jesus

With bleeding so central to this set of stories, many interpreters have suggested that, through them, Mark intends to overturn Levitical impurity laws.[79] Both women are ritually impure and contagious, these scholars argue, the woman because she has an irregular vaginal discharge and the girl because she is dead. Physical contact with either of them would render Jesus unclean for at least twenty-four hours. Moreover, by the time Mark was written, menstruation had become synonymous with defiling impurity in general. The notion that the Savior would be touched by a bleeding woman would have been perceived as offensive, even disgusting. The author of Ezra, for example, equated marriage with foreign women to intercourse with the "menstruous" people of the land, and the author of the Greek version of the biblical book of Esther compares Esther's Persian crown to a "menstruous rag."[80] An affirmation of the woman's and the girl's status as "daughter," irrespective of their bodily fluids and state of impurity, may well have been the point of Jesus's actions.

Still, a closer reading of Mark leads to the opposite conclusion. Jesus does not overturn purity laws, here or anywhere else in the Gospel's narrative. The issue is Jesus's power as a miraculous healer, not his violation of purity laws. First, the disciples want to know how Jesus could possibly recognize that someone has touched him given the size of the crowd

that was pressing in on him, any number of whom could have been ritually impure. Second, the mourners at Jairus's house laugh when Jesus
claims that the girl is sleeping rather than dead. They are not concerned
about purity but about the loss of a treasured child. Also, the disciples do
not worry that Jesus was touched—their concern was that he had been
touched by so many people he could not possibly identify any one individual in particular as having touched him. Similarly, those who laughed
did not question whether or not Jesus ought to touch the girl—they challenged the notion that he could help at all, given that she was dead. Jesus's
capacity to heal and perceive the true thoughts and intentions of others,
not his state of ritual purity, was at stake in these stories. Moreover, as
those familiar with Leviticus 15 would quickly realize, purity was simply
not a concern in this setting. These stories are set in Galilee, not in Judea,
so any ritual impurity that Jesus would have contracted by touching the
woman, the girl, or anyone in the crowd could easily have been removed
simply by taking an evening bath. Ritual impurity would have been a
problem only if Jesus had planned to visit the temple in Jerusalem later
that same day. Additionally, in the one instance in Mark when Jesus
could have overturned ritual impurity, he did not.[81]

At the beginning of the Gospel of Mark, Jesus encounters a leper who
begs to be healed. "Moved with pity," Mark reports, "Jesus stretched out
his hand and touched him" (1:41). Diseased skin, like genital discharges,
also rendered a body ritually impure and therefore ineligible for atten-
dance at God's sanctuary. Leviticus explains, "When a person has on the
skin of his body a swelling or an eruption or a spot, and it turns into a
leprous disease on the skin of his body, he shall be brought to Aaron
the priest or to one of his sons the priests" (13:2). The priests were to
examine the skin disease, determine its level of severity and contagion,
and exclude the person from worship for a period of seven days. If the
disease was chronic, the person was to be excluded until it abated. Once
healed, however, the formerly diseased person is to engage in a series of
ritual baths and offer sacrifices to God. With these instructions in mind,
Jesus commands the man to "show yourself to the priest, and offer for
your cleansing what Moses commanded, as a testimony to them" (Mark

1:44). In other words, Jesus affirms both the Levitical purity laws and
Levitical provisions regarding sacrifice. He does not hesitate to touch the
leper—after all, he could simply take a bath later—and, like the priestly
writers before him, he appears to regard ritual purity as an Israelite duty.
Jesus makes no specific ruling regarding genital discharges and skin diseases but, when encountering them, he appears to behave precisely in the
manner recommended in Leviticus.

Purity After the Temple

In 70 CE, the Roman general Titus burned the second temple to the
ground, putting an end to Israel's sacrificial cult. Still, Christians and
Jews continued to assume that one should maintain a state of purity when
approaching the divine—synagogues regularly included sources of water
for cleansing,[82] and, among Christians, the washing of baptism served as
the central initiatory rite.[83] Instructions regarding purification in the Didache, for example, an early-second-century Christian text of uncertain
provenance, insist that no one is to be invited to share in the community
meal unless they are washed in the waters of baptism: "Let no one eat or
drink from the Eucharistic meal unless they have first been baptized in
the name of the Lord."[84] The *Didascalia Apostolorum* (Teachings of the
Apostles), a third-century church order from Syria, juxtaposes the washing of baptism with the washing required of a woman after her period,
arguing that only baptism is required:

> *O woman, (if) in the seven days of your flux you regard yourself impure
> according to the second legislation—after seven days, therefore, how
> can you be purified without baptism? [If you bathe] you shall abrogate
> the perfect baptism of God which completely forgave your sins.*[85]

In other words, some Christian women were observing Leviticus
15, interpreting the passage in such a way that they refused to attend
church while menstruating and then bathing on the eighth day, before

reentering the community. The author of the *Didascalia* objected, insisting instead that these women should not observe the provisions of the "second legislation," the laws given to Moses after the incident involving the golden calf, which did not include menstrual isolation, but only those of the first legislation, that is, the original Ten Commandments. The only necessary washing, he argued, was the onetime washing of baptism.[86] The women, however, disagreed. And, as their disagreement suggests, Levitical purity laws remained a point of contention among Jews and Christians both, long after the destruction of the temple. Semen and menses remained a problem, but in the new circumstances of the second and third centuries, the implications of bodily pollution were far from clear.

Even before the elimination of the temple cult, some Jewish groups had extended the purity required of those preparing to visit God's sanctuary into other areas of life.[87] The Jews who wrote the Dead Sea Scrolls, for example, bathed regularly and often, though the precise meaning of their bathing continues to be debated.[88] According to the Gospels, John the Baptist also saw bathing as a fundamental symbol, in this case of repentance; he met his followers at the Jordan River and washed them in the running waters.[89] Some of these practices persisted once the temple was lost, including initiatory baptism among the Christians and, in Jewish synagogues, the requirement that a man who had recently ejaculated avoid recitation of certain benedictions.[90] The Tosefta, a late-antique Palestinian text, applies this principle to Torah study:

> *Men and women with irregular genital emissions, women who menstruate and parturients [women who had just given birth] . . . are permitted to read in the Torah, and to study Mishnah, midrash, religious law and aggadah [other sacred Jewish texts], but men who had a regular ejaculation are prohibited to do so.*[91]

As such, the Tosefta and the *Didascalia* agree about menstruation but disagree about semen—the *Didascalia* concludes that seminal emissions, like menstruation, require neither isolation nor washing,[92] but the

Tosefta welcomes menstruants and others with genital discharges, excluding only those who had recently ejaculated.

It is unlikely that the rabbis who compiled the Tosefta and the Christians who composed the *Didascalia* were aware of one another's writings. Still, their shared concern for the impact of genital discharges on the worship life of their communities indicates the continuing importance of Levitical purity requirements. For Jews, Torah study and prayer replaced the sacrifices on the altar. For Christians the sharing of the Eucharist became the central sacrificial rite. Both groups, however, retained the sense that their activities should involve cleanliness before God. So, for example, unaware of the advice of the *Didascalia,* the third-century Egyptian bishop Dionysius of Alexandria taught that menstruants should not attend church—obviously they should not "approach the holy table or touch the body and blood of Christ"—and advised men with recent seminal emissions to examine their consciences before taking the Eucharist.[93] The third-century *Apostolic Tradition,* an obscure text attributed to Hippolytus, bishop of Rome, also excludes menstruants, in this case from the rite of baptism: "But if a woman is in her time of menstruation, let her be set aside and receive baptism on another day."[94] Moreover, though the Jewish Sages ruled that the Torah was not subject to impurity, they nevertheless advised those exposed to semen to immerse before reading from it.[95] In other words, the holiness of the sanctuary needed to be preserved, whether the sanctuary was the site of the Eucharist, the baptismal pool, or the local synagogue liturgy.

The Pollution of Menstrual Blood

The application of Levitical purity regulations to the church and the synagogue was complemented by an even more pressing concern for personal purity, particularly when it came to the polluting power of menses. Among late-antique and early-medieval rabbis, the disabilities of the *niddah* (the menstruant) were transferred from an orientation toward the temple to family life, from Leviticus 15 and its instructions regarding the purity of God's sanctuary, to Leviticus 17 and the importance of avoiding sexual intercourse with a menstruant. The Levitical concern for preserving the purity of God's sanctuary was combined with advice regarding legitimate sexual relations and in such a way that the menstruant herself became a source of intimate contagion. Among early Christians, vaginal blood could symbolize the filth and fleshly degradation characteristic of women, a problem so acute that the *Proto-Gospel of James,* a popular account of the birth and childhood of Mary, sought to protect the Virgin from the potential stains of her own body. With men serving as the presumed leaders of both of these communities, attention to menstruation enforced the notion that men, and men alone, are the best managers of bodies and bodily products. Still, women were expected to guard their male family members from the dangerous pollutions flowing from their bodies, just as recent ejaculants were enjoined to protect God's sanctuary from the impurity of their semen.

Permitted to attend synagogue prayer and read from the Torah, menstruants were no longer barred from community worship, at least not initially. They were, however, instructed to take care when guarding their husbands and families from their contagious impurities. The *niddah,* the rabbis determined, might touch the objects in her own home, going about her usual chores in the usual way, but more intimate gestures like washing her husband's hands or feet were to be avoided, for they might lead to sexual temptation.[96] According to the Babylonian Talmud, however, a collection of rabbinic teachings compiled in Persia during the fifth and seventh centuries CE, an increasingly strict standard of observance was imposed:[97]

> *R. Zera said: The daughters of Israel have accepted this severity upon themselves, that even if they see but one drop of blood the size of a mustard seed, they regard themselves as impure, and count seven clean days.*[98]

The "seven clean days," also known as the "white days," extended the period of time in which a husband and wife may not engage in sexual relations to up to two weeks.[99] Eventually, this same requirement was applied to synagogue worship as well, effectively excluding women from the synagogue service for two weeks of every month.[100] As one Palestinian rabbi explained: "What is the fence which the Torah made about its words? Lo, it says 'Do not come near a woman during her period of uncleanness to uncover her nakedness.'"[101] Thus, maintaining purity within the home—and, by the sixth century, outside of the home as well—became a shared responsibility of men and women alike, though women alone bore the disability of their monthly bleeding.

Given the importance of establishing when, exactly, sexual intercourse was permitted, the rabbis also discussed such topics as the colors of vaginal blood, the significance of these colors for purity (not all colors indicated menses), and the location from which the blood flow originated, all of which could determine when intimacy could be initiated. Displaying remarkable expertise in the observation of women's discharges, the Mishnah Niddah, for example, decreed that blood the colors of red, black, saffron, muddy water, and diluted wine were to be regarded as impure, though there was less certainty regarding the color yellow.[102] Given the inherent danger of menstrual blood, such concerns were in order. Those who violated *niddah* provisions, the Sages warned, could find themselves facing disease, mishap, or even death. For example, a wife who failed to guard her husband from exposure might cause him to develop boils, and she herself risked divine punishment for her lapse in the form of death during childbirth.[103]

Mary's Period

Early Christian writings may not have contemplated the colors of vaginal blood, but they were concerned with the significance of menstrual defilement, particularly when considering the purity of Jesus's mother, Mary. The late-second-century *Proto-Gospel of James,* for example, organizes Mary's childhood in such a way that she is untouched by menstruation.[104] Attributed to James, brother of the Lord, and a "protogospel" in the sense that it tells the story of Mary and Jesus before Jesus reaches adulthood, this book recounts the births and childhoods of both Mary and Jesus. Pregnant before the onset of menses, breastfed by her mother only after her first eighty days of life, and untouched by the delivery of the infant Jesus, Mary was protected from the taint of uterine fluids through-out her entire life. Equally interested in Mary's discharges, the North African Christian Tertullian makes the opposite argument: the excep-tional filth of childbirth, a filth that plagues both Mary and all women, is taken as an exceptionally convincing proof of the mercy of a God who would not shrink even from the dirt of a woman's womb. In both cases, however, vaginal discharges are regarded as revolting.

Composed, at least in part, as an answer to accusations of fornication and adultery lodged against Mary, the *Proto-Gospel of James* sought to protect Mary at every turn, including from the possibility that she could have been polluted by her own body.[105] Apparently, by the late second cen-tury, such a defense was needed. According to at least one second-century anti-Christian polemicist, Mary was a convicted adulteress, driven out by her husband when she conceived a child by a soldier named Panthera.[106] Similar charges—or fears about them—may have already informed the earlier infancy narratives of Matthew and Luke, both of which explicitly defend Mary's virginity,[107] but the *Proto-Gospel* goes further. Not only was Mary engaged to Joseph, but she was also raised as a pure virgin in the temple and betrothed only after Joseph was selected as her part-ner by a divinely inspired sign.[108] When she was found to be pregnant, the priests were shocked, quite naturally concluding that she and Joseph had engaged in premarital sexual intercourse. Vehemently declaring in-nocence, the holy couple submitted to an ordeal designed to uncover any possible fornication, drinking a concoction that would reveal their trans-gression if guilty or, conversely, demonstrate their purity.[109] When they passed this test, the priest declared, "If the Lord God has not revealed your sins, neither do I condemn you." Following the birth of Jesus, the *Proto-Gospel* adds another miraculous detail: not only was Mary a pure virgin when she became pregnant, but she remained virginal even after Jesus was born. Thus, when the local Hebrew midwife, Salome, dared to doubt that Mary's hymen could be intact, she was dramatically and miraculously rebuked. Inserting her finger to test the holy mother's condition, her hand shriveled and she realized her terrible mistake.

As Jennifer Glancy has shown, these details work to guard Mary from contact with uterine and vaginal blood, both her own and that of her mother. Mary's purity was so complete, the *Proto-Gospel* suggests, that the problems identified by Leviticus 15 never troubled her at all. First, she was protected from the impure bleeding of her mother. Careful not to nurse her precious daughter for eighty days—that is, for the fourteen days of her initial purification and then the additional sixty-six days before she was permitted to visit God's sanctuary—Anna also guarded her daughter from defilement. Since ancient medical writers believed that milk was reprocessed uterine blood, the eighty days of her purification kept the tiny virgin from inadvertently drinking her mother's tainted postpartum blood.[110] Once the eighty days were over, however, Anna took Mary to her breast, nursing her until she was old enough to be dedicated to the temple. When she turned twelve, the problem of vaginal discharges was once again at hand. Knowing she was ripe for the onset of menses, the priests had no choice but to exclude Mary from her temple home, sending her to live with Joseph. Dwelling under Joseph's care, Mary miraculously conceives Jesus, without any involvement from Joseph and probably before her bleeding had begun. Miraculously, even after giving birth to Jesus, her purity remains complete, as is evidenced by her decision to place the infant at her breast. Unlike her mother, Anna, Mary nursed Jesus immediately, probably because the polluting fluids associated with childbirth never tainted her womb. "The birth of Jesus does not pollute her," Glancy concludes, a hunch that is confirmed when Salome discovers that her hymen has yet to be torn.[111]

To the writer of the *Proto-Gospel,* Mary's purity necessarily protects Jesus's own divine status. By contrast, Tertullian viewed Mary's pollution as the ultimate proof of divine compassion, expressed in the Savior's willingness to be born of a woman. Those who would dare to claim that Jesus never put on flesh, never entered the "sewer" of a woman's womb, he argues, are seriously mistaken. Both Christ's fleshly birth and his fleshly death are required, "that by His own nativity He might regenerate our birth, and might further by His death also dissolve our death."[112] And so, by calling into question the reality of his birth, his emergence from "the impure and shameful tortures of parturition" and "the filthy, troublesome, contemptible issues of the puerperal labour itself," these heretics overturn their own salvation.[113] Interpreting menstruation and childbirth as distressingly dirty, polluting activities, Tertullian and the *Proto-Gospel of James* turn to Mary and her fluids either to defend Jesus's exceptional perfection or to emphasize the exceptional degradation he willingly endured simply by being born at all.

The *Proto-Gospel of James* may be unique in its desire to protect the virgin Mary from any taint of menstrual pollution, and Tertullian's description of Mary's filthy womb may be otherwise unknown in Christian writings, but later Christians also found vaginal discharges to be a worthy theological and practical topic. For example, writing to Pope Gregory the Great in the late sixth century (597 CE), Augustine of Canterbury wanted to know how long a woman needed to wait between childbirth and returning to church. He was also concerned to identify whether a woman's menstrual period should exclude her from communion, a practice with which he appeared to be familiar. Gregory answered the first question by citing Leviticus 15: "she is to abstain for a male child thirty-three days and sixty-six days for a female."[114] In other words, she should be excluded from worship, though it is not a sin if she attends. Then, alluding to Leviticus 17, Gregory reminded Augustine that a wife is not permitted to approach her husband during her menstrual period, though she may attend worship, a principle Gregory affirmed by citing the gospel story of the bleeding woman. When it comes to receiving the Eucharist, however, a pious woman will abstain: "She must not therefore be forbidden to receive the mystery of the holy communion during those days [of her flow]. But if anyone out of profound respect does not presume to do it, she is to be commended."[115] Gregory may have regarded menstruation as natural rather than as a result of sin, but he still found it defiling. A scrupulously pious Christian woman, he concluded, will not allow the holy, sacrificial meal to enter her polluted body.

Circumcision, Semen, and the
Products of a Woman's Womb

As this survey of biblical, Jewish and Christian, attitudes toward bodily fluids and parts has shown, human flesh and its products have captured the imaginations of biblical writers and interpreters for millennia. Whether pursuing immortality through the production of offspring or longing for resurrection bodies, Israelites, Judeans, Jews, and Christians have quite literally inscribed their theological and social convictions on their flesh. A penis without a foreskin could therefore signify Canaanite identity, fidelity to the covenant of Abraham, loyalty to the Hasmonean dynasty, superior personal hygiene, a serious commitment to sexual self-control, and/or a sincere desire to approach God's presence. By contrast, a penis with a foreskin could demonstrate that Gentiles are made holy by faith, that spirit, not flesh, is what matters to God, and/or that Judaism was totally superseded by Christianity and Christ's sacrificial foreskin.

Care in the handling of genital discharges could also support a range of possible meanings. Barring menses and semen from God's sacred precincts could enforce patrilineal descent, rationalize the importance of sacrifice, and/or display a healthy, pious respect for the purity God expects from his people. Exposure to semen or menses could be treated as a matter of indifference, a topic of great practical and theological concern, and/or a symbol of God's willingness to endure the worst of what flesh has to offer. Clearly, interpreters of foreskins and bodily fluids have been attempting to flesh out what it means to be both human and faithful to God for quite some time, with no definitive conclusion in sight.

Such a stunning diversity of approaches to circumcision, semen, and menses, perhaps more than any other topic covered in this book, contradicts the notion that God's Word speaks with one voice about anything, especially the human body, genitalia, and sex. Biblical teachings regarding bodies and their fluids invite the frank admission that biblical principles cannot be—and have not been—applied to contemporary life in anything like a straightforward way. The tremendous gap between a world where bodies can be imagined to rise again, in the flesh, and a world where resurrections, if they can occur at all, must be scientifically manufactured, is almost too great to span. And yet, as ever developing responses to circumcision, semen, and menstruation also demonstrate, the capacity to imagine God's involvement in the mundane, everyday experience of being human has never waned. Biblical writers wanted to know what their bodies meant to God. Biblical interpreters have been equally interested in this topic, investing sacred texts with meanings that can hardly have been envisioned by their predecessors.

Conclusion

So I Hear You Have Five Husbands . . .

In the fourth chapter of the Gospel of John, the writer tells a story about an encounter between Jesus and a woman that sets the stage for the rest of the book. Passing through Samaria, a region of Judea-Palestine just to the north of Judea proper, a tired and thirsty Jesus stops by a well identified as the very same well where, centuries earlier, the biblical patriarch Jacob once drew water for his flocks.[1] " 'Give me a drink' " (v. 7), Jesus orders a local woman when she arrives. Acknowledging the sometimes rocky relationship between Judeans and Samaritans, she responds, "How is it that you, a Jew, ask a drink of me, a woman of Samaria?" (v. 9). Jesus then launches into a comparison of the kind of water he offers—living water that quenches thirst forever—and the water she was about to draw, which can quench thirst only temporarily. "Sir, give me this water," she requests, "so that I may never be thirsty or have to keep coming here to draw water" (v. 15). Instead of answering directly, he tells her to go get her husband. She responds, "I have no husband," an assessment Jesus confirms. She has actually had five husbands, he points out, "and the one you have now is not your husband" (vv. 17–18). Astonished at his ability to describe her life to her, she calls him a prophet, accepting his declaration that he is the Messiah and then sharing her newfound knowledge with the people of her town.

Though the Gospel offers no judgment regarding her marital status or her many husbands, later interpreters have been fascinated by this detail. How could Jesus have spoken with such a promiscuous woman? Could Jesus love a woman such as this? Taking the story literally, the early-third-century North African Christian Tertullian expressed shock at her behavior, labeling the woman both an adulteress and a prostitute. Only the Lord would grant forgiveness to such a disreputable sinner, Tertullian argued, and Christians in his own day should not expect to be treated so leniently.[2] John Chrysostom, the fourth-century bishop of Antioch, also regarded her as an outrageous sinner. If such a terrible sinner could accept Jesus's correction without resentment, he pointed out, inquiring further into the Lord's teachings, then what excuse do other Christians have for their easy ignorance? "Let us, then, be ashamed," Chrysostom declared, "and let us now blush . . . neither the time of day, nor her interest in anything else, nor any other thing diverted her from her quest for knowledge."[3] According to these interpretations, the woman is exemplary precisely because she was so disreputable. A woman so obviously guilty of sexual sin provides an excellent proof of both the mercy of Christ and the transformative potential of an encounter with him.[4]

Alternatively, perhaps the evangelist intended the story of the woman and her husbands to teach a lesson about something other than sexual sin. Perhaps these characters are to be understood as symbols for something else. After all, John is the most "spiritual" of the Gospels, filled with symbols and mysteries just waiting to be unpacked,[5] and, just before his encounter with the Samaritan woman, John's Jesus tells the Pharisee Nicodemus not to trust literal interpretations of words, but to look beyond fleshly understanding. Readers should therefore focus their attention not on the woman and her sins per se, but on what she and her husbands might stand for. Writing in the early third century, Origen of Alexandria adopted this approach. Regarding the husbands as symbols of the five senses, he concluded that the woman's mistake involved the pursuit first of sensual objects and then of theological error. Yet it was not too late, Origen declared, either then or now. By admitting that she did not have a husband—that is, that she was not interpreting scripture properly—she opened herself to Christ, and in this way she overcame both her senses and her ignorance, becoming a bride of the divine bridegroom. Later Christians can follow her example and regain a truly divine understanding.[6] The great Latin theologian Augustine of Hippo adopted a similar point of view.[7] Thanks to her encounter with the divine Word, Augustine claimed, the Samaritan woman was led away from sensual delight and ignorance and toward her one true husband, Christ.[8]

Less enamored with metaphorical depictions of God and his "wife," whether "she" is Israel, the Church, or believers in general, more recent interpreters have regarded the woman and her husbands as symbols of the people of Samaria, not as metaphors for Christian heresy. Among contemporary biblical scholars, the motif of the five husbands is commonly understood to represent the illegitimate worship of the Samaritan people, an interpretation supported on the basis of Israel's history. When the northern kingdom of Israel was lost in 722 BCE, immigrants from five other cities were brought in to occupy the land, carrying their foreign gods with them (see 2 Kgs. 17:24–41). As a result, the northern kingdom of Israel was no longer regarded as properly Israelite by the writers of 2 Kings, a sentiment promoted even more vigorously once the exiles from Judah returned from Babylon in the sixth century BCE. Loyal to a god they worshipped on Mount Gerizim, instead of in Jerusalem, the Samaritans understood the first five books of the Hebrew Bible to be sacred, but ignored the rest. The woman's "husbands," then, stand for the idolatrous worship of the Samaritans, who were not viewed as fully "Jewish" by their neighbors. Her sixth lover—a man who, Jesus states, is not even her husband—represents Samaritan impiety during Jesus's own day. The Gospel's invitation to the woman is therefore an invitation to the Samaritans as a whole to put aside their idolatrous worship and join in the worship of Yhwh's Messiah, an invitation they are depicted as eagerly accepting.[9] Alternatively, perhaps this story is designed to teach a lesson to Christian men about how women should be treated. When the disciples come upon Jesus and the woman speaking with one another, they are "astonished," though they keep their opinion to themselves. Sensing their discomfort, Jesus calls their attention to the surrounding fields, observing that they lay ripe for the harvest. He concludes, "I sent you to reap that for which you did not labor," a reference to the welcome reception he received among the Samaritans who were convinced by the labors of this woman. The woman, not the disciples, was the conduit of the Gospel to the Samaritans. As such, scholar Sandra Schneiders points out, Jesus's discourse confirms the worst fear of men who refuse to take women seriously: "that they are neither the originators nor the controllers of the Church's mission."[10] The scene therefore undermines the notion that men, not women, are the only appropriate conduits of the Gospel while also affirming the role of women as evangelists and teachers in the church.

Yet, which of these interpretations is correct? With so many different ways of reading this story, it can be difficult to determine what the evangelist might have meant. Does this story demonstrate the mercy of a God who would enter into conversation with a sexual sinner, so long as she changes her ways? Or does it emphasize the importance of turning aside from objects that satisfy the five senses? Or perhaps it exemplifies the universal message of the Christian faith, directed at the Samaritans as well as at the Jews and taught by women as well as men. Is the woman herself a miserable sinner, the first Samaritan evangelist, a symbol of the Church, an ideal heretic, or the perfect convert? Are her husbands jilted lovers, stand-ins for idolatry, or metaphors pointing to the problem of theological error? Was the Samaritan at the well a real historical woman with actual husbands who really did encounter Jesus, or was she merely an invention of the evangelist, an ideal type whose historical existence is beside the point? The story of the Samaritan woman, like so many of the stories encountered in this book, proves once again that the meaning of the Bible cannot easily be controlled. This story has no single meaning. Therefore, the issue for readers of the Gospel is not whether a particular interpretation is valid but whether it is valuable, and why.

Sex, Desire, and Biblical Interpretation

As a New Testament scholar and pastor, I am sometimes asked to lead Bible studies at local churches, including my own. Studies of Paul and women or of the Bible and sexuality are especially popular topics these days, though I have also taught courses on, for example, biblical perspectives on war and violence or the circumstances surrounding the production of particular New Testament books. Whatever I am teaching, however, I usually begin by asking participants what they wish the Bible said about the topic at hand. Do we wish that the Bible would reject war as a political strategy? Or perhaps we believe that the Bible should support defensive if not offensive wars. Do we wish that the Bible would confirm gay marriage, instead of rejecting it as so many Christians insist? Or perhaps our concern has to do with the role of women. Perhaps we wish that Paul had not told women to be silent and learn from their husbands at home, especially since talkative and independent women can be found throughout the Bible just as often as silent, obedient women. Whatever we wish for, I point out, probably can be found somewhere in the Bible, which is why it is so important to admit that we have wishes, whatever they may be. We are not passive recipients of what the Bible says, but active interpreters who make decisions about what we will believe and what we will affirm. Admitting that we have wishes, and that our wishes matter, is therefore the first step to developing an honest and faithful interpretation.

Once upon a time, the followers of Jesus knew that they were interpreting the Bible, not simply extracting truth from a set of divinely inspired texts. The apostle Paul, for example, openly admitted that he offered creative interpretations of earlier biblical passages. Discussing the story of Abraham, Sarah, and Hagar, he observed: "It is written that Abraham had two sons, one by a slave woman and the other by a free woman." From this passage he draws an allegory: "These women are two covenants. One woman, in fact, is Hagar, from Mount Sinai, bearing children for slavery. . . . [She] corresponds to the present Jerusalem, for she is in slavery with her children. But the other woman corresponds to the Jerusalem above; she is free, and she is our mother" (Gal. 4:22–26). Putting aside the question of what, precisely, Paul was saying when he brought up this story—this issue continues to be hotly debated among scholars—it is sufficient for our purposes to observe that Paul is offering an allegorical interpretation. The apostle was not interested in the history of what happened during Abraham's lifetime. He did not place the episodes of Hagar and Sarah in their larger biblical contexts. He was not worried about the original Hebrew words of Genesis. Instead, he equated Gentiles who desire to live according to the law with Ishmael, the son of a slave woman, and Gentiles who live according to (his) gospel with Isaac, the son of a free woman, conflating sons with mothers, mountains with cities, and rival theological opinions with both. In this way, Paul employed a common ancient interpretive strategy, arguing that one thing actually means something else entirely and thereby finding in Hagar and Sarah, Ishmael and Isaac another proof of his conviction that Gentiles ought not to adopt Jewish law. For Paul, the two sons of Abraham and their mothers become symbols of what it means to live either "according to the flesh" or "according to the promise," an argument that is only marginally related to the Abraham cycle as found in Genesis.

The author of the Gospel of Matthew provides another obvious example. This evangelist was equally free in his interpretive approach, linking the life and teachings of Jesus to loosely connected biblical prophecies, to important biblical characters, and to scriptural patterns, all while showing little concern for the literal or historical meanings of his sources. His well-crafted infancy narrative is particularly striking in this regard. Employing a Jewish interpretive style familiar to his own time, he reads biblical prophesy as predictive of his current circumstances. Using typology, an interpretive method that presents biblical characters and episodes as types that prefigure persons and events that take place much later, he weaves narrative elements drawn from Exodus into the story of Jesus's birth. Finally, adapting a verse from Isaiah 7 to the circumstances of Jesus's conception, he suggests that Mary's virginity was a fulfillment of prophecy, but does so by depending upon the Greek translation of Isaiah rather than the Hebrew original. As he put it, "All this took place to fulfill what had been spoken by the Lord through the prophet: 'Look, the virgin (Greek: *parthenos*) shall conceive and bear a son" (1:22–23), yet the Hebrew simply reads "young woman" (Hebrew: *almah*). In none of these examples does Matthew work to preserve the original contexts of a biblical episode or saying. Instead, applying prophetic teachings to Jesus's birth or developing typological parallels between Moses and Jesus, he completely transforms the meaning of his scriptural proofs. Paul and Matthew, it would seem, had no qualms about imaginative reappropriation, or about reading their own theological convictions into biblical texts. They let their readers know that they were actively interpreting, not simply repeating, what the Bible already said.

Early Christians were also forthright about their interpretive methods. Irenaeus of Lyons, for example, a mid-second-century bishop, suggests that the faith of the church guaranteed the truth of the scriptures, not the scriptures the church. He explains:

> *The church, as we have said before, though disseminated throughout the whole world, carefully guards this preaching and this faith which she has received, as if she dwelt in one house. She likewise believes these things as if she had but one soul and the one and the same heart; she preaches, teaches and hands them down harmoniously, as if she possessed but one mouth.*[12]

Yet "she" does not depend on the Bible for her message, but on the interpretation of the Bible put forward by the true church. Since the church guarantees the authenticity of the faith, membership in the proper orthodox community is a necessary requirement of anyone who wants to know what God thinks about anything. Reading the Bible alone will not help.

Though eventually declared a heretic himself, Origen of Alexandria promoted a similar perspective. In fact, combating views he regarded as heretical was a principal aim of his *Commentary on John*. When he decided that the story of the Samaritan woman was "about" the necessary discipline of the five senses and the surpassing of error introduced by false doctrine, he did so because he wanted to contradict the interpretations put forward by an earlier theologian with whom he disagreed, a fellow by the name of Heracleon. Envisioning the Samaritan woman as the ideal heretic, converted after a conversation with Jesus, the Word of God, he exhorted his audience to emulate her example by turning away from Heracleon's reading of the gospel. Recognizing that the Gospel of John contains no single meaning and that he was presenting one possible interpretation, Origen presents a range of interpretive possibilities, including Heracleon's, not a definitive answer to either this story or any other gospel passage. As these and other ancient interpreters acknowledged, the truth of the Bible is never obvious, but always in need of further thought and study.

Nowadays, the sense that reading scripture is a creative, imaginative act has too often been lost, despite the creativity it took for New Testament writers and early Christians to claim that the law and the prophets are, when read correctly, all about Jesus Christ. Paul, Matthew, Irenaeus, and Origen came to the Bible with convictions about what should be found in its pages and, employing a variety of interpretive methods, they found what they wanted. But, unlike many contemporary readers, they did not attempt to hide their interpretive work from their audiences. Instead, they sought to persuade their readers that their interpretations were valuable by revealing the principles they brought to bear on the texts they read, whether they were arguing that Gentiles should come to God as Gentiles, that Jesus's birth was miraculous, or that the church is the best arbiter of divine truth. They did not assume that quoting a few choice verses out of context could serve as sufficient proof of what the entire Bible says and therefore of what God says as well.

It is time for us to admit that we, too, are interpreters who hope to find our convictions reflected in biblical texts, and have been all along. Looking to the Bible for straightforward answers about anything, including sex, can lead only to disappointment. When read as a whole, the Bible provides neither clear nor consistent advice about sex and bodies, as the material presented in this book demonstrates. If one set of biblical books interprets polygamy as a sign of God's blessing, another set argues that celibacy is the best option for the faithful. If one biblical writer condemns

those who engage in sex before marriage, others present premarital seduction as central to God's plan. Just about every biblical commandment
is broken, and not only by biblical villains. Biblical heroes like Abraham,
Moses, and David also violate the commandments of Exodus, Deuteronomy, and Leviticus, and Jesus is represented radically reinterpreting
earlier scriptural teachings, including commandments regarding divorce.
When it comes to sex, the Bible is often divided against itself.

It is therefore a mistake to pretend that the Bible can define our ethics
for us in any kind of straightforward way: such an interpretive strategy
will only lead us astray while also preventing us from taking the Bible
as seriously as we should. Even more tragically, a refusal to acknowledge
that we are active interpreters might make it seem as if the only possible choice is between accepting the Bible as literally true or rejecting the
Bible altogether. Christians should not and need not be asked to make
this choice. Since neither the Bible nor a particular interpretation can
limit what particular stories and teachings must mean, it is up to readers
to decide what a biblically informed and faithful sexual morality might
look like. If the New Testament writers were willing to admit that they
were constructing their theological and moral perspective with biblical
texts but not because of them, then what is preventing readers today from
adopting the same strategy? The Bible provides neither a shortcut to the
real work of interpretation nor a simple solution to the important task of
figuring out what it means to be human and yet in love with God.

Touching Jesus

According to the Gospel of John, when Mary Magdalene arrived at Jesus's tomb three days after his crucifixion, she stood by, crying. Peering
into his grave, she saw two angels sitting at the place where his body had
been laid, dressed in dazzling white. Jesus's body, however, was gone.
Frantic, she ran out of the tomb and into a man she did not recognize,
who asked her why she was crying. "They have taken away my Lord,"
she responded, "and I don't know where they put him!" (20:13, my trans-

lation). When the man spoke her name, however, she realized what had happened—she was speaking with Jesus himself, raised from the dead. Yet, before she had a chance to embrace him, he gave her a strict order, "Do not touch me! For I have not yet ascended to my Father" (my translation). Instructing her to share the news of his resurrection with the other disciples, he sent her on her way.

Just a few verses later, the longing to touch the resurrected Jesus is mentioned again, this time by the apostle Thomas. "Unless I see the mark of the nails in his hands, and put my finger in the mark of the nails and my hand in his side," Thomas declared, "I will not believe" (v. 25). When Jesus did appear, however, presenting his scarred flesh to his doubting disciple, Thomas failed to touch him. Or if he did, the Gospel left this detail out. The directive in John, both to Mary and to Thomas, was to look but not to touch, even though the body of Jesus was recognizably his own, scarred by his horrific death on a cross. Both disciples recognized him, and both saw his wounds, but both were denied the chance to embrace their beloved friend.

Perhaps the frustration of a Mary or a Thomas at their inability to touch the body of the man they loved can serve as a metaphor for our own inability to capture the meaning of the Bible. Mary and Thomas longed to hold the body of Jesus, I imagine, because they genuinely loved him and so wanted contact not only with his words but with his flesh. They wanted real, material confirmation that somehow, miraculously, he had survived. And yet Jesus disappointed them. They did not get to touch his body, but only look. After a time, he left them behind with nothing but words, memories, God's spirit, and, in the end, books. I wonder, however, if they ever lost the wish that they could touch Jesus, just one more time.

The desire to touch the Bible, to find in its pages some kind of final solution to the problems we face or the worries that trouble us, is, I think, akin to the wish of a Mary or a Thomas that a physical Jesus would remain behind, with them. But, according to John anyway, that is not what Mary and Thomas got. Instead, they got a Holy Spirit to comfort them and a group of believers who once loved Jesus too. Finally, they got the Gospel of John, written so that they, and others like them, "might come to believe that Jesus is the Messiah" (v. 31). But a book is not quite the same as direct, unmediated access to a God who might just solve for us, once and for all, what we should do and what we should think. Books and fleshly bodies are human products, born in particular places at particular times and with particular concerns in mind, biblical books included.

Left behind with human books and human bodies but without simple solutions in sight, the Bible, with all its contradictions, can seem like an unsatisfactory source of comfort, but it does not have to be so. By admitting that we, too, have longings and commitments, that we, too, are invested not only in God's body but in the body of biblical texts and the bodies of those whom we love, we acknowledge both our limitations and our desires, opening ourselves up to the divine Word instead of closing our minds and hearts by acting as if we already know what God thinks and wants. Mary and Thomas were not able to touch Jesus, but, according to John anyway, they did see him. And what did they see? When they finally encountered Jesus, they met a resurrected body that was able to move through doors and walls but was nevertheless marked by wounds. If Jesus's body was any indication, then, bodily redemption does not require physical perfection but faithfulness. Scarred by the holes in his hands and the wound in his side, the body of God's Messiah was recognizable by its history, by the life and death it had known. The Bible is similar. Marked by the human histories and vulnerable lives of the people who wrote it and also by the ongoing interpretations of those who have read it, the Bible is not perfect, but it can still be regarded as beautiful, particularly when we do not try to force it to mean just one thing.

In the meantime, however, human beings need human touch, as both Mary and Thomas knew. Anyone who would use God and the Bible to deny touch, love, and affection to others has failed to present a valuable interpretation, not only of the Bible but also of what it means to be human, whether or not some biblical passage somewhere can be found to support their claims. Those who attempt to belittle or demean a class of people, denying them rights on the basis of an unexamined interpretation of a few biblical passages, are expressing not God's will but their own limited human perspective, backed up by a shallow and self-serving reading of the biblical text. No one should rejoice when Jezebel is eaten by dogs. Slavery is never acceptable, whatever the Bible says. And it is a tragedy, not a triumph, every time some young person somewhere is crushed by the weight of taunting and shame inspired by cruelty masquerading as righteousness. If the Bible is truly the word of God, as Christians have claimed for centuries, then surely it deserves to be treated better than this. If human bodies matter to God as much as some ancient Israelites, Jewish Sages, and early Christians taught, then surely they deserve both protection and high regard, no matter what. The Samaritan woman desired living water capable of quenching thirst forever, not still water trapped in a bucket and available for one thirsty afternoon. When it comes to the Bible, may we imitate her example, seeking abundant life in all the interpretations we offer.

Acknowledgments

I could never have written this book without the support and encouragement of my parents, Sandra and Charles Wright. My mother was a particularly crucial participant in the project—she read every page, helped prepare the bibliography, and made brilliant suggestions at every turn—and of course Dad was always there backing us up. Thanks also to Aunt Mary, Uncle Jim, and Colleen, my amazing support team in Fayette, Maine. I also owe a particular debt of gratitude to Kathryn House—her comments on early drafts have been essential—and to Bart Ehrman, who assisted me at every turn. A number of colleagues read portions of the manuscript, offering helpful suggestions and pointing me toward just the right bibliography. In this regard, I particularly want to thank my colleagues in Hebrew Bible, Alejandro Botta and Kathryn Pfisterer Darr. My thinking on sexuality and the Bible has been deeply influenced by rich conversations with members of Boston University's Gender and Sexuality Reading Group, particularly Gina Cogan, Patricia Larash, Ashley Mears, Eugenio Menegon, Erin Murphy, Suzanne O'Brien, Carrie Preston, Deborah Swedberg, Zsuzsanna Várhelyi, and J. Keith Vincent. Other colleagues have also been amazingly supportive, especially Kecia Ali, Dale Andrews, Deborah Belle, David Eckel, David Frankfurter, Paula Fredriksen, Kyna Hamill, Laura Harrington, Robert Allan Hill, Jonathan Klawans, Irit Kleiman, Deeana Klepper, Maurice

Lee, Marcie Lenk, Stephen Prothero, Shelly Rambo, Dana Robert, James Walters, Michael Zank, and my wonderful deans Mary Elizabeth Moore and Bryan Stone. Once again, Elizabeth Castelli rescued me at just the right moment. Thank you, Elizabeth.

Portions of this project were presented at the conference "Carnal Knowledge: Sexuality in Religion, History and Culture" and to a lecture series sponsored by the LGBTQ Ministry at Marsh Chapel, Boston University. I would like to thank Deborah Belle for inviting me to participate in "Carnal Knowledge" and also for her crucial support and feedback over the last few years. I would also like to congratulate the students and staff of the LGBTQ Ministry for their important contributions to life at BU. Thanks to their work, BU is a safer, more enjoyable community for all.

While finishing up the manuscript for this book, I was busy teaching Women and Religion, Introduction to the New Testament and Core Curriculum Humanities: Late Antiquity and the Medieval World. My students and teaching fellows were very kind as I tried to balance writing with lecturing and grading. I remain grateful to them for their patience and for their inspirational enthusiasm. I have been privileged to work with truly wonderful students over the course of my career, none more amazing than this past semester.

I would be remiss if I did not also acknowledge the many faithful Christian leaders who have made it possible for me to read the Bible in the way I do, and also the church communities that continue to form and inspire me. Many thanks to the Reverend Suzanne Woolston Bossert, the Reverend Robert Castle, the Reverend Patricia Coughlin, the Reverend James Holiman, the Reverend Doctor Earl Kooperkamp, the Reverend Ashlee Wiest-Laird, the Reverend David J. Wood, and Pastor Carl Storms, whom I still miss very much. Thanks also to the First Baptist Church in Jamaica Plain, Massachusetts; the First Baptist Church, Mount Vernon, Maine; the United Parish in Brookline, Massachusetts; St. Mary's Episcopal Church, New York City; Falls of Schuylkill Baptist Church, Philadelphia; the Illinois Disciples Foundation; and the First Baptist Church of West Hartford, Connecticut.

Many, many thanks are also due to the team at HarperOne, especially Claudia, Julie, Lisa, Mark, Suzanne, and, above all, Roger Freet. Roger's careful editing and regular encouragement have meant the world to me.

I have dedicated this book to my partner, Stefan. Together we have raised two wonderful sons, who continue to delight and surprise us. Thank you, Axel and Leander, for enriching our lives more than I can say. And, above all, thank you, Stefan. It has been a privilege to build a life with you.

Notes

INTRODUCTION

1. Emily White, *Fast Girls: Teenage Tribes and the Myth of the Slut* (New York: Scribner, 2002).

2. Leora Tanenbaum, *Slut! Growing Up Female with a Bad Reputation* (repr. New York: HarperCollins, 2000).

3. For more about Phoebe Prince, see, for example, Kevin Cullen, "The Untouchable Mean Girls," *Boston Globe,* January 24, 2010, www.boston.com/news/local/massachusetts/articles/2010/01/24/the_untouchable_mean_girls?mode=PF

4. *Revolve 2007: The Complete New Testament* (Nashville: Nelson, 2006), vi.

5. *Revolve,* 97.

6. *Revolve,* 104.

7. *Revolve,* 107.

8. *Revolve,* 142.

9. "Memorandum of Law, Brief *Amicus Curiae,* of the Ethics and Religious Liberty Commission of the Southern Baptist Convention," Case no. 09-CV–2292 VRW, Submitted by David L. Llewellyn Jr. and William C. Duncan, Attorneys for *Amicus Curiae,* Ethics and Religious Liberty Commission of the Southern Baptist Convention, http://erlc.com/documents/pdf/perry-v-schwarzenegger-brief-amicus-curiae-erlc.pdf (accessed January 14, 2010).

10. "To characterize religious support for marriage as unconstitutional animus threatens the ability of religious people to participate in public debate," "Brief *Amicus Curiae,*" 5.

11. For an alternative Baptist point of view, see, for example, the publications of

the Association of Welcoming and Affirming Baptists, a coalition of Baptist churches, organizations, and individuals committed to welcoming and affirming all persons, without regard for sexual orientation. Information is available at: www.wabaptists.org.

12. Owen S. Rachleff, *An Illustrated Treasury of Bible Stories,* 2 vols. (New York: Abradale, 1970). The story of Jezebel is retold in volume 1, pages 209–10, 216–20, 230–31.

13. Thomas Jefferson, *Notes on the State of Virginia,* Query 18, "Manners," edited with introduction and notes by William Peden, Institute of Early American History and Culture (Chapel Hill: Univ. of North Carolina Press, 1955), 163.

14. J. K. Paulding, *Slavery in the United States* (New York: Harper, 1836), 29–30.

15. See Jennifer A. Glancy, *Slavery in Early Christianity* (New York: Oxford Univ. Press, 2002).

16. David L. Thurmond, "Some Roman Slave Collars in *CIL,*" *Athenaeum* 82 (1994): 459–93; Keith Bradley, *Slavery and Society at Rome* (Cambridge: Cambridge Univ. Press, 1994); Lauren Hackwith Petersen, "Clothes Make the Man: Dressing the Roman Freedman's Body," in *Bodies and Boundaries in Graeco-Roman Antiquity,* ed. Thorsten Fögen and Mireille M. Lee (Berlin: De Gruyter, 2009), 181–241 (190).

17. Joyce Reynolds, "Roman Inscriptions 1971–5," *Journal of Roman Studies* 66 (1976): 174–99 (196).

18. As Frederick Douglass put it, describing allusions to Ephesians in his own, nineteenth-century context: "The slaveholding ministers preach up the divine right of the slaveholders to property in their fellow-men. The southern preachers say to the poor slave, 'Oh! If you wish to be happy in time, happy in eternity, you must be obedient to your masters; their interest is yours." Frederick Douglass, "The Church and Prejudice," a speech delivered at the Plymouth Church Anti-Slavery Society, December 23, 1841, in *Frederick Douglass: Selected Speeches and Writings,* ed. Philip S. Foner, abridged and adapted by Yuval Taylor (Chicago: Lawrence Hill Books, 1999), 3–4. For further discussion of the use of the Bible in the context of American slavery, see the excellent essay by J. Albert Harrill, "The Use of the New Testament in the American Slave Controversy: A Case History in the Hermeneutical Tension between Biblical Criticism and Christian Moral Debate," *Religion and American Culture* 10.2 (2000): 149–86. Also see the excellent study of the Bible and African American history by Vincent L. Wimbush, *The Bible and African Americans: A Brief History* (Minneapolis: Fortress, 2003).

19. Daniel R. Goodwin, *Southern Slavery in Its Present Aspects, Containing a*

Reply to a Late Work of the Bishop of Vermont on Slavery (New York: Lippincott, 1864; repr. New York: Negro Universities Press, 1969), 114, 118.

20. Frederick Douglass, speech in New York City, 1859, in *The Frederick Douglass Papers, Series One: Speeches, Debates and Interviews,* vol. 3: *1855–1863,* ed. John W. Blassingame (New Haven: Yale Univ. Press, 1985), 258. Cited and discussed in Harrill, "Use of the New Testament," 160–61.

21. "We Are the American Baptists," www.abc-usa.org/WhoWeAre/Identity/Bible/tabid/59/Default.aspx (accessed January 22, 2010).

22. On Esther as a Jewish response to colonial oppression and minority status, see Sidnie Ann White, "Esther: A Feminine Model for Jewish Diaspora," in *Gender and Difference in Ancient Israel,* ed. Peggy L. Day (Philadelphia: Fortress, 1989), 161–77. On the complex political implications of Esther, see Itumeleng J. Mosala, "The Implications of the Text of Esther for African Women's Struggle for Liberation in South Africa," in *The Postcolonial Biblical Reader,* ed. R. S. Sugirtharajah (London: Blackwell, 2006), 134–41.

23. Phyllis Trible, "Exegesis for Storytellers and Other Strangers," *Journal of Biblical Literature* 114.1 (1995): 3–19 (4).

24. Athalya Brenner, *The Israelite Woman* (Sheffield: Sheffield Univ. Press, 1985), 23–25.

25. Trible, "Exegesis for Storytellers," 3–19.

26. Paysha Stockton and Beth Daley, "Blaze Damages Historic Church," *Boston Globe,* January 19, 2005, www.boston.com/news/local/articles/2005/01/19/blaze_destroys_historic_church/ (accessed January 31, 2010).

27. Brian Ballou, "Five years after fire, Jamaica Plain church set to rise from ashes: Congregation set to worship in building today," *Boston Globe,* January 17, 2010, www.boston.com/news/local/massachusetts/articles/2010/01/17/five_years_after_fire_jamaica_plain_church_set_to_rise_from_ashes/ (accessed January 31, 2010).

28. Ashlee Wiest-Laird, "A New Beginning," preached at the First Baptist Church of Jamaica Plain on January 17, 2010.

29. Ashlee Wiest-Laird, citing Martin Luther King Jr., "The Strength to Love," in *A Testament of Hope: The Essential Writings and Speeches of Martin Luther King Jr.,* ed. James Melville Washington (San Francisco: HarperOne, 1990), 491–518 (515).

CHAPTER 1: *The Bible and the Joy of Sex*

1. "No Second Chance" instructional video. This video was once distributed through the Sex Respect program (www.sexrespect.com), though it appears to have been pulled from their online store. For more information, see Susan

Rose, "Going Too Far? Sex, Sin and Social Policy," *Social Forces* 84.2 (2005): 1207–32 (1208).

2. And, even worse, they violate God's plan. From *Why Wait? 24 Reasons for Abstinence* (Torrance, CA: Rose, 2003) we learn that there are twelve biblically based and twelve medically based reasons to avoid sex while waiting for "God's perfect plan": heterosexual marriage. Josh McDowell, author of *Why True Love Waits: The Definitive Book on How to Help your Kids Resist Sexual Pressure* (Carol Stream, IL: Tyndale, 2002), instructs both parents and kids that God's Word is nonnegotiable when it comes to premarital sex—it is forbidden. Still, he acknowledges abstinence can be a struggle. Desires are strong because God has designed men and women in such a way that they long for one another, but those who fail to wait until marriage to fulfill their desires are fooling themselves. God intends us for married love, not the free exercise of our sexual passions.

3. J. Cheryl Exum, "In the Eye of the Beholder: Wishing, Dreaming, and *Double Entendre* in the Song of Songs." In Black, Boer, and Runions, *Labour of Reading,* 71–86.

4. Josephus, *Contra Apion* 1.38. See Karel van der Toorn, *Scribal Culture and the Making of the Hebrew Bible* (Cambridge: Harvard Univ. Press, 2007), 260–61.

5. For a list of the contents of these manuscripts and Athanasius's thirty-ninth *Festal Letter,* see T. C. Skeat, "Sinaiticus, Vaticanus and Constantine," in *The Collected Biblical Writings of T. C. Skeat,* ed. J. K. Elliott, Supplements to Novum Testamentum 113 (Leiden: Brill, 2004), 193–237 (213).

6. F. W. Dobbs-Allsopp, "Late Linguistic Features in Song of Songs," in *Perspectives on the Song of Songs,* ed. Anselm C. Hagedorn (Berlin: De Gruyter, 2006), 27–77 (65).

7. Ellen F. Davis, *Proverbs, Ecclesiastes, and the Song of Songs* (Louisville: Westminster John Knox, 2000), 231–302. Compare R. Abraham b. Isaac ha-Levi TaMaKH's *Commentary on the Song of Songs,* English translation with introduction and commentary by Leon A. Feldman, Studia Semitica Neerlandica 9 (The Netherlands: Van Gorcum, 1970). Writing in the fourteenth century, Rabbi Abraham reads the ending of the *Song* as an anticipation of the redemption of Israel and the restoration of the temple.

8. J. Cheryl Exum, *The Song of Songs: A Commentary* (Louisville: Westminster John Knox, 2006), 47–63.

9. Suggested though not pursued by Michael Goulder, *The Song of Fourteen Songs,* JSOT Supplement Series 36 (Sheffield: JSOT, 1986), 16. See discussion in Fiona C. Black, "What Is My Beloved? On Erotic Reading and the Song of Songs," in Black et al., *Labour of Reading,* 35–52 (48–9).

10. English translation of Song of Songs 2:7 from Exum, *The Song of Songs,* 117. For further discussion, see Chana Bloch and Ariel Bloch, *The Song of Songs* (Berkeley: Univ. of California Press, 1998), 151–52; and Davis, *Proverbs, Ecclesiastes, and the Song of Songs,* 252–53, though she rejects this reading.

11. Bloch and Bloch, *Song of Songs,* 178.

12. Marvin H. Pope, *Song of Songs: A New Translation with Introduction and Commentary,* Anchor Bible 7C (New York: Doubleday, 1977); Davis, *Proverbs, Ecclesiastes, and the Song of Songs,* 247. But see Bloch and Bloch, *Song of Songs,* 145.

13. See Black, "What Is My Beloved?" 47: "[Pornographic] reading I think, in effect denies the text its erotic freedom by rushing through foreplay, stripping and *taking* it before it has had the chance to show a little skin." Also see Exum, "Eye of the Beholder."

14. See especially Roland Boer, *Knockin' on Heaven's Door* (London: Routledge, 1999) and "The Second Coming: Repetition and Insatiable Desire in the Song of Songs," *Biblical Interpretation* 8.3 (2000): 276–301.

15. Origen, *Commentary on the Song of Songs,* Prologue, trans. Rowan A. Greer, *Origen: An Exhortation to Martyrdom, Prayer, and Selected Works* (Classics of Western Spirituality) (Mahwah, NJ: Paulist Press, 1979), 218.

16. Virginia Burrus and Stephen D. Moore, "Unsafe Sex: Feminism, Pornography, and the Song of Songs," *Biblical Interpretation* 11.1 (2003): 24–52 (esp. 39–40); Carey Ellen Walsh, *Exquisite Desire: Religion, the Erotic, and the Song of Songs* (Minneapolis: Fortress, 2000), 35–37.

17. Exum, *Song of Songs,* 198–99.

18. Alicia Ostriker, "A Holy of Holies: The Song of Songs as Countertext," in *The Song of Songs: A Feminist Companion to the Bible (Second Series),* ed. Athalya Brenner and Carole R. Fontaine (Sheffield: Sheffield Academic, 2000), 36–54; Phyllis Trible, *God and the Rhetoric of Sexuality* (Philadelphia: Fortress, 1978), 144–65. But see Exum, *Song of Songs,* 25–28 and Fiona C. Black, "Unlikely Bedfellows: Allegorical and Feminist Readings of Song of Songs 7.1-8," in Brenner and Fontaine, *Song of Songs,* 127–29.

19. Thus, some scholars conclude that the last verse is spoken by the man, not the woman.

20. Interpreters often seek to solve this problem by adding marginal notes and other textual apparatuses that mark the speaker in some way.

21. See the excellent discussion in Black, "Unlikely Bedfellows," 104–29.

22. Augustine, *On Christian Doctrine* 2.12, trans. R. P. H. Green, *Augustine. De Doctrina Christiana* (Oxford: Clarendon, 1995), 63.

23. Rashi, *The Megilloth and Rashi's Commentary with Linear Translation,* trans.

Avraham Schwartz and Yisroel Schwartz (New York: Hebrew Linear Classics, 1983), 134, discussed by Black, "Unlikely Bedfellows," 109.

24. Nicholas of Lyra, *The Postilla on the Song of Songs,* ed. and trans. James George Kiecker (Milwaukee: Marquette Univ. Press, 1998), 67.

25. Mary Dove, ed. and trans., *The* Glossa Ordinaria *on the Song of Songs* (Kalamazoo: Western Michigan Univ., 2004), 82–83.

26. *Mishnah Yadaim* 3.5: "R. Akiva said: God forbid that any man in Israel ever disputed concerning the Song of Songs, saying that it does not make the hands unclean [that is, that it is not canonical], for the whole world is not worth the day on which the Song of Songs was given to Israel, for all the scriptures are holy, but the Song of Songs is the holiest of the holy." Translated and discussed by John Barton, "The Canonicity of the Song of Songs," in Hagedorn, *Perspectives on the Song of Songs,* 1–7 (3).

27. Daniel Boyarin, *Intertextuality and the Reading of the Midrash* (Bloomington: Indiana Univ. Press, 1990), 105–29. Also see Judith A. Kates, "Entering the Holy of Holies: Rabbinic Midrash and the Language of Intimacy," in *Scrolls of Love: Ruth and the Song of Songs,* eds. Peter S. Hawkins and Lesleigh C. Stahlberg (Fordham: Fordham Univ. Press, 2006), 201–9.

28. Origen, *Commentary on the Song of Songs,* Prologue, trans. Greer. Origen also read the Song as an allegory for the unity of Gentiles and Jews that becomes possible only in Christ. Though he was declared a heretic later on, Origen's interpretation of the Song greatly impressed his contemporaries and has continued to influence Song commentary to the present day. See E. Ann Matter, *The Voice of My Beloved: The Song of Songs in Western Medieval Christianity* (Philadelphia: Univ. of Pennsylvania Press, 1990), 25–31.

29. Elizabeth A. Clark, "Origen, the Jews, and the Song of Songs," in Hadedorn, *Perspectives on the Song of Songs,* 274–93.

30. Gregory of Nyssa, *Commentary on the Song of Songs,* Homily 5, trans. Casimir McCambley, *Saint Gregory of Nyssa. Commentary on the Song of Songs,* The Archbishop Iakovos Library of Ecclesiastical and Historical Sources 12 (Brookline, MA: Hellenic College Press, 1987).

31. Howard Eilberg-Schwartz, *God's Phallus and Other Problems for Men and Monotheism* (Boston: Beacon, 1994), 164–67.

32. Origen, *Homilies on the Song of Songs* 1.2–3, trans. R. P. Lawson, *Origen. The Song of Songs: Commentary and Homilies,* Ancient Christian Writers 26 (Westminster, MD: Newman, 1957).

33. William of St. Thierry, *Brevis Commentatio* 6–7, trans. Denys Turner, *Eros and Allegory: Medieval Exegesis of the Song of Songs,* Cistercian Studies 156 (Kalamazoo: Cistercian Publications, 1995), 280–82.

34. Bernard of Clairvaux, *Sermons on the Song of Songs* 3.1.1. Translated and discussed by Matter, *Voice,* 125–27.

35. Matter, *Voice,* 136–38. Also see Stephen D. Moore, "The Song of Songs in the History of Sexuality," *Church History* 69.2 (1000): 328–49.

36. Caroline Walker Bynum, *Holy Feast and Holy Fast: The Religious Significance of Food to Medieval Women* (Berkeley: Univ. of California Press, 1987), 94.

37. Fiona Griffiths, *The Garden of Delights: Reform and Renaissance for Women in the Twelfth Century* (Philadelphia: Univ. of Pennsylvania Press, 2007), 136–39; Bynum, *Holy Feast,* 116–18.

38. Moore, "Song of Songs," 328–49; Burrus and Moore, "Unsafe Sex," 32–33.

39. Sara Ahmed, *The Cultural Politics of Emotion* (Edinburgh: Univ. of Edinburgh Press, 2004), 152.

40. Ahmed, *Cultural Politics,* 153–54. Also see Judith Butler, "Is Kinship Always Already Heterosexual?" *Differences: A Journal of Feminist Cultural Studies* 13.1 (2002): 14–44.

41. I have often replaced the NRSV translation of "Yhwh"—"the LORD"— with the divine name Yhwh, as printed in the Hebrew text. The translation "LORD" attempts to preserve the tradition of printing the vowels for "Adonai" (Lord) with the consonants for the name Yhwh so that, when encountering the divine name, readers pronounce the word "Adonai" instead.

42. See, for example, Trible, *God and the Rhetoric of Sexuality,* 166–99; Danna Nolan Fewell and David M. Gunn, "'A Son Is Born to Naomi!' Literary Allusions and Interpretation in the Book of Ruth," in *Women in the Hebrew Bible: A Reader,* ed. Alice Bach (New York: Routledge, 1999), 233–39; Tikva Frymer-Kensky, *Reading the Women of the Bible* (New York: Schocken Books, 2002), 238–56; Musa W. Dube, "Divining Ruth for International Relations," in *Postmodern Interpretations of the Bible: A Reader,* ed. A. K. M. Adam (St. Louis: Chalice Press, 2001), 67–79, but see her ultimate rejection of this reading, 76–77.

43. See esp. Mieke Bal, *Lethal Love: Feminist Literary Readings of Biblical Love Stories* (Bloomington: Indiana Univ. Press, 1987), 68–88.

44. Robert L. Hubbard Jr., *The Book of Ruth* (Grand Rapids: Eerdmans, 1988), 39–42; André Lacocque, *The Feminine Unconventional: Four Subversive Figures in Israel's Tradition* (Minneapolis: Fortress, 1990), 84–116, discussed by Edward L. Greenstein, "Reading Strategies and the Story of Ruth," in Bach, *Women in the Hebrew Bible,* 211–31 (216).

45. Trible, *God and the Rhetoric of Sexuality,* 182; Katheryn Pfisterer Darr, *Far More Precious Than Jewels: Perspectives on Biblical Women* (Louisville: Westminster John Knox, 1991), 65; Tod Linafelt, "Ruth," in *Ruth and Esther,* eds. Tod Linafelt and Timothy K. Beal (Collegeville, MD: Liturgical Press, 1999), 49.

46. Ellen F. Davis, "Beginning with Ruth: An Essay on Translating," in Hawkins and Stahlberg, *Scrolls of Love,* 33–43 (37–38). The translation "valorous woman" is adopted from Davis.

47. Rebecca Alpert wonders if their love was not, in fact, erotic ("Finding our Past: A Lesbian Interpretation of the Book of Ruth," in *Reading Ruth: Contemporary Women Reclaim a Sacred Story,* ed. Judith A. Kates and Gail Twerksy Reimer [New York: Ballantine Books, 1994], 91–96).

48. Trible, *God and the Rhetoric of Sexuality,* 195.

49. Fewell and Gunn, "A Son Is Born to Naomi!" 238.

50. Roland Boer, *Marxist Criticism of the Bible* (Sheffield: Sheffield Academic, 2003), 76–86.

51. Suggested by Bal, *Lethal Love,* 81–82.

52. Darr, *More Precious Than Jewels,* 61–63.

53. John Chrysostom, *Homilies on Matthew* 3.5, ed. and trans. Philip Schaff, Nicene and Post-Nicene Fathers, series 1, vol. 10, *Chrysostom: Homilies on the Gospel of Saint Matthew* (repr. Peabody, MA: Hendrickson, 1995), 17.

54. Dube, "Divining Ruth," 72–79.

55. See esp. Kwok Pui-Lan, "Finding a Home for Ruth: Gender, Sexuality and the Politics of Otherness," in *New Paradigms for Bible Study: The Bible in the Third Millennium,* ed. Robert M. Fowler, Edith Blumhofer, and Fernando F. Segovia (London: Clark, 2004), 137–56.

56. Lesleigh Cushing Stahlberg, "Modern Day Moabites: The Bible and the Debate about Same-Sex Marriage," *Biblical Interpretation* 16.5 (2008): 442–75.

57. Hence, many have sought to identify the underlying sources of these books, the dates of their composition, and the date of the final editing process. See esp. Leonhard Rost, *The Succession to the Throne of David,* trans. Michael Rutter and David Gunn (Sheffield: Phoenix, 1982).

58. J. Cheryl Exum, *Tragedy and Biblical Narrative: Arrows of the Almighty* (Cambridge: Cambridge Univ. Press, 1992), 80; David Jobling, *1 Samuel* (Collegeville, MD: Liturgical Press, 1998), 90.

59. Susan Ackerman, *When Heroes Love: The Ambiguity of Eros in the Stories of Gilgamesh and David* (New York: Columbia Univ. Press, 2005), 187–88.

60. See esp. Tom Horner, *Jonathan Loved David: Homosexuality in Biblical Times* (Philadelphia: Westminster John Knox, 1978), though the antiquity of 1 and 2 Samuel makes it difficult to draw direct parallels between the love of Jonathan for David and homosexual love as understood today. Also see David Halperin, *One Hundred Years of Homosexuality: And Other Essays on Greek Love* (New York: Routledge, 1990); David Gunn, *The Fate of King Saul* (Sheffield: Sheffield Academic, 1980); Ackerman, *When Heroes Love,* esp. 153–54; 165–66; 194–99.

61. Hence, Simon Parker views citations of the relationship between Jonathan and David as a warrant for homosexuality to be an inappropriate misreading of the ancient evidence ("The Hebrew Bible and Homosexuality," *Quarterly Review* 11.1 [1991]: 6–20 [10–11]). For further discussion of the "love" terminology associated with covenants, see J. A. Thompson, "The Significance of the Verb *Love* in the David-Jonathan Narratives in 1 Samuel," *Vetus Testamentum* 24 (1974): 334–39; William L. Moran, "The Ancient Near Eastern Background of the Love of God in Deuteronomy," *Catholic Biblical Quarterly* 25 (1963): 77–87. But also see Susan Ackerman, "The Personal Is Political: Covenantal and Affectionate Love ('AHEB, 'AHABA) in the Hebrew Bible," *Vetus Testamentum* 52.4 (2002): 437–58.

62. Discussed by Saul M. Olyan, " 'Surpassing the Love of Women': Another Look at 2 Samuel and the Relationship of David and Jonathan," in *Authorizing Marriage? Canon, Tradition, and Critique in the Blessing of Same-Sex Unions,* ed. Mark D. Jordan with Meghan T. Sweeney and David M. Mellott (Princeton: Princeton Univ. Press, 2006), 7–16 (8–9).

63. Olyan, " 'Surpassing the Love of Women'," 9–16.

64. Ackerman, *When Heroes Love,* 192–94; also see 221–26.

65. Even before ascending to the throne, David had married Ahinoam, probably a former wife of Saul, and Abigail, the wife of his rival Nabal. After being installed in Jerusalem, he takes several additional wives and likely inherits the remaining wives and concubines of Saul's household. See Jon D. Leveson and Baruch Halpern, "The Political Import of David's Marriages," *Journal of Biblical Literature* 99.4 (1980): 507–18.

66. See Ken Stone, *Practicing Safer Texts: Food, Sex and Bible in Queer Perspective* (London: Clark, 2005), 74–81; Regina Schwartz, "Adultery in the House of David: The Metanarrative of Biblical Scholarship and the Narratives of the Bible," in *Women in the Hebrew Bible,* 335–50.

67. See Randall C. Bailey, *David in Love and War: The Pursuit of Power in 2 Samuel 10–12,* JSOT Supplement Series 75 (Sheffield: Sheffield Academic, 1990), 83–123; R. N. Whybray, *The Succession Narrative: A Study of II Sam. 9–20 and I Kings 1 and 2,* Studies in Biblical Theology, 2nd Series 9 (London: SCM, 1968). Foreign women are regularly depicted as a source of Israel's troubles, which is one of the reasons the book of Ruth seems so surprising.

CHAPTER 2: *Biblical Marriage*

1. Peggy Pascoe, "Miscegenation Law, Court Cases, and Ideologies of 'Race' in Twentieth-Century America," *Journal of American History* (1996): 44–69.

2. Charles F. Robinson II, "Legislated Love in the Lone Star State: Texas and Miscegenation," *Southwestern Historical Quarterly* 108.1 (2004): 65–87.

3. Dara Orenstein, "Void for Vagueness: Mexicans and the Collapse of Miscegenation Law in California," *Pacific Historical Review* 74.3 (2005): 367–407.

4. For a discussion of the two creation stories, written from a historical-critical perspective, see Claus Westermann, *Genesis 1–11: A Commentary,* trans. John Scullion (Minneapolis: Augsburg Fortress, 1984), 157–58.

5. Trible, *God and the Rhetoric of Sexuality,* 12–23, 72–143.

6. On *adamah* as fertile, arable soil, see Theodore Hiebert, *The Yahwist's Landscape: Nature and Religion in Early Israel* (Oxford: Oxford Univ. Press, 1996), 34–38.

7. Robert A. J. Gagnon, *The Bible and Homosexual Practice: Text and Hermeneutics* (Nashville: Abingdon Press, 2001), 62.

8. Christopher Seitz, *Word Without End: The Old Testament as Abiding Witness* (Grand Rapids: Eerdmans, 1998), 273. Cited and discussed by Stone, *Safer Texts,* 23.

9. Allen Verhey, *Remembering Jesus: Christian Community, Scripture and the Moral Life* (Grand Rapids: Eerdmans, 2002), 215.

10. Carol Meyers, *Discovering Eve: Ancient Israelite Women in Context* (New York and Oxford: Oxford Univ. Press, 1988), 111–15: "The physical risks related to childbearing constituted a gender-specific life threat" (113).

11. Genesis Rabbah 8.1, discussed and translated by Wayne A. Meeks, "The Image of the Androgyne: Some Uses of a Symbol in Earliest Christianity," *History of Religions* 13.3 (1974): 165–208 (186). Also see Arnold M. Goldberg, *Untersuchungen über die Vorstellung von der Schekhinah in der Frühen Rabbinischen Literatur,* Studia Judaica 5 (Berlin: Gruyter, 1969), 352–54. Goldberg collects together the rabbinic commentary on Genesis 1:27 and offers a German translation.

12. Daniel Boyarin, *Carnal Israel: Reading Sex in Talmudic Culture* (Berkeley: Univ. of California Press, 1993), 42–46.

13. Meeks, "Androgyne," esp. 180–89.

14. Bentley Layton, trans., *The Gnostic Scriptures: Ancient Wisdom for the New Age,* Anchor Bible Reference Series (New York: Doubleday, 1987), 343.

15. Gregory of Nyssa (fourth century CE) comments that, "sexual division was a departure from the 'prototype,' Christ, the 'image' of God the Father, since in Christ there is 'no male and female.'" (Elizabeth A. Clark, *Reading Renunciation: Asceticism and Scripture in Early Christianity* [Princeton: Princeton Univ. Press, 1999], 127).

16. Boyarin, *Carnal Israel,* 46.

17. Stone, *Safer Texts,* 28–29; Clark, *Reading Renunciation,* 180–83; Peter Brown, *The Body and Society: Men, Women and Sexual Renunciation in Early Christianity* (New York: Columbia Univ. Press, 1988), 295–98. James Barr

argues on literary grounds that the book of Genesis assumes the opposite: Adam and Eve did engage in sexual intercourse (*The Garden of Eden and the Hope of Immortality* [Minneapolis: Fortress, 1993], esp. 66–67).

18. See further Elaine Pagels, *Adam, Eve and the Serpent* (New York: Random House, 1988).

19. As Bernard F. Batto puts it, "Like the Atrahasis [a Babylonian creation myth], the Yahwist's myth purports to explain the proper place of human-kind within the cosmos by showing that 'our world' is the result of a series of inchoate attempts by an inexperienced creator to achieve a workable cre-ation. . . . Like the Gilgamesh [another Babylonian myth], the Yahwist sets forth immortality as a divine prerogative that is denied to humankind. But the genius of the Yahwist is that he brought together these disparate mythi-cal themes into a highly original composition that placed Israelite religious and national traditions at the center of the cosmic story": *Slaying the Dragon: Mythmaking in the Biblical Tradition* (Louisville, KY: Westminster John Knox, 1992), 47.

20. English translation of the Atrahasis myth by Stephanie Dalley, *Myths from Mesopotamia* (Oxford: Oxford Univ. Press, 1991), 9–38 (14–17); discussed by Batto, *Slaying the Dragon,* 50–51 and Stone, *Safer Texts,* 36–37.

21. *Gilgamesh* 2.3.1–37, trans., Alexander Heidel, *The Gilgamesh Epic and Old Testament Parallels* (Chicago: Univ. of Chicago Press, 1946), 28–29.

22. *Gilgamesh* 11.267–89. Heidel, *Gilgamesh Epic,* 91–92. On the loss of a chance at immortality as the central theme of Genesis 2–3, see Barr, *Garden of Eden,* esp. 21–56. Also see Stone, *Safer Texts,* 40–41.

23. Hiebert, *Yahwist's Landscape,* 33–38.

24. Meyers, *Discovering Eve,* 54–57, 59–63.

25. Meyers, *Discovering Eve,* 165–68. Also see Ronald A. Simkins, "Gender Construction in the Yahwist Creation Myth," in *Genesis,* ed. Athalya Brenner, The Feminist Companion to the Bible, 2nd series, 1 (Sheffield: Sheffield Academic, 1998), 32–52.

26. Simkins, "Gender Construction," 52.

27. See Tikva Frymer-Kensky, "Virginity in the Bible," in *Gender and Law in the Hebrew Bible and the Ancient Near East,* ed. Victor H. Matthews, Ber-nard M. Levinson, and Tikva Frymer-Kensky, JSOT Supplement Series 262 (Sheffield: Sheffield Academic, 1998), 77–96. The display of the bloody sheets vindicates the honor of the parents and shames the bridegroom "in one fell swoop" (95).

28. Moshe Weinfeld, *Deuteronomy 1–11: A New Translation with Introduction and Commentary,* Anchor Bible (New York: Doubleday, 1991), 1–84. For a helpful review of this scholarship, see John Van Seters, *A Law Book for*

the Diaspora: Revision in the Study of the Covenant Code (New York and London: Oxford Univ. Press, 2003), 3–46, though Van Seters reviews this scholarship primarily to discount it. Also see Brevard S. Childs, *Exodus: A Commentary* (Chatham: Mackay, 1974), 451–88. For an exploration of the importance of the rewriting of the Exodus laws by the writer(s) of Deuteronomy, see Bernard M. Levinson, *Deuteronomy and the Hermeneutic of Legal Innovation* (New York and Oxford: Oxford Univ. Press, 1997).

29. Weinfeld, *Deuteronomy,* 37–53; Norbert Lohfink, "The Cult Reform of Josiah of Judah: 2 Kings 22–23 as a Source for the History of the Israelite Religion," in *Ancient Israelite Religion: Essays in Honor of Frank Moore Cross,* ed. Patrick D. Miller Jr., Paul D. Hanson, and S. Dean McBride (Philadelphia: Fortress, 1987), 459–75.

30. For an overview of these problems, see Calum M. Carmichael, *The Origins of Biblical Law: The Decalogues and the Book of the Covenant* (Ithaca: Cornell Univ. Press, 1992), 1–21.

31. Carmichael makes the ingenious suggestion that the order of the laws is related to the narrative structure of Genesis, responding to questions that might come up in light of Genesis with legal rulings appropriate to the case. Thus, laws regarding married Hebrew slaves and slave concubines rule on the experiences of Jacob, Leah, and Rachel while Jacob was serving as a slave in Laban's household (see Gen. 29:1–31:55). See Carmichael, *Origins of Biblical Law,* 79–97. While attractive, this hypothesis cannot be conclusively proven.

32. Code of Hammurabi §117, in *Law Collections from Mesopotamia and Asia Minor,* trans. Martha T. Roth, Writings from the Ancient World 6 (Atlanta: Scholars Press, 1995), 103.

33. Carolyn Pressler, "Wives and Daughters, Bond and Free: Views of Women in the Slave Laws of Exodus 21:2–11," in *Gender and Law in the Hebrew Bible and the Ancient Near East,* ed. Victor H. Matthews, Bernard Levinson, and Tikva Freymer-Kensky (Sheffield: Sheffield Academic, 1998), 147–72 (164–65).

34. These rules are complex and textually unstable. For further discussion, see William H. C. Propp, *Exodus 19–40: A New Translation with Introduction and Commentary,* Anchor Bible (New York: Doubleday, 2006), 197–201.

35. See further Victor H. Matthews, "The Anthropology of Slavery in the Covenant Code," in *Theory and Method in Biblical and Cuneiform Law: Revision, Interpolation and Development,* ed. Bernard M. Levinson, JSOT Supplement Series 181 (Sheffield: Sheffield Academic, 1994), 119–35.

36. Raymond Westbrook, "The Female Slave," in Matthews, Levinson, and Freymer-Kensky, *Gender and Law,* 214–38 (215–17).

37. Walter Brueggemann is particularly interested in the economic implications of Deutoronomy's theological emphasis here (*Deuteronomy,* Abingdon New Testament Commentaries [Nashville: Abingdon, 2001], 164–70).

38. Compare the Middle Assyrian Law §55 (ca. 1076 BCE) regarding a raped virgin: "If he [the fornicator] has no wife, the fornicator shall give 'triple' the silver as the value of the maiden to her father; her fornicator shall marry her; he shall not reject (?) her. If the father does not desire it so, he shall receive 'triple' silver for the maiden, and he shall give his daughter in marriage to whomever he chooses." (Roth, *Law Collections,* 175).

39. Freymer-Kensky, "Virginity in the Bible," 91.

40. Phyllis Bird, *Missing Persons and Mistaken Identities: Women and Gender in Ancient Israel* (Minneapolis: Augsburg Fortress, 1997), 24–25.

41. See, for example, Sumerian Excise Tablet §8 (Roth, *Law Collections,* 44); Code of Hammurabi §§137–50, 170–71 (Roth, *Law Collections,* 107–9, 113–14); Middle Assyrian Laws §§12–18, 23–24, 55–56 (Roth, *Law Collections,* 157–62, 174–75); Hittite Laws §§ 28a, 29 (Roth, *Law Collections,* 221). For a comparison of biblical laws involving adultery and those in Egyptian sources, see Pnina Galpaz-Feller, "Private Lives and Public Censure: Adultery in Ancient Egypt and Biblical Israel," *Near Eastern Archaeology* 67.3 (2004): 152–61.

42. As Gayle Rubin has famously observed: "Women are given in marriage, taken in battle, exchanged for favors, sent as tribute, traded, bought and sold. . . . Men are of course also trafficked—but as slaves, hustlers, athletic stars, serfs, or as some other catastrophic social status, rather than as men" ("The Traffic in Women: Notes on the 'Political Economy' of Sex," in *Toward an Anthropology of Women,* ed. Rayna R. Reiter [New York and London: Monthly Review Press, 1975], 157–210 [175–76]).

43. While it is true that in antiquity adoption bestowed full paternity on the adopted son, with all its privileges of inheritance and blessing and therefore that Joseph's paternity connects Jesus to David, the interpretation I am pursuing here concludes that Jesus's descent from Joseph is also designed to underscore the importance of fictive kinship ties to the gospel authors. For this point of view, see Janice Capel Anderson and Stephen D. Moore, "Matthew and Masculinity," in *New Testament Masculinities,* ed. Stephen D. Moore and Janice Capel Anderson, Semeia 45 (Atlanta: Society of Biblical Literature, 2003), 67–91 (72–76). Moore and Capel Anderson also connect Matthew's vision of fatherhood to his use of the term "brother" which is "the special domain of the disciple" (76). For a discussion of Joseph as Jesus's foster father, see Raymond E. Brown, *The Birth of the Messiah: A Commentary on the Infancy Narratives in Matthew and Luke* (New York: Doubleday, 1993), 138–43.

44. On Jesus's decidedly antifamily and antihousehold stance, see also Dale B. Martin, *Sex and the Single Savior: Gender and Sexuality in Biblical Interpretation* (Louisville: Westminster John Knox, 2006), 94–97, 104–6.

45. Justin Martyr, *1 Apology* 29, in Leslie William Barnard, trans., *St. Justin Martyr. The First and Second Apologies,* Ancient Christian Writers 56 (New York: Paulist, 1997), 43.

46. This episode is reported by Eusebius of Caesarea (*History of the Church* 6:8.1–3). Not everyone is convinced by the historicity of Eusebius's account. See Matthew Keuffler, *The Manly Eunuch: Masculinity, Gender Ambiguity, and Christian Ideology in Late Antiquity* (Chicago: Univ. of Chicago Press, 2001), 260–61.

47. Canon 1 of the Council of Nicaea: "If any one in sickness has been subjected by physicians to a surgical operation, or if he has been castrated by barbarians, let him remain among the clergy; but, if any one in sound health has castrated himself, it behooves that such a one, if [already] enrolled among the clergy, should cease [from his ministry], and that from henceforth no such person should be promoted. But, as it is evident that this is said of those who willfully do the thing and presume to castrate themselves, so if any have been made eunuchs by barbarians, or by their masters, and should otherwise be found worthy, such men the Canon admits to the clergy." English translation edited by Henry R. Percival, *The Seven Ecumenical Councils of the Undivided Church,* Nicene and Post-Nicene Fathers, Second Series 14 (New York: Charles Scribner, 1900; repr. Peabody, MA: Hendrikson, 1995), 8.

48. Clark, *Reading Renunciation,* 90–92.

49. Anderson and Moore, "Matthew and Masculinity," 88–90.

50. Late antique rabbis recommended that the husband initiate the divorce by giving his wife a document called a *get,* which terminated the marriage and made it possible for the woman to enter into a subsequent marriage legally. Josephus, a Jewish historian and contemporary of the author of Mark, also thought that Jewish custom requires the husband to initiate the divorce (*Antiquities* 15.259–60). See further Rachel Biale, *Women and Jewish Law: The Essential Texts, Their History, and Their Relevance for Today* (New York: Schocken Books, 1984), 70–101.

51. For example, in one surviving second-century Jewish marriage contract, there is a provision indicating that the bride had the right to demand the return of her dowry, thus giving her the option of terminating her marriage (Ross Shepard Kraemer, "Women's Judaism(s) at the Beginning of Christianity," in *Women and Christian Origins,* ed. Mary Rose D'Angelo and Ross Shepard Kraemer [New York and Oxford: Oxford Univ. Press, 1999], 50–79 [60]). Also see Martin, *Single Savior,* 132; Bernadette Brooten, "Konnten

Frauen im alten Judentum die Scheidung betreiben? Überlengungen zu Mark 10, 11–12 und Kor 7, 1–11," *Evangelische Theologie* 42 (1982): 65–80.

52. On the "exception clause," see Martin, *Single Savior,* 134–37. Martin reads this statement not as allowing separation from a sexually immoral wife, but removing the guilt from a man who divorces his wife and therefore makes her an adulteress. Since she was already engaged in illicit sexual behavior, the man is not responsible for making her an adulteress. She has already done this herself.

53. Here I am following Martin's analysis.

54. Martin, *Single Savior,* 137.

55. See David C. Parker, *The Living Text of the Gospels* (Cambridge: Cambridge Univ. Press, 1997), 72–94.

56. Summarized and excerpted from Parker, *Living Text,* 75–91.

CHAPTER 3: *The Evil Impulse*

1. Gretel C. Kovach, "Pastor's Advice for Better Marriage: More Sex," *New York Times,* November 23, 2008, www.nytimes.com/2008/11/24/us/24sex.html.

2. Roy Appleton, "Grapevine pastor wants married couples to have sex every day for a week," *Dallas Morning News,* November 11, 2008.

3. Kovach, "Pastor's Advice." Also see the many books, CDs, videos, and other products produced by and for Reverend Young at www.edyoung.com.

4. Kovach, "Pastor's Advice."

5. See Brenda Brasher, *Godly Women: Fundamentalism and Female Power* (New Brunswick, NJ: Rutgers Univ. Press, 1998); Julie Ingersoll, *Evangelical Christian Women: War Stories in the Gender Battles* (New York: New York Univ. Press, 2003); Dawne Moon, *God, Sex and Politics: Homosexuality and Everyday Theologies* (Chicago: Univ. of Chicago Press, 2004).

6. See Amy-Jill Levine, "Diaspora as Metaphor: Bodies and Boundaries in the Book of Tobit," in *Diaspora Jews and Judaism: Essays in Honor of and Dialogue with A. Thomas Kraebel,* ed. J. Andrew Overman and Robert S. MacLenham (Atlanta: Scholars Press, 1992), 115–17.

7. As we will see in chapter 5, the habit of blaming foreign women for sexual misconduct was widespread.

8. For an overview, see Daniel N. Schowalter and Steven J. Friesen, eds., *Urban Religion in Roman Corinth: Interdisciplinary Approaches* (Cambridge: Harvard Univ. Press, 2005). On prostitution in Corinth, see John R. Lanci, "The Stones Don't Speak and the Texts Tell Lies: Sacred Sex at Corinth," in Schowalter and Friesen, *Urban Religion,* 205–20 and Stephanie Budin, *The Myth of Sacred Prostitution in Antiquity* (Cambridge: Cambridge Univ. Press, 2008), esp. 113–52.

9. Daniel Boyarin, "Internal Opposition in Talmudic Literature: The Case of the Married Monk," *Representations* 36 (1991): 87–113 (92–93); Boyarin, *A Radical Jew: Paul and the Politics of Identity* (Berkeley: Univ. of California Press, 1994), 191–93. Also see Judith Plaskow, *Standing Again at Sinai: Judaism from a Feminist Perspective* (San Francisco: Harper and Row, 1990), 179–83; Rachel Biale, *Women and Jewish Law,* 121–27.

10. Translated and discussed by Biale, *Women and Jewish Law,* 125.

11. Also see Peter Brown, *Body and Society,* 53–56; Elizabeth Castelli, "Interpretations of Power in 1 Corinthians," *Semeia* 54 (1992): 197–222; Dale Martin, "Paul without Passion: On Paul's Rejection of Desire in Sex and Marriage," in, *Single Savior,* 65–76; Dale Martin, *The Corinthian Body* (New Haven: Yale Univ. Press, 1995), 209.

12. Dale Martin, "*Arsenokoitês* and *Malakos*: Meanings and Consequences," in *Single Savior,* 37–50.

13. See M. K. Hopkins, "The Age of Roman Girls at Marriage," *Population Studies* 18.3 (1965): 309–27; Brent D. Shaw, "The Age of Roman Girls at Marriage: Some Reconsiderations," *Journal of Roman Studies* 77 (1987): 30–46; Susan Treggiari, *Roman Marriage: Iusti Coniuges from the Time of Cicero to the Time of Ulpian* (Oxford: Clarendon, 1991), 398–403; Michael Satlow, *Jewish Marriage in Antiquity* (Princeton: Princeton Univ. Press, 2001), 105–11.

14. As the third-century CE Roman jurist Papinian explained, "The *lex Julia* [on punishing adulteries] applies only between free persons" (*Digest of Justinian* 48.5.6, trans., Alan Watson, *The Digest of Justinian* [Philadelphia: Univ. of Pennsylvania Press, 1985]). See further Thomas A. J. McGinn, *Prostitution, Sexuality and the Law in Ancient Rome* (New York and Oxford: Oxford Univ. Press, 1998), 195–96; Treggiari, *Roman Marriage,* 281.

15. Watson, *Digest of Justinian* 25.7.3.

16. See further Elizabeth Castelli, "Paul on Women and Gender," in Kraemer and D'Angelo, *Women and Christian Origins,* 221–35.

17. See Kathy Gaca, *The Making of Fornication: Eros, Ethics and Political Reform in Greek Philosophy and Early Christianity* (Berkeley: Univ. of California Press, 2003), 140–41.

18. Most important, see Bernadette Brooten, *Love Between: Early Christian Responses to Female Homoeroticism* (Chicago: Univ. of Chicago Press, 1996) and the comprehensive review of Brooten's work in Elizabeth Castelli, ed., "Lesbian Historiography Before the Name?" *GLQ* 4 (1998). Other important studies include Diana M. Swancutt, "'The Disease of Effemination': The Charge of Effeminacy and the Verdict of God (Romans 1:18–2:16)," in Moore and Capel Anderson, *New Testament Masculinities,* 193–234; Dale

Martin, "*Arsenokoitês* and *Malakos*: Meanings and Consequences," in *Single Savior,* 37–50; Jennifer Wright Knust, *Abandoned to Lust: Sexual Slander and Ancient Christianity.* Gender, Theory, Religion (New York: Columbia Univ. Press, 2005), esp. 64–66.

19. The bibliography on this topic is immense. Particularly helpful studies include: Kenneth Dover, *Greek Homosexuality* (Cambridge: Harvard Univ. Press, 1978); Halperin, *One Hundred Years of Homosexuality;* Aline Rousselle, *Porneia: On Desire and the Body in Antiquity,* trans. Felicia Pheasant (London: Blackwell, 1988); Craig A. Williams, *Roman Homosexuality* (New York and London: Oxford Univ. Press, 1999); John J. Winkler, *The Constraints of Desire: The Anthropology of Sex and Gender in Ancient Greece* (New York and London: Routledge, 1990). Ruth Mazo Karras has written a helpful review of the scholarship; see her "Review Essay: Active/Passive, Acts/ Passions: Greek and Roman Sexualities," *American Historical Review* 105.4 (2000): 1250–65.

20. W. A. Oldfather, trans., *Epictetus* 1, LCL13, in Arrian's *Discourses of Epictetus* 2.10.17–18 (Cambridge: Harvard Univ. Press, 1925), 278–79. On the "monstrosity" of women who desire women, see Brooten, *Love Between Women.*

21. *CIL* 14.3565.2–7; *CLE* 1504, translated and discussed by Williams, *Roman Homosexuality,* 22. Also see Amy Richlin, *The Garden of Priapus: Sexuality and Aggression in Roman Humor* (New York and Oxford: Oxford Univ. Press, 1986 [2nd ed. 1992]).

22. Acceptance of love between free men and enslaved or recently freed youths was so widespread that, a century after Paul, the emperor Hadrian publicly celebrated his youthful lover, Antinous, adorning his palaces with images of his beloved and, after Antinous's untimely death, founding a memorial cult in the young man's honor. See Williams, *Roman Homosexuality,* 56–61.

23. See O. Larry Yarbrough, *Not Like the Gentiles: Marriage Rules in the Letters of Paul,* SBL Dissertation Series 80 (Atlanta: Scholars Press, 1985), 68–76.

24. Cora B. Lutz, trans., "Musonius Rufus: The Roman Socrates," *Yale Classical Studies* 10 (1947): 3–147 (87–89).

25. Plutarch, *Advice to the Bride and Groom,* trans. Donald Russell. *Plutarch's "Advice to the Bride and Groom" and "A Consolation to His Wife,"* ed. Sarah B. Pomeroy (New York and Oxford: Oxford Univ. Press, 1999), 5–13 (7).

26. On prostitution in the ancient world, see McGinn, *Prostitution.* On Paul's disregard for slave prostitutes, see Glancy, *Slavery in Early Christianity,* 39–70.

27. Helmut Koester, "Imperial Ideology and Paul's Eschatology in 1 Thessalonians," in *Paul and Empire: Religion and Power in Roman Imperial Soci-*

ety, ed. Richard A. Horsley (Harrisburg: Trinity Press International, 1997), 158–66.

28. Also see 1 Corinthians 15:20. There Paul states that Jesus is the "first fruits of those who have died," implying that the harvest has begun and the general resurrection will take place that same season.

29. For an excellent overview of the reception of Paul's views in the writings of later New Testament writers, see Margaret Y. MacDonald, "Rereading Paul: Early Interpreters of Paul on Women and Gender," in Kraemer and D'Angelo, *Women and Christian Origins,* 236–53.

30. Origen, *Homilies on Hebrews,* preserved by Eusebius, *Ecclesiastical History* 6.27.7, G. A. Williamson, trans., rev. trans. Andrew Louth, *Eusebius: The History of the Church from Christ to Constantine* (New York: Penguin Classics, 1965, rev. ed. 1989), 202.

31. The New Testament letter 2 Thessalonians, which may not actually be by Paul, also acknowledges the problem of forgeries: "We beg you . . . not to be quickly shaken in mind or alarmed, either by spirit or by word or by letter, as though from us." (2 Thessalonians 2:1–2). In other words, the Thessalonians were in possession of a letter identified with Paul and his companions Silvanus and Timothy that had upset them. This letter, 2 Thessalonians argues, should be recognized as false.

32. See J. K. Elliott, *The Apocryphal New Testament: A Collection of Apocryphal Christian Literature in an English Translation Based on M. R. James* (Oxford: Clarendon, 1993), 353–54, 380–82, 546–54.

33. For more information regarding Colossians and its likely identity as a pseudepigraphical letter attributed to but not written by Paul, see James D. G. Dunn, *The Epistles to Colossians and Philemon* (Grand Rapids: Eerdmans, 1996); Eduard Lohse, *Colossians and Philemon* (Philadelphia: Fortress Press, 1971). On the "household code" in Colossians, see Margaret Y. MacDonald, *The Pauline Churches: A Socio-Historical Study of Institutionalization in the Pauline and Deutero-Pauline Writings* (Cambridge: Cambridge Univ. Press, 1988); Mary Rose D'Angelo, "Colossians," in *Searching the Scriptures,* vol. 2, *A Feminist Commentary,* ed. Elisabeth Schüssler Fiorenza (New York: Crossroad, 1994), 313–24; David Balch and Carolyn Osiek, *Families in the New Testament World* (Louisville: Westminster John Knox Press, 1997), 118–21. The work of Elisabeth Schüssler Fiorenza remains central to this discussion. See her now classic work *In Memory of Her: A Feminist Theological Reconstruction of Christian Origins* (New York: Crossroad, 1989), esp. 251–59.

34. Lutz, "Musonius Rufus," 67.

35. On Ephesians and the household codes, see Sarah J. Tanzer, "Ephesians" in

Schüssler Fiorenza, *Searching the Scriptures,* 325–48 and *In Memory of Her,* 266–70.

36. *Oeconomicus* 10.9–12, trans. Sarah B. Pomeroy, *Xenophon Oeconomicus: A Social and Historical Commentary* (Oxford: Clarendon, 1994), 163. On the idealized wife of the *Oeconomicus,* see Sheila Murnaghan, "How a Woman Can Be More Like a Man: The Dialogue Between Isomachus and His Wife in Xenophon's *Oeconomicus,*" *Helios* 15.1 (1988): 9–22, with response by Anthony Gini, "The Manly Intellect of His Wife: Xenophon 'Oeconomicus' 7," *Classical World* 86.6 (1993): 483–86.

37. Pomeroy, "The *Oeconomicus* after Xenophon," in *Xenophon Oeconomicus,* 68–90 (69–73).

38. On topics and rhetorical exercises, see Raffaella Cribiore, *Gymnastics of the Mind: Greek Education in Hellenistic and Roman Egypt* (Princeton: Princeton Univ. Press, 2001), esp. 220–35. As Teresa Morgan points out, a series of sayings memorized and copied by schoolboys includes several about the household: "A good woman saves a man's household in one quotation, his *bios* [life as a citizen] in another" (136). Children were also explicitly taught to honor their fathers and to consider women primarily in their role as wives (138). See her study, *Literate Education in the Hellenistic and Roman Worlds* (Cambridge: Cambridge Univ. Press, 1998). On the popularity of the topic in later Greek philosophical works, see Sarah B. Pomeroy, *Goddesses, Whores, Wives, and Slaves: Women in Classical Antiquity* (New York: Schocken Books, 1975), 132–36; Sarah B. Pomeroy, *Women in Hellenistic Egypt: From Alexander to Cleopatra* (New York: Schocken Books, 1984), 67–71. On the reception of these works in Roman contexts, see Treggiari, *Roman Marriage,* 205–27.

39. I'm taking the lead here from Jennifer A. Glancy, "Protocols of Masculinity in the Pastoral Epistles," in *New Testament Masculinities,* ed. Stephen D. Moore and Janice Capel Anderson, Semeia Studies 45 (Atlanta: Society of Biblical Literature, 2003), 235–64.

40. Like most contemporary scholars, I am assuming that these letters were forged in Paul's name. They are not mentioned in Christian writings until the third century, and even then their authenticity was disputed. Nevertheless, they were ultimately accepted as Pauline and, by the fourth century, were included in the developing canon lists of the orthodox churches. For further discussion, see J. D. Quinn, "Timothy and Titus, Epistles to," *Anchor Bible Dictionary* 6:560–71.

41. This topic will be addressed at greater length in the next chapter.

42. *katastrêniaô*—the precise meaning of this word is unclear.

43. 1 Timothy 5:11; compare 5:6: "the widow who lives for pleasure is dead even while she lives."

44. See 1 Timothy 2:8; 3:1–10; 4:8; 6:11–12; 2 Timothy 2:1–3, 15, 22; 4:3–5; Titus 1:6–15. See further Glancy, "Protocols of Masculinity"; Mary Rose D'Angelo, "'Knowing How to Preside Over His Own Household': Imperial Masculinity and Christian Asceticism in the Pastorals, *Hermas,* and Luke-Acts," in *New Testament Masculinities,* 265–95 (271–76); Mary Rose D'Angelo, "*Eusebeia*: Roman Imperial Family Values and the Sexual Politics of 4 Maccabees and the Pastorals," *Biblical Interpretation* 11.2 (2003):139–65.

45. D'Angelo, "Imperial Masculinity," 274.

46. D'Angelo, "Imperial Masculinity," 277.

47. See Jouette Bassler, "The Widow's Tale: A Fresh Look at 1 Timothy 5:3–16," *Journal of Biblical Literature* 103 (1984): 232–41; Margaret Y. MacDonald, *Early Christian Women and Pagan Opinion: The Power of the Hysterical Woman* (Cambridge: Cambridge Univ. Press, 1996), esp. 157–77.

48. See Charlotte Methuen, "'Virgin Widow': A Problematic Social Role for the Early Church?" *Harvard Theological Review* 90.3 (1997): 285–98; Jan Bremmer, "Pauper or Patroness: The Widow in the Early Christian Church," in *Between Poverty and the Pyre: Moments in the History of Widowhood,* ed. Laurens van den Bosch (London: Routledge, 1995), 35.

49. Ignatius, *Letter to the Smyrneans* 13, in Bart D. Ehrman, ed. and trans., *The Apostolic Fathers,* vol. 1, LCL 24 (Cambridge: Harvard Univ. Press, 2003), 309.

50. Ehrman, *Apostolic Fathers,* 1:315.

51. *Acts of Paul,* trans. J. K. Elliott, *The Apocryphal New Testament* (Oxford: Clarendon, 1993), 364–72 (365).

52. Methuen, "Virgin Widow," 293–97. See further Susanna Elm, *Virgins of God: The Making of Asceticism in Late Antiquity* (Oxford: Clarendon, 1994).

53. Treggiari, *Roman Marriage,* 69: "Maternity was the only way for a woman to escape from the requirement that she be under lifelong guardianship. Free-born women qualified for freedom from guardianship if they had three children; freedwomen who were under the guardianship of their patron or his male descendants needed for children to escape."

54. Gaius, *Institutes* 1.44, translated and discussed by Judith Evans Grubbs, *Women and the Law in the Roman Empire* (London and New York: Routledge, 2002), 24–25.

55. "To women the Julian Law gave a grace period of one year from the death of a husband and six months from a divorce, but the Papian Law gave two years from the death of a husband and one year and six months from a divorce" (*Tituli Ulpiani* 14), translated and discussed by Treggiari, *Roman Marriage,* 73.

56. Glancy, "Protocols of Masculinity," 238–49. Also see Knust, *Abandoned to Lust.*

57. Charla Muller with Betsy Thorpe, *365 Nights: A Memoir of Intimacy* (New York: Berkeley, 2008); Douglas A. Brown, *Just Do It: How One Couple Turned Off the TV and Turned On Their Sex Lives for 101 Days (No Excuses!)* (New York: Three Rivers, 2009).

58. Appleton, "Grapevine pastor wants married couples to have sex."

CHAPTER 4: *Sexual Politics*

1. Jerry Falwell, *The 700 Club,* September 13, 2001, quoted in Laurie Goodstein, "Falwell's Finger Pointing Inappropriate, Bush Says," *New York Times* (September 15, 2001), A15.

2. Christians invented the name "Jehovah" on the basis of an erroneous understanding of the Hebrew name for God, Yhwh. According to Jewish tradition, one is not supposed to speak the divine name. Hence, when printing the name Yhwh, Hebrew Bibles print the consonants YHWH with the vowels for the word *Adonai,* or "Lord." When encountering YHWH in the Hebrew while reading aloud, one says "Adonai," or "Lord," instead. "Jehovah" combines the consonants of YHWH with the vowels for Adonai, inventing a name for God that does not actually appear in the biblical text. Nevertheless, the name Jehovah has enjoyed a long history in English Bibles and is still employed in the Authorized [King James] Version today.

3. Kelly Boggs, "Islam through a glass darkly," Southern Baptist Convention—Southern Baptist Churches Annual Meeting 2002 Newsroom (June 13, 2002), www.sbcannualmeeting.org/sbc02/newsroom/newspage. asp?ID=285; Susan Sachs, "Baptist Pastor Attacks Islam, Inciting Cries of Intolerance," *New York Times* (June 15, 2002), A10.

4. The Bible's preferred terms for "not part of Israel," "not Jewish" or "not Christian" include *goy, goyah, goyyim* (Hebrew "non-Israelite") and *ethnos, ethnê* (Greek "nation, people" or "non-Jew") but not "pagan." Pagan is from the Latin word *paganus,* a word associated with those from small villages, which was first applied to non-Christians in the fourth and fifth centuries. See Gillian Clark, *Christianity and Roman Society,* Key Themes in Ancient History (Cambridge: Cambridge Univ. Press, 2004), 35–37.

5. The precise date and circumstances of the book of Hosea are difficult to determine. According to most modern scholars, it is likely that the book was the product of a prophetic school rather than one prophet and was edited several times, reaching its final form long after the eighth century BCE, when Hosea the prophet was first delivering oracles to Israel. The first three chapters of the book, however, are usually considered to be the earliest. They were probably written just prior to the fall of Israel to the Assyrians in 721 BCE. For further discussion, see Gale A. Yee, "'She Is Not My Wife and I

Am Not Her Husband': A Materialist Analysis of Hosea 1–2," *Biblical Interpretation* 9.4 (2001): 345–83 and Gale A. Yee, *Composition and Tradition in the Book of Hosea: A Redaction Critical Investigation,* SBL Dissertation Series 102 (Atlanta: Scholars Press, 1985).

6. This is a complicated passage and a complex metaphor. I would particularly like to thank my colleague Katheryn Pfisterer Darr for discussing it with me and for pointing me to some of the most important bibliography. For a recent appraisal, see Geraldine Bauman, *Love and Violence: Marriage as a Metaphor for the Relationship between YHWH and Israel in the Prophetic Books* (Collegeville, MN: Liturgical Press, 2003). For further discussion of Hosea's "wife of harlotry," see Yvonne Sherwood, *The Prostitute and the Prophet: Hosea's Marriage in Literary-Theoretical Perspective,* JSOT Supplement Series 212, Gender Culture, Theory 2 (Sheffield: Sheffield Academic, 1996).

7. See Katheryn Pfisterer Darr, "Ezekiel," in *The Women's Bible Commentary,* ed. Carol A. Newsom and Sharon H. Ringe (Louisville: Westminster John Knox, 1992), 183–90; Julie Galambush, *Jerusalem in the Book of Ezekiel: The City as Yahweh's Wife,* Society of Biblical Literature Dissertation Series 130 (Atlanta: Scholars Press, 1992); Linda Day, "Rhetoric and Domestic Violence in Ezekiel 16," *Biblical Interpretation* 8.3 (2000): 205–30; Peggy L. Day, "The Bitch Had It Coming to Her: Rhetoric and Interpretation in Ezekiel 16," *Biblical Interpretation* 8.3 (2000): 231–54. As Peggy Day notes, Ezekiel writes as if the Temple is still standing, though this does not necessarily imply that it was (234). On the date of Ezekiel and the circumstances of the exile, see Meindert Dijkstra, "The Valley of Dry Bones: Coping with the Reality of the Exile in the Book of Ezekiel," in *The Crisis of Israelite Religion: Transformation of Religious Tradition in Exilic and Post-Exilic Times,* ed. Bob Becking, Marjo C. A. Korpel (Leiden: Brill, 1999), 114–33; Rainer Albertz, *Israel in Exile: The History and Literature of the Sixth Century B.C.E.,* trans. David Green (Atlanta: Society of Biblical Literature, 2003); Moshe Greenberg, *Ezekiel 1–20,* Anchor Bible 22 (New York: Doubleday, 1983).

8. See Exodus 34:15–16; Leviticus 17:7; 20:1–9; Deuteronomy 7:1–6; Judges 2:17; 8:27; 1 Chronicles 5:25; 2 Kings 9:22; compare Acts 15:20–29; Revelation 9:20–21; 17:1.

9. See further Barbara R. Rossing, *The Choice Between Two Cities: Whore, Bride and Empire in the Apocalypse,* Harvard Theological Studies 48 (Harrisburg, PA: Trinity Press International, 1999); Frederick J. Murphy, *Fallen Is Babylon: The Revelation to John* (Harrisburg, PA: Trinity Press International, 1998); Catherine Keller, *Apocalypse Now and Then: A Feminist Guide to the End of the World* (Boston: Beacon Press, 1996); Leonard L. Thomp-

son, *The Book of Revelation: Apocalypse and Empire* (Oxford: Oxford Univ. Press, 2000); Elisabeth Schüssler Fiorenza, *Revelation: Vision of a Just World,* Proclamation Commentaries (Minneapolis: Fortress Press, 1991). Scholars are unanimous in viewing this "whore" as a personification of Rome, an identification that is made clear by the author when he identifies the city as "seated on many waters" (17:1), seven mountains "on which the woman is seated" (17:9), and "the great city that rules over the kings of the earth" (17:18).

10. William Foxwell Albright, *Archaeology and the Religion of Israel* (New York: Anchor Books, 1969), 75, 91. Also see his essay, "The Role of Canaanites in the History of Civilization," in *The Bible and the Ancient Near East: Essays in Honor of W. F. Albright,* ed. G. E. Wright (New York: Doubleday, 1961), 438–87, esp. 438: "Canaanite religion . . . adopted some of the most demoralizing cultic practices then existing in the Near East."

11. Similarly, describing the crime of infanticide, listed as one of the abominable acts characteristic of the Canaanites and Egyptians in Leviticus (18:1–30), F. E. Hirsch and J. K. Grider insisted that such an abhorrent practice was "quite foreign to the minds of the Hebrews," though some might have been tempted to sacrifice their children "when following the religious customs of the Canaanites." Once again, the Canaanites were presumed guilty and any poor behavior on the part of Israel was blamed on their negative influence. F. E. Hirsch and J. K. Grider, "Crime," in *The International Standard Bible Encyclopedia,* ed. Geoffrey W. Bromiley, et al. (Grand Rapids: Eerdmans, 1979), 816. As Lewis Bayles Paton concluded, the degrading influence of Canaanite religion was "a real menace" that required constant vigilance. Lewis Bayles Paton, "Canaanite Influence on the Religion of Israel," *The American Journal of Theology* 18.2 (1914): 205–24 (209). According to Paton, the Israelites had no choice but to purge their religion of the "contamination that it had contracted in its career of conquest" (224).

12. See, for example, Brian S. Rosner, "Temple Prostitution in 1 Corinthians 6:12–20," *Novum Testamentum* 40.4 (1998): 336–51.

13. See, for example, Charles K. Williams II, "Corinth and the Cult of Aphrodite," in *Corinthiaca: Studies in Honor of Darrell A. Amyx,* ed. Mario A. Del Chiaro and William R. Biers (Columbia: Univ. of Missouri Press, 1986), 12–24.

14. I would like to acknowledge the invaluable assistance of my colleague Alejandro Botta in the identification of the relevant bibliography for this section as well as the section (below), "Yhwh and his Asherah."

15. Phyllis Bird, "The Harlot as Heroine: Narrative Art and Social Presupposition in Three Old Testament Texts," in *Missing Persons,* 197–218 (199–201).

For an alternative point of view, see Richard S. Hess, *Israelites Religions: An Archaeological and Biblical Survey* (Grand Rapids: Baker Academic, 2007), 332–35. Hess leaves open the possibility that there may have been such prostitutes, though they are just as likely to have been nonpriestly employees of the temples.

16. Genesis 38. See discussion in Phyllis Bird, " 'To Play the Harlot': An Inquiry into an Old Testament Metaphor," in *Missing Persons and Mistaken Identities,* 219–36 (222–23).

17. Judges 16:1. See Phyllis Bird, "Prostitution in the Social World and Religious Rhetoric of Ancient Israel," in *Prostitutes and Courtesans in the Ancient World,* ed. Christopher A. Faraone and Laura McClure (Madison, WI: Univ. of Wisconsin Press, 2006), 40–58 (46).

18. Lipit-Ishtar Lawcode 27, in Roth, *Law Collections,* 31.

19. Middle Assyrian Laws 40, in Roth, *Law Collections,* 185–86. See further Sophie Lafont, "Middle Assyrian Laws," in *A History of Ancient Near Eastern Law,* ed. Raymond Westbrook (Leiden: Brill, 2003) 1: 521–63 (534).

20. Similarly, a document from sixth-century BCE Persia warns "Tabat-Ishar, daughter of Jashe'ijama" that she must not consort with "Kulu, son of Kalba"; if she does, she will be enslaved. Cyr. 307 (British Museum no. 74923), cited, translated and discussed by Martha T. Roth, "Marriage, Divorce and the Prostitute in Ancient Mesopotamia," in Faraone and McClure, *Prostitutes and Courtesans,* 21–39 (31). Roth includes several other examples of this sort of document in her discussion.

21. See esp. Delbert R. Hillers, "Analyzing the Abominable: Our Understanding of Canaanite Religion," *Jewish Quarterly Review* 75.3 (1985): 253–69 and Mark S. Smith, "Ugaritic Studies and Israelite Religion: A Retrospective View," *Near Eastern Archaeology* 65.1 (2002): 17–29.

22. Stephanie Lynn Budin, *The Myth of Sacred Prostitution in Antiquity* (Cambridge: Cambridge Univ. Press, 2008), 29–31, 45–47. Also see Ziony Zevit, *The Religions of Ancient Israel: A Synthesis of Parallactic Approaches* (New York: Continuum, 2001), 462–63.

23. Budin, *Sacred Prostitution,* 34–35; Zevit, *Religions of Ancient Israel,* 463: "In Israel, [the *qedesot*] may have been cultic poets and musicians, bearers of Syrian mythic traditions."

24. Budin, *Sacred Prostitution,* 23–26, 45–46.

25. RSV: "There shall be no cult prostitute of the daughters of Israel, neither shall there be a cult prostitute of the sons of Israel." NIV: "No Israelite man or woman is to become a shrine prostitute." KJV: "There shall be no whore of the daughters of Israel, nor a sodomite of the sons of Israel."

26. Translation my own.

27. Translation my own.

28. *Herodotus: The History* 1.199, trans. David Grene (Chicago: Univ. of Chicago Press, 1987), 124.

29. Herodotus, *History* 1.5.

30. See, for example, the assessment of Herodotus's description of Egypt by A. B. Lloyd, *Herodotus, Book ii. Introduction, Commentary 1–98*. 2 vols. (Leiden: Brill, 1975–1976); David Frankfurter, *Religion in Roman Egypt: Assimilation and Resistance* (Princeton: Princeton Univ. Press, 1998), 224–25; Ian Moyer, "Herodotus and an Egyptian Mirage: The Genealogies of the Theban Priests," *Journal of Hellenic Studies* 122 (2002): 70–90. On Herodotus's depiction of Babylon, see Richard A. McNeal, *Herodotus: Book 1* (Lanham, MD: Univ. Press of America, 1986), 185–87 and "The Brides of Babylon: Herodotus 1.196," *Historia: Zeitschrift für Alte Geschichte* 37.1 (1988): 54–71.

31. Cicero, *The Laws* 1.1.5., trans. Clinton Walker Keyes, in *Cicero,* vol. 16, Loeb Classical Library (Cambridge: Harvard Univ. Press, 1977), 301.

32. *Geography* 8.6.20, *The Geography of Strabo,* trans. Horace L. Jones, 8 vols., Loeb Classical Library (Cambridge: Harvard Univ. Press, 1917–1933), 4:189–91.

33. On the *heterai,* see Vinciane Pirenne-Delforge, *L'Aphrodite grecque. Contribution à l'étude de ses cultes et de sa personnalité dans le pantheon archaïque et classique* (Athens and Liège: Centre international de l'étude de la religion greque antique, 1994).

34. Lanci, "Stones Don't Speak, 205–20 (213).

35. For an overview on the history of Corinth, see Guy D. R. Sanders, "Urban Corinth: An Introduction," in Schowalter and Friesen, *Urban Religion in Roman Corinth,* 11–24.

36. See further Mary Beard and John Henderson, "'With This Body I Thee Worship' Sacred Prostitution in Antiquity," in *Gender and the Body in the Ancient Mediterranean,* ed. Maria Wyke (London: Blackwell, 1998), 56–74; Lanci, "Stones Don't Speak" 205–20; J. Albert Harrill, *The Manumission of Slaves in Early Christianity* (Tübingen: Mohr, 1998), 70–72; Jerome Murphy-O'Connor, *St. Paul's Corinth: Texts and Archaeology* (Collegeville, MI: Liturgical Press, 1990), 55–57.

37. Athenaeus, *The Learned Banquet* 13.573. trans. Charles B. Gulick, in *Athenaeus. The Deipnosophists.* 7 vols., Loeb Classical Library (Cambridge: Harvard Univ. Press, 1927–1941), 6:96–97.

38. For more on Athenaeus, see the essays in David Braund and John Wilkins, ed. *Athenaeus and His World: Reading Greek Culture in the Roman Empire* (Exeter: Univ. of Exeter Press, 2000).

39. See further Andrew McGowan, *Ascetic Eucharists: Food and Drink in Early*

Christian Ritual Meals (New York and Oxford: Oxford Univ. Press, 1999) and Jorunn Økland, *Women in Their Place: Paul and the Corinthian Discourse of Gender and Sanctuary Space,* JSNT Supplement Series 269 (Sheffield: Clark, 2004).

40. When she is finally reunited with her beloved, the maiden Callirhoe visits Aphrodite's temple and thanks her for her assistance: "[Callirhoe] put her hands on the goddess's feet, placed her face on them, let down her hair, and kissed them. 'Thank you, Aphrodite!'" (Chariton, *Chaereas and Callirhoe* 8.8.14), trans. B. P. Reardon, in *Collected Ancient Greek Novels,* ed. B. P. Reardon (Berkeley: Univ. of California Press, 1989), 21–124 (124). Also see Achilles Tatius's description of the pleasure women enjoy during sexual intercourse, which he describes as the "sensations named for Aphrodite" (*Leucippe and Clitophon* 2.37, trans. John J. Winkler, in Reardon, *Collected Ancient Greek Novels,* 175–284 [207]).

41. Pirenne-Delforge, *L'Aphrodite grecque,* 446–58.

42. Genesis 9:22–24. Devorah Steinmetz, "Vineyard, Farm, and Garden: The Drunkenness of Noah in the Context of Primeval History," *Journal of Biblical Literature* 113 (1994): 193–207 (200); Robert W. E. Forrest, "Paradise Lost Again: Violence and Obedience in the Flood Narrative," *Journal for the Study of the Old Testament* 62 (1994): 3–18 (15–16).

43. The association of various sons of Noah with particular peoples is not consistent across biblical sources. Nevertheless, as David Aaron has observed, "The curse of Ham's son, Canaan, makes perfect sense given the socio-political realities during the time Hebrew Scriptures were composed" ("Early Rabbinic Exegesis on Noah's Son Ham and the So-Called 'Hamitic Myth'," *Journal of the American Academy of Religion* 63.4 [1995]: 721–59 [733]). Aaron associates the curse of Canaan with the provisions in Leviticus specifying that, while Hebrew slaves had to be released periodically, foreign slaves could be enslaved in perpetuity.

44. For a recent review of the scholarship on this passage, see John Sietze Bergsma and Scott Walker Hahn, "Noah's Nakedness and the Curse on Canaan (Genesis 9:20–27)," *Journal of Biblical Literature* 121.1 (2005): 25–40.

45. Alan Baumgarten, "Myth and Midrash: Genesis 9:20–29," in *Christianity, Judaism, and Other Greco-Roman Cults: Studies for Morton Smith at Sixty,* ed. Jacob Neusner (Leiden: Brill, 1975), 3:55–71; Naomi Koltun-Fromm, "Aphrahat and the Rabbis on Noah's Righteousness in Light of Jewish-Christian Polemic," in *The Book of Genesis in Jewish and Oriental Exegesis,* ed. Judith Frishman and Lucas van Rompay (Leuven: Peeters, 1997), 57–72 (65–67).

46. "And Noah awoke from his wine, and knew what his youngest son had

done to him (Gen 9:24). Rav and Sameul differ, one maintains that he (Ham) castrated him, while the other says that he sexually abused him. He who says that he castrated him (reasons) because he cursed him (Ham) by his fourth son (Canaan), he (Ham) must have injured him (Noah) with respect to a fourth son. . . . Now, on the view that he emasculated him, it is right that he cursed him by his fourth son; but on the view that he abused him, why did he curse his fourth son: he should have cursed him (Ham)? Both indignities were perpetuated" (Babylonian Talmud, Sanhedrin 70a, trans. Koltun-Fromm, 67).

47. Philo of Alexandria, a first-century Jewish interpreter, offered a similar interpretation (*On Sobriety* 45–48). Preserved by Christians rather than Jews, Philo's writings may well have influenced Christian interpretations.

48. Methodius, *On Chastity* 2, trans. William R. Clark, in *Ante-Nicene Fathers*, vol. 6, *Gregory Thaumaturgus, Dionysius the Great, Julius Africanus, Anatolius and Minor Writers Methodius, Arnobius* (New York: Christian Literature Publishing, 1886; repr. Peabody, MA: Hendrickson, 1995), 309–55 (348).

49. Ambrose of Milan, *On the Duties of the Clergy* 18.79.

50. See further Stephen Haynes, *Noah's Curse: The Biblical Justification of American Slavery* (New York and London: Oxford Univ. Press, 2002), 24–30.

51. Leviticus 20:17. See Frederick W. Bassett, "Noah's Nakedness and the Curse of Canaan, a Case of Incest?" *Vetus Testamentum* 21.2 (1971): 232–37 (233).

52. The use of the phrase "uncovering nakedness" in the context of narratives of invasion and conquest suggest that the latter interpretation is at least possible. For example, when the brothers of the biblical patriarch Joseph visit him in Egypt, he accuses them of being spies, eager to scout out the "nakedness of the land" so that they might invade (Genesis 42:1–17, esp. v. 9). Warning the Babylonians that God plans to punish them, the prophet Nahum imagines Yhwh stating: "I . . . will lift up your skirts over your face; and I will let nations look on your nakedness and kingdoms on your shame!" (Nah. 3:5). A "naked" nation is therefore a nation that has been invaded and overthrown.

53. Deuteronomy 23:1; 27:20. This discussion repeats arguments made by Bergsma and Hahn, "Noah's Nakedness," esp. 34–40, though I disagree with their emphasis on the "heterosexual" nature of Ham's infraction. Also see Bassett, "Noah's Nakedness."

54. "The LORD struck the child that Uriah's wife bore to David" (2 Sam. 12:15). "And Absalom went in to his father's concubines in the sight of all Israel" (12:11; 16:22–23).

55. This story would go on in infamy as the curse of Canaan was transposed

and then transported to colonial America. Relabeling it the "curse of Ham," colonists identified Ham and his son Canaan with blackness and then invoked biblical authority to justify the eternal enslavement of Africans on American soil. See esp. Sylvester A. Johnson, *The Myth of Ham in Nineteenth-Century American Christianity: Race, Heathens, and the People of God* (New York: Palgrave Macmillan, 2004).

56. See Lori Rowlett, "Disney's Pocahontas and Joshua's Rahab in Postcolonial Perspective," in *Culture, Entertainment and the Bible,* ed. George Aichele, JSOT Supplement Series 309 (Sheffield: Sheffield Academic, 2000), 66–75.

57. "I will give to you, and to your offspring after you, the land where you are now an alien, all the land of Canaan, for a perpetual holding; and I will be their God" (Gen. 17:8).

58. The episode of Rahab and the spies is found in Joshua 2:1–21.

59. See further Erin Runions, "From Disgust to Humor: Rahab's Queer Affect," *Postscripts: The Journal of Sacred Texts and Contemporary Worlds* 4.1 (2008): 41–69; Phyllis Bird, "The Harlot as Heroine: Narrative Art and Social Presupposition in Three Old Testament Texts," in *Missing Persons and Mistaken Identities,* 197–218 (208–16).

60. Joshua 6:17, 19, 21. On the notion of *herem,* see Philip D. Stern, *The Biblical Herem: A Window on Israel's Religious Experience,* Brown Judaic Studies 211 (Atlanta: Scholars Press, 1991). On *herem* in the book of Joshua, see Richard D. Nelson, *Joshua: A Commentary,* Old Testament Library (Louisville: Westminster John Knox, 1997), 19–20, 93–95, 101–3.

61. The Moabite Stone, discussed by John J. Collins, "The Zeal of Phinehas: The Bible and the Legitimation of Violence," *Journal of Biblical Literature* 122.1 (2003): 3–21 (5).

62. On the date of the book of Joshua, see Richard D. Nelson, *Joshua: A Commentary,* The Old Testament Library (Louisville: Westminster John Knox Press, 1997), 2–9.

63. For a devastating account of the conquest narrative, as seen from the Canaanite perspective, see Robert Warrior, "Canaanites, Cowboys and Indians: Deliverance, Conquest, and Liberation Theology Today," *Christianity and Crisis* 49 (September 11, 1989): 261–65.

64. As Randall C. Bailey points out, the "sexualization of the indigene" in these stories legitimates the dispossession of the Canaanites from the land. See his essay, "He Didn't Even Tell Us the Worst of It!" *Union Seminary Quarterly Review* 59.1–2 (2005): 15–24 (20).

65. Judith E. McKinlay, "Rahab: A Hero/ine?" *Biblical Interpretation* 7.1 (1999): 44–57 (45). This verb is employed in the sense of to "lie down for the

purpose of sexual intercourse" in Genesis 19:33–35; 30:15–16; Exodus 22:16; Deuteronomy 22:22; Numbers 5:19, and elsewhere.

66.   Dana Nolan Fewell and David M. Gunn, *Gender, Power, and Promise: The Subject of the Bible's First Story* (Nashville: Abingdon, 1993), 120–21.

67.   The precise contours of Hebrew settlement in the land of Canaan/Israel remains hotly debated, with some suggesting that there must have been some sort of conquest and others arguing that the entry of Yhwhists into Canaan was entirely peaceful. Nevertheless, few would argue that the Joshua narrative is "historical" in any modern sense. For a range of opinions on the matter, see, for example, George Mendenhall, "The Hebrew Conquest of Palestine," *The Biblical Archaeologist* 25 (1962): 66–87; Albrecht Alt, *Essays on Old Testament History and Religion,* trans. Robert Wilson (Garden City, NY: Doubleday/Anchor Books, 1966); Robert G. Boling, *Joshua: A New Translation with Notes and Commentary* (Garden City, NY: Doubleday, 1982), 74–88; Israel Finkelstein, *The Archaeology of the Israelite Settlement* (Jerusalem: Israelite Exploration Society, 1988); Mark S. Smith, *The Early History of God: Yahweh and the Other Deities in Ancient Israel* (San Francisco: Harper & Row, 1990); Israel Finkelstein, "Ethnicity and Origin of the Iron I Settlers in the Highlands of Canaan: Can the Real Israel Stand Up?" *The Biblical Archaeologist* 59.4 (1996): 198–212; Susan Niditch, *Ancient Israelite Religion* (New York and Oxford: Oxford Univ. Press, 1997), 10–14; Zevit, *Religions of Ancient Israel,* 114–15 n. 48.

68.   Michael G. Hasel, "Israel in the Merneptah Stele," *Bulletin of the American Schools of Oriental Research* 296 (1994): 45–61.

69.   John Huehnergard, "Languages of the Ancient Near East," *Anchor Bible Dictionary,* vol. 4 (New York: Doubleday, 1992), 155–70. I would particularly like to thank my colleague Alejandro Botta for his assistance with the Canaanite languages.

70.   Niditch, *Ancient Israelite Religion,* 10–14.

71.   See Lester L. Grabbe, "'Canaanite': Some Methodological Observations in Relation to Biblical Study," in *Ugarit and the Bible: Proceedings of the International Symposium on Ugarit and the Bible,* ed. G. J. Brooke, A. H. W. Curtis, and J. F. Healey, Ugeritisch-biblisch Literatur 11 (Münster: Ugarit-Varlag, 1994).

72.   Judith M. Hadley, "The Khirbet el-Qom Inscription," *Vetus Testamentum* 37.1 (1987): 50–62 (51). William Shea offers a slightly different reconstruction and translation, suggesting that Uriyahu's slave had an asherah, not Uriyahu himself. See his "The Khirbet el-Qom Tomb Inscription Again," *Vetus Testamentum* 60.1 (1990): 110–16. Also see Judith M. Hadley, *The Cult of Asherah in Ancient Israel and Judah: Evidence for a Hebrew Goddess,* Cambridge Oriental Publications 57 (Cambridge: Cambridge Univ. Press, 2000)

and Saul M. Olyan, *The Cult of Yahweh in Israel,* SBL Monograph Series 24 (Atlanta: Scholars Press, 1988), 23–25.

73. Olyan in particular makes this argument. Also see Niditch, *Ancient Israelite Religion,* 20–22.

74. Smith, *Early History of God,* 49–55. Also see John Day, *Yahweh and the Gods and Goddesses of Canaan,* JSOT Supplement Series 265 (Sheffield: Sheffield Academic, 2000); Zevit, *Religions of Ancient Israel.*

75. For an overview of the archaeological evidence, see Hess, *Israelite Religions,* 297–332.

76. Also see Stone, *Safer Texts,* 57–64.

77. As one particularly strident website puts it, holding California responsible for ruining the rest of the United States: "California leads the way in moral rot, feminism, liberal agendas, homosexuality, wacko environmental laws, the highest prison population, scams, false prophets, cults and sadly, divorce. I say this kindly, but to America's shame. . . . I think Lex Luthor was on to something when he wanted to nuke the San Andreas' fault line and plunge California into the Pacific Ocean. Curse you Superman!" David J. Stewart, "Divorce Rate 75.54% in California!!!" www.jesus-is-savior.com/Evils%20 in%20America/Divorce/california.htm. For an alternative point of view, see Dan Hurley, "Divorce Rate: It's Not as High as You Think," *New York Times* April 19, 2005, http://query.nytimes.com/gst/fullpage.html?res=9805E2DE1 F3EF93AA25757C0A9639C8B63.

78. For a helpful overview of Israelite concerns regarding purity and sacrifice, see esp. Jonathan Klawans, *Impurity and Sin in Ancient Judaism* (New York and Oxford: Oxford Univ. Press) and *Purity, Sacrifice, and the Temple: Symbolism and Supersessionism in the Study of Ancient Judaism* (New York and Oxford: Oxford Univ. Press, 2006), 49–74.

79. See esp. Mary Douglas, *Purity and Danger: An Analysis of Concepts of Pollution and Taboo* (repr. London: Routledge, 1991), 41–57 and her updated version of this thesis, *Leviticus as Literature* (New York and Oxford: Oxford Univ. Press, 1999), esp. 134–45. Milgrom does not fully accept Douglas's point of view, though he is persuaded that separation and distinction are the main principles driving the dietary laws (Jacob Milgrom, *Leviticus 1–16: A New Translation with Introduction and Commentary* [Anchor Bible New York: Doubleday, 2000], vol. 1, 721–36). On the issue of blood, see William K. Gilders, *Blood Ritual in the Hebrew Bible: Meaning and Power* (Baltimore, MD: Johns Hopkins Univ. Press, 2004).

80. I follow Saul M. Olyan here in translating this phrase as literally as possible. See his essay, " 'And with a Male You Shall Not Lie the Lying Down of a

Woman': On the Meaning and Significance of Leviticus 18:22 and 20:13," *Journal of the History of Sexuality* 5.2 (1994): 79–206.

81. This discussion is heavily informed by the detailed and helpful analysis of Jacob Milgrom, *Leviticus 17–22: A New Translation with Introduction and Commentary* (Anchor Bible New York: Doubleday, 2000).

82. Gershon Hepner, "Abraham's Incestuous Marriage with Sarah a Violation of the Holiness Code," *Vetus Testamentum* 53.2 (2003): 143–55.

83. Calum M. Carmichael suggests that Leviticus intends to respond directly to these ancestral infractions, shaping the list of laws in light of narratives in Genesis. See his *Law, Legend and Incest in the Bible: Leviticus 18–20* (Cornell: Cornell Univ. Press, 1997).

84. Tirzah Meacham, "The Missing Daughter: Leviticus 18 and 20," *Zeitschrift für die Alttestamentliche Wissenschaft* 109. 2 (1997): 254–59 (258).

85. Jonathan R. Ziskind, "The Missing Daughter in Leviticus XVIII," *Vetus Testamentum* 46.1 (1996): 125–30.

86. Roth, *Law Collections,* 110–11. For further discussion of these laws, see Raymond Westbrook, "Old Babylonian Law," in *A History of Ancient Near Eastern Law,* 1: 361–430 (418).

87. Hittite Laws 187–200, trans. Harry A. Hoffner Jr., in Roth, *Law Collections,* 236–37.

88. See Meacham, "Missing Daughter," 254–55.

89. Ziskind, "Missing Daughter," 125–30.

90. See Exodus 22:16–17 and Deuteronomy 22:13–21, as discussed in chapter 2. Also see Judith Romney Wegner, "Leviticus," in Newsom and Ringe, *Women's Bible Commentary,* 36–44 (41).

91. Milgrom, *Leviticus 17–22,* 1528.

92. Here I am following Milgrom, *Leviticus 17–22,* 1567. Also see Stephen F. Bigger, "The Family Laws of Leviticus 18 in Their Setting," *Journal of Biblical Literature* 98.2 (1979): 187–203.

93. Olyan, "With a Male You Shall Not," 181–82.

94. Olyan, "With a Male You Shall Not," 184.

95. Olyan, "With a Male You Shall Not," 185.

96. Many English translations render *tebhel* as "it is a perversion," but, as Mary Douglas pointed out in 1966, this is incorrect. *Tebhel* is a rare Hebrew word, with a very specific meaning involving inappropriate mixing. See her *Purity and Danger,* 53.

97. Daniel Boyarin, "Are There Any Jews in the 'History of Sexuality'?" *Journal of the History of Sexuality* 5.3 (1995): 333–55 (342–43).

98. Boyarin, "Are There Any Jews," 343.

99. Bigger, "Family Laws," 195–96, 202. Also see Olyan, "With a Male You Shall Not," 201–6.

100. Ackerman, *When Heroes Love,* 165–66.

101. See Carol A Newsom, "Woman and the Discourse of Patriarchal Wisdom: A Study of Proverbs 1–9," in *Women in the Hebrew Bible: A Reader,* ed. Alice Bach (New York and London: Routledge, 1999), 93.

CHAPTER 5: *Strange Flesh*

1. Rainer Maria Rilke, *Duino Elegies,* First Elegy, trans. J. B. Leishman and Stephen Spender (New York: Norton, 1939), 21.

2. Rilke, *Duino Elegies,* 21.

3. Rilke explained, "The angel of the *Elegies* is the being who vouches for the recognition of a higher degree of reality in the invisible.— Therefore 'terrible' to us, because we, its lovers and transformers, still depend on the visible." Quoted and translated by Leishman and Spender, *Duino Elegies,* 87. For further discussion, see Kathleen L. Komar, *Transcending Angels: Rainer Maria Rilke's Duino Elegies* (Lincoln: Univ. of Nebraska Press, 1987), esp. 25–27, 39, 41–45.

4. For example, in his poem "The Angels," he states: "They all have tired mouths and bright seamless souls. And a longing (as for sin) sometimes haunts their dreams." Rainer Maria Rilke, "The Angels," in *The Book of Images,* translated with German on facing pages by Edward Snow, rev. ed. (New York: Farrar, Straus and Giroux, 1994), 31.

5. Tamara C. Eskenazi and Eleanore P. Judd, "Marriage to a Stranger in Ezra 9–10," in *Second Temple Studies,* vol. 2, *Temple Community in the Persian Period,* ed. Tamara C. Eskenazi and Kent H. Richards, JSOT Supplement Series 175 (Sheffield: JSOT Press, 1994), 266–72; Klawans, *Impurity and Sin,* 43–66; Christine E. Hayes, *Gentile Impurities and Jewish Identities: Intermarriage and Conversion from the Bible to the Talmud* (New York and Oxford: Oxford Univ. Press, 2002), esp. 68–73; Harold C. Washington, "Israel's Holy Seed and the Foreign Women of Ezra-Nehemiah: A Kristevan Reading," *Biblical Interpretation* 11 (2003): 427–37.

6. Michael Segal, *The Book of Jubilees: Rewritten Bible, Redaction, Ideology and Theology* (Leiden: Brill, 2007), 103–4.

7. For a full survey of the evidence, see the excellent study by Annette Yoshiko Reed, *Fallen Angels and the History of Judaism and Christianity: The Reception of Enochic Literature* (Cambridge: Cambridge Univ. Press, 2005).

8. See George W. E. Nickelsburg "The Books of Enoch at Qumran: What We Know and What We Need to Think About," in *Antikes Judentum und*

frühes Christentum. Festschrift für Hartmut Stegemann zum 65. Geburstag, ed. B. Kollmann and others (Berlin: De Gruyter, 1998), 99–113; J. T. Milik, *The Books of Enoch: Aramaic Fragments of Qumran Cave 4* (Oxford: Clarendon, 1976).

9. On the relationship between Jude and 1 Enoch, see James C. VanderKam, "1 Enoch, Enochic Motifs, and Enoch in Early Christian Literature," in *The Jewish Apocalyptic Heritage in Early Christianity,* ed. James C. VanderKam and William Adler, Compendia Rerum Iudaicarum ad Novum Testamentum 4 (Minneapolis: Fortress, 1996), 35–40.

10. See Reed, *Fallen Angels,* 84–101. English translations of the fragments of Jubilees and Enoch found among the Dead Sea Scrolls are available in Florentino García Martínez, ed. and W. G. E. Watson, trans., *The Dead Sea Scrolls Translated: The Qumran Texts in English* (Leiden: Brill, 1996).

11. 1 Enoch 6–7. See Matthew Black, trans. *The Book of Enoch or 1 Enoch: A New English Edition* (Leiden: Brill, 1985), 28.

12. Black, *Book of Enoch,* 28–29.

13. Black, *Book of Enoch,* 31.

14. Jubilees 5.1. Also see Sibylline Oracle 1.90–103; Jude 6–7; 1 Peter 3:19; 2 Peter 2:4–10; 2 Baruch 56. For further discussion, see James VanderKam, *The Book of Jubilees* (Sheffield: Sheffield Academic, 2001), esp. 34–35 and Segal.

15. Sibylline Oracle 1.90–103. On the First Sibylline Oracle, see Reed, *Fallen Angels,* 108–9 and John J. Collins, "The Sibylline Oracles," in *Jewish Writings of the Second Temple Period,* ed. Michael E. Stone (Philadelphia: Fortress, 1984), 331–44 (332).

16. Testament of Naphtali 3. On the *Testaments of the Twelve Patriarchs,* see Marinus de Jonge, *Pseudepigrapha of the Old Testament as Part of Christian Literature: the Case of the Testaments of the Twelve Patriarchs and the Greek Life of Adam and Eve,* Studia in Veteris Testamenti pseudepigrapha 18 (Leiden: Brill, 2003) and Robert A. Kugler, *The Testaments of the Twelve Patriarchs* (Sheffield: Sheffield Academic, 2001).

17. R. H. Charles, trans., "The Book of Jubilees," in *Apocrypha and Pseudepigrapha of the Old Testament,* vol. 2. (Oxford: Clarendon, 1913), 1–82 (20).

18. A. F. J. Klijn, trans., "2 (Syriac Apocalypse of) Baruch," in *Old Testament Pseudepigrapha*, vol. 1, *Apocalyptic Literature and Testaments,* ed. James H. Charlesworth (New York: Doubleday, 1983), 621–52 (641).

19. It is quite difficult to establish the date of the Testament of Job with any certainty. Some would argue that it is not a Jewish book at all but was composed by Christians as late as the second century CE. Still, others would suggest that it was written by Jews as early as the first century BCE. For an

overview, see Russell P. Spittler, "The Testament of Job: A History of Research and Interpretation," in *Studies on the Testament of Job,* ed. Michael A. Knibb and Pieter W. van der Horst (Cambridge: Cambridge Univ. Press, 1989), 17–19.

20. Testament of Job 48. Russell P. Spittler, trans., "Testament of Job," in *Old Testament Pseudepigrapha,* vol. 1, *Apocalyptic Literature and Testaments,* ed. James H. Charlesworth (New York: Doubleday, 1983), 829–68 (865–66). For discussion, see Randall D. Chestnutt, "Revelatory Experiences Attributed to Biblical Women in Early Jewish Literature," in *Women Like This: New Perspectives on Jewish Women in the Greco-Roman World,* ed. Amy-Jill Levine (Atlanta: Scholars Press, 1991), 107–43 (115–24); Pieter W. van der Horst, "Images of Women in the Testament of Job," in Knibb and van der Horst, *Testament of Job,* 93–116 (101–6); Susan Garrett, "The 'Weaker Sex' and the Testament of Job," *Journal of Biblical Literature* 112.1 (1993): 55–70; and Rebecca Lesses, "Amulets and Angels: Visionary Experience in the Testament of Job and the Hekhalot Literature," in *Heavenly Tablets: Interpretation, Identity and Tradition in Ancient Judaism,* ed. Lynn LiDonnici and Andrea Lieber, Supplements to the Journal for the Study of Judaism 119 (Leiden: Brill, 2007), 49–74.

21. Tertullian, *On the Veiling of Virgins* 7.3–8.1, Geoffrey D. Dunn, trans., *Tertullian,* The Early Church Fathers (London: Routledge, 2004), 108. For further discussion, see Mary Rose D'Angelo, "Veils, Virgins and the Tongues of Men and Angels," in *Off with Her Head! The Denial of Women's Identity in Myth, Religion and Culture,* ed. Howard Eilberg-Schwartz and Wendy Doniger (Berkeley: Univ. of California Press, 1995), 131–64.

22. I have altered the NRSV translation to emphasize the specificity of the shared sins of the angels and Sodom: in both cases, lusting after "strange flesh" (*sarkos heteras*) was involved.

23. Richard J. Bauckham, *Jude, 2 Peter,* Word Biblical Commentary 50 (Waco: Word Books, 1983), 11–12; Duane F. Watson, "The Letter of Jude," in *The New Interpreter's Bible,* vol. 12 (Nashville: Abingdon Press, 1998), 475; J. Daryl Charles, *Literary Strategy in the Epistle of Jude* (Scranton: Univ. of Scranton Press, 1993), 25–48; Duane F. Watson, *Invention, Arrangement, and Style: Rhetorical Criticism of Jude and 2 Peter,* SBL Dissertation Series 104 (Atlanta: Scholars Press, 1988), 29–79; Knust, *Abandoned to Lust.*

24. Also see Donald Senior, *1 and 2 Peter* (Wilmington, DE: Michael Glazier, 1980); Jerome Neyrey, *2 Peter, Jude: A New Translation with Introduction and Commentary,* Anchor Bible (New York: Doubleday, 1993); Watson, *Invention, Arrangement, and Style.* The text of Jude is remarkably unstable. For

an excellent and thorough discussion of the issues, see Tommy Wasserman, *The Epistle of Jude: Its Text and Transmission,* Coniectanea Biblical New Testament Series 43 (Stockholm: Almqvist and Wiksell International, 2006).

25. Joseph Cardinal Ratzinger for the Congregation for the Doctrine of the Faith, "Letter to the Bishops of the Catholic Church on the Pastoral Care of Homosexual Persons," October 1, 1986, www.vatican.va/roman_curia/congregations/cfaith/documents/rc_con_cfaith_doc_19861001_homosexual-persons_en.html. Also see Eugene F. Rogers Jr., ed. *Theology and Sexuality: Classic and Contemporary Readings,* Blackwell Readings in Modern Theology (London: Blackwell, 2002), 249–58.

26. "Letter to the Bishops," paragraphs 6, 10. 15.

27. Mark D. Jordan, *The Invention of Sodomy in Christian Theology* (Chicago: Univ. of Chicago Press, 1997), esp. 29–58.

28. Jordan, *Invention of Sodomy,* 45–66.

29. See, for example, Philo's *Life of Abraham* 133–36, trans. F. H. Colson, *Philo,* vol. 6, Loeb Classical Library 289 (Cambridge: Harvard Univ. Press, 1935), 68–71.

30. For a general overview of these stories and their place within the Abraham cycle, see J. Van Seters, *Abraham in History and Tradition* (New Haven: Yale Univ. Press, 1975), 202–26.

31. The proposition that, above all, these stories are about the importance of hospitality is widely accepted among biblical scholars. See, for example, Claus Westermann, *Genesis 12–36: A Commentary,* trans. John J. Scullion (Minneapolis: Augsburg, 1985), 272–309.

32. Hermann Gunkel, *Genesis,* trans. Mark E. Biddle (originally published Göttingen: Vandenhoek & Ruprecht, 1901; repr. Macon, GA: Mercer Univ. Press, 1997), 206–8.

33. As Martti Nissinen shows, the demand "to know" (*yada*) the angels is a demand that they be permitted to engage in sexual intercourse with them, *Homoeroticism in the Biblical World: A Historical Perspective,* trans. Kirsi Stjerna (Minneapolis: Fortress Press, 1998), 46.

34. If, as most modern scholars assume, Genesis and Judges both attained their current form long after the events they describe purportedly took place, perhaps while kings were ruling in Israel, then these two books were edited and rewritten together. See Gale A. Yee, "Ideological Criticism: Judges 17–21 and the Dismembered Body," in *Judges and Method: New Approaches in Biblical Studies* (Minneapolis: Fortress Press, 1995), 146–67, esp. 164–65.

35. A helpful, close reading of this story may be found in Susan Niditch, *Judges: A Commentary,* Old Testament Library (Louisville: Westminster John Knox, 2008), 185–94.

36. T. Desmond Alexander, "Lot's Hospitality: A Clue to His Righteousness," *Journal of Biblical Literature* 104.2 (1985): 289–91 (291).

37. As Phyllis Trible points out, the rape of a daughter or concubine would be "good" in comparison to permitting the rape of a male guest (*Texts of Terror: Literary-Feminist Readings of Biblical Narratives* [Philadelphia: Fortress, 1984], 74). Also see Mary Anna Bader, *Sexual Violation in the Hebrew Bible: A Multi-Methodological Study of Genesis 34 and 2 Samuel 13,* Studies in Biblical Literature 18 (New York and Frankfurt: Peter Lang, 2006), 41–42 and Yee, "Ideological Criticism," 163.

38. Westermann, *Genesis 12–36,* 297–98. Also see Yee, "Ideological Criticism," 164–65.

39. Compare Helena Zlotnick, *Dinah's Daughters: Gender and Judaism from the Hebrew Bible to Late Antiquity* (Philadelphia: Univ. of Pennsylvania Press, 2002), 41. Also see Ken Stone, *Sex, Honor, and Power in the Deuteronomistic History,* Journal for the Study of the Old Testament Supplement Series 234 (Sheffield: Sheffield Academic, 1996), 75–84.

40. Niditch, *Judges,* 190–94.

41. Who were these women? See Eskenazi and Judd, "Marriage to a Stranger," 266–72 and Shaye J. D. Cohen, *The Beginnings of Jewishness: Boundaries, Varieties, Uncertainties* (Berkeley: Univ. of California Press, 1999), 243–44. Whether these women were truly "foreign" or Judean women left behind at the time of the exile, they were assimilated to the category "Gentile"—they had become *like* foreigners and hence could not be tolerated.

42. Peter R. Bedford, "Diaspora: Homeland Relations in Ezra-Nehemiah," *Vetus Testamentum* 52.2 (2002): 147–65 (154–55 n. 13).

43. See Deuteronomy 7:1–4. For further discussion, see Shaye J. D. Cohen, "From the Bible to the Talmud: The Prohibition of Intermarriage," *Hebrew Annual Review* 7 (1983): 23–39; Hayes, "Intermarriage and Impurity in Ancient Jewish Sources," Harvard Theological Review 92 (1999): 10–13; Hayes, *Gentile Impurities,* esp. 24–34; and Klawans, *Impurity and Sin,* 43–45.

44. For discussion, see Niditch, *Judges,* 208–11.

45. Cohen, *Beginnings of Jewishness,* 243–44; Hayes, *Gentile Impurity,* 27–33; Klawans, *Impurity and Sin,* 44–46.

46. Bader, *Sexual Violation,* 61–69.

47. On this story, see Susanne Scholz, *Rape Plots: A Feminist Cultural Study of Genesis 34,* Studies in Biblical Literature 13 (New York: Peter Lang, 2000). For an alternative reading, see Zlotnick, *Dinah's Daughters,* 33–56 and Lyn M. Bechtel, "What If Dinah Is Not Raped? (Genesis 34)," *Journal for the Study of the Old Testament* 62 (1994): 19–36.

48. See Deuteronomy 22:28–30. Still this law would not have been extended to include a Hivvite like Shechem.

49. Bader, *Sexual Violation,* 28, 38–40.

50. Zlotnick, *Dinah's Daughters,* 48.

51. As Shaye J. D. Cohen has ably demonstrated, the rabbinic view that in cases of intermarriage Jewish identity passes through the female line cannot be found prior to the codification of the Mishnah. See *Beginnings of Jewishness,* 283–307.

52. Deuteronomy 17:17. See Claudia V. Camp, "1 and 2 Kings," in Newsom and Ringe, *Women's Bible Commentary,* 96–109 (102).

53. Famously, King Ahab married Jezebel, the Phoenician princess and devotee of the god Baal (see 1 Kings 16:31), leading to both idolatry and bloodshed in Israel. For further discussion, see the introduction.

54. See Klawans, *Impurity and Sin,* 22–26.

55. Washington, "Israel's Holy Seed," 427–37.

56. David Biale, *Eros and the Jews: From Biblical Israel to Contemporary America* (Berkeley: Univ. of California Press, 1997), 30.

57. Hayes, "Intermarriage and Impurity," 13.

58. See esp. Claudia V. Camp, *Wise, Strange and Holy: The Strange Woman and the Making of the Bible,* Journal for the Study of the Old Testament Supplement Series 320, Gender, Culture, Theory 9 (Sheffield: Sheffield Academic, 2000), 40–43; Herbert R. Marbury, "The Strange Woman in Persian Yehud: A Reading of Proverbs 7," in *Approaching Yehud: New Approaches to the Study of the Persian Period,* ed. Jon L. Berquist, Semeia 50 (Atlanta: Society of Biblical Literature, 2007), 167–83; Gale Yee, *Poor Banished Children of Eve: Women as Evil in the Hebrew Bible* (Minneapolis: Augsburg Fortress, 2003), 135–66.

59. Joseph Blekinsopp, "The Social Context of the 'Outsider Women' in Proverbs 1–9," *Biblica* 72 (1991): 457–73.

60. Marbury, "Strange Woman," 174, Yee, *Poor Banished Children,* 153–56.

61. For more extensive discussion of these issues, see esp. Cohen, *Beginnings of Jewishness;* Erich Gruen, *Heritage and Hellenism: The Reinvention of Jewish Tradition* (Berkeley: Univ. of California Press, 1998); John M. G. Barclay, *Jews in the Mediterranean Diaspora: From Alexander to Trajan (323 BCE–117 CE)* (Edinburgh: Clark, 1996); Louis H. Feldman, *Jew and Gentile in the Ancient World: Attitudes and Interactions from Alexander to Justinian* (Princeton: Princeton Univ. Press, 1993); Martin Goodman, ed., *Jews in a Graeco-Roman World* (Oxford: Clarendon, 1998); Tessa Rajak, *The Jewish Dialogue with Greece and Rome: Studies in Cultural and Social Interaction* (Leiden:

Brill, 2001); Seth Schwartz, *Imperialism and Jewish Society, 200 BCE to 640 CE* (Princeton: Princeton Univ. Press, 2001).

62. Pseudo-Aristeas 139. R. J. H. Shutt, ed. "Letter of Aristeas," in *Old Testament Pseudepigrapha,* vol. 2, *Expansions of the "Old Testament"* Anchor Bible (New York: Doubleday, 1985), 7–34 (22). For further discussion, see Gruen, *Heritage and Hellenism,* 118–20 and Barclay, *Jews in the Mediterranean Diaspora,* 138–50.

63. Jubilees 30, 7–9. Charles, "Jubilees," 58. For discussion, see Betsy Halpern-Amaru, *The Empowerment of Women in the Book of Jubilees,* Supplements to the Study of Judaism 60 (Leiden: Brill, 1999), esp. 7, 27–28, 111–21, 155–56.

64. Non-Jews appear to have known about this rhetoric. Famously, the Roman historian Tacitus argued that the Jews "sit apart at meals, and they sleep apart, and although as a race they are prone to lust, they abstain from intercourse with foreign women; yet among themselves nothing is unlawful" (Tacitus *Histories* 5.4–5). Clifford H. Moore, trans., *Tacitus. The Histories Books IV-V,* Loeb Classical Library 111 (Cambridge: Harvard Univ. Press, 1952).

65. Yet one should regard these claims as rhetorical, not as representative of "what happened" in an obvious way. See Michael Satlow, *Jewish Marriage in Antiquity,* 134–61.

66. Justin Martyr, *Second Apology,* Greek text edited by Edgar J. Goodspeed, *Die altesten Apologeten* (Göttingen: Vandenhoeck & Ruprecht, 1914), 78–89 (82). English translation my own.

67. Justin, *First Apology* 54, *Second Apology* 7. For further discussion, see Reed, *Fallen Angels,* 162–66, 170–74.

68. Justin Martyr, *First Apology* 15.6–7.

69. Greek text Goodspeed, 103. English translation A. Lukyn Williams, *Justin Martyr: The Dialogue with Trypho,* Christian Literature Series 1 (London: SPCK; New York: MacMillan, 1930), 165. For discussion, see Knust, *Abandoned to Lust,* 148–52; Michael Mach, "Justin Martyr's *Dialogue cum Tryphone Iudaeo* and the Development of Christian Anti-Judaism," in *Contra Iudaeos: Ancient and Medieval Polemics Between Christians and Jews,* ed. Ora Limor and Guy G. Stroumsa (Tügbingen: Mohr/Siebeck, 1996), 27–47; Tessa Rajak, "Talking at Trypho: Christian Apologetic as Anti-Judaism in Justin's *Dialogue with Trypho the Jew,*" in *Apologetics in the Roman Empire,* ed. Mark J. Edwards and others (Oxford: Clarendon, 1999), 58–80.

70. The author of the New Testament book 1 Peter, for example, asserted that the followers of Christ are "a chosen race, a royal priesthood, a holy nation, God's own people" (2:9), and Paul claimed that the Gentiles had become the adopted children of God by means of their faith: "If you belong to

Christ, then you are Abraham's offspring, heirs according to the promise" Gal. 3:29). See the excellent discussion of these and other passages in Caroline Johnson Hodge, *If Sons, Then Heirs: A Study of Kinship and Ethnicity in the Letters of Paul* (New York and London: Oxford Univ. Press, 2007), esp. 67–77. On genealogical speculation among the early Christians, see esp. Denise Kimber Buell, *Why This New Race? Ethnic Reasoning in Early Christianity* (New York: Columbia Univ. Press, 2005).

71. Paul advises Gentile followers of Jesus to remain married to their unbelieving spouses, if they possibly can (see 1 Cor. 7:12–16); the author of 1 Peter advises wives to obey unbelieving husbands so that the husbands might be won over to Christ (see 1 Pet. 3:1–2); Justin tells a story involving a Christian woman who had no choice but to separate from her impious non-Christian husband (*Second Apology* 2); legendary accounts of the miracles and teachings of the apostles suggest that the apostles interrupted engagements and marriages to unbelievers, encouraging women to adopt celibacy over marriage (see, for example, the *Acts of Paul and Thecla,* the *Acts of John,* and the *Acts of Thomas*). For discussion, see MacDonald, *Early Christian Women and Pagan Opinion,* esp. 188–213, 244–48.

72. Satlow, *Jewish Marriage,* 155–57.

73. The Babatha archive, for example, a collection of contracts, letters, and other documents belonging to a woman named Babatha and dating from early-second-century Judea, includes both Babatha's own marriage contract, in Aramaic, as well as that of her daughter, rendered in Greek, which includes the promise that she will be supported "in accordance with Greek custom." Babatha herself may not have been Jewish—Babatha is an unusual name, particularly for a Jew—though she married a Jewish soldier in the Roman army named Judah, becoming his second wife. Still, there is no reason to believe that Babatha was *not* Jewish (Jews often took non-Jewish names), and, however Ezra might regard her ancestry, she appears to have regarded herself as a full member of the Jewish community living around the Dead Sea at the time. Martin Goodman, "Babatha's Story," a review of Y. Yadin, *The Documents from the Bar Kokhba Period in the Cave of Letters: Greek Papyri,* ed. N. Lewis and *Aramaic and Nabatean Signatures and Subscriptions,* ed. Y. Yadin and G. C. Greenfield, *Journal of Roman Studies* 81 (1991): 169–75 (174). See further Hannah Cotton, "A Cancelled Marriage Contract from the Judean Desert," *Journal of Roman Studies* 84 (1994): 64–86 and "The Guardianship of Jesus son of Babatha: Roman and Local Law in the Province of Arabia," *Journal of Roman Studies* 83 (1993): 94–108; Ross Shepard Kraemer, "On the Meaning of the Term 'Jew' in Greco-Roman Inscriptions," *Harvard Theological Review* 82.1 (1989): 35–53.

74. Patrick Wolfe, "Land, Labor and Difference: Elementary Structures of Race," *The American Historical Review* 106.3 (2001): 866–905 (872–73).

75. Scott L. Malcomson, *One Drop of Blood: The American Misadventure of Race* (New York: Farrar, Straus and Giroux, 2000), esp. 73–90.

76. See especially the reaction to the marriages of two educated Cherokee men to the daughters of Connecticut luminaries in the mid–1800s (Malcomson, *One Drop of Blood*, 70–73).

CHAPTER 6: *Bodily Parts*

1. A sensationalist account of these events may be found in Larry Johnson's book, *Frozen: My Journey into a World of Cryonics, Deception and Death* (New York: Vanguard Press, 2009). For more on Ted Williams and the controversy raised by his decision to be frozen, see Raja Mishra, "Williams Estate Halts Legal Inquiry on Cryonics Pact," *Boston Globe* August 9, 2002, A1. Among several other tributes to Ted Williams by Boston fans, see Brian McQuarrie and Raphael Lewis, "Across New England, a Sense of Loss and Fond Memories," *Boston Globe* July 6, 2002, A1.

2. Alcor Life Extension Foundation, www.alcor.org/, accessed April 30, 2010. See further, Arlene Sheskin, *Cryonics: A Sociology of Death and Bereavement* (New York: Irvington Press, 1979), 12–14; George P. Smith II, *Medical-Legal Aspects of Cryonics: Prospects for Immortality* (Washington, D.C.: Catholic Univ. Press of America, 1983), 15–23.

3. The general consensus at the moment seems to be that circumcision can slow the spread of certain sexually transmitted diseases, particularly HIV. Hence, the World Health Organization is currently recommending the practice. For an overview, see Michael T. Brady, "Newborn Circumcision: Routine or Not Routine, That Is the Question," *Archives of Pediatric and Adolescent Medicine* 164 (January 2010): 94–96.

4. On menstruation today, see Lara Freidenfelds, *The Modern Period: Menstruation in Twentieth-Century America* (Baltimore: The Johns Hopkins University Press, 2009). On changing ideas about menstruation in Western history, see the essays in Etienne Van de Walle and Elisha P. Renne, *Regulating Menstruation: Beliefs, Practices, Interpretations* (Chicago: Univ. of Chicago Press, 2001).

5. Notions of the afterlife in the Hebrew Bible are highly complex. For an excellent overview, see Kevin Madigan and Jon D. Levenson, *Resurrection: The Power of God for Christians and Jews* (New Haven: Yale Univ. Press, 2008), 45–68.

6. According to the Dead Sea Scrolls, when the Messiah comes he will "heal the sick and resurrect the dead"—they will be renewed, revived, healed,

raised up, and placed in an eternal kingdom (4Q521). See Emile Puech, "Une Apocalypse messianique [4Q521]," *Revue de Qumran* 15 (1992): 475–619, and John J. Collins, "The Works of the Messiah," *Dead Sea Discoveries* 1.1 (1994): 98–112. On resurrection among the Pharisees, see Claudia Setzer, "Resurrection of the Dead as Symbol and Strategy," *Journal of the American Academy of Religion* 69.1 (2001): 65–101, and *Resurrection of the Body in Early Judaism and Early Christianity: Doctrine, Community, and Self-Definition* (Leiden: Brill, 2004). The apostle Paul, himself a Pharisee ("as to the law a Pharisee," Phil. 3:5), was also emphatic about the resurrection.

7. The Hebrew is *"orlim."* See, for example, Judges 14:3; 15:18; 1 Samuel 31:4; 2 Samuel 1:20.

8. "So shall my covenant be in your flesh an everlasting covenant" (Gen. 17:13). Shaye J. D. Cohen, *Why Aren't Jewish Women Circumcised? Gender and the Covenant in Judaism* (Berkeley: Univ. of California Press, 2005), 9–12.

9. See Westermann, *Genesis 12–36*, 264–71.

10. See J. Alberto Soggin, *Joshua: A Commentary,* Old Testament Library (Philadelphia: Westminster Press, 1972), 68; A. Graeme Auld, *Joshua Retold: Synoptic Perspectives* (Edinburgh: Clark, 1998), 12–14.

11. Herodotus, *Histories* 2.104.

12. As we've already noted, "feet" is a euphemism for penis.

13. Shaye J. D. Cohen, "A Brief History of Jewish Circumcision Blood," in *The Covenant of Circumcision: New Perspectives on an Ancient Jewish Rite,* ed. Elizabeth Wyner Mark (Hanover, NH: Brandeis Univ. Press, 2003), 30–42 (31).

14. Deuteronomy 10:16; compare Leviticus 26:40–42.

15. *Orlim,* Jeremiah 9:26.

16. See Ezekiel 28:10; 31:18; 32:19–26.

17. Feldman, *Jew and Gentile in the Ancient World,* 153–55.

18. 1 Maccabees 1:14–15. See further Gruen, *Heritage and Hellenism,* 29–31 and Nissan Rubin, *"Brit Milah*: A Study of Change of Custom."

19. William Whitson, trans., *Jewish Antiquities* 13.257–58, 438.

20. For discussion, see Cohen, *Beginnings of Jewishness,* 15–23.

21. Feldman, *Jew and Gentile in the Ancient World,* 155.

22. Horace, *Satires* 1.5.100, 1.9.69–70. Latin text with notes by Edward P. Morris, *Horace: The Satires* (Norman: Univ. of Oklahoma Press, 1974), 95, 129.

23. Juvenal, *Satire* 14.96–100, trans. G. G. Ramsay, *Juvenal and Persius,* Loeb Classical Library 91 (Cambridge: Harvard Univ. Press, rev. ed. 1940), 273. Compare Tacitus, *Histories* 5.4.

24. Suetonius, *Life of Domitian* 12, Latin text, trans. J. C. Rolfe, *Suetonius,* vol. 2, Loeb Classical Library 38 (Cambridge: Harvard Univ. Press, rev. ed., 1997), 346–47.

25. Alan Kerkeslager offers the particular example of a comedic text that makes fun of a naked athlete carrying a "Jewish load," that is, displaying a circumcised penis in the contest. See his essay, "Maintaining a Jewish Identity in the Greek Gymnasium: A 'Jewish Load' in *CPJ* 3.519 (= P. Schub. 37 = P. Berol. 13406)," *Journal for the Study of Judaism* 28.1 (1997): 12–33. Also see Shaye J. D. Cohen, "'Those Who Say They are Jews and Are Not': How Do You Know a Jew in Antiquity When You See One?" in *Diasporas in Antiquity,* ed. Shaye J. D. Cohen and Ernest S. Frerichs, Brown Judaic Studies 288 (Atlanta: Scholars Press, 1992), 1–45.

26. Ra'anan Abusch (Boustan), "Circumcision and Castration under Roman Law in the Early Empire," in *The Covenant of Circumcision,* 75–86 (75). Also see Cohen, *Beginnings of Jewishness,* 39–49; Martin Goodman, *Rome and Jerusalem: The Clash of Ancient Civilizations* (New York: Vintage Books, 2009), 160–68, 278–79.

27. Philo of Alexandria, *Questions and Answers on Genesis* 3.46–48, trans. Ralph Marcus, *Philo,* Supplement, vol. 1, *Questions and Answers on Genesis,* Loeb Classical Library (Cambridge: Harvard Univ. Press, 1953), 241–47.

28. F. H. Colson, trans., *Philo,* vol. 7, Loeb Classical Library (Cambridge: Harvard Univ. Press, 1937), 100–101.

29. *Special Laws* 1.7–10. Colson, *Philo,* vol. 7, 104–5.

30. See further David Biale, *Eros and the Jews,* 38–40.

31. Soranus, *On Gynecology* 1.43, trans. Owsei Temkin (Baltimore: Johns Hopkins Univ. Press, 1956), 42–43; Galen, *On the Usefulness of the Parts of the Body,* 14.2.300, trans. Margaret Tallmadge May (Ithaca: Cornell Univ. Press, 1968), 2:630–31.

32. Galen, *Parts of the Body,* 15.2.346, 2:660–61.

33. As Howard Eilberg-Schwartz puts it, circumcision "symbolically enables the penis to more effectively discharge its divinely allotted task. That task, as suggested by the content of the covenant, is to impregnate women and produce offspring" (*The Savage in Judaism: An Anthropology of Israelite Religion and Ancient Judaism* [Bloomington and Indianapolis: Indiana Univ. Press, 1990], 148).

34. Eilberg-Schwartz, *Savage,* 150.

35. Philo, *Questions and Answers on Genesis* 3.50; Marcus, *Philo,* 1:251.

36. *Genesis Rabbah* 46.2, trans. Maurice Simon, 390.

37. Eilberg-Schwartz, *Savage,* 154.

38. On the association between circumcision and desire in rabbinic literature, see David Biale, *Eros and the Jews,* 39.

39. *Genesis Rabbah* 46.4. Simon, 391. For discussion, see Eilberg-Schwartz, *God's Phallus,* 172–73.

40. As Howard Eilberg-Schwartz observes, a woman's little finger was treated elsewhere in rabbinic literature as a particularly erotic part of her body, so lovely that whoever touches it may as well have touched "that place," that is, her vagina (Eilberg-Schwartz, *God's Phallus,* 172).

41. *Genesis Rabbah* 48.2 (on Genesis 18:1), 406. See Simon and Wolfson, 192–93.

42. Epistle of Barnabas 9.4, trans. Bart D. Ehrman, *Apostolic Fathers,* vol. 2, Loeb Classical Library 25 (Cambridge: Harvard Univ. Press, 2003), 44–45.

43. Epistle of Barnabas 9.8.

44. Justin Martyr, *Dialogue with Trypho* 16, ed. Miroslav Marcovich, *Iustini Martyris. Dialogus cum Tryphone,* Patristiche Texte und Studien 47 (Berlin: De Gruyter, 1997), 96–97. Thomas Falls, trans., *Saint Justin Martyr: The First Apology, the Second Apology, Dialogue with Trypho, Exhortation to the Greeks, Discourse to the Greeks, The Monarchy or the Rule of God,* Fathers of the Church 6 (Washington, D.C.: Catholic Univ. Press, 1948), 172.

45. Mary T. Boatwright, *Hadrian and the Cities of the Roman Empire* (Princeton: Princeton Univ. Press, 2000), 196–203; Seth Schwartz, *Imperialism and Jewish Society 200 BCE to 640 CE* (Princeton: Princeton Univ. Press, 2001), 105–61.

46. "But if some, due to their instability of will, desire to observe as many of the Mosaic precepts as possible—precepts which we think were instituted because of [Israel's] hardness of heart—while at the same time they place their hope in Christ, and if they desire to perform the eternal and natural acts of justice and piety, yet wish to live with us as Christians and believers, as I already stated, not persuading them to be circumcised like themselves, or to keep the Sabbath, or to perform any other similar acts, then in my opinion we Christians should receive them and associate with them in every way as kinsmen and brethren (*Dialogue with Trypho* 47; Patrische Texte und Studien 47), 147, Fathers of the Church 6, 218.

47. Nina E. Livesy, "Theological Identity Making: Justin's Use of Circumcision to Create Jews and Christians," *Journal of Early Christian Studies* 18.1 (2010): 51–79.

48. Boyarin, *Radical Jew,* esp. 106–35.

49. See Romans 3:30–31; compare Galatians 5:6; 6:14.

50. See further Hodge, *If Sons, Then Heirs,* esp. 87–89.

51. Judith 14:9. Cohen, *Beginnings of Jewishness,* 130.

52. Cohen, *Beginnings of Jewishness,* 263–397; Shaye J. D. Cohen, "Was Timothy Jewish (Acts 16:1–3)? Patristic Exegesis, Rabbinic Law, and Matrilineal Descent," *Journal of Biblical Literature* 105.2 (1986): 251–68; Shaye J. D. Cohen, "The Origins of the Matrilineal Principle in Rabbinic Law," *AJS Review* 10.1 (1985): 19–53; and Irene Levinskaya, *The Book of Acts in Its Diaspora Setting* (Grand Rapids: Eerdmans, 1996), 12–18. Against Cohen, Levins-

kaya concludes that Acts 16 may well be early evidence of the later rabbinic principle (16–18).

53. Augustine *Epistle* 116.12.1. Cited and discussed by Cohen, "Was Timothy Jewish?" 258.

54. As a number of scholars have observed, this author shows a particular interest in all matters Roman—only Luke-Acts identifies Paul as a Roman citizen and insists upon the innocence of both Jesus and Paul vis-à-vis Roman law.

55. Watson, *Digest of Justinian* 23.44.1.

56. For further discussion, see Treggiari, *Roman Marriage,* 43–51.

57. Ignatius of Antioch, *To the Philadelphians* 6.1, my translation.

58. Ignatius, *Philadelphians* 6.1. See further Shaye J. D. Cohen, "Judaism without Circumcision and 'Judaism' without 'Circumcision' in Ignatius," *Harvard Theological Review* 95.4 (2002): 395–415.

59. Justin Martyr, *Dialogue with Trypho* 67.6, my translation. For discussion, see Andrew S. Jacobs, "Dialogical Differences: (De-)Judaizing Jesus' Circumcision," *Journal of Early Christian Studies* 15.3 (2007): 291–335 (300–304).

60. Origen, *Against Celsus* 5.48. See Jacobs, "Dialogical Differences," 309.

61. Ambrose, *Commentary on the Gospel According to Luke* 2.55. Translated and discussed by Andrew Jacobs, "Passing: Jesus' Circumcision and Strategic Self-Sacrifice," in *Ancient Mediterranean Sacrifice: Images, Acts, Meanings,* ed. Jennifer Knust and Zsuzsanna Várhelyi (New York and Oxford: Oxford Univ. Press), forthcoming.

62. See further Amy G. Remensnyder, "Legendary Treasure at Conques: Reliquaries and Imaginative Memory," *Speculum* 71.4 (1996): 884–906 (892–97); Caroline Walker Bynum, *Wonderful Blood: Theology and Practice in Late Medieval Germany and Beyond* (Philadelphia: Univ. of Pennsylvania Press, 2007, esp. 90–98; Elizabeth Pastan, "Charlemagne as Saint? Relics and the Choice of Window Subjects at Chartres Cathedral" in *The Legend of Charlemagne in the Middle Ages: Power, Faith and Crusade,* ed. Matthew Gabriele and Jace Stuckey (New York: Palgrave Macmillan, 2008), 97–136 (116–18).

63. Quoted and discussed in Bynum, *Wonderful Blood,* 98.

64. On the history of the word "onanism," which first appears in 1719, see Jean Stengers and Anne van Neck, *Masturbation: The History of a Great Terror,* trans. Kathryn Hoffman (New York: Palgrave Macmillan, 2001), 53–54.

65. See especially Simon-Andre Tissot, *L'onanism, ou Dissertation physique sur les maladies produits par la masturbation* (1760), quoted and discussed by Stengers and van Neck, *Masturbation,* 70.

66. David L. Gollaher, "From Ritual to Science: The Medical Transformation of Circumcision in America," *Journal of Social History* 28 (1994): 5–34.

67. J. M. McGee (1882), quoted and discussed by Gollaher, "Ritual to Science," 11.

68. E. J. Spratling, "Masturbation in the Adult," quoted and discussed by Robert Darby, "The Masturbation Taboo and the Rise of Routine Male Circumcision: A Review of the Historiography," *Journal of Social History* 36.3 (2003): 737–57 (49). Also see Robert Darby, *A Surgical Temptation: The Demonization of the Foreskin and the Rise of Circumcision in Britain* (Chicago: Univ. of Chicago Press, 2005) and, for a slightly different view, Thomas Laqueur, *Solitary Sex: A Cultural History of Masturbation* (New York: Zone Books, 2003).

69. Gollaher, "Ritual to Science," 21.

70. Jonathan Klawans, *Purity, Sacrifice, and the Temple: Symbolism and Supersessionism in the Study of Ancient Judaism* (New York and Oxford: Oxford Univ. Press, 2006), esp. 53–56.

71. On the particular importance of blood in the Israelite cult, see William K. Gilders, *Blood Ritual in the Hebrew Bible: Meaning and Power* (Baltimore: Johns Hopkins Univ. Press, 2004).

72. Klawans, "Pure Violence: Sacrifice and Defilement in Ancient Israel," *Harvard Theological Review* 94.2 (2001): 135–57 (151); compare *Purity, Sacrifice, and the Temple*, 65.

73. Nancy Jay, "Sacrifice as a Remedy for Having Been Born a Woman," in *Women, Gender, Religion: A Reader*, ed. Elizabeth Castelli (New York: Palgrave, 2001), 174–94.

74. Also see Nancy Jay, *Throughout Your Generations Forever: Sacrifice, Religion, and Paternity* (Chicago: Univ. of Chicago Press, 1992), xxiii–xxvii and, on Israel in particular, 94–111.

75. Cohen, *Why Aren't Jewish Women Circumcised?*, 20.

76. Charlotte Elisheva Fonrobert, *Menstrual Purity: Rabbinic and Christian Reconstructions of Biblical Gender*, Contraversions (Stanford: Stanford Univ. Press, 2000), 43–46.

77. Fonrobert, *Menstrual Purity*, 46.

78. Mary Rose D'Angelo, "(Re)presentations of Women in the Gospels: John and Mark," in Kraemer and D'Angelo, *Women and Christian Origins*, 143. Also see Frances Taylor Gench, *Back to the Well: Women's Encounters with Jesus in the Gospels* (Knoxville: Westminster John Knox Press, 2004), 98.

79. See, for example, Joanna Dewey, "The Gospel of Mark," in Fiorenza, *Searching the Scriptures*, 481–82.

80. Ezra 9:2, 11–12. Additions to the book of Esther 14:15–16. Washington, "Israel's Holy Seed," 427–37; Adele Reinhartz, "The Greek Book of Esther," in Newsom and Ringe, *Women's Bible Commentary*, 86–92.

81. Fonrobert offers a similar reading of this passage, *Menstrual Purity*, 188–96.

82. On synagogue founts and other evidence of extratemple purity rites, see

John C. Poirier, "Purity Beyond the Temple in the Second Temple Era," *Journal of Biblical Literature* 122.2 (2003): 247–65 (256–59). Several basins and a water reservoir were found at the synagogue at Delos (see Monika Trümper, "The Oldest Original Synagogue Building in the Diaspora: The Delos Synagogue Reconsidered," *Hesperia* 73 [2004]: 513–98). Similar items have been discovered at other synagogues as well (Lee I. Levine, *The Ancient Synagogue: The First Thousand Years,* 2nd edition [New Haven: Yale Univ. Press, 2005], 331–33).

83. As Cohen has shown, Jews also employed baptism in conversion rituals, *Beginnings of Jewishness,* 208–22.

84. *Didache* 9.5. For further discussion, see Huub van de Sandt, " 'Do Not Give What Is Holy to the Dogs' (Did 9:5D and Matt 7:6A): The Eucharistic Food of the Didache in Its Jewish Purity Setting," *Vigiliae Christianae* 56.3 (2002): 223–46.

85. Didascalia 26. Critical edition of the Syriac with English translation by Arthur Vööbus, *The Didascalia Apostolorum in Syriac,* CSCO 401–2; 407–8, Scriptores Syri 175–76; 179–80 (Louvain: Secrétariat du Corpus SCO, 1979). Citation here from 402:258 (Syriac) and 408:241 (English). Greek and Latin fragments edited by Erik Tidner, *Didascalia Apostolorum, Canonum ecclesiastorum, Traditionis apostolicae versiones Latinae* (Berlin: Akademie-Verlag, 1963).

86. See Fonrobert's extensive and convincing discussion of this passage (*Menstrual Purity,* 179–85) and also David Brakke, "The Problematization of Nocturnal Emissions in Early Christian Syria, Egypt, and Gaul," *Journal of Early Christian Studies* 3.4 (1995): 419–60 (424–27).

87. Shaye J. D. Cohen, "Purity and Piety: The Separation of Menstruants from the Sancta," in *Daughters of the King: Women and the Synagogue,* ed. Susan Grossman and Rivka Haut (New York: Jewish Publication Society, 1992), 106.

88. See Jodi Magness, *The Archaeology of Qumran and the Dead Sea Scrolls* (Grand Rapids: Eerdmans, 2002), esp. 134–57 and Jonathan D. Lawrence, *Washing in Water: Trajectories of Ritual Bathing in the Hebrew Bible and Second Temple Literature* (Atlanta: Society of Biblical Literature, 2006), 160–84 (173–83). On responses to seminal emissions, vaginal blood, and childbirth in the Dead Sea Scrolls, see Martha Himmelfarb, *A Kingdom of Priests: Ancestry and Merit in Ancient Judaism* (Philadelphia: Univ. of Pennsylvania Press, 2006), 85–101.

89. See Matthew 3:1–12; Mark 1:1–8; Luke 3:1–9; John 1:19–28.

90. Cohen, "Purity and Piety," 106, citing Mishnah *Berakhot* 3.4–6.

91. Tosefta Berakhot 2:13. Translated and discussed by Fonrobert, *Menstrual Purity,* 173.

92. *Didascalia* 26. CSCO 402:259–60; 408:242–43. See Brakke, "Nocturnal Emissions," 426.

93. Brakke, "Nocturnal Emissions," 433–34.

94. *Apostolic Tradition* 20.6. This section of the *Apostolic Tradition* survives only in Sahidic, Arabic, and Ethiopic, though a parallel can be found in the *Canons of Hippolytus*. See the translation of all these texts, as well as discussion, in *The Apostolic Tradition: A Commentary* by Paul F. Bradshaw, Maxwell E. Johnson and L. Edward Phillips, Hermeneia (Minneapolis: Fortress, 2002), 104–10. For discussion, see Shaye J. D. Cohen, "Menstruants and the Sacred in Judaism and Christianity," in *Women's History and Ancient History,* ed. Sarah B. Pomeroy (Chapel Hill: Univ. of North Carolina Press, 1991), 273–99 (287–88).

95. Cohen, "Menstruants," 283–84.

96. Rachel Biale, *Women and Jewish Law,* 161–62.

97. Charlotte Elisheva Fonrobert and Martin S. Jaffee's introduction to *The Cambridge Companion to the Talmud and Rabbinic Literature* offers a helpful overview of the difficulties in dating these rabbinic texts (Cambridge: Cambridge Univ. Press, 2007), 1–14. In this same volume, also see Jeffrey L. Rubenstein, "Social and Institutional Settings of Rabbinic Literature," 58–74.

98. bNiddah 66a. Quoted and discussed by Cohen, "Menstruants and the Sacred," 277–78.

99. Jonah Steinberg, "From a 'Pot of Filth' to a 'Hedge of Roses' (and Back)," *Journal of the Feminist Studies of Religion* 13.2 (1997):5–26 (9).

100. This principle is introduced in the sixth or seventh centuries by the *Beraita de Nidda*. See Cohen, "Menstruants," 285–86.

101. Leviticus 18:19, *Avot de-Rabbi Nathan* A, 2. Cited and discussed by Judith R. Baskin, *Midrashic Women: Formations of the Feminine in Rabbinic Literature* (Hanover, NH: Brandeis Univ. Press, 2002), 25.

102. Fonrobert, *Menstrual Purity,* 53–54, 106, discussing Mishnah Niddah 5:1, 2:6–7.

103. Steinberg, 12.

104. Jennifer A. Glancy, *Corporal Knowledge: Early Christian Bodies* (New York and Oxford: Oxford Univ. Press, 2010), 109–17.

105. P. A. Van Stempvoort, "The Protevangelium Jacobi: The Sources of its Theme and Style and their Bearing on its Date," in *Studia Evengelica,* vol. 3, ed. F. L. Cross, 410–26. Texte und Untersuchungen zur Geschichte der Altchristlichen Literatur 88 (Berlin: Akademie-Verlag, 1964), 425.

106. Origen, *Against Celsus* 1.28, 32. Greek text edited with French translation by Marcel Borret, *Origène. Contre Celse.* vol. 1, *Livres I et II*, SC 132 (Paris:

Les Éditions du Cerf, 2005), 150, 162–64; Henry Chadwick, trans., *Origen: Contra Celsum* (Cambridge: Cambridge Univ. Press, 1953), 28, 31–32.

107.   Matthew 1:3, 5, 18–23; Luke 1:27–38. Brown, *Birth of the Messiah,* 534–42; Jane Schaberg, *The Illegitimacy of Jesus*; John A. Darr, "Belittling Mary: Insult Genre, Humiliation and the Early Development of Mariology," in *From the Margins 2: Biblical Women and Their Afterlives,* ed. Christine Joynes and Christopher Rowland (Sheffield: Sheffield Phoenix Press, 2009).

108.   *Proto-Gospel of James* 7.1–3; 9.1–2.

109.   *Proto-Gospel of James* 16.1–2; compare Numbers 5:11–31.

110.   Glancy, *Corporal Knowledge,* 114. On Tertullian's understanding of blood and pollution, also see Blake Leyerle, "Blood Is Seed," *Journal of Religion* 81.1 (2001): 26–48.

111.   Glancy, *Corporal Knowledge,* 114.

112.   Tertullian *Against Marcion* 3.9.

113.   Tertullian, *Against Marcion* 3.11. Glancy, *Corporal Knowledge,* 120–22.

114.   Letter of Gregory to Augustine (597 CE), preserved by Bede in his *Ecclesiastical History* 1.27, trans. J. A. Giles, *The Venerable Bede's Ecclesiastical History of England, also the Anglo-Saxon Chronicle* (London: George Bell & Sons, 1894), 46.

115.   Gregory to Augustine, in Giles, *Venerable Bede's Ecclesiastical History,* 48.

CONCLUSION

1.   Genesis 29:1–10; John 4:12. Though Genesis does not identify a particular well as "Jacob's well," later tradition did, establishing a pilgrimage site there.

2.   Tertullian. *On Modesty (De pudicitia)* 11.1.

3.   John Chrysostom, *Homilies on the Gospel of John* 32, trans. Sister Thomas Aquinas Goggin, *Saint John Chrysostom. Commentary on Saint John the Apostle and Evangelist,* vol. 1. *Homilies 1–47,* Fathers of the Church (New York: Fathers of the Church, 1957), 319.

4.   Writing in 1966, the modern biblical scholar Raymond Brown agreed. "Jews were allowed only three marriages," he comments. "If the same standard was applicable among the Samaritans, then the woman's life has been markedly immoral" (*The Gospel according to John (i–xii)*, Anchor Bible [New York: Doubleday, 1966], 171). He adds, "It is useless to ask what would have happened if she had returned with her paramour" (171).

5.   The classic discussion is that by Maurice Wiles, *The Spiritual Gospel: The Interpretation of the Fourth Gospel in the Early Church* (Cambridge: Cambridge Univ. Press, 1960).

6.   Origen of Alexandria. *Commentary on John* 13, trans. Joseph W. Trigg, *Origen,* The Early Church Fathers (London and New York: Routledge,

1998), 151–78.

7. Augustine. *Homilies on John* 15.22, trans. Edmund Hill, *Saint Augustine. Homilies on John 1–40* (New York: Augustinian Heritage Institute, 2009), 288.

8. See further Jocelyn McWhirter, *The Bridegroom Messiah and the People of God: Marriage in the Fourth Gospel,* Society for New Testament Studies Monograph Series 138 (Cambridge: Cambridge Univ. Press, 2006).

9. For an overview of this interpretation see Craig R. Koester, " 'The Savior of the World' (John 4:42)," *Journal of Biblical Literature* 109.4 (1990): 665–80 (669–73).

10. Sandra Schneiders, *The Revelatory Text: Interpreting the New Testament as Sacred Scripture* (San Francisco: HarperSanFrancisco, 1991), 195. Also see Frances Gench, *Back to the Well,* 118–20.

11. Irenaeus of Lyons, *Against the Heresies* 1.10.1–2, trans. Dominic Unger, rev. by John J. Dillon, *St. Irenaeus of Lyons, Against the Heresies,* Ancient Christian Writers (Mahwah, NJ: Paulist Press, 1992), 49.

Bibliography

Aaron, David. "Early Rabbinic Exegesis on Noah's Son Ham and the So-Called 'Hamitic Myth'." *Journal of the American Academy of Religion* 63.4 (1995): 721–59.

Abu-Salieh, S. A. Aldeeb. "Muslims' Genitalia in the Hands of the Clergy: Religious Arguments about Male and Female Circumcision." In *Male and Female Circumcision: Medical, Legal, and Ethical Considerations in Pediatric Practice,* edited by George C. Denniston, Frederick Mansfield Hodges, and Marilyn Fayre Milos, 131–72. Proceedings of the Fifth International Symposium on Sexual Mutilations: Medical, Legal and Ethical Considerations in Pediatric Practice, held August 5–7, 1998, in Oxford, England. New York: Plenum Publishers, 1999.

Ackerman, Susan, "The Personal Is Political: Covenantal and Affectionate Love ('AHEB, 'AHABA) in the Hebrew Bible." *Vetus Testamentum* 52.4 (2002): 437–58.

———. *When Heroes Love: The Ambiguity of Eros in the Stories of Gilgamesh and David*. New York: Columbia Univ. Press, 2005.

Ahmed, Sara. *The Cultural Politics of Emotion*. Edinburgh: Univ. of Edinburgh Press, 2004.

Albertz, Rainer. *Israel in Exile: The History and Literature of the Sixth Century B.C.E.* Translated by David Green. Atlanta: Society of Biblical Literature, 2003.

Albright, William Foxwell. *Archaeology and the Religion of Israel*. New York: Anchor Books, 1969.

———. "The Role of Canaanites in the History of Civilization." In *The Bible and the Ancient Near East: Essays in Honor of W. F. Albright,* edited by G. E. Wright, 438–87. New York: Doubleday, 1961.

Alexander, T. Desmond. "Lot's Hospitality: A Clue to His Righteousness." *Journal of Biblical Literature* 104.2 (1985): 289–91.

Ali, Kecia. *Sexual Ethics and Islam: Feminist Reflections on Qur'an, Hadith and Jurisprudence.* Oxford: OneWorld Publications, 2006.

Alpert, Rebecca. "Finding Our Past: A Lesbian Interpretation of the Book of Ruth." In *Reading Ruth: Contemporary Women Reclaim a Sacred Story,* edited by Judith A. Kates and Gail Twerksy Reimer, 91–96. New York: Ballantine Books, 1994.

Alt, Albrecht. *Essays on Old Testament History and Religion.* Translated by Robert Wilson. Garden City, NY: Doubleday/Anchor Books, 1966.

Anderson, Janice Capel, and Stephen D. Moore. "Matthew and Masculinity." In *New Testament Masculinities,* edited by Stephen D. Moore and Janice Capel Anderson, 67–91. Semeia 45. Atlanta: Society of Biblical Literature, 2003.

Athenaeus. *The Learned Banquet.* Translated by Charles B. Gulick, *Athenaeus. The Deipnosophists.* 7 vols. Loeb Classical Library. Cambridge: Harvard Univ. Press, 1927–1941.

Augustine. *De Doctrina Christiana.* Translated by R. P. H. Green. Oxford: Clarendon, 1995.

———. *Homilies on John.* Translated by Edmund Hill. *Saint Augustine. Homilies on John 1–40.* New York: Augustinian Heritage Institute, 2009.

Auld, A. Graeme. *Joshua Retold: Synoptic Perspectives.* Edinburgh: Clark, 1998.

Bach, Alice, ed. *Women in the Hebrew Bible: A Reader.* New York and London: Routledge, 1999.

Bader, Mary Anna. *Sexual Violation in the Hebrew Bible: A Multi-Methodological Study of Genesis 34 and 2 Samuel 13.* Studies in Biblical Literature 18. New York and Frankfurt: Peter Lang, 2006.

Bailey, Randall C. *David in Love and War: The Pursuit of Power in 2 Samuel 10–12.* JSOT Supplement Series 75. Sheffield: Sheffield Academic, 1990.

———. "He Didn't Even Tell Us the Worst of It!" *Union Seminary Quarterly Review* 59.1–2 (2005): 15–24.

Bal, Mieke. *Lethal Love: Feminist Literary Readings of Biblical Love Stories.* Bloomington, IN: Indiana Univ. Press, 1987.

Balch, David, and Carolyn Osiek. *Families in the New Testament World.* Louisville: Westminster John Knox Press, 1997.

Barclay, John M. G. *Jews in the Mediterranean Diaspora: From Alexander to Trajan (323 BCE–117 CE).* Edinburgh: Clark, 1996.

Barnard, Leslie William, trans. *St. Justin Martyr. The First and Second Apologies.* Ancient Christian Writers 56. New York: Paulist, 1997.

Barr, James. *The Garden of Eden and the Hope of Immortality.* Minneapolis: Fortress, 1993.

Barton, John. "The Canonicity of the Song of Songs." In *Perspectives on the Song of Songs,* edited by Anselm Hagedorn, 1–7. Berlin: De Gruyter, 2006.

Baskin, Judith R. *Midrashic Women: Formations of the Feminine in Rabbinic Literature.* Hanover, NH: Brandeis Univ. Press, 2002.

Bassett, Frederick W. "Noah's Nakedness and the Curse of Canaan, a Case of Incest?" *Vetus Testamentum* 21.2 (1971): 232–37.

Bassler, Jouette. "The Widow's Tale: A Fresh Look at 1 Timothy 5:3–16." *Journal of Biblical Literature* 103 (1984): 232–41.

Batto, Bernard F. *Slaying the Dragon: Mythmaking in the Biblical Tradition.* Louisville: Westminster John Knox, 1992.

Bauckham, Richard J. *Jude, 2 Peter.* Word Biblical Commentary 50. Waco: Word Books, 1983.

———. *Jude, 2 Peter.* Vol. 12 of *The New Interpreter's Bible.* Nashville: Abingdon, 1998.

Baumann, Gerlinde. *Love and Violence: Marriage as a Metaphor for the Relationship between YHWH and Israel in the Prophetic Books.* Collegeville, MN: Liturgical Press, 2003.

Baumgarten, Alan. "Myth and Midrash: Genesis 9:20–29." In *Christianity, Judaism, and Other Greco-Roman Cults: Studies for Morton Smith at Sixty,* edited by Jacob Neusner, 55–71. Leiden: Brill, 1975.

Beal, Timothy K. *Esther.* Berit Olam: Studies in Hebrew Narrative and Poetry. Collegeville, MD: Liturgical Press, 1999.

Beard, Mary, and John Henderson. "With This Body I Thee Worship: Sacred Prostitution in Antiquity." In *Gender and the Body in the Ancient Mediterranean,* edited by Maria Wyke, 56–75. London: Blackwell, 1998.

Bechtel, Lyn M. "What If Dinah Is Not Raped? (Genesis 34)." *Journal for the Study of the Old Testament* 62 (1994): 19–36.

Bedford, Peter R. "Diaspora: Homeland Relations in Ezra-Nehemiah." *Vetus Testamentum* 52.2 (2002): 147–65.

Bergsma, John Sietze, and Scott Walker Hahn. "Noah's Nakedness and the Curse on Canaan (Genesis 9:20–27)." *Journal of Biblical Literature* 121.1 (2005): 25–40.

Biale, David. *Eros and the Jews: From Biblical Israel to Contemporary America.* Berkeley: Univ. of California Press, 1997.

Biale, Rachel. *Women and Jewish Law: The Essential Texts, Their History, and Their Relevance for Today.* New York: Schocken Books, 1984.

Bigger, Stephen F. "The Family Laws of Leviticus 18 in Their Setting." *Journal of Biblical Literature* 98.2 (1979): 187–203.

Bird, Phyllis, *Missing Persons and Mistaken Identities: Women and Gender in Ancient Israel.* Minneapolis: Augsburg Fortress, 1997.

———. "Prostitution in the Social World and Religious Rhetoric of Ancient Israel." In *Prostitutes and Courtesans in the Ancient World,* edited by Christopher Faraone and Laura McClure, 40–58. Madison: Univ. of Wisconsin Press, 2006.

Black, Fiona C. "What Is My Beloved? On Erotic Reading and the Song of Songs." In *The Labour of Reading: Desire, Alienation, and Biblical Interpretation,* edited by Fiona C. Black, Roland Boer, and Erin Runions, 35–52. Semeia 36. Atlanta: Society of Biblical Literature, 1999.

———. "Unlikely Bedfellows: Allegorical and Feminist Readings of Song of Songs 7.1-8." In *The Song of Songs: A Feminist Companion to the Bible,* 2nd series, edited by Athalya Brenner and Carole R. Fontaine, 104–29. Sheffield: Sheffield Academic, 2000.

Black, Matthew. *The Book of Enoch or 1 Enoch,* A New English Edition. Leiden: Brill, 1985.

Blekinsopp, Joseph. "The Social Context of the 'Outsider Women' in Proverbs 1–9." *Biblica* 72 (1991): 457–73.

Bloch, Ariel, and Chana Bloch. *The Song of Songs.* Berkeley: Univ. of California Press, 1998.

Boatwright, Mary T. *Hadrian and the Cities of the Roman Empire.* Princeton: Princeton Univ. Press, 2000.

Boer, Roland. *Knockin' on Heaven's Door: The Bible and Popular Culture.* London: Routledge, 1999.

———. "The Second Coming: Repetition and Insatiable Desire in the Song of Songs." *Biblical Interpretation* 8.3 (2000): 276–301.

———. *Marxist Criticism of the Bible.* Sheffield: Sheffield Academic, 2003.

Boggs, Kelly. "Islam through a glass darkly." Southern Baptist Convention— Southern Baptist Churches Annual Meeting 2002 Newsroom (13 June 2002), available on-line: http://www.sbcannualmeeting.org/sbc02/newsroom/news-page.asp?ID=285.

Boling, Robert G. *Joshua: A New Translation with Notes and Commentary.* Garden City, NY: Doubleday, 1982.

Boustan, Ra'anan (Abusch). "Circumcision and Castration under Roman Law in the Early Empire." In *The Covenant of Circumcision: New Perspectives on an Ancient Jewish Rite,* edited by Elizabeth Wyner Mark, 75–86. Lebanon, NH: Univ. Press of New England/Brandeis Univ. Press, 2003.

Boyarin, Daniel. "Are There Any Jews in the 'History of Sexuality'?" *Journal of the History of Sexuality* 5.3 (1995): 333–55.

———. *Carnal Israel: Reading Sex in Talmudic Culture.* Berkeley: Univ. of California Press, 1993.

———. "Internal Opposition in Talmudic Literature: The Case of the Married Monk." *Representations* 36 (1991): 87–113.

———. *Intertextuality and the Reading of the Mishnah.* Bloomington: Indiana Univ. Press, 1990.

———. *A Radical Jew: Paul and the Politics of Identity.* Berkeley: Univ. of California Press, 1994.

Bradshaw, Paul F., Maxwell E. Johnson, and L. Edward Phillips. *The Apostolic Tradition: A Commentary.* Hermeneia. Minneapolis: Fortress, 2002.

Brady, Michael T. "Newborn Circumcision: Routine or Not Routine, That Is the Question." *Archives of Pediatric and Adolescent Medicine* 164 (January 2010): 94–96.

Brakke, David. "The Problematization of Nocturnal Emissions in Early Christian Syria, Egypt, and Gaul." *Journal of Early Christian Studies* 3.4 (1995): 419–60.

Braund, David, and John Wilkins, ed. *Athenaeus and His World: Reading Greek Culture in the Roman Empire.* Exeter: Univ. of Exeter Press, 2000.

Bremmer, Jan. "Pauper or Patroness: The Widow in the Early Christian Church."

In *Between Poverty and the Pyre: Moments in the History of Widowhood,* edited by Laurens van den Bosch, 31–57. London: Routledge, 1995.

Brooten, Bernadette. "Konnten Frauen im alten Judentum die Scheidung betreiben? Überlengungen zu Mark 10, 11–12 und Kor 7, 1–11." *Evangelische Theologie* 42 (1982): 65–80.

———. *Love Between: Early Christian Responses to Female Homoeroticism.* Chicago: Univ. of Chicago Press, 1996.

Brown, Peter. *The Body and Society: Men, Women and Sexual Renunciation in Early Christianity.* New York: Columbia Univ. Press, 1988.

Brown, Raymond E. *The Birth of the Messiah: A Commentary on the Infancy Narratives in Matthew and Luke.* New York: Doubleday, 1993.

———. *The Gospel according to John (i–xii).* Anchor Bible. New York: Doubleday, 1966.

Brueggemann, Walter. *Deuteronomy.* Abingdon New Testament Commentaries. Nashville: Abingdon, 2001.

Budin, Stephanie Lynn. *The Myth of Sacred Prostitution in Antiquity.* Cambridge: Cambridge Univ. Press, 2008.

Buell, Denise Kimber. *Why This New Race? Ethnic Reasoning in Early Christianity.* New York: Columbia Univ. Press, 2005.

Burrus, Virginia, and Stephen D. Moore. "Unsafe Sex: Feminism, Pornography, and the Song of Songs." *Biblical Interpretation* 11.1 (2003): 24–52.

Butler, Judith. "Is Kinship Always Already Heterosexual?" *Difference: A Journal of Feminist Cultural Studies* 13.1 (2002):14–44.

Bynum, Caroline Walker. *Holy Feast and Holy Fast: The Religious Significance of Food to Medieval Women.* Berkeley: Univ. of California Press, 1987.

———. *Wonderful Blood: Theology and Practice in Late Medieval Germany and Beyond.* Philadelphia: Univ. of Pennsylvania Press, 2007.

Camp, Claudia V. "1 and 2 Kings." In *The Women's Bible Commentary,* edited by Carol A. Newsom and Sharon H. Ringe, 96–109. Louisville: Westminster John Knox, 1992.

———. *Wise, Strange and Holy: The Strange Woman and the Making of the Bible.* Journal for the Study of the Old Testament Supplement Series 320. Gender, Culture, Theory 9. Sheffield: Sheffield Academic, 2000.

Canons of the Council of Nicea. Translated by Henry R. Percival. *The Seven Ecu-*

menical Councils of the Undivided Church. Nicene and Post-Nicene Fathers, Second Series 14. New York: Charles Scribner, 1900. Repr. Peabody, MA: Hendrikson, 1995.

Carmichael, Calum M. *Law, Legend and Incest in the Bible: Leviticus 18–20.* Ithaca, NY: Cornell Univ. Press, 1997.

————. *The Origins of Biblical Law: The Decalogues and the Book of the Covenant.* Ithaca: Cornell Univ. Press, 1992.

Castelli, Elizabeth A. "Interpretations of Power in 1 Corinthians." *Semeia* 54 (1992): 197–222.

————. "Paul on Women and Gender." In *Women and Christian Origins,* edited by Mary Rose D'Angelo and Ross Shepard Kraemer, 221–35. Oxford: Oxford Univ. Press, 1999.

————, ed. "Lesbian Historiography Before the Name?" *GLQ* 4 (1998).

Chariton, *Chaereas and Callirhoe.* Translated by B. P. Reardon, in *Collected Ancient Greek Novels,* edited by B. P. Reardon, 17–124. Berkeley: Univ. of California Press, 1989.

Charles, J. Daryl. *Literary Strategy in the Epistle of Jude.* Scranton: Univ. of Scranton Press, 1993.

Charles, R. H. "The Book of Jubilees." In *Apocrypha and Pseudepigrapha of the Old Testament,* Vol. 2. Oxford: Clarendon, 1913.

Chestnutt, Randall D. "Revelatory Experiences Attributed to Biblical Women in Early Jewish Literature." In *Women Like This: New Perspectives on Jewish Women in the Greco-Roman World,* edited by Amy-Jill Levine, 107–26. Atlanta: Scholars Press, 1991.

Childs, Brevard S. *Exodus: A Commentary.* Chatham, MA: Mackay, 1974.

Cicero, Marcus Tullius. *De legibus.* Translated by Clinton Walker Keyes. *Cicero.* Vol. 16, *De republica. De legibus.* Loeb Classical Library: Cambridge: Harvard Univ. Press, 1977.

Clark, Gillian. *Christianity and Roman Society: Key Themes in Ancient History.* Cambridge: Cambridge Univ. Press, 2004.

Clark, Elizabeth A. "Origen, the Jews, and the Song of Songs." In Hagedorn, *Perspectives on the Song of Songs,* 274–93.

————. *Reading Renunciation: Asceticism and Scripture in Early Christianity.* Princeton: Princeton Univ. Press, 1999.

Cohen, Shaye J. D. "A Brief History of Jewish Circumcision Blood." In Wyner Mark. *Covenant of Circumcision,* 30–42.

———. *The Beginnings of Jewishness: Boundaries, Varieties, Uncertainties.* Berkeley: Univ. of California Press, 1999.

———. "From the Bible to the Talmud: The Prohibition of Intermarriage," *Hebrew Annual Review* 7 (1983): 23–39.

———. "Judaism without Circumcision and 'Judaism' without 'Circumcision' in Ignatius." *Harvard Theological Review* 95.4 (2002): 395–415.

———. "Menstruants and the Sacred in Judaism and Christianity." In *Women's History and Ancient History,* edited by Sarah B. Pomeroy. Chapel Hill: Univ. of North Carolina Press, 1991.

———. "The Origins of the Matrilineal Principle in Rabbinic Law," *AJS Review* 10.1 (1985): 19–53.

———. "Purity and Piety: The Separation of Menstruants from the Sancta." In *Daughters of the King: Women and the Synagogue,* edited by Susan Grossman and Rivka Haut, 103–16. New York: Jewish Publication Society, 1992.

———. "'Those Who Say They Are Jews and Are Not': How Do You Know a Jew in Antiquity When You See One?" In *Diasporas in Antiquity,* edited by Shaye J. D. Cohen and Ernest S. Frerichs. Brown Judaic Studies 288. Atlanta: Scholars Press, 1992.

———. "Was Timothy Jewish (Acts 16:1–3)? Patristic Exegesis, Rabbinic Law, and Matrilineal Descent." In *Journal of Biblical Literature* 105.2 (1986), 251–68.

———. *Why Aren't Jewish Women Circumcised? Gender and the Covenant in Judaism.* Berkeley: Univ. of California Press, 2005.

Collins, John J. "The Sibylline Oracles." In *Jewish Writings of the Second Temple Period,* edited by Michael E. Stone, 331–44. Assen, the Netherlands: VanGorcum; Philadelphia: Fortress Press, 1984.

———. "The Works of the Messiah." *Dead Sea Discoveries* 1.1 (1994): 98–112.

———. "The Zeal of Phinehas: The Bible and the Legitimation of Violence." *Journal of Biblical Literature* 122.1 (2003): 3–21.

Colson, F. H., trans., *Philo,* Vol. 7, *On the Decalogue. On the Special Laws, books 1–3.* Loeb Classical Library. Cambridge: Harvard Univ. Press, 1937.

Cotton, Hannah. "A Cancelled Marriage Contract from the Judean Desert." *Journal of Roman Studies* 84 (1994): 64–86.

————. "The Guardianship of Jesus Son of Babatha: Roman and Local Law in the Province of Arabia." *Journal of Roman Studies* 83 (1993): 94–108.

Cribiore, Raffaella. *Gymnastics of the Mind: Greek Education in Hellenistic and Roman Egypt.* Princeton: Princeton Univ. Press, 2001.

Dalley, Stephanie. *Myths from Mesopotamia.* Oxford: Oxford Univ. Press, 1991.

D'Angelo, Mary Rose. "Colossians." In *Searching the Scriptures.* Vol. 2, *A Feminist Commentary,* edited by Elisabeth Schüssler Fiorenza, 313–24. New York: Crossroad, 1994.

————. "*Eusebeia*: Roman Imperial Family Values and the Sexual Politics of 4 Maccabees and the Pastorals." *Biblical Interpretation* 11.2 (2003): 139–65.

————. "'Knowing How to Preside Over His Own Household': Imperial Masculinity and Christian Asceticism in the Pastorals, *Hermas,* and Luke-Acts." In Moore and Anderson, *Masculinities,* 265–95.

————. "(Re)presentations of Women in the Gospels: John and Mark." In Kraemer and D'Angelo. *Women and Christian Origins.*

————. "Veils, Virgins and the Tongues of Men and Angels." In *Off with Her Head! The Denial of Women's Identity in Myth, Religion and Culture*, edited by Howard Eilberg-Schwartz and Wendy Doniger, 131–64. Berkeley: Univ. of California Press, 1995.

Darby, Robert. *A Surgical Temptation: The Demonization of the Foreskin and the Rise of Circumcision in Britain.* Chicago: Univ. of Chicago Press, 2005.

————."The Masturbation Taboo and the Rise of Routine Male Circumcision: A Review of the Historiography." *Journal of Social History* 36.3 (2003): 737–57.

Darr, John A. "Belittling Mary: Insult Genre, Humiliation and the Early Development of Mariology." In *From the Margins 2: Biblical Women and Their Afterlives*, edited by Christine Joynes and Christopher Rowland. Sheffield: Sheffield Phoenix Press, 2009.

Darr, Kathryn Pfisterer. *Far More Precious Than Jewels: Perspectives on Biblical Women.* Louisville: Westminster John Knox, 1991.

————. "Ezekiel." In Newsom and Ringe. *Women's Bible Commentary,* 183–90.

Davis, Ellen F. "Beginning with Ruth: An Essay on Translating." In *Scrolls of Love: Ruth and the Song of Songs,* edited by Peter S. Hawkins and Lesleigh Cushing Stahlberg, 33–43. Fordham: Fordham Univ. Press, 2006.

————. *Proverbs, Ecclesiastes, and the Song of Songs.* Louisville: Westminster John Knox, 2000.

Day, John. *Yahweh and the Gods and Goddesses of Canaan.* JSOT Supplement Series 265. Sheffield: Sheffield Academic, 2000.

Day, Linda. "Rhetoric and Domestic Violence in Ezekiel 16." *Biblical Interpretation* 8.3 (2000): 205–30.

Day, Peggy L. "The Bitch Had It Coming to Her: Rhetoric and Interpretation in Ezekiel 16." *Biblical Interpretation* 8.3 (2000): 231–54.

de Jonge, Marinus. *Pseudepigrapha of the Old Testament as Part of Christian Literature: The Case of the Testaments of the Twelve Patriarchs and the Greek Life of Adam and Eve.* Studia in Veteris Testamenti pseudepigrapha 18. Leiden: Brill, 2003.

Dewey, Joanna. "The Gospel of Mark." In *Searching the Scriptures.* Vol. 2, *A Feminist Commentary,* edited by Elisabeth Schüssler Fiorenza. New York: Crossroad, 1994.

Didascalia Apostolorum. Translated by Arthur Vööbus. *The Didascalia Apostolorum in Syriac.* CSCO 401–2; 407–8, Scriptores Syri 175–76; 179–80. Louvain: Secrétariat du Corpus SCO, 1979.

The Digest of Justinian. Edited and translated by Alan Watson. 4 vols. Philadelphia: Univ. of Pennsylvania Press, 1985.

Dijkstra, Meindert. "The Valley of Dry Bones: Coping with the Reality of the Exile in the Book of Ezekiel." In *The Crisis of Israelite Religion: Transformation of Religious Tradition in Exilic and Post-Exilic Times,* edited by Bob Becking, Marjo C. A. Korpel, 114–33. Leiden: Brill, 1999.

Dobbs-Allsopp, F. W. "Late Linguistic Features in Song of Songs." In Hagedorn, *Perspectives on the Song of Songs,* 27–77.

Douglas, Mary. *Leviticus as Literature.* New York and Oxford: Oxford Univ. Press, 1999.

————. *Purity and Danger: An Analysis of Concepts of Pollution and Taboo.* Repr. London: Routledge, 1991.

Dove, Mary, ed. and trans. *The Glossa Ordinaria on the Song of Songs.* Kalamazoo: Western Michigan University, 2004.

Dover, Kenneth. *Greek Homosexuality.* Cambridge: Harvard Univ. Press, 1978.

Dube, Musa W. "Divining Ruth for International Relations." In *Postmodern Inter-*

pretations of the Bible: A Reader, edited by A. K. M. Adam, 67–79. St. Louis, MO: Chalice Press, 2001.

Dunn, Geoffrey D., trans., *Tertullian.* The Early Church Fathers. London: Routledge, 2004.

Dunn, James D. G. *The Epistles to Colossians and Philemon.* Grand Rapids: Eerdmans, 1996.

Ehrman, Bart D., ed. and trans. *The Apostolic Fathers.* 2 vols. Loeb Classical Library 24–25. Cambridge: Harvard Univ. Press, 2003.

Eilberg-Schwartz, Howard. *God's Phallus and Other Problems for Men and Monotheism.* Boston: Beacon Press, 1994.

———. *The Savage in Judaism: An Anthropology of Israelite Religion and Ancient Judaism.* Bloomington: Indiana Univ. Press, 1990.

Elliott, J. K. *The Apocryphal New Testament.* Oxford: Clarendon, 1993.

Elm, Susanna. *Virgins of God: The Making of Asceticism in Late Antiquity.* Oxford: Clarendon, 1994.

Epictetus. *The Discourses.* Translated by W. A. Oldfather, *Epictetus. The Discourses as Reported by Arrian, the Manual, and Fragments,* 2 vols. Loeb Classical Library. Cambridge: Harvard Univ. Press, 1925.

Eskenazi, Tamara C., and Eleanore P. Judd. "Marriage to a Stranger in Ezra 9–10." In *Second Temple Studies.* Vol. 2, *Temple Community in the Persian Period,* edited by Tamara C. Eskenazi and Kent H. Richards, 266–72. JSOT Supplement Series 175. Sheffield: JSOT Press, 1994.

Eusebius of Caesarea. *Ecclesiastical History.* Translated by Kirsopp Lake, John Ernest Leonard, and Hugh Jackson Lawlor. *Eusebius. The Ecclesiastical History,* 2 vols. Loeb Classical Library. Cambridge: Harvard Univ. Press, 1926–1932.

Exum, J. Cheryl. "In the Eye of the Beholder: Wishing, Dreaming, and *Double Entendre* in the Song of Songs." In *The Labour of Reading: Desire, Alienation and Biblical Interpretation,* edited by Fiona Black, Roland Boer, and Erin Runions, 71–86. Atlanta: Society of Biblical Literature, 1999.

———. *The Song of Songs: A Commentary.* Louisville: Westminster John Knox, 2006.

———. *Tragedy and Biblical Narrative: Arrows of the Almighty.* Cambridge: Cambridge Univ. Press, 1992.

Faraone, Christopher, and Laura McClure, ed. *Prostitutes and Courtesans in the Ancient World*. Madison: Univ. of Wisconsin Press, 2006.

Feldman, Louis H. *Jew and Gentile in the Ancient World: Attitudes and Interactions from Alexander to Justinian*. Princeton: Princeton Univ. Press, 1993.

Fewell, Dana Nolan, and David M. Gunn. *Gender, Power, and Promise: The Subject of the Bible's First Story*. Nashville: Abingdon, 1993.

———. "'A Son is Born to Naomi!' Literary Allusions and Interpretation in the Book of Ruth." In *Women in the Hebrew Bible: A Reader,* edited by Alice Bach, 233–39, New York and London: Routledge, 1999.

Finkelstein, Israel. *The Archaeology of the Israelite Settlement*. Jerusalem: Israelite Exploration Society, 1988.

———. "Ethnicity and Origin of the Iron I Settlers in the Highlands of Canaan: Can the Real Israel Stand Up?" *The Biblical Archaeologist* 59.4 (1996): 198–212.

Fiorenza, Elisabeth Schüssler. *In Memory of Her: A Feminist Theological Reconstruction of Christian Origins*. New York: Crossroad, 1989.

———. *Revelation: Vision of a Just World*. Proclamation Commentaries. Minneapolis: Fortress, 1991.

———, ed. *Searching the Scriptures*. Vol. 2, *A Feminist Commentary*. New York: Crossroad, 1994.

Fonrobert, Charlotte Elisheva, and Martin S. Jaffee. Introduction to *The Cambridge Companion to the Talmud and Rabbinic Literature*. Cambridge: Cambridge Univ. Press, 2007.

———. *Menstrual Purity: Rabbinic and Christian Reconstructions of Biblical Gender*. Contraversions. Stanford: Stanford Univ. Press, 2000.

Forrest, Robert W. E. "Paradise Lost Again: Violence and Obedience in the Flood Narrative," *Journal for the Study of the Old Testament* 62 (1994): 3–18.

Fox, M., and M. Thomson. "A Covenant with the Status Quo? Male Circumcision and the New BMA Guidance to Doctors." *Journal of Medical Ethics* 31.8 (2005): 463–69.

Frankfurter, David. *Religion in Roman Egypt: Assimilation and Resistance*. Princeton: Princeton Univ. Press, 1998.

Freidenfelds, Lara. *The Modern Period: Menstruation in Twentieth-Century America*. Baltimore: Johns Hopkins Univ. Press, 2009.

Frymer-Kensky, Tikva. *Reading the Women of the Bible*. New York: Schocken, 2002.

————. "Virginity in the Bible." In *Gender and Law in the Hebrew Bible and the Ancient Near East,* edited by Victor H. Matthews, Bernard M. Levinson, and Tikva Frymer-Kensky, 77–96. JSOT Supplement Series 262. Sheffield: Sheffield Academic, 1998.

Gaca, Kathy. *The Making of Fornication: Eros, Ethics and Political Reform in Greek Philosophy and Early Christianity.* Berkeley: Univ. of California Press, 2003.

Gagnon, Robert A. J. *The Bible and Homosexual Practice: Text and Hermeneutics.* Nashville: Abingdon, 2001.

Galambush, Julie. *Jerusalem in the Book of Ezekiel: The City as Yahweh's Wife.* Society of Biblical Literature Dissertation Series 130. Atlanta: Scholars Press, 1992.

Galen. *On the Usefulness of the Parts of the Body.* Translated by Margaret Tallmadge. 2 vols. Ithaca: Cornell Univ. Press, 1968.

Galpaz-Feller, Pnina. "Private Lives and Public Censure: Adultery in Ancient Egypt and Biblical Israel," *Near Eastern Archaeology* 67.3 (2004): 152–61.

Garrett, Susan. "The 'Weaker Sex' in the Testament of Job." *Journal of Biblical Literature* 112.1 (1993): 55–70.

Gench, Frances Taylor. *Back to the Well: Women's Encounters with Jesus in the Gospels.* Louisville: Westminster John Knox, 2004.

Gilders, William K. *Blood Ritual in the Hebrew Bible: Meaning and Power.* Baltimore: Johns Hopkins Univ. Press, 2004.

Gini, Anthony. "The Manly Intellect of His Wife: Xenophon *Oeconomicus* 7." *Classical World* 86.6 (1993): 483–86.

Glancy, Jennifer A. *Corporal Knowledge: Early Christian Bodies.* New York and Oxford: Oxford Univ. Press, 2010.

————. "Protocols of Masculinity in the Pastoral Epistles." In Moore and Anderson, *Masculinities,* 235–64.

————. *Slavery in Early Christianity.* New York and Oxford: Oxford Univ. Press, 2002.

Goldberg, Arnold M. *Untersuchungen über die Vorstellung von der Schekhinah in der Frühen Rabbinischen Literatur.* Studia Judaica 5. Berlin: De Gruyter, 1969.

Gollaher, David L. "From Ritual to Science: The Medical Transformation of Circumcision in America." *Journal of Social History* 28 (1994): 5–36.

————. *Circumcision: A History of the World's Most Controversial Surgery.* New York: Basic Books, 2000.

Goodman, Martin. "Babatha's Story: A Review of Y. Yadin, *The Documents from the Bar Kokhba Period in the Cave of Letters: Greek Papyri*. Edited by N. Lewis; *Aramaic and Nabatean Signatures and Subscriptions*. Edited by Y. Yadin and G. C. Greenfield," *Journal of Roman Studies* 81 (1991): 169–75.

———. *Rome and Jerusalem: The Clash of Ancient Civilizations*. New York: Vintage Books, 2009.

Goodman, Martin, ed. *Jews in a Graeco-Roman World*. Oxford: Clarendon, 1998.

Goodstein, Laurie. "Falwell's Finger Pointing Inappropriate, Bush Says." *New York Times,* September 15, 2001, A15.

Goulder, Michael. *The Song of Fourteen Songs*. JSOT Supplement Series 36. Sheffield: JSOT, 1986.

Grabbe, Lester L. "'Canaanite': Some Methodological Observations in Relation to Biblical Study." In *Ugarit and the Bible: Proceedings of the International Symposium on Ugarit and the Bible*, edited by G. J. Brooke, A. H. W. Curtis, and J. F. Healey. Ugeritisch-biblisch Literatur 11. Münster: Ugarit-Varlag, 1994.

Greenberg, Moshe. *Ezekiel 1–20*. Anchor Bible 22. New York: Doubleday, 1983.

Greenstein, Edward L. "Reading Strategies and the Story of Ruth." In Bach, *Women in the Hebrew Bible,* 211–32.

Gregory the Great. "Letter to Augustine." In *The Venerable Bede's Ecclesiastical History of England: Also the Anglo-Saxon Chronicle*. Translated by J. A. Giles. London: George Bell & Sons, 1894.

Gregory of Nyssa. *Commentary on the Song of Songs*. Translated by Casimir McCambley, *Saint Gregory of Nyssa. Commentary on the Song of Songs*. The Archbishop Iakovos Library of Ecclesiastical and Historical Sources 12. Brookline, MA: Hellenic College Press, 1987.

Grene, David. *Herodotus: The History*. Chicago: Univ. of Chicago Press, 1987.

Griffiths, Fiona. *The Garden of Delights: Reform and Renaissance for Women in the Twelfth Century*. Philadelphia: Univ. of Pennsylvania Press, 2007.

Grubbs, Judith Evans. *Women and the Law in the Roman Empire*. London and New York: Routledge, 2002.

Gruen, Erich. *Heritage and Hellenism: The Reinvention of Jewish Tradition*. Berkeley: Univ. of California Press, 1998.

Gunkel, Hermann. *Genesis*. Translated by Mark E. Biddle. Originally published Göttingen: Vandenhoek & Ruprecht, 1901; repr. Macon, GA: Mercer Univ. Press, 1997.

Gunn, David. *The Fate of King Saul.* Sheffield: Sheffield Academic, 1980.

Hadley, Judith M. *The Cult of Asherah in Ancient Israel and Judah: Evidence for a Hebrew Goddess.* Cambridge Oriental Publications 57. Cambridge: Cambridge University, 2000.

————."The Khirbet el-Qom Inscription." *Vetus Testamentum* 37.1 (1987): 50–62.

Hagedorn, Anselm C., ed. *Perspectives on the Song of Songs*, 27–77. Berlin: De Gruyter, 2006.

Halperin, David. *One Hundred Years of Homosexuality: And Other Essays on Greek Love.* New York: Routledge, 1990.

Halpern-Amaru, Betsy. *The Empowerment of Women in the Book of Jubilees.* Supplements to the Study of Judaism 60. Leiden: Brill, 1999.

Harrill, J. Albert, *The Manumission of Slaves in Early Christianity.* Tübingen: Mohr, 1998.

Hasel, Michael G. "Israel in the Merneptah Stele." *Bulletin of the American Schools of Oriental Research* 296 (1994): 45–61.

Hayes, Christine E. *Gentile Impurities and Jewish Identities: Intermarriage and Conversion from the Bible to the Talmud.* New York and Oxford: Oxford Univ. Press, 2002.

Haynes, Stephen. *Noah's Curse: The Biblical Justification of American Slavery.* New York and London: Oxford Univ. Press, 2002.

Heidel, Alexander. *The Gilgamesh Epic and Old Testament Parallels.* Chicago: Univ. of Chicago Press, 1946.

Hepner, Gershon. "Abraham's Incestuous Marriage with Sarah a Violation of the Holiness Code." *Vetus Testamentum* 53.2 (2003): 143–55.

Hess, Richard S. *Israelite Religions: An Archaeological and Biblical Survey.* Grand Rapids: Baker Academic, 2007.

Hiebert, Theodore. *The Yahwist's Landscape: Nature and Religion in Early Israel.* Oxford: Oxford Univ. Press, 1996.

Hillers, Delbert R. "Analyzing the Abominable: Our Understanding of Canaanite Religion." *Jewish Quarterly Review* 75.3 (1985): 253–69.

Himmelfarb, Martha. *A Kingdom of Priests: Ancestry and Merit in Ancient Judaism.* Philadelphia: Univ. of Pennsylvania Press, 2006.

Hirsch, F. E., and J. K. Grider. "Crime." In *The International Standard Bible Encyclopedia,* edited by Geoffrey W. Bromiley, et al. Grand Rapids: Eerdmans, 1979.

Hodge, Caroline Johnson, *If Sons, Then Heirs: A Study of Kinship and Ethnicity in the Letters of Paul.* New York and London: Oxford Univ. Press, 2007.

Hoffman, Lawrence A. *Covenant of Blood: Circumcision and Gender in Rabbinic Judaism.* Chicago: Univ. of Chicago Press, 1996.

Horner, Tom. *Jonathan Loved David: Homosexuality in Biblical Times.* Philadelphia: Westminster John Knox, 1978.

Hopkins, M. K. "The Age of Roman Girls at Marriage." *Population Studies* 18.3 (1965): 309–27.

Hubbard, Jr., Robert L. *The Book of Ruth.* Grand Rapids: Eerdmans, 1988.

Huehnergard, John. "Languages of the Ancient Near East." *Anchor Bible Dictionary.* Vol. 4, 155–70. New York: Doubleday, 1992.

Irenaeus of Lyons. *Against the Heresies.* Translated by Dominic J. Unger with revisions by John J. Dillon. Ancient Christian Writers. New York: Paulist Press, 1992.

Jacobs, Andrew S. "Dialogical Differences: (De-)Judaizing Jesus' Circumcision." *Journal of Early Christian Studies* 15.3 (2007): 291–335.

———. "Passing: Jesus' Circumcision and Strategic Self-Sacrifice." In *Ancient Mediterranean Sacrifice: Images, Acts, Meanings,* edited by Jennifer Knust and Zsuzsanna Várhelyi. New York and Oxford: Oxford Univ. Press, forthcoming.

Jay, Nancy. "Sacrifice as Remedy for Having Been Born a Woman." In *Women, Gender, Religion: A Reader,* edited by Elizabeth A. Castelli. New York: Palgrave, 2001.

———. *Throughout Your Generations Forever: Sacrifice, Religion, and Paternity.* Chicago: Univ. of Chicago Press, 1992.

Jobling, David. *1 Samuel.* Collegeville, MD: Liturgical Press, 1998.

John Chrysostom. *Homilies on Matthew.* Edited and translated by Philip Schaff. *Nicene and Post-Nicene Fathers.* Series 1, Vol. 10, *Chrysostom: Homilies on the Gospel of Saint Matthew.* Repr. Peabody, MA: Hendrickson, 1995.

———. *Homilies on the Gospel of John.* Translated by Sister Thomas Aquinas Goggin. *Saint John Chrysostom. Commentary on Saint John the Apostle and Evangelist.* Vol. 1, *Homilies 1–47.* Fathers of the Church. New York: Fathers of the Church, 1957.

Johnson, Larry, with Scott Baldyga. *Frozen: My Journey into the World of Cryonics, Deception and Death.* New York: Vanguard, 2009.

Johnson, Sylvester A. *The Myth of Ham in Nineteenth-Century American Christianity: Race, Heathens, and the People of God.* New York: Palgrave Macmillan, 2004.

Jordan, Mark D. *The Invention of Sodomy in Christian Theology.* Chicago: Univ. of Chicago Press, 1997.

Josephus. *Against Apion.* Translated by H. St. J. Thackeray. *Josephus. The Life. Against Apion.* Loeb Classical Library. Cambridge: Harvard Univ. Press, 1926.

Justin Martyr. *First and Second Apology.* Greek text edited by Edgar J. Goodspeed, *Die altesten Apologeten.* Göttingen: Vandenhoeck & Ruprecht, 1914.

———. *The Dialogue with Trypho.* Translated by A. Lukyn Williams. Christian Literature Series 1. London: SPCK; New York: MacMillan, 1930.

Juvenal. *Satires.* Translated by G. G. Ramsay. *Juvenal and Persius.* Loeb Classical Library. Cambridge: Harvard Univ. Press, rev. ed. 1940.

Karras, Ruth Mazo. "Review Essay: Active/Passive, Acts/Passions: Greek and Roman Sexualities," *American Historical Review* 105.4 (2000): 1250–65.

Kates, Judith A., "Entering the Holy of Holies: Rabbinic Midrash and the Language of Intimacy." In Hawkins and Stahlberg, *Scrolls of Love.*

Keller, Catherine. *Apocalypse Now and Then: A Feminist Guide to the End of the World.* Boston: Beacon Press, 1996.

Kerkeslager, Alan. "Maintaining a Jewish Identity in the Greek Gymnasium: A 'Jewish Load' in *CPJ* 3.519 (= P. Schub. 37 = P. Berol. 13406)." *Journal for the Study of Judaism* 28.1 (1997): 12–33.

Kister, M. J. "'And He Was Born Circumcised' . . . Some Notes on Circumcision in Hadith." *Oriens* 34 (1994): 10–30.

Klawans, Jonathan. *Impurity and Sin in Ancient Judaism.* New York and Oxford: Oxford Univ. Press, 2000.

———. *Purity, Sacrifice, and the Temple: Symbolism and Supersessionism in the Study of Ancient Judaism.* New York and Oxford: Oxford Univ. Press, 2006.

Klijn, A. F. J. "2 (Syriac Apocalypse of) Baruch." In *Old Testament Pseudepigrapha.* Vol. 1, *Apocalyptic Literature and Testaments,* edited by James H. Charlesworth. New York: Doubleday, 1983.

Knibb, Michael A., and Pieter W. Van Der Horst, ed. *Studies on the Testament of Job.* Cambridge: Cambridge Univ. Press, 1989.

Knust, Jennifer Wright. *Abandoned to Lust: Sexual Slander and Ancient Christianity.* Gender, Theory, Religion. New York: Columbia Univ. Press, 2005.

Koester, Craig R. "'The Savior of the World' (John 4:42)," *Journal of Biblical Literature* 109.4 (1990): 665–80.

Koester, Helmut. "Imperial Ideology and Paul's Eschatology in 1 Thessalonians." In *Paul and Empire: Religion and Power in Roman Imperial Society,* edited by Richard A. Horsley, 158–66. Harrisburg: Trinity Press International, 1997.

Koltun-Fromm, Naomi. "Aphrahat and the Rabbis on Noah's Righteousness in Light of Jewish-Christian Polemic." In *The Book of Genesis in Jewish and Oriental Exegesis,* edited by Judith Frishman and Lucas van Rompay, 57–72. Leuven: Peeters, 1997.

Komar, Kathleen L. *Transcending Angels: Rainer Maria Rilke's Duino Elegies.* Lincoln: Univ. of Nebraska Press, 1987.

Kovács, Éva, and Júlia Vajda. "Circumcision in Hungary after the Shoah." In *The Covenant of Circumcision: New Perspectives on an Ancient Jewish Rite,* edited by Elizabeth Wyner Mark. Hanover and London: Brandeis Univ. Press, 2003.

Kraemer, Ross Shepard. "On the Meaning of the Term 'Jew' in Greco-Roman Inscriptions." *Harvard Theological Review* 82.1 (1989): 35–53.

———. "Jewish Women and Women's Judaism(s) at the Beginning of Christianity." In Kraemer and D'Angelo. *Women and Christian Origins,* 50–79.

Kueffler, Matthew. *The Manly Eunuch: Masculinity, Gender Ambiguity, and Christian Ideology in Late Antiquity.* Chicago: Univ. of Chicago Press, 2001.

Kugler, Robert A. *The Testaments of the Twelve Patriarchs.* Sheffield: Sheffield Academic, 2001.

Lacocque, André. *The Feminine Unconventional: Four Subversive Figures in Israel's Tradition.* Minneapolis: Fortress, 1990.

Lafont, Sophie. "Middle Assyrian Laws." In *A History of Ancient Near Eastern Law,* edited by Raymond Westbrook. Leiden: Brill, 2003.

Lanci, John. "The Stones Don't Speak and the Texts Tell Lies: Sacred Sex at Corinth." In *Urban Religion in Roman Corinth: Interdisciplinary Approaches,* edited by Daniel N. Schowalter and Steven J. Friesen. Harvard Theological Studies 53. Cambridge: Harvard Univ. Press, 2005.

Laqueur, Thomas. *Solitary Sex: A Cultural History of Masturbation.* New York: Zone Books, 2003.

Lawrence, Jonathan D. *Washing in Water: Trajectories of Ritual Bathing in the*

Hebrew Bible and Second Temple Literature. Atlanta: Society of Biblical Literature, 2006.

Layton, Bentley. *The Gnostic Scriptures: Ancient Wisdom for the New Age.* Anchor Bible Reference Series. New York: Doubleday, 1987.

Lesses, Rebecca. "Amulets and Angels: Visionary Experience in the Testament of Job and the Hekhalot Literature." In *Heavenly Tablets: Interpretation, Identity and Tradition in Ancient Judaism,* edited by Lynn LiDonnici and Andrea Lieber, 49–74. Supplements to the Journal for the Study of Judaism 119. Leiden: Brill, 2007.

Letter of Aristeas. Translated by R. J. H. Shutt. In *Old Testament Pseudepigrapha.* Vol. 2, *Expansions of the "Old Testament."* Edited by James Charlesworth. Anchor Bible. New York: Doubleday, 1985.

Levenson, Jon D., and Baruch Halpern. "The Political Import of David's Marriages." *Journal of Biblical Literature* 99.4 (1980): 507–18.

Levine, Amy-Jill. "Diaspora as Metaphor: Bodies and Boundaries in the Book of Tobit." In *Diaspora Jews and Judaism: Essays in Honor of and Dialogue with A. Thomas Kraebel,* edited by J. Andrew Overman and Robert S. MacLenham, 105–18. Atlanta: Scholars Press, 1992.

Levine, Lee I. *The Ancient Synagogue: The First Thousand Years.* 2nd ed. New Haven: Yale Univ. Press, 2005.

Levinskaya, Irene. *The Book of Acts in Its Diaspora Setting.* Grand Rapids: Eerdmans, 1996.

Levinson, Bernard M. *Deuteronomy and the Hermeneutic of Legal Innovation.* New York and Oxford: Oxford Univ. Press, 1997.

Leyerle, Blake. "Blood Is Seed." *Journal of Religion* 81.1 (2001): 26–48.

Linafelt, Tod. *Ruth.* Berit Olam: Studies in Hebrew Narrative and Poetry. Collegeville, MD: Liturgical Press, 1999.

Livesy, Nina E., "Theological Identity Making: Justin's Use of Circumcision to Create Jews and Christians." *Journal of Early Christian Studies* 18.1 (2010): 51–79.

Lloyd, A. B. *Herodotus,* Book ii. Introduction, Commentary 1–98. 2 vols. Leiden: Brill, 1975–1976.

Lohfink, Norbert. "The Cult Reform of Josiah of Judah: 2 Kings 22–23 as a Source for the History of the Israelite Religion." In *Ancient Israelite Religion: Essays in*

Honor of Frank Moore Cross, edited by Patrick D. Miller Jr., Paul D. Hanson, and S. Dean McBride, 459–75. Philadelphia: Fortress, 1987.

Lohse, Eduard. *Colossians and Philemon.* Hermeneia. Philadelphia: Fortress, 1971.

Lutz, Cora B. "Musonius Rufus: The Roman Socrates," *Yale Classical Studies* 10 (1947): 3–147.

MacDonald, Margaret Y. *Early Christian Women and Pagan Opinion: The Power of the Hysterical Woman.* Cambridge: Cambridge Univ. Press, 1996.

———. "Rereading Paul: Early Interpreters of Paul on Women and Gender." In Kraemer and D'Angelo. *Women and Christian Origins,* 236–53.

———. *The Pauline Churches: A Socio-Historical Study of Institutionalization in the Pauline and Deutero-Pauline Writings.* Cambridge: Cambridge Univ. Press, 1988.

Mach, Michael. "Justin Martyr's *Dialogue cum Tryphone Iudaeo* and the Development of Christian Anti-Judaism." In *Contra Iudaeos: Ancient and Medieval Polemics Between Christians and Jews,* edited by Ora Limor and Guy G. Stroumsa, 27–48. Texts and Studies in Medieval and Early Modern Judaism 10. Tübingen: Mohr/Seibeck, 1996.

MacQuarrie, Brian, and Raphael Lewis. "Across New England, a Sense of Loss and Fond Memories." *Boston Globe,* July 6, 2002, A1.

Madigan, Kevin, and Jon D. Levenson. *Resurrection: The Power of God for Christians and Jews.* New Haven: Yale Univ. Press, 2008.

Magness, Jodi. *The Archaeology of Qumran and the Dead Sea Scrolls.* Grand Rapids: Eerdmans, 2002.

Malcomson, Scott L. *One Drop of Blood: The American Misadventure of Race.* New York: Farrar, Straus and Giroux, 2000, esp. 73–90.

Marbury, Herbert R. "The Strange Woman in Persian Yehud: A Reading of Proverbs 7." In *Approaching Yehud: New Approaches to the Study of the Persian Period,* edited by Jon L. Berquist. Semeia 50. Atlanta: Society of Biblical Literature, 2007.

Martin, Dale B. *The Corinthian Body.* New Haven: Yale Univ. Press, 1995.

———. *Sex and the Single Savior: Gender and Sexuality in Biblical Interpretation.* Louisville: Westminster John Knox, 2006.

Martínez, Florentino García, ed., and W. G. E. Watson, trans. *The Dead Sea Scrolls Translated: The Qumran Texts in English.* Leiden: Brill, 1996.

Mathews, Victor H., Bernard M. Levinson, and Tikva Frymer-Kensky, ed. *Gender and Law in the Hebrew Bible and the Ancient Near East.* JSOT Supplement Series 262. Sheffield: Sheffield Academic, 1998.

Matter, E. Ann. *The Voice of My Beloved: The Song of Songs in Western Medieval Christianity.* Philadelphia: Univ. of Pennsylvania Press, 1990.

Matthews, Victor H., "The Anthropology of Slavery in the Covenant Code." In *Theory and Method in Biblical and Cuneiform Law: Revision, Interpretation and Development,* edited by Bernard M. Levinson, 119–35. JSOT Supplement Series 181. Sheffield: Sheffield Academic, 1994.

McGinn, Thomas A. J. *Prostitution, Sexuality and the Law in Ancient Rome.* New York and Oxford: Oxford Univ. Press, 1998.

McGowan, Andrew. *Ascetic Eucharists: Food and Drink in Early Christian Ritual Meals.* New York and Oxford: Oxford Univ. Press, 1999.

McKinlay, Judith E. "Rahab: A Hero/ine?" *Biblical Interpretation* 7.1 (1999): 44–57.

McNeal, Richard A. "The Brides of Babylon: Herodotus 1.196." *Historia: Zeitschrift für Alte Geschichte* 37.1 (1988): 54–71.

———. *Herodotus: Book 1.* Lanham, MD: Univ. Press of America, 1986.

McWhirter, Jocelyn. *The Bridegroom Messiah and the People of God: Marriage in the Fourth Gospel.* Society for New Testament Studies Monograph Series 138. Cambridge: Cambridge Univ. Press, 2006.

Meacham, Tirzah. "The Missing Daughter: Leviticus 18 and 20." *Zeitschrift für die Alttestamentliche Wissenschaft* 109.2 (1997): 254–59.

Meeks, Wayne A. "The Image of the Androgyne: Some Uses of a Symbol in Earliest Christianity." *History of Religions* 13.3 (1974): 165–208.

Mendenhall, George. "The Hebrew Conquest of Palestine." *The Biblical Archaeologist* 25 (1962): 66–87.

Methodius. *The Symposium: A Treatise on Chastity.* Translated and edited by William R. Clark. In the Ante-Nicene Fathers. Vol. 6, Gregory Thaumaturgus, Dionysius the Great, Julius Africanus, Anatolius and Minor Writers Methodius, Arnobius. New York: Christian Literature Publishing, 1886; repr. Peabody, MA: Hendrickson, 1995.

Methuen, Charlotte. "'Virgin Widow': A Problematic Social Role for the Early Church?" *Harvard Theological Review* 90.3 (1997): 285–98.

Meyers, Carol. *Discovering Eve: Ancient Israelite Women in Context.* New York and Oxford: Oxford Univ. Press, 1988.

Milgrom, Jacob. *Leviticus 17–22: A New Translation with Introduction and Commentary.* Anchor Bible. New York: Doubleday, 2000.

Milik, J. T. *The Books of Enoch: Aramaic Fragments of Qumran Cave 4.* Oxford: Clarendon, 1976.

Mishra, Raja. "Williams Estate Halts Legal Inquiry on Cryonics Pact." *Boston Globe,* August 9, 2002, A1.

Moore, Stephen D. "The Song of Songs in the History of Sexuality." *Church History* 69.2 (2000): 328–49.

Moore, Stephen D., and Janice Capel Anderson, ed. *New Testament Masculinities,* 67–91. Semeia 45. Atlanta: Society of Biblical Literature, 2003.

Moran, William L. "The Ancient New Eastern Background of the Love of God in Deuteronomy." *Catholic Biblical Quarterly* 25 (1963): 77–87.

Morgan, Teresa. *Literate Education in the Hellenistic and Roman Worlds.* Cambridge: Cambridge Univ. Press, 1998.

Morris, Edward P. *Horace: The Satires.* Norman: Univ. of Oklahoma Press, 1974.

Moyer, Ian. "Herodotus and an Egyptian Mirage: The Genealogies of the Theban Priests." *Journal of Hellenic Studies* 122 (2002): 70–90.

Murnaghan, Sheila. "How a Woman Can Be More Like a Man: The Dialogue Between Isomachus and His Wife in Xenophon's *Oeconomicus.*" *Helios* 15.1 (1988): 9–22.

Murphy, Frederick J. *Fallen Is Babylon: The Revelation to John.* Harrisburg, PA: Trinity Press International, 1998.

Murphy-O'Connor, Jerome. *St. Paul's Corinth: Texts and Archaeology.* Collegeville, MN: Liturgical Press, 1990.

Nelson, Richard D. *Joshua: A Commentary.* The Old Testament Library. Louisville: Westminster John Knox, 1997.

Newsom, Carol A. "Woman and the Discourse of Patriarchal Wisdom: A Study of Proverbs 1–9." In Bach, *Women in the Hebrew Bible.*

Newsom, Carol A., and Sharon H. Ringe, ed. *The Women's Bible Commentary.* Louisville: Westminster John Knox, 1992.

Neyrey, Jerome. *2 Peter, Jude: A New Translation with Introduction and Commentary.* Anchor Bible. New York: Doubleday, 1993.

Nicholas of Lyra. *The Postilla on the Song of Songs.* Translated by James George Kiecker. Milwaukee, WI: Marquette Univ. Press, 1998.

Nickelsburg, W. E. "The Books of Enoch at Qumran: What We Know and What We Need to Think About." In *Antikes Judentum und frühes Christentum. Festschrift für Hartmut Stegemann zum 65. Geburstag,* edited by B. Kollmann, W. Reinbold, H. Stegemann, and A. Steudel, 99–113. Berlin: De Gruyter, 1998.

Niditch, Susan. *Ancient Israelite Religion.* New York and Oxford: Oxford Univ. Press, 1997.

———. *Judges: A Commentary.* Old Testament Library. Louisville: Westminster John Knox, 2008.

Nissinen, Martti. *Homoeroticism in the Biblical World: A Historical Perspective.* Translated by Kirsi Stjerna. Minneapolis: Fortress, 1998.

Økland, Jorunn. *Women in Their Place: Paul and the Corinthian Discourse of Gender and Sanctuary Space.* JSNT Supplement Series 269. Sheffield: Clark, 2004.

Olyan, Saul M. *Asherah and the Cult of Yahweh in Israel.* SBL Monograph Series 24. Atlanta: Scholars Press, 1988.

———. " 'And with a Male You Shall Not Lie the Lying Down of a Woman': On the Meaning and Significance of Leviticus 18:22 and 20:13." *Journal of the History of Sexuality* 5.2 (1994): 79–206.

———. " 'Surpassing the Love of Women': Another look at 2 Samuel 1:26 and the Relationship of David and Jonathan." In *Authorizing Marriage? Canon, Tradition, and Critique in the Blessing of Same-Sex Unions,* edited by Mark D. Jordan with Meghan T. Sweeney and David M. Mellott, 7–16. Princeton: Princeton Univ. Press, 2006.

Origen. *Prologue to the Commentary on the Song of Songs.* Translated by Rowan A. Greer. *Origen: An Exhortation to Martyrdom, Prayer, First Principles: Book IV, Prologue to the Commentary on the Song of Songs, Homily XXVII on Numbers.* Classics of Western Spirituality. Mahwah, NJ: Paulist, 1979.

———. *Homilies on the Song of Songs.* Translated by R. P. Lawson. *Origen. The Song of Songs: Commentary and Homilies.* Ancient Christian Writers 26. Westminster, MD: Newman, 1957.

———. *Contra Celsum.* Edited and translated (French) by Marcel Borret, *Origène. Contre Celse.* Vol. 1, *Livres I et II.* SC 132. Paris: Les Éditions du Cerf, 2005. English translation by Henry Chadwick. *Origen: Contra Celsum.* Cambridge: Cambridge Univ. Press, 1953.

————. *Commentary on John* 13. Translated by Joseph W. Trigg. *Origen.* The Early Church Fathers. London and New York: Routledge, 1998.

Ostriker, Alicia. "A Holy of Holies: The Song of Songs as Countertext." In Brenner and Fontaine. *Song of Songs: A Feminist Companion,* 36–54.

Pagels, Elaine. *Adam, Eve and the Serpent.* New York: Random House, 1988.

Parker, David C. *The Living Text of the Gospels.* Cambridge: Cambridge Univ. Press, 1997.

Parker, Simon. "The Hebrew Bible and Homosexuality." *Quarterly Review* 11.1 (1991): 6–20.

Pastan, Elizabeth. "Charlemagne as Saint? Relics and the Choice of Window Subjects at Chartres Cathedral" In *The Legend of Charlemagne in the Middle Ages: Power, Faith and Crusade,* edited by Matthew Gabriele and Jace Stuckey. New York: Palgrave Macmillan, 2008.

Paton, Lewis Bayles. "Canaanite Influence on the Religion of Israel." *The American Journal of Theology* 18.2 (1914): 205–24.

Philo of Alexandria. *Life of Abraham.* Translated by F. H. Colson. *Philo,* Vol. 6. Loeb Classical Library. Cambridge: Harvard Univ. Press, 1935.

————. *Questions and Answers on Genesis.* Translated by Ralph Marcus. *Philo.* Supplement, Vol. 1, *Questions and Answers on Genesis.* Loeb Classical Library. Cambridge: Harvard Univ. Press, 1953.

Pirenne-Delforge, Vinciane. *L'Aphrodite grecque. Contribution à l'étude de ses cultes et de sa personnalité dans le pantheon archaïque et classique.* Athens and Liège: Centre international de l'étude de la religion greque antique, 1994.

Plaskow, Judith. *Standing Again at Sinai: Judaism from a Feminist Perspective.* San Francisco: Harper and Row, 1990.

Plutarch. *Advice to the Bride and Groom.* Translated by Donald Russell. In *Plutarch's Advice to the Bride and Groom and A Consolation to His Wife,* edited by Sarah B. Pomeroy, 5–13. New York and Oxford: Oxford Univ. Press, 1999.

Poirier, John C. "Purity Beyond the Temple in the Second Temple Era." *Journal of Biblical Literature* 122.2 (2003): 247–65.

Pomeroy, Sarah B. *Goddesses, Whores, Wives, and Slaves: Women in Classical Antiquity.* New York: Schocken Books, 1975.

————. *Women in Hellenistic Egypt: From Alexander to Cleopatra.* New York: Schocken Books, 1984.

————. *Xenophon Oeconomicus: A Social and Historical Commentary.* Oxford: Clarendon, 1994.

Pope, Marvin H. *Song of Songs: A New Translation with Introduction and Commentary.* Anchor Bible 7C. New York: Doubleday, 1977.

Pressler, Carolyn. "Wives and Daughters, Bond and Free: Views of Women in the Slave Laws of Exodus 21:2–11." In Mathews, Levinson, and Frymer-Kensky, *Gender and Law,* 147–72.

Propp, William H. C. *Exodus 19–40: A New Translation with Introduction and Commentary.* Anchor Bible. New York: Doubleday, 2006.

Puech, Emile. "Une Apocalypse messianique (4Q521)." *Revue de Qumran* 15 (1992): 475–519.

Pui-Lan, Kwok. "Finding a Home for Ruth: Gender, Sexuality and the Politics of Otherness." In *New Paradigms for Bible Study: The Bible in the Third Millennium,* edited by Robert M. Fowler, Edith Blumhofer, and Fernando F. Segovia, 137–56. London: Clark, 2004.

Rajak, Tessa. "Talking at Trypho: Christian Apologetic as Anti-Judaism in Justin's *Dialogue with Trypho the Jew.*" In *Apologetics in the Roman Empire,* edited by Mark J. Edwards, Martin Goodman, Simon Price, and Christopher Rowland. Oxford: Clarendon, 1999.

————. *The Jewish Dialogue with Greece and Rome: Studies in Cultural and Social Interaction.* Leiden: Brill, 2001.

Rashi, *The Megiloth and Rashi's Commentary with Linear Translation,* trans. Avraham Schwartz and Yisroel Schwartz. New York: Hebrew Linear Classics, 1983.

Ratzinger, Joseph Cardinal, for the Congregation for the Doctrine of the Faith, "Letter to the Bishops of the Catholic Church on the Pastoral Care of Homosexual Persons," October 1, 1986, www.vatican.va/roman_curia/congregations/cfaith/documents/rc_con_cfaith_doc_19861001_homosexual-persons_en.html.

Reardon, B. P., ed. *Collected Ancient Greek Novels.* Berkeley: Univ. of California Press, 1989.

Reed, Annette Yoshiko. *Fallen Angels and the History of Judaism and Christianity: The Reception of Enochic Literature.* Cambridge: Cambridge Univ. Press, 2005.

Reinhartz, Adele. "The Greek Book of Esther." In Newsom and Ringe. *Women's Bible Commentary,* expanded edition.

Remensnyder, Amy G. "Legendary Treasure at Conques: Reliquaries and Imaginative Memory," *Speculum* 71.4 (1996): 884–906.

Richlin, Amy. *The Garden of Priapus: Sexuality and Aggression in Roman Humor.* New York and Oxford: Oxford Univ. Press, 1986 (2nd ed. 1992).

Rilke, Rainer Maria. *The Book of Images.* Translated with German on facing pages by Edward Snow, rev. ed. New York: Farrar, Straus and Giroux, 1994.

———. *Duino Elegies.* Translated by J. B. Leishman and Stephen Spender. New York: Norton, 1939.

Rogers Jr., Eugene F., ed. *Theology and Sexuality: Classic and Contemporary Readings.* Blackwell Readings in Modern Theology. London: Blackwell, 2002.

Rosner, Brian S. "Temple Prostitution in 1 Corinthians 6:12–20." *Novum Testamentum* 40.4 (1998): 336–51.

Rossing, Barbara R. *The Choice Between Two Cities: Whore, Bride and Empire in the Apocalypse.* Harvard Theological Studies 48. Harrisburg, PA: Trinity Press International, 1999.

Rost, Leonhard. *The Succession to the Throne of David,* trans. Michael Rutter and David Gunn. Sheffield: Phoenix, 1982.

Roth, Martha T. *Law Collections from Mesopotamia and Asia Minor.* Writings from the Ancient World 6. Atlanta: Scholars Press, 1995.

———. "Marriage, Divorce and the Prostitute in Ancient Mesopotamia." In Faraone and McClure, ed. *Prostitutes and Courtesans.*

Rousselle, Aline. *Porneia: On Desire and the Body in Antiquity.* Translated by Felicia Pheasant. London: Blackwell, 1988.

Rowlett, Lori. "Disney's Pocahontas and Joshua's Rahab in Postcolonial Perspective." In *Culture, Entertainment and the Bible,* edited by George Aichele, 66–75. JSOT Supplement Series 309. Sheffield: Sheffield Academic, 2000.

Rubenstein, Jeffrey L. "Social and Institutional Settings of Rabbinic Literature." In Fonrobert and Jaffee, *Cambridge Companion to the Talmud.*

Rubin, Gayle. "The Traffic in Women: Notes on the 'Political Economy' of Sex." In *Toward an Anthropology of Women,* edited by Rayna R. Reiter, 157–210. New York and London: Monthly Review Press, 1975.

Runions, Erin. "From Disgust to Humor: Rahab's Queer Affect." *Postscripts: The Journal of Sacred Texts and Contemporary Worlds* 4.1 (2008): 41–69.

Sachs, Susan. "Baptist Pastor Attacks Islam, Inciting Cries of Intolerance." *New York Times,* June 15, 2002, A10.

Sanders, Guy D. R. "Urban Corinth: An Introduction." In Schowalter and Friesen, *Urban Religion.*

Satlow, Michael. *Jewish Marriage in Antiquity.* Princeton: Princeton Univ. Press, 2001.

Schaberg, Jane. *The Illegitimacy of Jesus: A Feminist Theological Interpretation of the Infancy Narratives.* San Francisco: Harper and Row, 1987.

Schneiders, Sandra. *Revelatory Text: Interpreting the New Testament as Sacred Scripture.* San Francisco: HarperSanFrancisco, 1991.

Scholz, Susanne. *Rape Plots: A Feminist Cultural Study of Genesis 34.* Studies in Biblical Literature 13. New York: Peter Lang, 2000.

Schowalter, Daniel, and Steven J. Friesen, ed. *Urban Religion in Roman Corinth: Interdisciplinary Approaches.* Cambridge: Harvard Univ. Press, 2005.

Schwartz, Regina. "Adultery in the House of David: The Metanarrative of Biblical Scholarship and the Narratives of the Bible." In Bach, *Women in the Hebrew Bible.*

Schwartz, Seth. *Imperialism and Jewish Society 200 BCE to 640 CE.* Princeton: Princeton Univ. Press, 2001.

Segal, Michael. *The Book of Jubilees: Rewritten Bible, Redaction, Ideology and Theology.* Leiden: Brill, 2007.

Seitz, Christopher. *Word Without End: The Old Testament as Abiding Witness.* Grand Rapids: Eerdmans, 1998.

Senior, Donald. *1 and 2 Peter.* Wilmington, DE: Michael Glazier, 1980.

Setzer, Claudia. *Resurrection of the Body in Early Judaism and Early Christianity: Doctrine, Community, and Self-Definition.* Leiden: Brill, 2004.

———. "Resurrection of the Dead as Symbol and Strategy," *Journal of the American Academy of Religion* 69.1 (2001): 65–101.

Shaw, Brent D. "The Age of Roman Girls at Marriage: Some Reconsiderations." *Journal of Roman Studies* 77 (1987): 30–46.

Shea, William. "The Khirbet el-Qom Tomb Inscription Again." *Vetus Testamentum* 60.1 (1990): 110–16.

Sherwood, Yvonne. *The Prostitute and the Prophet: Hosea's Marriage in Literary-*

Theoretical Perspective. JSOT Supplement Series 212. Gender, Culture, Theory 2. Sheffield: Sheffield Academic, 1996.

Sheskin, Arlene. *Cryonics: A Sociology of Death and Bereavement.* New York: Irvington, 1979.

Simkins, Ronald A. "Gender Construction in the Yahwist Creation Myth." In Brenner and Fontaine, *Feminist Companion to the Bible*, 32–52.

Skeat, T. C. "Sinaiticus, Vaticanus and Constantine." In *The Collected Biblical Writings of T. C. Skeat.* Edited by J. K. Elliott, 193–237. Supplements to Novum Testamentum 113. Leiden: Brill, 2004.

Smith II, George P. *Medical-Legal Aspects of Cryonics: Prospects for Immortality.* Washington, D.C.: Catholic Univ. Press of America, 1983.

Smith, Mark S. *The Early History of God: Yahweh and the Other Deities in Ancient Israel.* San Francisco: Harper & Row, 1990.

———. "Ugaritic Studies and Israelite Religion: A Retrospective View." *Near Eastern Archaeology* 65.1 (2002): 17–29.

Soggin, J. Alberto. *Joshua: A Commentary.* Old Testament Library. Philadelphia: Westminster, 1972.

Soranus. *On Gynecology.* Translated by Owsei Temkin. Baltimore: Johns Hopkins Univ. Press, 1956.

Spittler, Russell P. *Old Testament Pseudepigrapha.* Vol. 1, *Apocalyptic Literature and Testaments.* Edited by James H. Charlesworth. New York: Doubleday, 1983.

———. "The Testament of Job: A History of Research and Interpretation." In *Studies on the Testament of Job,* edited by Michael A. Knibb and Pieter W. van der Horst. Cambridge: Cambridge Univ. Press, 1989.

Stahlberg, Lesleigh Cushing. "Modern Day Moabites: The Bible and the Debate about Same-Sex Marriage." *Biblical Interpretation* 16.5 (2008): 442–75.

Steinberg, Jonah. "From a 'Pot of Filth' to a 'Hedge of Roses' (and Back): Changing Theorizations of Menstruation in Judaism." *JFSR* 13.2 (1997): 5–26.

Steinmetz, Devorah. "Vineyard, Farm, and Garden: The Drunkenness of Noah in the Context of Primeval History." *Journal of Biblical Literature* 113 (1994): 193–207.

Stengers, Jean, and Anne van Neck. *Masturbation: The History of a Great Terror.* Translated by Kathryn Hoffman. New York: Palgrave Macmillan, 2001.

Stern, Philip D. *The Biblical Herem: A Window on Israel's Religious Experience.* Brown Judaic Studies 211. Atlanta: Scholars Press, 1991.

Stone, Ken. *Practicing Safer Texts: Food, Sex and Bible in Queer Perspective.* London: Clark, 2005.

———. *Sex, Honor, and Power in the Deuteronomistic History.* JSOT Supplement Series 234. Sheffield: Sheffield Academic, 1996.

Strabo. *The Geography.* Translated by Horace L. Jones. *The Geography of Strabo,* 8 vols. Loeb Classical Library. Cambridge: Harvard Univ. Press, 1917–1933.

Suetonius. *Lives of the Deified Emperors.* Translated by J. C. Rolfe. *Suetonius.* 2 vols. Loeb Classical Library 38. Cambridge: Harvard Univ. Press, rev. ed., 1997.

Swancutt, Diana M. "'The Disease of Effemination': The Charge of Effeminacy and the Verdict of God (Romans 1:18–2:16)." In Moore and Anderson. *Masculinities.*

Tacitus, Achilles. *The Histories.* Translated by Clifford H. Moore. *Tacitus. The Histories Books IV-V.* Loeb Classical Library. Cambridge: Harvard Univ. Press, 1952.

Tanzer, Sarah J. "Ephesians." In Fiorenza. *Searching the Scriptures,* 325–48.

Tatius. *Leucippe and Clitophon.* Translated by John J. Winkler. In Reardon, *Ancient Greek Novels,* 170–284.

Tertullian. *On Modesty (De pudicitia).* Translated by Rudolph Arbesmann, Sister Emily Joseph Daly, and Edwin A. Quain. *Tertullian. Disciplinary, Moral and Ascetical Works.* Fathers of the Church. Washington, D.C.: The Catholic Univ. of America Press, 1985.

Testament of Job, The. In Spittler, *Old Testament Pseudepigrapha.*

Thompson, J. A. "The Significance of the Verb *Love* in the David-Jonathan Narratives in 1 Samuel." *Vetus Testamentum* 24 (1974): 334–39.

Thompson, Leonard L. *The Book of Revelation: Apocalypse and Empire.* Oxford: Oxford Univ. Press, 2000.

Treggiari, Susan. *Roman Marriage: Iusti Coniuges from the Time of Cicero to the Time of Ulpian.* Oxford: Clarendon, 1991.

Trible, Phyllis. *God and the Rhetoric of Sexuality.* Philadelphia: Fortress, 1978.

———. *Texts of Terror: Literary Feminist Readings of Biblical Narratives.* Philadelphia: Fortress Press, 1984.

Trümper, Monika. "The Oldest Original Synagogue Building in the Diaspora: The Delos Synagogue Reconsidered." *Hesperia* 73 (2004): 513–98.

Van der Horst, Pieter W. "Images of Women in the Testament of Job." In Knibb and Van der Horst, *Testament of Job*.

VanderKam, James C. *The Book of Jubilees.* Sheffield: Sheffield Academic, 2001.

———. "1 Enoch, Enochic Motifs, and Enoch in Early Christian Literature." In *The Jewish Apocalyptic Heritage in Early Christianity,* edited by James C. VanderKam and William Adler, 35–40. Compendia Rerum Iudaicarum ad Novum Testamentum 4. Minneapolis: Fortress, 1996.

Van Der Toorn, Karel. *Scribal Culture and the Making of the Hebrew Bible.* Cambridge: Harvard Univ. Press, 2007.

Van de Sandt, Huub. "'Do Not Give What Is Holy to the Dogs' (Did 9:5D and Matt 7:6A): The Eucharistic Food of the Didache in Its Jewish Purity Setting." *Vigiliae Christianae* 56.3 (2002): 223–46.

Van de Walle, Etienne, and Elisha P. Renne. *Regulating Menstruation: Beliefs, Practices, Interpretations.* Chicago: Univ. of Chicago Press, 2001.

Van Seters, John. *Abraham in History and Tradition.* New Haven: Yale Univ. Press, 1975.

———. *A Law Book for the Diaspora: Revision in the Study of the Covenant Code.* New York and London: Oxford Univ. Press, 2003.

Van Stempvoort, P. A. "The Protevangelium Jacobi: The Sources of Its Theme and Style and Their Bearing on Its Date." In *Studia Evengelica,* Vol. 3, edited by F. L. Cross, 410–26. Texte und Untersuchungen zur Geschichte der Altchristlichen Literatur 88. Berlin: Akademie-Verlag, 1964.

Verhey, Allen. *Remembering Jesus: Christian Community, Scripture and the Moral Life.* Grand Rapids: Eerdmans, 2002.

Walsh, Carey Elle. *Exquisite Desire: Religion, The Erotic, and the Song of Songs.* Minneapolis: Fortress, 2000.

Warrior, Robert. "Canaanites, Cowboys and Indians: Deliverance, Conquest, and Liberation Theology Today" *Christianity and Crisis* 49 (September 11, 1989): 261–65.

Washington, Harold C. "Israel's Holy Seed and the Foreign Women of Ezra-Nehemiah: A Kristevan Reading." *Biblical Interpretation* 11 (2003): 427–37.

Wasserman, Tommy. *The Epistle of Jude: Its Text and Transmission.* Coniectanea

Biblical New Testament Series 43. Stockholm: Almqvist and Wiksell International, 2006.

Watson, Duane F. *Invention, Arrangement and Style: Rhetorical Criticism of Jude and 2 Peter*. SBL Dissertation Series 104. Atlanta: Scholars Press, 1988.

———. "The Letter of Jude." In *The New Interpreter's Bible*. Vol. 12, 471–500 Nashville: Abingdon, 1998.

Wegner, Judith Romney. "Leviticus." In Newsom and Ringe. *Women's Bible Commentary*, 36–44.

Weinfeld, Moshe. *Deuteronomy 1–11: A New Translation with Introduction and Commentary*. Anchor Bible. New York: Doubleday, 1991.

Westbrook, Raymond. "The Female Slave." In Mathews, Levinson, and Frymer-Kensky, *Gender and Law*, 214–38.

———. "Old Babylonian Law." In *History of Ancient Near Eastern Law*, 361–430.

———, ed. *History of Ancient Near Eastern Law*. Leiden: Brill, 2003.

Westermann, Claus. *Genesis 1–11: A Commentary*. Translated by John J. Scullion. Minneapolis: Augsburg Fortress, 1984.

———. *Genesis 12–36: A Commentary*. Translated by John J. Scullion. Minneapolis: Augsburg Fortress, 1985.

Whybray, R. N. *The Succession Narrative: A Study of II Sam. 9–20 and I Kings 1 and 2*. Studies in Biblical Theology, 2nd Series 9. London: SCM, 1968.

Wiles, Maurice F. *The Spiritual Gospel: The Interpretation of the Fourth Gospel in the Early Church*. Cambridge: Cambridge Univ. Press, 1960.

William of Saint Thierry. *Brevis Commentatio*. Translated by Denys Turner. *Eros and Allegory: Medieval Exegesis of the Song of Songs*. Cistercian Studies 156. Kalamazoo: Cistercian Publications, 1995.

Williams II, Charles K. "Corinth and the Cult of Aphrodite." In *Corinthiaca: Studies in Honor of Darrell A. Amyx,* edited by Mario A. Del Chiaro and William R. Biers. Columbia: Univ. of Missouri Press, 1986.

Williams, Craig A. *Roman Homosexuality*. New York and London: Oxford Univ. Press, 1999.

Winkler, John J. *The Constraints of Desire: The Anthropology of Sex and Gender in Ancient Greece*. New York and London: Routledge, 1990.

Wolfe, Patrick. "Land, Labor and Difference: Elementary Structures of Race." *American Historical Review* 106.3 (2001): 866–905 (872–73).

Wyner Mark, Elizabeth, ed. *The Covenant of Circumcision: New Perspectives on an Ancient Jewish Rite*. Hanover and London: Brandeis Univ. Press, 2003.

Yarbrough, O. Larry. *Not Like the Gentiles: Marriage Rules in the Letters of Paul*. SBL Dissertation Series 80. Atlanta: Scholars Press, 1985.

Yee, Gale A. *Composition and Tradition in the Book of Hosea: A Redaction Critical Investigation*. SBL Dissertation Series 102. Atlanta: Scholars Press, 1985.

———. "Ideological Criticism: Judges 17–21 and the Dismembered Body." In *Judges and Method: New Approaches in Biblical Studies*. Minneapolis: Fortress, 1995.

———. *Poor Banished Children of Eve: Women as Evil in the Hebrew Bible*. Minneapolis: Augsburg Fortress, 2003.

———. " 'She Is Not My Wife and I Am Not Her Husband': A Materialist Analysis of Hosea 1–2." *Biblical Interpretation* 9.4 (2001): 345–83.

Zevit, Ziony. *The Religions of Ancient Israel: A Synthesis of Parallactic Approaches*. New York: Continuum, 2001.

Ziskind, Jonathan R. "The Missing Daughter in Leviticus XVIII." *Vetus Testamentum* 46.1 (1996): 125–30.

Zlotnick, Helena. *Dinah's Daughters: Gender and Judaism from the Hebrew Bible to Late Antiquity*. Philadelphia: Univ. of Pennsylvania Press, 2002.

Index